D0856157

Fanny von Arnstein

Hilde Spiel

Fanny von Arnstein

A Daughter of the Enlightenment
1758–1818

Translated by
Christine Shuttleworth

BERG
New York/Oxford
Distributed exclusively in the USA and Canada by
St Martin's Press, New York

First published in 1991 by
Berg Publishers Limited
Editorial offices:
165 Taber Avenue, Providence, RI 02906, USA
150 Cowley Road, Oxford, OX4 1JJ, UK

Translated from the German *Fanny von Arnstein oder Die Emanzipation*,
copyright Fischer
Taschenbuch Verlag, 1978

British Library Cataloguing in Publication Data

Spiel, Hilde
  Fanny von Arnstein: A Daughter of the Enlightenment, 1758–1818
  1. Austria. Vienna. Jews. Social life
  I. Title II. Fanny von Arnstein oder die Emanzipation.
  English
  943.613004924

  ISBN 0–85496–179–8

Library of Congress Cataloging-in-Publication Data
Spiel, Hilde.
  [Fanny von Arnstein, English]
  Fanny von Arnstein: A Daughter of the Enlightenment, 1758–1818 /
Hilde Spiel; translated by Christine Shuttleworth, – 1st English ed.
    p. cm.
  Translation of: Fanny von Arnstein.
  Includes bibliographical references.
  ISBN 0–85496–179–8
  1. Arnstein, Fanny von, 1758–1818,
2. Jews–Austria–Vienna–Biography.
3. Jews–Austria–Emancipation. 4. Vienna (Austria)–Biography. I.
Title.
DS135.A93A76713 1991
943.6'1300492402–dc20
[B]

90–389
CIP

Printed in Great Britain by
Billing & Sons Ltd, Worcester

Contents

For the rest I have written quite impartially and without premeditation, and favoured neither Jews nor Christians, and therefore have no fear of reproaches on this account. I have always borne in mind the precept that one should not draw conclusions about whole nations from the examples of individuals, which I recognize as unjust. Therefore I have taken great care to avoid anything which might be misinterpreted either by Christians or by Jews and be detrimental to one party; and this I considered to be my duty.

Joh. Balthasar König, *Annalen der Juden in den deutschen Staaten* (Berlin, 1790)

Preface

In the gentle light of everyday life, we are borne along by two realities. One accompanies us from the day of our entrance into the world to our dying day. The other flows around us from the beginnings of humanity and through us until the end of all earthly life. Over most of us the stream of history rushes on its way uncaring; it washes the traces of our existence into the depths, to efface them for ever. We alter its course as little as would a small pebble, loosened from the bank and driven along with the current for a while.

To halt the course of world events, or even to turn them in a new direction, is granted only to few. Like dams, boulders or continually whirling eddies, the impact they have on their epoch seems to interrupt the flow of history. It is not always necessary to take vigorous action in order to gain this significance. There are some who are placed by chance at a turning of the stream of time, where it is joined by more than one tributary. Like a small island, resting unharmed amid the convergence of waters, they endure as marks of a change of course. Not by their deeds, but merely by their being, they achieve immortality.

It is not however without a measure of greatness that such people earn their claim to imperishable existence. The woman whose life is recorded here did not strive to obstruct or promote the progress of events. But she was conscious of her origins, of what people, in what times and what place she was born, and she filled her place in history with grace, spirit and dignity. Her place of birth was a Europe torn by the battles of kings, by the uprising of nations, by war and revolution. Her time extended from the Dark Ages of thought through the Age of Enlightenment to the returning twilight of reaction. Her people was that of which Tacitus had said that it was like no other on earth, and which paid for its otherness with constant humiliation and mortal danger. Yet for a short moment she procured for it equality of rank. In her person the great ones of the world recognised a being of similar worth. In her they honoured what had been despised for thousands of years.

Preface

When she died, Felix Mendelssohn's mother mourned in her 'the most interesting woman in Europe'. This she was not by any means. She was only to be found where Europe was most interesting. Among the heroines of emancipation in Europe she was merely the first, not the cleverest. She was no intellectual phenomenon like Rahel Varnhagen, nor a romantically fanciful one like Dorothea Schlegel, nor an erotic–sentimental one like poor Henriette Herz. She was a social phenomenon which operated by its emanations alone. It is not without reason we have no letter of hers, and very few documents from her own hand. Her ephemeral figure, her intangible charm have been preserved only in the mirror of her contemporaries. But the outward form that was hers became her image. It was neither a prophet nor a wise woman, but a great lady, who became a symbol of the liberation of women and the emancipation of the Jews.

Acknowledgements

The present work could have been begun, but hardly brought to a reasonably satisfying conclusion without the generous help which I have received from members of the Pereira-Arnstein family. Although some of them are now deceased, I should like to record my gratitude to them.

In the first place I must express my thanks to Baroness Marie Rosine von Pereira-Arnstein, née Countess Mensdorff-Pouilly, for having entrusted to me valuable documents for examination, and for the tireless patience with which she herself contributed to their decipherment. I am equally indebted to Baron Fritz von Pereira-Arnstein, in whose hospitable house, Schloss Rothenturn in Carinthia, I found letters, notes and pictures of inestimable value for my work. Baronesses Lily von Pereira and Maria von Skrbensky did me the kindness of placing significant documents at my disposal.

I owe important clues concerning the Berlin family of my heroine to Frau Karoline Cauer, who, connected by marriage with the Mendelssohn and Itzig families, was in a position to provide me, among other documents, with Cäcilie Eskeles's letter of 1809 from the besieged city of Vienna.

The indispensable but unfortunately fragmentary data from private sources needed to be supplemented by contemporary references which lay hidden in numerous documents and reports. To collect and examine this material would have been impossible without the help of a number of scholars and archivists. I would like to name above all Dr Hanns Jäger-Sunstenau, who offered me access to all the files and records of the Viennese City Archives; Professor Dr Erika Weinzierl, whose help was essential in the Austrian State Archives; Professor Dr Hanns Leo Mikoletzky, the extremely helpful director of the archives of the Finanz-und Hofkammer; Professor Dr Goldinger of the Adelsarchiv; Dr Hedwig Kraus of the archive of the Gesellschaft der Musikfreunde; as well as the assistants and officials of the Austrian National Library and City Library of Vienna. Frau Ilse R. Wolff of the Wiener Library,

London, gave me sympathetic and encouraging support.

Among the private researchers who readily offered advice and information were Dr Jacob Jacobson of Worcester and Dr Siegfried Ascher of Haifa, with a quantity of genealogical data; the noted musicologists Professor O. E. Deutsch and Dr Heinz Schöny; Mr J. Christopher Herold, author of an excellent biography of Madame de Staël, and Dr Maria Ullrichovà, an expert on the same subject; Professor Dr Edwin Redslob; my fatherly friend Dr Franz Kobler; Professor Hadumod Bussmann; Countess Maria Lanckoronska, and that most charming expert on the local history of Vienna, Herr Siegfried Weyr.

Last but nevertheless foremost I want to thank the translator, my daughter Christine Shuttleworth, for her resolve, tirelessly pursued with, to me at least, the greatest possible success, to find a suitable equivalent for every shade of meaning in this complicated web of history and biography. She has also compiled a new and greatly improved index. It is now her book as well as mine.

–1–

The Mildness of the Hohenzollerns

In the early summer of 1776, a young couple of quality, and without visible flaw, were seated in a berline which was driving south, with frequent changes of horses and by deliberate daily stages by way of Dresden and Prague, to the imperial capital. The Prussian bride and Viennese bridegroom were fashionably attired: the lady in a narrow-waisted crinoline, lace sleeves and deep *décolleté*, the gentleman with pigtail and bag-wig, in knee-breeches which were entirely concealed by his top-boots and coat-tails; his unbuckled dagger lay beside him on the seat.

They were accompanied by a valet and lady's-maid, who were following in a second carriage with ample luggage, as was fitting for the daughter of a man who was in a position to provide 70,000 thalers as dowry for her and each of her nine sisters; and no less so for the son of a man whose estate, a decade later, was to amount to three-quarters of a million gulden in Viennese currency. The bride had left a *palais* in the Burgstrasse in Berlin and a country seat near the Schlesisches Tor in order to move into an elegant town house on the Graben in Vienna. Her father, like her bridegroom's, was well versed in associating with monarchs. He stood as near to the King's throne as his *palais* to the royal residence on the Kupfergraben. He was separated from the ordinary citizen, as were the aristocracy, by an unbridgeable gulf.

A gulf also lay between the two countries to which the young couple belonged. When the bride was born, two years of the Seven Years' War had passed. Even the peace of which she soon became conscious could not reconcile Prussia and Austria. That bitter fight in the heart of Europe, which had enriched the father of the bride as he helped his King to victory, left the two nations in deep, never quite eradicated opposition. True, both were now experiencing a fresh impetus which brought renewed prosperity to the drained provinces of one country as of the other; true, they had, together with Russia, each taken their share of helpless Poland; true, the obstinate spirit of reform of Frederick the Great was encroaching upon the hereditary lands of the Habsburgs and taking hold, if not of the Empress, at least of her son – who had twice admiringly shaken the hand of the former enemy – as well as of her Chancellor, Kaunitz, a cautious Voltairean and a patient man. But a new quarrel was at hand. Two years after the couple's marriage, Prussian and Austrian soldiers, sent to war by their rulers for the sake of Bavaria, were to confront each other again in northern Bohemia. They did not fight; they simply dug up each other's potatoes. But the love between the two countries did not grow any greater on that account.

The bridal couple in the berline had every reason not to become involved in these dissensions. Nevertheless, throughout their lives an invisible line of separation ran between them, which sometimes seemed to light up like a red warning signal. At seventeen years of age, the girl had exchanged her own home for an Austrian one. She was nearing fifty-seven when it was said of her, in a private communication at the time of the Congress of Vienna, that the lady was 'scandaleusement prussienne'. Tall and slim, with a long, straight nose and beautiful, slightly prominent pale blue eyes, she stood out among the plump, delicately boned little Viennese ladies as a Berliner, if not as a north German, while her freshness, her ready wit and her restless vivacity unmistakably derived from the sharp clear air of her native city. The bridegroom, ten years older, but in his future marriage decidedly of more subdued powers of comprehension and slower intellect, had the good-humoured, expressionless face and soft chin of so many Austrian citizens. In short, were it not for certain features such as a slight fullness of the lips or slope of the nose that almost imperceptibly hinted at a more ancient origin, they were both passable representatives of their nations. But they were not quite as passable as all that.

For when, on the second or third day of the journey, the berline stopped in front of the city gate of Dresden, the carriage was surrounded by Saxon toll-collectors who demanded the travellers' documents, which they inspected closely with offensive glances at their elegant clothing and demeanour, finally imposing the modest but humiliating personal toll of twenty groschen. A few weeks later, in August of the same year, the same experience befell a more famous man. Moses Mendelssohn, the author of *Phaedon* and Kant's successful rival for the Prussian Academy prize, was also forced at the gates of Dresden to pay the toll which was otherwise imposed only in the case of cattle and pigs. A Saxon friend of the philosopher who heard of the matter persuaded the authorities to refund the twenty groschen to Mendelssohn, whereupon the latter passed it, 'increased tenfold', to the city's poor-box. Although the bridal couple too had, for certain reasons, in the end been excused payment, this moment made a deep impression on the girl's mind. For in her notebook, one of the few documents from her own hand that survives, is found a verse by Moses Ephraim Kuh, who had five years earlier undergone similarly humiliating experiences elsewhere in Saxony. This touchingly naïve man, himself a *Douanier* of poetry, had expressed his resentment in a little dialogue between the '*Zöllner* [toll-collector] at E.' and a travelling Jew:

Z. Du, Jude, mußt drey Thaler Zoll erlegen.
J. Drey Thaler? Soviel Geld? mein Herr, weswegen?
Z. Das fragst du noch? weil du ein Jude bist.
   Wärst du ein Türk', ein Heid', ein Atheist,
   So würden wir nicht einen Deut begehren,
   Als einen Juden müssen wir dich scheren.
J. Hier ist das Geld! – Lehrt euch dies euer Christ?

[T. Thou, Jew, must pay three thalers toll.
 J. Three thalers? So much money? Sir, wherefore?
 T. Canst thou ask that? Because thou art a Jew.
   Wert thou a Turk, heathen or atheist,
   We would not ask of thee a single farthing,
   But as thou art a Jew, thou must be shorn.
 J. Here is your money! Does your Christ teach you thus?]

The bridal couple drove on, along the Elbe, through 'Saxon Switzerland' into the hereditary land of Bohemia and here, through waving yellow corn, to the old city of Prague. The June sky was blue. But a shadow had fallen over the newly married pair and accompanied them on their way, over the stony hills of the borderland into Lower Austria, through the dark green Waldviertel down into the plain as far as the river, broad and rushing, that guided them into the outskirts of Vienna. Here too, when their post-horses came to a halt at the custom-house opposite Leopoldstadt and the bride, her gaze turned upon the grey walls and high towers of the imperial residence, listened to the sentry's brusque questions about residential authorisation and toleration document, here too the shadow did not lift. It had hovered over her people since the earliest days and in the splendid, easy-going capital of the Holy Roman Empire it was even a few shades darker than at home in royal Berlin.

It was from there that, when Leopold I drove out the Viennese Jews in 1670, a number of distinguished heads of families sent a request for protection and accommodation to Frederick William, the Great

Elector of Brandenburg. Sadly they complained to his ambassador in Vienna, a certain Andreas Neumann, 'that the earth and the world, which God had after all created for all mankind, were equally closed against them'. The Great Elector, moved by pious mildness and political astuteness, decided that since their people had been tolerated in the electorate from the days of his ancestor Johann Georg henceforth he should provide sanctuary for fifty of them. The Marches and the duchy of Krossen, like the rest of Germany, were still suffering the consequences of the Thirty Years' War. The land was devastated, the population scanty and impoverished; trade was languishing. Frederick William expected from the immigrants that mercantile advantage which they had been bringing for some time to his newly acquired urban community of Halberstadt. He opened his gates to the Viennese Jewry, set their annual protection fee at eight thalers, allowed them to buy houses and guaranteed their privileges for twenty years. Before this period had expired, they were absolved from the personal toll which was not abolished in Saxony until a century later.

This reasonable treatment, such as they had never received in any other part of Germany, must have gone to their heads to the extent that they began to behave as though they were human beings like any others. They began to wrangle and to squabble with each other, slandered and defrauded each other and here and there rose to riches and high position, only to leave the rest of their community behind them. In this way, in the last years of the Elector and even more so at the court of that lover of art and architecture, Frederick I, the jeweller Jost Liebmann had become very influential. The King valued him highly. Jost went in and out at court, and after his death his widow enjoyed the same favour. She rose so high that 'together with her children she was accorded favourable treatment above the rest of Jewry', and even enjoyed the privilege of appearing unannounced in Frederick's private apartments, which particularly annoyed the Crown Prince. The *Liebmannin*, it is said, was a very beautiful woman, whose company was not by any means unpleasing to the King. Once the Crown Prince is said to have been ungracious to her in his father's presence, whereat the latter reproved him for his sharpness of tone, so as to arouse in the Crown Prince 'bitter feelings against anything which appeared *Liebmännisch*, which, however, he was only able to practise when he became King himself'.

Even though Frederick I had inherited the clemency of the Great Elector, and though he had fallen into the snares of the jeweller's widow, the provincial regulations that he imposed upon the Jews of the Brandenburg Marches in 1700 were not entirely to their advantage. None of them was allowed to own retail shops or stalls unless they had already had them in 1690. With that practised eye for financial advantage characteristic of German princes, whether Habsburgs, Hohenzollerns, Wittelsbachs or whoever they were, in dealing with Jews, Frederick increased their annual protection money to 2,000 ducats. No one could contract a marriage without first disbursing a gold gulden. In exchange they were permitted to maintain three houses of worship, one for the *Liebmannin* and her followers, one for the almost as powerful Koppel Riess, and a third for the rest of the community.

This last ordinance immediately set the Jews at loggerheads. Those who had arrived only decades ago from Vienna and those who had long been resident in the north of Germany had no wish to worship their God together. A certain Markus Magnus, servant and favourite of the Crown Prince, tried to edge the *Liebmannin* out of her privileged position. In the course of time the greatest disturbance and confusion prevailed in the community, and in the end Magnus and the widow took each other to court. The headstrong adversaries came up before a commission which included the privy councillor for finance Freiherr von Bartholdi, the *Liebmannin* took refuge behind the King, who proceeded to undermine the conciliatory work of the commission, which was already achieving some success – in short, the building of the Berlin temple was accompanied by a storm of complaints and intrigue, until at last the irritable Jews were mollified and in 1712 the foundation stone was laid.

A further, worse affliction, which likewise was contrived by one of their own number, remained to be suffered by the Jews of the electorate in Frederick's reign. With zealous servility, their former fellow-believer Franz Wentzel, who had been baptised, drew the authorities' attention to the fact that a passage in the Hebrew prayer *Olenu* insulted the person of the Saviour in the most scandalous fashion. For in this prayer, which was uttered twice a day and as many as three times on the Sabbath, 'the Jews conducted themselves blasphemously' at the words 'we kneel and bow, but not before the hanged Jesus', when they spat 'as if at an abomination' and jumped slightly away from the spot where they stood. 'This blasphemy,' explained Wentzel, 'is not printed in any prayer-book, but a space is left for it and it is constantly drummed into the impressionable children and learnt by heart by them.'

Since the medieval accusations of desecration of the Host and ritual murder, no complaint as grave as this had been made against Jews. Urged on by his ecclesiastics, the King gave orders for the most exact and searching inquiry; the elders of all the Jewish communities in Brandenburg were summoned to Küstrin and each of them, under severe and individual cross-examination, was directed to give his interpretation of the prayer *Olenu*. Some said that they did utter this prayer, but not the words in question. Others translated 'Hevel verick', which according to Wentzel referred to 'the hanged Jesus', as meaning fools, heathens or idolaters. A third group pointed out that the prayer *Olenu* was composed by the prophet Joshua, and therefore before the appearance of the Christians' Messiah. Since their ancestors had been accustomed 3,000 years ago to spit at a certain point in the prayer, they did the same, but 'they spat not in mockery of any person'.

The only way out of this confusion appeared to be to constrain the Jews, in swearing the dreadful oath imposed upon them of old, to abjure any evil intention expressed by this prayer. This they were prepared to do. But the King, perhaps following the whispered suggestion of the *Liebmannin*, but more likely his own judgement, enacted a decree with the regal solicitude which that good and shrewd sovereign, a follower of Leibniz's doctrine, bestowed upon even the most despised of his subjects. In this decree he banned the use of the words 'Hevel verick', the spitting and jumping away from the spot, but at the same time freed them from the painful necessity of the oath:

> When we gaze with merciful eyes upon the poor Jewish people, that our God has made subject to us in our lands, we do wish right heartily that this people, that the Lord loved so greatly of old, and did choose for his own from all other peoples, should at last be freed from their blindness, and be brought into a communion with us in our faith in the Messiah and Saviour of the world, born of their own line: Whereas however the great work of conversion belongs to the spiritual kingdom of Christ, and our temporal power has no place in it, and we yield up all power over the conscience of mankind to the Lord of all Lords; therefore we must await the time and the hour which our merciful God has chosen to enlighten them, according only to His own gracious will, suffering them meanwhile with patience, and using means towards their conversion with love and gentleness; . . . while yet we deem ourselves most dutifully bound to resist and mightily to oppose the evil of their rising up against Christ Jesus, our Lord and Saviour, and His Kingdom.

The questionable practices of the prayer *Olenu* were now forbidden to them 'from now until time eternal', but no intention to offend was associated with this ban:

> Yet we are graciously pleased to expect that the Jews will show the most
> submissive obedience to this our decree, which we have devised in the
> most gracious consideration that they were once the people beloved of
> God, and are the friends of our Saviour in the flesh, with love, pity and
> mercy towards them . . . since therein is nothing in the smallest degree
> contrary to their religion, ceremonies, precepts or customs . . . They
> who are now willing to follow obediently our most gracious and most
> earnest desire may, like other loyal subjects, enjoy our sovereign pro-
> tection and safeguard.

These were the words of a Prussian king in 'Cölln an der Spree'
in 1703, when no one in any other corner of the German states
wished to be reminded of the 'fleshly friendship' of the wretched
Jews with the Saviour. It was the first sign of benevolent intentions
towards the Jews since the days of their great, gracious and just
protector Charles V. It was the flaring up of a humane sympathy
which was to find an echo in Frederick I's great-grandchildren, but
also in both learned and simple men of his nation before the century
came to an end.

His son, however, opposed to his father's attitude for the reasons
already mentioned, dealt differently with this matter, according to
his own judgement. He had no love, nor even consideration for this
foreign community which had failed to integrate with its hosts
whether from lack of goodwill or simple reluctance. But at first he
showed himself, as was his nature, in most cases as just as he was
stern. To be sure, the *Liebmannin*, whose beauty had vanished with
age, and through her quarrelsome presumption, was forbidden
access to court once he had ascended the throne, put under a
ten-month-long house arrest and denied under pain of heavy penalties any claim to the estate of the late King, who had been in her
debt to the tune of some 100,000 thalers. After this severe treatment
she was again admitted to the very highest protection, but she died,
bowed down by grief, a year after the death of Frederick I. Before
her death she asked that her royal friend's most beautiful gift, a
gold necklace, should be buried with her. Markus Magnus, who
had inveighed against her on behalf of the Crown Prince, was now
also removed by the King from his presence.

With the sense of justice which was characteristic of the 'soldier-
King' and which he manifested everywhere, in his new regulations
concerning the Jews he annulled the heavy restrictions which had
been placed on them since 1671. Nor did he have any objection to
being well rewarded for these mitigations. Eight thousand thalers –

perhaps as much as 28,000, if other accounts are to be trusted – were the price for rescinding his father's decrees of 1700 and abolishing the yellow patch which the Jews had had to wear throughout the Middle Ages as a mark of Cain. In addition, the Jews' existing conditions were improved, as for example by a new law by which the children of privileged persons were allowed to remain in the country after certain statutory payments had been made, and a widow's right to protection could be passed on to a second husband.

The reign of Frederick William I thus began more favourably than one might have assumed from his early bitterness 'against anything which appeared *Liebmännisch*'. It would have remained equally benevolent, if in 1721 he had not been roused to the greatest fury by the Jews. The *Münzjude* (Jewish mint-master) Veit had died with an outstanding debt of more than 100,000 thalers. However rich he had been in his lifetime, his fortune was not to be found after his death, and no one admitted to knowing what had become of it. Veit, known in all his dealings as an honest man, had certainly departed this life at a moment as convenient for his debtors as it was inconvenient for his creditors. But the King refused to believe that no ready cash was available, persisted in his opinion that the whole Jewish community was concealing its whereabouts, and decided overnight to outlaw them. This he did on 15 August, in the presence of the chief court minister Jablonsky, having had every one of them driven into their temple.

A year later the father of our bride was born.

While the travelling carriage – its occupants having been inspected and deemed worthy to pass within the walls of Vienna – drove up the steep Rotenthurmstrasse, past the cathedral of St Stephen and along the Graben, the lady from Berlin may have recalled with some melancholy the wide avenues and prospects of her native city. Here the houses stood in untidy rows, narrow-chested and poky, crowding around the cathedral like unruly sheep around their shepherd, allowing no glimpse of courtyards, gardens, fountains or patches of blue sky. Only a little later, her compatriot Friedrich Nicolai was to find fault with these 'narrow, crooked, uneven alleys' in blunter terms than the young woman dared to utter that day: 'Handsome squares there are few, and none of the monuments on these has a fine appearance. Thus the city of Vienna itself for the most part makes no very remarkable impression.' As for the *Pestsäule* (plague memorial column) on the Graben, upon which from now on her eye would fall every morning, Nicolai found it 'hideous, a monstrous hotchpotch of unconnected things. No connoisseur of art, accustomed to the contemplation of simple and noble works of sculpture, can gaze with any pleasure at this mass of ungrouped figures piled ineffectually on top of one another.' At home, in his opinion, far better taste was shown in these matters.

Not only the worthy Nicolai, a Prussian pedant and puritan, who was so shocked by the passionate baroque of the *Pestsäule*, placed the great Frederick's Berlin high above Maria Theresa's Vienna. The bride's father, too, born within the dark confines of his community, saw in the exemplary proportions, the military straightness of the streets, the punctiliously rounded towers, geometric squares and rigorously simple façades of his city an assurance that order reigned there – both in its architecture and in the disposition of its King. Gone were the days when the despotism of the ruler showed itself to be as fickle in favour as in disfavour. Gone were the alternating spring-like mildness and April tempests of the capricious sovereign, gone too the pragmatic justice of the soldier-King, which a sudden suspicion could sweep aside.

Awakened by the sharp, bright intellect of the French *encyclopédistes*, a new intelligence was at work, as rectilinear as its perspectives. No gentle pity for the people whom the Lord had once loved and then rejected, no mystic dream of their conversion through strict discipline, no sentimentality derived from hatred or partiality disturbed the judgement of this King. Whatever he did was dictated by reason. Out of the sand of the Marches a new and mighty city began to emerge. Like his father, Frederick William I, with whom otherwise he had little in common, Frederick the Great clung to the saying: 'The fellow has money – let him build!' Where the money came from was of little concern to him, as long as it helped the city to grow and flourish. Like the soldier-King he planned to populate it generously – with Protestants from Salzburg, from Bohemia, wherever they might come from. In this motley community there was a firmly delineated place for the Jews whom he esteemed lightly, but found useful. Since 1572, the Hohenzollerns had tolerated them in their electorate. Within limits, which were as strictly drawn as ever, he answered for their safety.

In the first decade of his reign the only change was that their restrictions were subjected to a thorough and sensible examination. As the source of this, Manitius, the secretary of finance, named 'the *odium religiosum* emanating *ex papatu*', which 'is the origin of all misfortune and of the spirit of persecution in the world'. This aversion, however, in his opinion was a thing of the past. Nevertheless, in the event the revised general patent of 1750 was not much more benevolent than the previous ones had been. It allowed a slightly increased number of family members; otherwise things stayed much the same. The attitude of the royal aesthete towards the Jews was unaltered; he enclosed them like his parade grounds, fencing them in with restrictions. But his sense of proportion, to which there was much reference in the new patent, directed them to their safe and proper place within these limits.

This place, as in the days of the Great Elector, they owed solely to their usefulness. As military suppliers they were of great service to Frederick, who was embroiled in wars from the first day of his accession. The moment soon came, however, when they were able to demonstrate their usefulness to the highest degree. Shortly before the King invaded Saxony in order to take possession for the third and last time of Silesia, he concluded a coinage contract with the court jeweller, a protected Jew called Veitel Ephraim, by which he transferred to him the coinage of all the currencies in his states. With this Ephraim there began the rise of a small number of families, closely knit by marriage, who some decades later were to exercise a decided influence on the social scene in Berlin. These were the 'juifs de Frédéric le Grand', whose business sense and understanding of finance contributed as much to Prussia's greatness as did their daughters to a fruitful union of his hereditary nobility with the nobility of intellect and art.

Their rise stemmed from obscure transactions, which often aroused animosity, between the family heads and their ambitious King. It brought them out of overcrowded dwellings where they clung closely together with their abundant children and hangers-on, into splendid palaces, near the throne. Its origins were Frederick's intense desire to obtain ever greater power and richer landed property for himself and Prussia, no less than the dubious methods of his mint-masters in procuring for him the means to do so. This they did, like so many devoted servants of German princely courts before them, by dint of repeated debasement of the coinage, sometimes of positive counterfeiting.

In the guild of court Jews, which had been set up long since, but attained genuine status only in the eighteenth century, the coiners were always in the most vulnerable position. Since the right of coinage had passed from the Emperor to all, even the most insignificant, of his princes and bishops, the various currencies of the

Holy Roman Empire had lost their firm value. Their gold or silver content went up and down unremittingly. The German silver mines, moreover, had become exhausted since the Thirty Years' War, the princes found themselves obliged to import precious metals from abroad, and this trade was not only problematic because of the annual rise in the price of silver but also fraught with danger, since the law of many states completely prohibited their export.

As usual, the thankless task, to which no self-respecting merchant would subject himself, fell to the Jews in their arduous struggle for social advancement. A number of them carried it out quietly and without reproach, obtaining silver and coining money as their ruler had ordained. But as soon as it occurred to such a ruler to devalue his currency, those who had followed his orders were held up to execration. This was what happened to Veitel Ephraim, whom Frederick the Great, before the Third Silesian War, instructed to exchange the good old coins of the realm for others which he had minted to a lower value than the nominal one, and provided with a deceptive silver sheen.

> Von außen schön, von innen schlimm,
> Außen Friedrich, innen Ephraim!

[Outwardly good, evil within, / Outside Frederick, inside Ephraim!]

This song was soon heard in the Prussian states, and after the King's invasion of Saxony had succeeded and his mint-masters brought into circulation new coins of one-third the former value and low silver content, these were contemptuously referred to as 'Ephraimites'. Nevertheless these ruses, which emptied the pockets of the little man, were the only way to conduct a war of seven years' duration against an overwhelmingly powerful coalition without imposing extortionate taxes or incurring tax debts. Moreover, it was the King who went astray, with his money-clippers by his side.

If the rise of the Friderician Jews took place in a twilight of dubious practices, it took place also in an atmosphere of quarrelling and calumny, like that which had prevailed in the Berlin community at the time of the *Liebmannin* and of Markus Magnus. For soon after, when Ephraim had been promoted from a mere supplier of silver to lessee of the coinage, an opposition party came into being whose sole object was to edge him out of his post. In October 1755, this party, consisting of Herz Gompertz, the husband of Ephraim's sister Clara, a certain Daniel Itzig and his brother-in-law Moses Isaac, managed to get the lease of all six state mints transferred from Ephraim to itself. How this was accomplished is no longer apparent; probably the opposition outbid Ephraim for the lease.

When, however, the *Münzjuden* began to reproach each other publicly to the effect that they had lowered the value of the coins as well as raising the price of silver too high, the King, under similar pressure to that of his grandfather Frederick I, ordered them not to trouble him with such proceedings. During the war the feuds between the hostile though closely related groups continued. The administration of the coinage wavered between the two parties, while not only the King, but also his general commissioners and superintendents, were adept at playing one party off against the other. It was not till 1758, when Ephraim's most dangerous opponents, Major-General von Retzow and his own brother-in-law Herz Gompertz, were dead, that he succeeded in forming a consortium with their former partners Moses Isaac and Daniel Itzig, which took over all the King's coinage commissions.

Daniel Itzig is the man, among all these confused and unedifying machinations, with whom we will now be concerned. When, greatly respected and advanced in years, he passed away a few months before the turn of the century, the controversial beginnings of his career were forgotten. This patriarch, whose name was to adorn the family trees not only of rich businessmen, great artists and eminent scholars, but also of blue-blooded scions of the ancient aristocracy, had won the favour of his King through the most devoted services. That in doing so he did not overlook his own interests is not to be denied. Nevertheless, the way in which he freed himself and his children's children from the burden of poverty and ignominious birth was, although less romantic, in no way less honourable than that of the robber knights who from the safety of their castles had lain in wait to prey on passing strangers. Above all it took courage – the courage to make unpleasant decisions which must inevitably come up against resistance; the courage to play scapegoat to an ambitious and, as we will see, disloyal employer; the courage to call down on his head the irrational hate of the community; finally, the courage to take upon himself the venomous excesses of the reproach of future generations – for example, of Carlyle, who spoke years later of the 'foul swollen creatures' Ephraim and Itzig, 'rolling in foul wealth by the ruin of their neighbours', although in the well-authenticated way of life of the latter at least, there is no evidence of merciless self-interest, but much of his great philanthropic and charitable nature.

Daniel Itzig enjoyed better favour among his more impartial contemporaries than he did with Carlyle. In a 'Characterisation of Berlin' published in Philadelphia in 1764 his noble 'character and irreproachable way of life' were particularly mentioned. On an official occasion Frederick William II referred to his 'well-known respectable conduct and selfless behaviour'. And the worthy Johann Balthasar König, a contemporary historian, makes the general observation that 'the Jews' behaviour was excellent in the conduct of this business', and that it was to be doubted 'that the Christians would have manifested so much delicacy and subtlety if the business had been entrusted to their care'. Yet it was not König's well-considered account but the intemperate judgement of Carlyle which was considered fit to establish the image of these men in the consciousness of later times – for history is no less fallible and prejudiced than her most malicious chronicler.

> He was of tall, noble proportions, of gentle, beautiful physiognomy, had a keen, penetrating, but friendly gaze; altogether a benevolent, captivating being and at the same time one who commanded respect, in a word, he was a very handsome man. His whole bearing, manner and behaviour bespoke manly dignity, it was as if he were from the very beginning called to higher things, as if he were created by nature for gentle manners and good taste, in order to be able to move in refined circles.

Such was the glorified picture of Daniel Itzig which survived among his co-religionists. Today one would hesitate to call him a handsome man. The small portrait preserved at a Carinthian castle by one of his descendants shows a paterfamilias of serious but gentle mien, whose pointed nose and reflectively pursed lips manifest that cunning and circumspection with whose help he had risen to become the most powerful man among Prussian Jewry. Only his large, sea-blue eyes express the leaning towards gentle manners and good taste reported by his eulogist. His wife, Mariane, who in the course of a long marriage bore him sixteen children, had the same bright, clear eyes. As we have seen, they were inherited by his daughter, the bride of our story.

Daniel's origins cannot be pursued very far back, certainly not into the Middle Ages as in the case of so many German Jewish families. We know only that his grandfather Daniel Jafe lived in Grätz, and in 1679 celebrated the birth of a son, Isaac, who later went to Berlin, where he took up horse-trading. This Isaac (or Itzig) Daniel Jafe, who appears in 1714 on the list of tolerated Jews, was from time to time allowed to sell horses to Frederick William I. Apart from his son Daniel, born to him in his forty-fourth year, he had three sons and two daughters, including Bela, who brought her brother into her husband's coinage business. Daniel Itzig, 'from the very beginning called to higher things', must have shown early promise as a skilled financier, for he was only thirty-two when, with his brother-in-law Moses Isaac and the latter's associate Herz Gompertz, he took over the lease of the six mints in Berlin, Magdeburg, Cleve, Aurich, Breslau and Königsberg.

His youth was marked by sorrow. At eighteen he lost his father. That he proved a good son and brother to his family – his mother died at an advanced age – is undoubted. Otherwise the manufacturer Benjamin Elias Wulff of Dessau would never have given him his daughter's hand in marriage, for Daniel was living in modest circumstances when he courted Mariane (or Miriam) in 1748. The Wulffs, on the other hand, were among the most distinguished families of their faith in Germany. Mariane's great-grandfather Moses Benjamin Wulff had, in rivalry with Jost Liebmann, served the Great Elector as court supplier, until Liebmann's intrigues ruined him, drove him out of the Brandenburg Marches and brought him to Anhalt-Dessau.

This Wulff, who was known as the 'long Jew' from his impressive stature, was one of the first and most brilliant of the great princely courtiers, and administered the coinage of the Duke of Gotha and Altenberg. A quarrel of long standing with the house of Gotha, however, brought poverty to his heirs, impelling them to seek their fortune anew in the Prussian capital. But in Dessau, at the time when the hunchbacked boy Moses Mendelssohn was growing up there, the esteem in which the Wulff family was held was as high as it had ever been. Daniel's marriage to Mariane could not but redound to his honour. It was the start of his rise to success in Berlin. He soon became an agent and a few years later a partner to Herz Gompertz, his wife bore him a child every year, and even if the latest regulations permitted only two of his offspring to settle in the city, he lulled himself in the hope that with the favourable passage of time his residence might continue to be granted to him together with all his nearest and dearest.

His first attempts to prove of service to the King did not work out too well. In 1752 Daniel first entered the coinage business, still as a middleman to Gompertz, who was supplying silver for the new mint at Stettin. Current coinage and small denominations were to be minted there, not only for Pomerania, but for the province of Prussia too. The commission was however carried out in defiance of instructions: more small coins than directed were brought into circulation, better coins already in circulation were melted down for re-use and in the end, contrary to the agreement, even the standard of coinage was debased. The King was dissatisfied, reproved the entrepreneurs and their 'almost unrestrainable scheming and despicable behaviour', and gave orders to his agent Graumann 'rather to conduct dealings with respectable Christian tradespeople'. But his trust in the latter proved misplaced. They either declined Graumann's request that they should take over deliveries, or they delivered too little and at unacceptably high prices. And so, with the King's tacit agreement, a year later Graumann went back to his *Münzjuden*, who knew how to indemnify themselves against the excessively low silver rate imposed upon them. In March 1754, even they were no longer able to take on the burden of the difficult commission with its low profit margin and gave up the business, upon which the Stettin mint finally had to be closed down.

This débâcle with which Daniel Itzig's first dealings with the King were to end was due not only to the 'scheming and despicable behaviour' of the coinage entrepreneurs but also to the unrealistic terms imposed upon them. One thing is certain: as soon as he achieved equal rights in his partnership with Gompertz and in later associations, he gave no occasion for complaints, but was in the habit of carrying on his business reliably and enjoyed the highest possible approval. Frederick's mistrust of him and his partner had been banished when, in 1755, they received from him responsibility for the six Prussian mints.

In the following year the King's forces invaded Silesia. The war began to consume money: some 170 million thalers before it was brought to a victorious end. Of this sum, 29 million thalers were covered by a brassage (mint charge) of metal suitable for coinage, the greater part of which came into being through the dealings of Gompertz, Itzig, Isaac and, once again, Ephraim. In the course of time the thaler's nominal value was repeatedly reduced, until it had sunk by one-third. But more and more of this money was needed, and it seemed more and more difficult to get enough gold and silver into the country. The risks and costs incurred by the entrepreneurs were massive, their profit only an 8 per cent share of the price of the metal, while all the profit on the coinage went into the war fund. In the end they took so little pleasure in their job that, in 1760, they tried to buy themselves out for 200,000 thalers. But the King refused to release them from their contract.

Frederick's *Münzjuden* had become indispensable to him. No longer did he dispute the integrity of their dealings; he did not even hesitate at the end of the war to give his formal approval to the account for the brassage revenue of the past year. It was granted to them in the following words:

> Since His Royal Majesty has deigned henceforth to administer his coinage in his own most gracious person, and since the hitherto general suppliers of coinage Ephraim and Sons and Daniel Itzig have presented their accounts, and their deliveries of coin up to this time have been examined and found to be correct: therefore in consideration of this general supplying of coinage hitherto entrusted to them, His Royal Majesty has most graciously granted his complete approval to the aforesaid Ephraim and Sons and Daniel Itzig and excused them from all further claim on this account.

It would certainly have been pleasant to them to see this announcement made public in the newspapers; but when they made this request to the King, he would not allow it. Now that Austria was vanquished and Prussia's glory had been achieved, he had no interest in drawing attention to the oppressive measures and questionable means which had helped him to this victory. In truth, he had never concealed the fact that he himself was the originator of this first Prussian inflation. But now he wanted his dealings with the *Münzjuden* to sink into oblivion, and so the token of their loyalty that they demanded from him was denied them. The profit they had made, and the certainty of being permitted to maintain their residence in Berlin with the King's approval and with all their children, were their only rewards. Perhaps, as a historian later wrote, this in itself was a proof that they had gained their fortune honestly and that their efforts had been genuinely of service to the welfare of Prussia. Be that as it may, they got no more, and had to make the best of it.

Those who had been the most vehement opponents at the beginning of the war were closely united when it ended. While Hohenzollern and Habsburgs strove with each other at Hochkirch, the enemies Itzig and Ephraim were concluding their own separate peace. At the moment when they buried their differences, the last danger that the position at court of one or the other could be destroyed was cleared out of the way. Now they set to work together to do the King's dirty work. Together they remained as hostages for three days and nights in General Tottleben's headquarters during the Russian invasion, while other Jews were forced to pay out fees and sweeteners. Together they fulfilled the double and contradictory office of being Frederick's most obedient servants and scapegoats, while at the same time dignified and respected elders of their community. Their place at the foot of the throne seemed secure for all that. And so it was not by chance, but an intentional and conspicuous symbol, that they now established themselves within view of the royal residence.

Where Daniel Itzig was living in that autumn of 1758, when his partnership with Ephraim came into being, under what roof the eighth of his sixteen children was born on 29 November, is unknown. Whatever landed property he acquired in his life had not yet fallen to his lot. Still in the obscurity of an overpopulated district, somewhere in this rapidly expanding city of Berlin, his fourth daughter came into the world. She was seven years old when the reconstruction of a row of houses in the Burgstrasse had been completed and her father was able to move into his city mansion. As much as was possible for a man of his origins at that time, he had achieved.

Here, by the side of the Spree, whose opposite shore bordered the palace park, under the clear, wide sky of the Marches, in a victorious country, of whose rise every simple citizen felt part – so much the more a man who had contributed greatly to it – here, in steadily improving prosperity, surrounded by a flock of siblings, a little girl was growing up, whose name was Franziska, but who answered to the pet name *Vögelchen* (Birdie). She had forgotten the terrors of war, which had made only a muted impression on her mind, as she had forgotten the narrow confines of her first home. A kindly mother, beloved older sisters, an abundance of domestic servants, cared for the child and above all spared her the knowledge that the calm peace and security of this house were still doubtful and endangered. Outside those walls her father's rank and station were no greater than the lowest idler in the Prussian state saw fit to allow him. And if one were looking out for enemies and for those ready to mock or insult, there were as many of these close at hand as there had once been among the Russians and the Austrians.

The little girl was without doubt approaching a moment which would be like the sudden awakening from a pleasant dream. Yet when it came this moment would not bring with it the cruel severity with which it fell upon children of earlier and future generations. In times of tranquillity and, indeed, hope, ill-will vanishes and benevolence increases. Thus the signs of a better future were multiplying in that time of Prussia's youth. Even the members of a despised faith were to be allowed to harvest the fruits of peace. More and more often those who lived by a trade were allowed that 'general privilege' that made them equal to Christian merchants. And while the heads of families whose financial acumen had helped Frederick to win his war were now devoting their energies to turning his country from a little agrarian state into a great mercantile power, their women and children were cultivating the arts and social life.

Those among them, however, whose ambitions were directed at the acquisition, not of property and influence, but of knowledge and wisdom, equally found themselves receiving new, previously unattained honours. In June of the year in which the Peace of Hubertusburg had been signed, a dissertation, 'On Evidence in the Metaphysical Sciences', written in German, was honoured by the Prussian Academy in open session. Its author, 'well enough known here already through his writings, the indigenous Jew Moses Mendelssohn', received the prize of 50 ducats, while his rival Kant obtained only the so-called 'accessit'. Four years later a book was published that was to bring greater and purer fame to him and his kin than all the outward pomp and splendour of their more prosperous fellow-believers. It was *Phaedon* – a much admired work, the first philosophical piece of writing read by the young Goethe, the spur to Mendelssohn's friendship with Herder, a passport to the world of German intellect and a monument of transcendental speculation, although it was knocked from its pedestal when Kant's *Critique of Pure Reason* was published and Fichte, Hegel and Schelling appeared upon the scene.

Meanwhile, little Franziska's father, a friend and patron of the philosopher, was climbing the ladder of earthly success, with deliberation and a proper sense of his own patriarchal dignity. In the last winter of the war he had acquired his own factory, the ironworks Sorge und Voigtsfelde in the Harz, close to the border of Brunswick. It had been the King's wish to develop Prussian industry, in order to be less dependent on expensive imports of goods. Daniel Itzig set up three more foundries, and by the year 1765 he had already invested 100,000 thalers in foundry works. When he later sold them to the mining board in exchange for an equally high annuity for his family he had already added to his enterprises an oil-mill, an English leather factory and, together with his father-in-law, a silk factory.

He had, in compliance with Frederick's wishes, become a manufacturer as well as a coiner and financier. Certainly he still took part in coinage transactions, but above all, since he had been a co-founder of the Royal Bank, he proudly regarded himself as Frederick's court banker. He seems to have parted company with Ephraim soon after the Peace of Hubertusburg, as can be assumed from a letter addressed to him in the handwriting of Gotthold Ephraim Lessing. In this document General von Tauentzien, whose secretary Lessing was, confirmed to Daniel Itzig that Ephraim's claim against him for certain business shares was unjustified.

In royal favour, as well as in esteem within his own province, Daniel was rapidly beginning to overtake his former rival and later partner. In the same first year of peace he was named chief elder of the Jewish community in Berlin. The following summer he moved into his mansion, designed for him as a two-winged residence, unpretentiously elegant in the symmetry of its simple lines, in contrast to the more splendid Ephraim house nearby. This house in the Burgstrasse soon became a treasure-house of the fine arts. For now, having overcome the rigours of his youth, achieved his arduous rise and completed his fortieth year, he found himself able to develop those 'gentle manners and good taste' which were written in his face. Now he was truly moving in 'refined circles', not only of his own faith, but also among enlightened Christians.

Nicolai was his guest, and later, full of admiration, described the Itzig mansion with its valuable paintings, including Rubens' Ganymede, two musicians by Terborch and works by Watteau and Antoine Pesne, its well-constructed prayer-room and its bathroom, a great rarity at the time. There were many links with Lessing, Mendelssohn's long-standing friend. Whoever came to the Prussian capital and, in addition to the court, the nobility, the artists and scholars also wished to be introduced into Jewish circles, was taken first to Moses Mendelssohn, then to the house of the man who was now known as the *Judenfürst*, or Jewish Prince. August von Henning, later a Danish councillor of state, wrote in his description of Berlin in 1772 which has survived into our times:

> The Jewish colony is considerable; it comprises four hundred families, estimated at two thousand persons. It has the great advantage of enjoying even greater distinction from the fame of its scholars than from the beauty of its ladies. A letter from Reimarus brought me into the house of the famous Mendelssohn. At the mansion of the banker Itzig I often see the learned Friedländer, who is much esteemed in the cultured world. Itzig has sixteen children, of whom some already have situations in their

own right, and others are just at the age when beauty begins to unfold. The charm of the daughters' beauty is heightened by their talents, particularly for music, and by a finely developed intellect.

It was Franziska, at nearly fourteen years old, whose beauty he saw unfolding. The older sisters – the first-born Hanna, Bella, whose grandson was to be Felix Mendelssohn, and the twenty-year-old Blümchen – were all married by this time, and the younger ones were still in the nursery. It later became clear how rich the musical talent of this fourth daughter would prove to be. She and her sisters also took delight in the theatre, and it may well be that an event recorded in the memoirs of Henriette Herz took place in their midst. 'As early as my ninth year, that is in about 1773,' Henriette told her biographer J. Fürst, 'I attended the performance of a tragedy in the house of a Jewish banker. It was *Richard III* – by what author I cannot remember – and the daughters of the house had taken the female roles. The impression of this, the first dramatic performance I ever saw, was an inextinguishable one.'

It seems an obvious conclusion that she enjoyed the drama by the unknown author – probably, as Fürst assumes, C. S. Weiss, a popular playwright of the time – in the beautiful, large garden in the suburb of Kölln which Daniel Itzig already owned at that time. This park had been extensively remodelled by its owner with the help of the court gardener, Heidert. Now it contained, according to Friedrich Nicolai in his description of Berlin, 'apart from hedges, arcades and shady plantations for one's delight, several thousand fruit-trees of the best varieties. Here also is a garden theatre in the open air. Likewise there are various statues by Knöfler of Dresden'.

No trace remains for posterity of the histrionic power with which those young ladies so inextinguishably impressed on the memory of Henriette Herz a *Richard III* which was not even by Shakespeare. As transitory as the living performance is the testimony of an aesthetic disposition which is often the only creative streak to be found in great merchants! Daniel Itzig, who was perhaps 'called to higher things', who, had he himself been a grandchild and heir, would have aspired to and attained what his own grandchildren and heirs attained, expressed his propensity for beauty, his love of nobility in a garden. This garden, enclosed in a rectangular piece of land, cut off diagonally at the lower edge, between the Köpenicker Strasse and the Schlesisches Tor, whose design and ornamentation were comparable at that time only with those of the castle grounds of Sanssouci, has long ago disappeared from the face of the earth. It lives on only in a sketch in the Nicolai book and in a melancholy account that appeared in the *Vossische Zeitung* on 3 May 1865, on the occasion of its final destruction.

In this, the rondels and bosquets of the park, which had already become a wilderness, are praised, together with its sculptures and vases on pedestals, its colossal figures, its benches and staircases in the best style of the Friderician age. The statues were from the hands of masters – Cupids, some furnished with the attributes of Greek gods and heroes, some with other emblems; nymphs and satyrs; figures of children; busts of emperors and bejewelled women. 'Among the other sculptures,' the description ends, 'two fine vases, with winged dragons for handles, are particularly to be mentioned. The sundial should finally be noted, worked by Ring of Berlin, according to the inscription, after the invention of "Rab Israel Moses" in the year 1762, on a copper plate with detailed divisions, and set upon a dainty pedestal.'

The *Vossische Zeitung* had this to add, over 100 years ago, on the subject of Itzig and his transitory creation:

We held it to be our duty to recall these sculptures once more, before levers and crowbars banish them from the place allotted to them by an art-loving man in the days when Frederick's sun rose gloriously over our fatherland and the impulse of his creative genius provoked emulation in all spheres. Was it a high official of state, a cavalier of the favoured nobility, an important courtier sunning himself in the direct rays of royal grace, whose creation we admire here, endowed with all the splendour, abundance and prodigality in the use of space of the last century? No, this park, this garden, under whose old trees a kind of fairytale magic wafts towards us, all these weathered old mazes, devastated bowling-greens, these pavilions and bowers, between whose stones grass grows in luxuriance, ruined conservatories, almost marshy water-basins, these splendid avenues and salons of trees, these partly shattered and overthrown sculptures covered with moss and lichen – all these were planned and laid out by a man at the very foot of the ladder of citizenship of those days – a *Schutzjude* [tolerated Jew]. How characteristic of its time, how interesting in the history of our city is this work, a monument to the great King's spirit that penetrated into all the strata of society, a proof also of the spirit that was stirring among the Jews in the days of Lessing and Moses Mendelssohn and of how it adorned the patrician citizens of the German cities.

It is not only to prove her father's aesthetic taste but also to cast some light on Franziska's childhood, of which so little is known, that the park by the Schlesisches Tor has been described in all its particulars. This was the landscape of her childhood, which she later tried lovingly and laboriously to recreate in the Braunhirschengrund near Vienna. Here her feeling for splendour and beauty unfolded, here were the sources of her gaiety and love of life, here she learned, on the stone steps of the 'garden theatre in the open air', to move freely and yet with studied grace, here she found pleasure in rich social life, overcame, in her playing and dreaming, the curse of her people, glided, without carrying away any lasting damage, over the moment of recognition of her otherness. Untroubled, even high-spirited, she looked upon the world as would a little princess, without ever doubting that a life among the great and the wise of this earth was to be her lot.

In her crinoline, with powdered hair, distinguished from the children of the Prussian nobility only by certain religious observances and a vague mistrust towards the outside world, the daughter of the *Judenfürst* walked out into the daylight. After all, had not the King himself bestowed upon her father the highest rank which was to be given in the Jewish hierarchy? On 28 December 1775, Frederick had deigned 'to designate Daniel Itzig and Jacob Moses, hitherto the elders of the Jewry of these parts, because of their well-known excellent high reputation and their insight into the condition and the affairs of Jewry, as perpetual chief elders of the Jewish communities of all his several lands, and to confirm them most graciously in this title'. In the same winter, just before Franziska's seventeenth birthday, Itzig was granted a certificate by the Berlin police authorising the marriage of his fourth daughter 'to the foreign Jew Nathan Adam Arnsteiner' from Vienna.

The wedding took place in the following summer. The Arnsteiners had come to inspect the bride two years earlier: in September 1773 the imperial and royal court administrator Adam Isaac Arnsteiner had requested a passport for himself and his family 'for the purpose of travelling to Berlin, where his son wished to marry'. How and why Daniel Itzig chose the young Nathan Adam as his son-in-law is unknown. It is enough to say that both families belonged to that special aristocracy of court Jews, though it was not yet described in those terms, which was as widely ramified as it was tightly knit by intermarriage. Countless links bound one to the other. And if seniority counterbalances even the highest position, Arnsteiner, whose grandfather had served Emperor Joseph I, need not be ashamed to be seen beside the granddaughter of an occasional court supplier to an elector of the German Empire. After all, both houses had emerged from the obscurity of history at about the same time. If the court banker Daniel Itzig was now the most powerful man in Prussian Jewry, the court agent Adam Isaac Arnsteiner was among the most influential Jews of the imperial residence.

On the penultimate day of June 1776 the marriage was solemnised in Berlin, under the richly decorated canopy in the prayer-room of the 'Itzig city mansion'. The celebrations in those houses were famous, and not infrequently the nobility pleaded for the privilege of being allowed to attend them. Princess Amelia, the King's sister, for instance once visited a celebration of the Feast of Tabernacles, where the pretty little Henriette Herz was presented to her. Another sister of the great Frederick, the Queen Mother Ulrica of Sweden, in April 1772 invited herself to a Jewish wedding and was deeply impressed by the splendour and the fine manners which she saw there: 'What surprised me the most was the education that the people chosen by God gives its children. I truly believed that I was among persons of high rank and birth.'

Her brother, to whom she wrote thus at Potsdam, had a few malicious remarks to make. 'I confess to you, my dear sister,' he replied, 'that I would not have expected to find you at a Jewish wedding. You have certainly delighted all the children of the old law by your presence, but I fear greatly that the Hebrew music must have jarred on your ears. The Jews of Berlin are rich and have for some years found it to their taste to give their children a good education, in the hope that God will one day lend his ear again to his people and make them the rulers of the world. I must confess that I see few indications of this, but nothing lifts up one's soul so much as imagining that we are destined for something higher, and the Jews are filled with this notion.'

The wedding which Queen Ulrica had honoured with her presence had taken place in the same year as that of an older Itzig daughter, Blümchen, who had married the 'learned Friedländer', Moses Mendelssohn's pupil. Certainly, it had not been more splendid and solemn than Franziska's four years later. Neither one congregation nor the other, however, could delude itself into thinking that God would ever elevate its people to the mastery of the world. Appearances, as Frederick rightly remarked, did not support this view. Indeed, permission for this marriage had been given only on condition that the young couple should leave the country shortly afterwards. Not even the *Judenfürst* was allowed to keep his daughter and son-in-law in his house for as long as he wished. For even in the land of the great Frederick, who was very well able to appreciate the countless services of his Jewish subjects, there was indignation over every Jew who entered the country, and joy over each one who turned his back on it.

And so, after a last few days in her native city, the bride departed with the young man from Vienna who was almost a stranger to her. The image of the large-roomed, elegant house in the Burgstrasse in Berlin, the image of the patriarchal home, of her kindly parents and beloved siblings, of the garden in which she was safe from the world, with its well-groomed rondels and bosquets, its graceful nymphs and Cupids, accompanied her on her long journey. In the mountains of Saxony, in the forests of Bohemia, she dreamed of birch trees and sand. And when the berline came to a halt on the Graben in Vienna and her husband leaped to the pavement to help her down, as she stood there in silence, while a door opened in a narrow, tall, dark house, her blue eyes still reflected the gleam of the Brandenburg sky.

-2-

The Emperor's Minions

The Emperor's eyes too were blue. So blue that the court ladies named a colour after them, in which they had their gowns made *à la duchesse* and *à la toque*. The same colour was surprisingly becoming to the Emperor himself, as if to belie the gravity of that shrewd, parsimonious man. He preferred to dress simply, in the German or 'Werther' style, as it was called in those days, consisting of a long greatcoat, leather trousers and top-boots, which betrayed his martial sternness and perhaps also his admiration for Austria's main adversary. Frederick the Great was his model; yet he took up arms against him without a qualm when it became necessary. He had revered Voltaire as the King's teacher; yet he travelled through Switzerland without seeking out the philosopher in Ferney. In his discipline, his moderation and his sense of duty this exceptional Habsburg took after his robust ancestors of the Palatinate and Brunswick. Roman King and Emperor in the German realm, at home only a tolerated co-regent of his mother, the Austrian ruler, he shivered in the evening sunshine of the Theresian sovereignty, waiting for the dawn of enlightenment. Among his easy-going subjects he felt like a lonely, misunderstood stranger. Twice widowed, 'cold and passionless, looking at women as though they were statues', he did not share their tendencies towards extravagance. A frugal eater, whose meal of no more than six dishes was prepared by a single royal cook, he was untouched, even revolted by their gluttony.

'The god of the Viennese is their belly. They know no more pleasant entertainment than to feed. In summer, there is no garden that one enters where people are not eating from high-piled dishes laid out on every table; and for the most part chicken – fried chicken, braised chicken, roast chicken.' So wrote an *Engelländer* (Englishman) in his *Journey through Mannheim, Bavaria and Austria to Vienna*, which was published 'by his German friend L. A. F. v. B.' in the last year of Joseph II's reign, and perhaps even written in that year. It is only one of the numerous reports on countries, peoples and customs which were being rushed into print at a time when people were possessed by a veritable travel fever. They traversed the length and breadth of Europe noting, in the most painstaking detail, the dimensions, topography and population of its great cities, their public buildings, means of transport, quality of lighting, the birth and death rates of their inhabitants, how they spent their time and their money, the laws and regulations, religious, social and sexual customs, the names of the most important statesmen, philosophers, artists, collectors and scholars, the virtues and vices of the men and women, their songs and prayers, their bills of fare and their epitaphs, their appearance, their character and their temperament.

There is hardly an epoch in European history which has been described so frequently and so amply, with such naïve delight in discovery, as if one were dealing with exotic or savage tribes, with such pleasure in the characteristic and generalising detail. One learns almost too much, and the inconsistencies are many. Yet all these travellers' accounts, whether by genuine or bogus Englishmen, Frenchmen, Germans or Dutch, agree on one thing, that is the epicureanism and gluttony of the Viennese.

'Apart from eating, their greatest pleasure is their *Kasperl* [Punch and Judy] and their animal-baiting,' reports the *Engelländer* previously quoted. Another visitor, the Swabian Wilhelm Ludwig Wekhrlin, is of the opinion that 'both sexes love splendour, display and pleasure to the point of excess – faults that are not so much in their hearts as in their blood'. Admittedly he has seen 'consummate beauty among the women' and 'figures among the male sex which a Persian sultan might envy', but 'these gifts are obscured by the most insufferable self-love and vanity'. The Viennese ladies attract and repel him simultaneously. They are 'neither as coarse and strapping as Englishwomen, nor as delicate as Frenchwomen. They possess the sentiment of a Neapolitan, the coquetry of a French and the heart of a German woman.' Their pleasing traits however are 'balanced by an unforgivable tendency towards idleness and a comfortable life. To paint the emblem of a Viennese lady, one would have to follow the drawing by Carracus: a Venus with a tortoise at her feet.'

Moreover, however beautiful 'the scions of this climate' appear to him, he calls in question the purity of their blood-line: 'Vienna teems with French, Italians, Hungarians, Slavs, Jews and other nations. The original Austrians have disappeared. A magistrate told me yesterday that from the house of Starhemberg down to the town-crier who goes about the streets there is hardly a family left among us which can trace its Austrian ancestry in an undiluted lineage from its great-grandfather.'

The North Germans were the sharpest critics of the sensuality and selfishness of that nation in the south, in whose midst, as it happened, their overlord, the Emperor of the Holy Roman Empire, resided. In 1784 a Berliner wrote to a friend concerning the Viennese aristocracy: 'The young ones play, drive, ride, hunt, make love in warm countries, till they grow cold, beat their servants lame, ruin their tenants, squeeze money out of their stewards, often get their mistresses with child, but rarely their wives, know no other merit in them but that they have money, and wish for nothing more earnestly than that the virtue of women could be sold at auction, like old books and clothes.' Of the old, he said that they were 'wrathful, headstrong, proud, litigious, and keep their own followers, because in their old age they have not forgotten the habit of teasing people which still clings to them from their youth; they quarrel with their wives, are given over to gorging and guzzling, and let their children grow up blockheads'.

The ordinary people seemed to please him better, for they were 'trusty, hospitable, kindly, well-meaning', but liked to live 'in splendour and excess'. 'My dear fellow, I should in no way exceed the limits of the truth, were I perhaps to describe Vienna to you as the one place where the most gormandising takes place.' All this, however, this 'gluttony and debauchery makes the people here too lustful and lascivious, as the servant girls know only too well, when their gentlemen need to refresh themselves after dinner'. Nowhere else is 'female game so cheap as here, for you can eat yourself sick for twenty pence. You may easily, without trouble, find a *letto fornito* in any house, as there are in most inns in Italy.'

Finally, this Prussian subject emphatically rejected Vienna's claim to be a beautiful city. 'It has no spacious streets, no squares with buildings pleasant to the eye, no dominant similarity of the houses and no perspective views as have other German towns . . . Vienna is not a place which strikes one by its appearance; it needs an expert eye, and must be examined.'

If this anonymous correspondent was a thorn in the flesh of the country that had entertained him, in order afterwards to be exposed by him, his compatriot Friedrich Nicolai seemed a very dagger in its heart. When, at about the same time, the second volume of Nicolai's *Journey through Germany and Switzerland in the Year 1781* was published, in which his description of Vienna began, a storm of indignation arose in Austria and raged northwards to Berlin. The Viennese, hotheads and sensible people alike, were being forced to observe their own merciless portrait through the eyes of an upright, enlightened, tolerant but deadly serious Prussian.

'To abolish all the softness, love of comfort, thoughtlessness, idleness and constant dissipation that are so generally rife in Vienna, two future generations will certainly not suffice.' This was only one of the gloomy prophecies which Nicolai wove into his description of the court. Precise as in all things he said or did, he furnished proof of his assertion:

> A well-to-do citizen in Vienna is eating almost at every moment of the day. On rising, in summer he slurps down a few glasses of cream and enjoys the requisite quantity of croissants or French rolls to go with them. In the winter he dips his roll into milky coffee and, before going to mass, stuffs himself with a good helping of 'prayer sausages'. Before midday he is to be found in the cherry wine cellar in summer, or the mead cellar in winter, and has a cold snack while he is about it. For his midday meal he usually eats four dishes, and not a little of each. About four o'clock, he has a hearty afternoon tea; at five he goes to play skittles, when he takes some smoked belly of pork or chicken, as well as fried snails, scrambled eggs and roast loin of beef. Notwithstanding all this, he is able to consume a further three dishes at home towards eight o'clock, or he betakes himself to a tavern, dines on a hundred oysters and accompanies them with sweet wine. All who do not do so are called starvelings. My native land, Brandenburg, is frequently given the honour in Vienna of being called *Hungerland*.

The greed of the Viennese particularly enraged him because of its harmful effect on body and mind, its stultifying effect on the writers and thinkers of the city, regular spongers at the table of their patrons, of whom a satirist says:

> Sie schlecken beym Lungenbraten und Hendl,
> Fauscheln von Mauskatzen, Krapfen und Pfänzl,
> Und suchen Verstand, Genie, Witz und Laun
> Im Schnapfen und steyrischen Kapaun.

> [They gobble their roast beef and chicken, / Gloating over pancakes and doughnuts, / And seek reason, genius, good humour and wit / In snipe or woodcock and Styrian capon.]

In his reproaches, whether they were directed against sensual excesses or lack of spirituality, Nicolai hoped to find support among all right-minded people. And certainly a visitor from Berlin arriving in the capital of the German Empire in those days was bound to share Nicolai's opinion to a certain extent, even if he did not possess the writer's strict and unflinching sense of virtue. Whether he had grown up in the Protestant creed of the New Testament or according to the reasonable laws of the Old, he could not but deplore the abuses of bigotry and hypocrisy into which Christianity had here degenerated. For, like Nicolai, he would have observed in the dark old churches, glistening with gold, an almost superstitious reverence for dubious relics, a 'sliding around on one's knees' before every tinsel-decked shrine, together with the scarcely concealed sidelong glances of the ladies who had come straight from their lovers to divine service, or even the coquettish fervour of women of easy virtue at the last Mass at half past eleven in the Kapuzinerkirche, which was well known as the 'whores' Mass'. Like him, he would have met young clerics, 'all languishing and thirsting for pleasure in their celibate state', as well as the 'excessively great number of young and beautiful chambermaids, who appeared decked from head to foot in silk and gold lace'.

As far as the dearth of men of intellect was concerned, many a visitor from Berlin would have been convinced like Nicolai that 'Austria has not yet given us a writer deserving of the attention of the rest of Germany'. Without doubt there was in Berlin 'a very faulty knowledge of the political, literary, commercial and social circumstances of that other part of Germany'. And there was certainly some truth in the dictum coined by Lady Mary Wortley Montagu seventy years earlier, now confirmed by Nicolai, that 'getting a Lover is so far from loseing, that 'tis properly geting reputation, Ladys being much more respected in regard to the rank of their Lovers than that of their Husbands'.

But if the Berliner were here not to see, to censure and to depart again, but to linger awhile in Vienna, then for better or worse, sooner or later, he would have to learn to reconcile the two lifestyles. Perhaps the most charming work to have been published at that time in defence of the capital might then have fallen into his hands. Johann Friedel's *Letters from Vienna on Various Subjects to a Friend in Berlin* – published in the same year as Nicolai's second volume – corrected the balance in a refreshing way. Friedel nominated kind-heartedness as 'the most original trait of our populace', but admitted that not all foreigners were aware of this characteristic: 'We appear to them too stiff, too unfeeling. And why? Because we do not appear to melt away at every moment with sentimentality and soulfulness.'

Sensual enjoyment has rarely been advocated with more ingenuousness:

We sentimentalise less. A hundred times we visit smiling meadows or rose-decked avenues at sunrise, and hardly once do we notice the roses, the meadows or the sunrise. All that magic lies there before us, and seldom, very seldom do we say to ourselves more than: Upon my soul! now that's a pretty sight, truly. And therewith we saunter off to breakfast, enjoy it, feel cheerful and never give another thought to why we should feel so cheerful. It is with the pleasures of man as it is with beauty. The Graces please us, as long as we see them entire. But as soon as they are dissected in the anatomical theatre – gone is the susceptible feeling we would have at the sight of them. So it is with pleasure. As soon as the moral surgeon dissects the pleasure we have enjoyed – we yawn – it disgusts us at last. It is only affectation that prevents us from admitting this. We enjoy the pleasure; – you chatter about it. – We drink wine; you sing about it. We marry our pretty girls; you – Petrarchise over them. We kiss the bosom that pleases us; you write a poem about it. – We enjoy becoming fathers, you moralise about this pleasure. We pluck the roses and violets and hyacinths, – you paint them, and so on. Now which of us two is the more sensible?

A hedonistic view of the world opposed to an ethical–sentimental one – this is how the contrast between the two cities, imperial Vienna and royal Berlin, presents itself. Joseph II, by nature and upbringing attached to the moral rules of life, the 'dissecting' way of thinking of his Prussian subjects, in a great and futile experiment set about converting his compatriots to this very attitude. In vain! As long as the good-hearted, narrow-minded, motherly old Empress sat upon the throne, and hardly less after her death, though prevented from an excessively carefree satisfaction of their thirst for enjoyment by Joseph's Spartan reforming spirit, the Viennese gave themselves up to their *joie de vivre*.

They worked only when they had to do so, and much preferred to revel in idleness. They bustled in and out of inns, restaurants, dance-halls and promenades; they strolled in the Augarten and the Prater; they crowded to the animal-baitings where fierce dogs were set upon enfeebled donkeys, bears and lions to tear them in pieces for the general amusement, and they assembled in front of the pillories where a hundred strokes of the rod were being meted out to some thief. They rushed to the *Kasperl* show and laughed themselves silly over its coarse jests. They ate their fried and braised and roast chickens and drank the light, dry, rippling wine that grew on the slopes of the Vienna Woods. And when they had had their fill of laughter, food and drink, they took their evening stroll through the broadest of their crooked old city streets, signalled to a 'nymph' of the Graben and disappeared with her into one of those houses which did not scruple to rent out an empty bed or a *letto fornito* for a few hours. It would take more than a Prussian pedant, a Friedrich Nicolai, more than an idealistic monarch, to rob them of such joys. From time to time, wars and famines damped their animal spirits. But as soon as these were fanned into flame again by the return of prosperity and plentiful nourishment, once more the Viennese would fall to their pleasures in the traditional, earthy-sensual way.

This then was the city which had become the new home of the bride from Berlin. Her residence was in the Graben, that street of purveyors of fashion and of coffee-houses, of evening strollers and ladies of easy virtue, which was at the same time the domicile of the best society. It was surprising enough that the Arnsteiners had been permitted to settle here, and explained only by the special advantage enjoyed by Adam Isaac Arnsteiner through the imperial warrant which entitled him to establish his quarters 'in any place that he should consider most safe to take up his abode'. We know how much yearly rent Adam Isaac paid his landlord, Johann Baptist Contrini, every Martinmas: it was 2,690 gulden. For this he became possessor of nineteen reception rooms, ten bedrooms, three kitchens, three attics, two cellars, lodging for carriages, stabling for six horses, and a hay-loft, distributed over three storeys and some outbuildings in the courtyard.

The house known as 'No. 1175 in the city' was a splendid edifice, with a snarling lion leaping out from the ridge of the roof. A glazed alcove on the first floor provided a view of the Starhemberg fountain and, some distance away, the column of the Trinity whose disorganised mass Nicolai found so abominable. At ground-floor level there were the arched shop-fronts of the merchants Franz Hakel, Peter Oswald and Martin Vogl. On the third floor, besides accommodation for the Arnsteiners' coachmen, personal servants and kitchenmaids, was a small apartment occupied by a succession of tenants. And finally, Contrini, the landlord, had reserved for himself the use of a bedroom and a cellar. Otherwise, the sole ruler of the building was the court agent, Arnsteiner, with his wife Sibilla, his eldest son and his retinue, together with an indeterminate and changeable band of followers including clerks, bookkeepers and cashiers, who shared his protected status and were as devoted to him as slaves. Outside, instead of the barges of the Spree boatmen which passed in front of the palace in the Burgstrasse, carriages glided past, sedan-chairmen ran along, and the melancholy cries of Croatian hawkers of herbs, Bohemian women selling snails, and straw-cutters from Lombardy, drifted upwards. It was a foreign world. Franziska found it difficult to feel at home, and in a sense she never did.

To the Arnsteiners this was a familiar world, as if they had lived there from time immemorial. Eighty years are a long time in the history of an unsettled people who were constantly driven from one place to the next. And it was in about 1700 that the court agent's father had first set foot in this city – a slight young man from Arnstein near Würzburg, still unmarried and childless, who for his part became employed as a cashier by the great Samson Wertheimer, and thus came to share his privilege of protection. When he exchanged his sleepy Franconian village for the capital of the Holy Roman Empire, he had come to a place whose very soil seemed drenched with the ancient destiny of the Jews.

In the train of the Roman legions, the Jews had reached the Rhine, the Main and the Danube. Titus, who destroyed Jerusalem and drove them out of there, already regarded them as imperial servants, as objects, goods and chattels. This, too, was how they were seen by the Holy Roman Emperors, the heirs and successors of the Caesars, who as 'overlords and immediate arbiters over Jewry at large' reserved for themselves the right 'to keep Jews', well up to the days of Charles V. Under the Carolingians the Jews were allowed to ply their trades in Austria, and the Vienna of the Dukes of Babenberg allowed them their own streets and squares. In the eleventh and twelfth centuries, here and there some of their number achieved fame and wealth; in King Wratislaw's Bohemia, on the Wissehrad hill, for example, they were said to be rolling in gold and silver, and in neighbouring Hungary it was reported that they had become so mighty that many of the kingdom's greatest subjects were on the point of converting to Judaism. In Vienna, however, the crusaders and local citizens made sure that they were kept firmly in their place and continually clipped their wings.

Frederick the Warlike conceded them some public offices for a time, but it was a privilege which was soon removed. Forbidden to practise any trade, to farm, to join the army, to take up administrative posts, to practise law or medicine in any form, and restricted to the narrow and not always high-minded world of money and commerce, the Jews developed their talents to their own benefit and that of their prince. Immediately subject to him, neither part of the nation nor owing a duty to it, they 'stood at the side of any tyrant with untiring industry', assisted him in his state of constant shortage of funds by dint of inventing new royal prerogatives, taxes and duties and thus drew upon themselves the wrath of the populace, 'which was ready to run riot against them for the sake of every conflagration, every misfortune sent from heaven'. If ever their financial power should disappear through some stroke of fate, the ruler would have no further use for them. When, in 1406, the Jewish quarter of Vienna, behind the big square *am Hof*, went up in flames, the mob looted the houses that had been spared by the fire, while their occupants sat in the cellar, 'so as not to complete the plundering with a blood-bath'. They had no way of making good the loss of some 100,000 gulden either for themselves or Duke Frederick, who immediately came to view their usefulness in a less favourable light. Their community had not yet recovered from the consequences of this misfortune when a man called Israel, in the city of Enns, was accused of desecration of the Eucharist, and despite his denials under severe torture was found guilty.

Jews were now being captured throughout the duchy of Austria and deported across the frontier, mainly to Poland, but some were retained as hostages. Israel's wife 'strangled herself with her own veil. A rich Jew of Tuln drove a knife into his own heart. Many Jewesses in Mödling, in Berchtoldsdorf, throttled themselves, many veiled the faces of their friends and loved ones and opened their veins for them.' On 12 March 1421, all those in prison, including Jews of both sexes, were burnt to death on the meadow near the Viennese suburb of Erdberg, and their ashes scattered in the Danube. They had not wavered in their faith and had disdained to be saved through conversion. 'Now when the Jews were taken to be burnt,' says a report, 'they began to dance and leap as if going to a wedding. With loud shouts and words of comfort to each other, they begged each others' forgiveness and looked forward to bliss in the next world.' After this sacrificial procession, reminiscent of the martyrdoms of the early Christians, all their houses were made the property of the city, under the seal of the mayor and council.

In this way young Albert, Duke of Austria, who later acquired the title of King of Germany, first drove the Jews out of his duchy. For a long time they were banned from entering it. After many years of representations by their 'commander' Josel von Rosheim, Emperor Charles V granted them a privilege in the German Kingdom which simultaneously protected them and freed them from their imperial bondage. But the effects of his clemency did not extend as far as Vienna. 'Safe conduct in trading and travelling by land or water' was not granted to those who might have wished to return to this city. And as there were hardly any Jews to be found there when the decree was issued, its prohibition against expelling any who had been resident there at the time of the Emperor's accession did not greatly help matters. Those few who still remained in Vienna in 1551 were forced by Ferdinand I to wear the yellow armband. Even twenty years later, there were no more than seven families who were constrained by Maximilian II to wear a 'little yellow disc'.

Rudolf II – that eccentric Habsburg, who surrounded himself with alchemists and visionaries, astrologers and interpreters of dreams, painters and silversmiths, and drew the Jews of Prague to his court, not only for their money but for the sake of their cabbalistic mysticism – bestowed renewed favour upon them. He even created the concept of 'court Jews', chosen men who were not subject to the limitations of other members of their faith. Yet to the poor and simple among them, who had meanwhile settled in Vienna without any proper authorisation, but only as a result of occasional official negligence, this was not yet a sign of special graciousness. It was in Ferdinand II that they first saw their true protector. This sensible monarch agreed in 1619 to a confirmation of their rights and liberties, allowed them to build a house of worship and soon afterwards assigned them a part of the city as their place of residence – the 'Lower Werd', a district on the left-hand shore of the present Danube canal.

Here they were found and described by the traveller J. J. Müller from Weimar, in the year 1660, when he had reached 'the Jews' town, oddly situated in front of the Red Tower over the draw-bridge, and somewhat protected by its walls and gates'. In its streets sat 'those of the male sort, their heads covered by broad black caps, some in long gowns of black velvet and others in silk, as among others their *medicus*, and also a *chymicus*, who is consulted by the most distinguished cavaliers and others in the city of Vienna, in the same habit. Those of the above-mentioned who wear white woollen shawls are reputed to be men of law.'

Ferdinand's son had allowed them to live in peace in the Lower Werd and had even had them protected – at their own expense, it is true – by his musketeers at times of unrest and attacks by students. The youthful Leopold I too seemed well disposed towards them at first. When the advance of Turkish troops was imminent soon after his accession, the Jews were given permission to flee into the inner city in case of need. Leopold frequently gave orders to check the wrath of the populace against them, which broke out time and again through bitterness over the hardships of war. Despite many injustices and constant threat from Turks, Swedes and their own compatriots, those fifty years of peace in the Lower Werd were once seen by the Vienna Jews as their golden age. But their happiness was not to last. 'Those of Vienna', representatives of the city and guilds who stood to gain no direct benefit from the Jews' wealth were always devising new ways to drive them out and to seize their possessions and premises.

A conflagration in the newly built wing of the Hofburg, set off by the carelessness of a carpenter's mate, was laid at the door of Jewry. The bloody tumult that broke out after the arrest of a student who was mistreating a Jew was also blamed on them. They were reproached with collusion with the Turks, because they sometimes sent their children on exchange visits to their relatives in Turkish-occupied Hungary. Bishop Kollonitsch stirred up anger against them from the pulpit. And finally, in their eagerness to appropriate for themselves the Jews' business dealings, the Viennese merchants together with the city council declared themselves willing to reimburse the Emperor for the 10,000 gulden of annual tolerance payments.

Leopold hesitated, mindful of his father's example. In the end, however, he gave way to the constant pressure from 'those of Vienna', the reservations of his clergy and not least the pleas of his consort Margarethe Therese – a 'weak and delicate female, brought up rather for the profession of a nun than of a princess' – whose religious fervour stemmed from her native Inquisitorial Spain. His mind once made up, he carried out his intention in great haste. The feast of Corpus Christi in 1669 seemed to him an 'opportunity to take action *contra inimicos Christi*' which was not to be lost. At that time there were some 4,000 Jews living in 132 houses in the Lower Werd, a whole flourishing community with scholars, doctors, lawyers and men of culture and taste, who often entertained the bourgeoisie of Vienna and travelling scholars as guests. The first 1,400 were expelled as early as July. When they had departed, and wholesale expulsion was threatened, those who remained turned to the Emperor with 'humble sighs and entreaties dripping with blood', 'in the most gracious consideration that to be a Jew is in itself no crime', and because His Majesty 'would hold their extirpation no satisfaction for his tender disposition', to allow them to stay. This was refused with the declaration that 'execution is the soul of all wholesome resolutions'. A year later the Jews' town was empty. Leopold gave the district the name of his patron saint and had a church dedicated to him built on the site of the destroyed Jewish prayer-house.

The second expulsion, however thoroughly it destroyed the life of the community, at least proceeded without a blood-bath. Robbed of their immovable possessions, with only a few bundles heaped up on carts, they who had only recently walked in state 'in black velvet and silk' were passing out of the city gates of Vienna. Fifty families, as we know, set out for Berlin. Most of the others headed for the hereditary dominions of Bohemia and Moravia, where they were left unmolested and often given the surname of Wiener. Like their predecessors who had met death by fire on the Gänswiese at Erdberg, they were not shaken in their faith by any promises, though this might have been presumed in a 'people given to haggling and usury'. Full of indignation, the satirical versifier Matthias Abele reported the answer given by the weeping women in a distinguished Jewish household, where he had been invited for a farewell meal, to his suggestion that they should take refuge in the bosom of Christianity: 'They would rather let themselves be burnt alive than waver the breadth of a needle's point from their faith. I bethought myself that these accursed martyrs of the devil would persevere in their wickedness and obstinacy even up to their ears. I would sooner seek to wash a Moor white than to cleanse and purify such Jewish scum.'

The Swedish resident ambassador wrote in a similar vein to Queen Christina, who had interceded with the Holy See for the Vienna Jews: 'Yet this is greatly to be wondered at, that of three to four thousand souls who have emigrated within half a year, and are about to settle in Bohemia, Moravia and Silesia, not one should be found who might prepare himself in this their great affliction to think of changing their faith.'

Now they were gone. And the Viennese, to whom the business-minded Jews had been a thorn in the flesh, rejoiced. But the new landlords of the 'Leopoldstadt' did not pay their share of the 4,000 gulden tolerance money, the treasury found that it no longer had the option of obtaining short-term credit, and apart from finance certain kinds of retail trade came to a standstill, 'since the idleness of Christians and particularly of the Viennese,' as a treasury document remarked, 'is so great that they are unwilling to transact such business.' The imperial treasury found further grounds to deplore the departure of the Jews. It estimated at around 25,000 gulden the loss of revenue to the townspeople from rents for premises standing empty, the diminished market for foodstuffs and the decrease in business for merchants and companies. The loss of annual receipts from taxes, duties, levies and tolls formerly paid by the Jews was estimated at 40,000 gulden. Meanwhile Vienna was afflicted by the plague and, worse than ever before, by the Turks. Public credit was exhausted. Whereas 100,000 gulden could once have been procured in a day, the Emperor had for weeks not been able to borrow a tenth of that sum.

It was thus his top financial officials who finally advised him urgently to take in the Jews again, and, on the subject of the cost of their expulsion, wrote that 'doubtless, had your Imperial Majesty been advised earlier of this matter, your Majesty would not so lightly have agreed to such a general banishment'. The treasury also questioned the theological faculty of the University of Vienna as to what might stand in the way of a return of the Jews, and received the answer that their scruples were not insurmountable. Nevertheless, the Emperor was unable to share his treasury's viewpoint that fiscal considerations should serve as the guiding principle of government, and wished to see the matter weighed above all *'theologice*, then *politice* and finally *cameraliter'*. Since the political consequences of renewed admission for the Jews seemed too great a threat, even if the church should raise no objection to it, Leopold refused the treasury's suggestion.

As he was soon to realise, he did so to his own detriment. For at this late stage of absolutism the court Jews, whose privileges had been justified by almost superhuman achievements in the procurement of money and credit, had already become indispensable to the throne. Constant wars, the demands of ostentatious court life and the needs of the growing administrative machinery, were disrupting the domestic economy. Nobody was capable of preventing the 'witches' cauldron of state finance' from occasionally boiling over. But the court Jews, by means of long-term loans or supply of goods on credit, had continually blown cooling breezes over it so that the hellish brew should not flood the whole country. Whether one liked it or not, however, with the court Jews the matrix of a new community had been admitted. Had these men been without ties or responsibilities, thinking only of the advancement of themselves and their families, their services could have been bought more cheaply. But even in the highest positions they never lost solidarity with their own religious community. They remained its spiritual and sometimes even its religious leaders; they became its spokesmen in times of need. Not only that: they were the advance-guard of an army of the disinherited that was always on the move. Their victories were symbolic. Every honour bestowed upon them fell to the share of the most humble of their brethren.

Collectively the Jews had been driven out of Vienna. Singly they now returned – looked at askance by a people and clergy who had no use for them, and greeted with barely concealed relief by an Emperor and an exchequer to whom their use was only too evident. For ten years Leopold had hesitated to readmit them to the capital. But the wars against the Turks and French were bleeding the state coffers dry. His armies, led by Prince Eugene of Savoy, needed to be equipped. The coalition with Spain, Holland and England rested on Austria's power and influence. Not long after the expulsion the Emperor had already imposed the task of supplying his army with clothing and ammunition upon the Jew Samuel Oppenheimer in Heidelberg.

This man, the most skilful business magnate since the decline of the Fugger family, now military commissary of the great European coalition, was the first Jew to re-acquire the right to settle in Vienna. A second, who was to raise himself to equal power with Oppenheimer, Samson Wertheimer, was summoned to the imperial court for the same reasons. Both hailed from that meeting-point of three states, Hesse, Baden and Franconia, that lies in the heart of Germany and in the midst of its most delightful countryside. Both came to be the true embodiment of the court Jew of the era of absolute monarchy, far more than Oppenheimer's unfortunate relative Jew Süss had ever been, far more also than most of their contemporary kinsfolk.

They were men of unimaginable wealth and influence, who could conjure up out of thin air, perhaps not armies, but their pay and equipment. They carried out financial business which today would require a whole chain of banks, yet at the same time, in a Europe of countless petty states each with its own tax-collecting system, of inadequate means of communication, of unregulated markets and unstable currencies, they were able to supply every conceivable kind of commodity – from jewellery, wines and confectionery for the Emperor's household, timber for the construction of his palaces and fodder for his stables, to all the materials of war for his armies and ships for his new Danube fleet. By special privilege, they owned houses in Vienna, in Worms and in Frankfurt, and vineyards on the slopes of the Vienna Woods. They lived like true kings of their tribe, exercised generous hospitality and, when they died, left their children costly proofs of princely favour such as could not be matched in splendour by any statesman or diplomat. Samson Wertheimer's will, for example, includes a list of gifts which reveals, if nothing else, the range of his high connections:

A portrait of the King of Poland set with brilliants, ditto of the Elector of Mainz, ditto of the Elector Palatine set with diamonds, Elector of Bavaria a portrait with brilliants, Elector of Mainz ditto brilliants, a portrait with diamonds and rubies of his Grace the Duke of Wolfenbüttel, ten chains of honour, one from his Imperial Majesty now reigning, one from their Imperial Majesties Leopold and Joseph of most blessed memory. Item, from her Majesty the Empress Amelia, two from his Royal Majesty of Poland. One from the Elector of Mainz, ditto the Elector Palatine, ditto the Elector of Trier, and lastly one from the Duke of Saxe-Gotha with likeness attached, of which two are set with small diamonds.

Despite such lavishly bestowed favour, such intimacy with many thrones, these and all other men who were once again able to settle in Vienna were more strictly limited in their rights than their predecessors in the Lower Werd. They were forbidden to form a community, their acts of worship could be carried out only individually and in secret, and their residence was legal only as long as their privileges were renewed by the Emperor. They were there merely 'on sufferance', although the nation's financial credit stood or fell by them. In this paradox an era is revealed which almost daily, as Prince Eugene wrote, provided an example of how 'a charming woman, a black-robed priest or a bearded Jew decided the fate of nations'. But so closely knotted were the financial bonds between the treasury and the court agents that even the ingenious Oppenheimer was finally destroyed by the exchequer's promissory notes, which were widely ramified, barely comprehensible and insufficiently guaranteed, so that his fortune of millions turned out at his death to be no more than a mass of irrecoverable debts.

His nephew, Wertheimer, who succeeded him in 1703 in the position of court banker, was not only a wiser but also a more careful man. Only five years later, at the height of his reputation, he gave up the conduct of the imperial business, which was taken over by his son Wolf, while he himself went into honourable retirement. In 1718 a young cousin from Lippe-Detmold described him as 'the great, respected, famous Herr Samson Wertheim, who in the common parlance is known as the Jewish emperor'. Here in Vienna, 'where the richest Jews of Europe' had their homes, Wertheimer had 'full many palaces and gardens'. Ten of the Emperor's soldiers stood guard outside his gates at all times, 'by special favour of the Emperor among many other privileges allowed him'. He was said to be so wealthy that 'he hath given to each of his children two hundred thousand Dutch gulden against their marriage, and of his children there are six'. Moreover, he performed many good acts, so it was said, among the poor of his Jewish brethren, throughout Europe, as far as Poland and 'even unto the Holy Land, to Jerusalem, where he is called lord of the land'. He was honoured not only as a dignitary, but as a scholar who had written many important sermons, designated his younger son to the study of religion and created innumerable schools.

It was the service of this man, the mightiest of his faith in the Holy Roman Empire, which was entered by the first of the Arnsteiners. He may or may not have been a relative of Samson, having travelled from his native Franconia to seek his fortune under Samson's protection. He may or may not have appeared on the list of Samson's 'kith and kin' as early as 1699, as 'S. Wertheimer's bookkeeper', who was resident at the house of the court Jew Schneider. Born in about 1682, he first set foot in the capital around the turn of the century, where he probably began his career as a humble cashier. In 1710, however, he was already travelling to Amsterdam as Samson's bookkeeper with the 'newly appointed chief manager Wolf Wertheimer' in order to redeem the 'mortgaged' jewellery of the King of Spain and bring it to Vienna.

This was the first important commission undertaken by Wolf, after declaring himself ready to 'follow in his father's footsteps and most humbly and obediently perform useful duties for your Imperial Majesty'. That he chose Isaac Arnsteiner for his companion in this undertaking casts some light on the position that Arnsteiner had meanwhile achieved in Samson's employ. Together with Wolf's father-in-law, the court Jew of electoral Mainz at Frankfurt am Main, they were both granted passports to travel to Linz, entry to which 'in those dangerous times' – the plague was rife – was denied to Jews. They travelled on, unhindered, to Amsterdam and forthwith delivered to Joseph I the Habsburg treasures that had been pawned by his brother. Isaac Arnsteiner carried out occasional commissions for Joseph's brother, Charles VI, who ascended the imperial throne in the following year. But his proper office became that of court agent to the widowed Empress Amelia, a Brunswick by birth, whom he served faithfully until her death.

Arnsteiner's career began and blossomed in the shadow of the great Wertheimer, and came to an end with his death. Like Wertheimer and the other members of the privileged circle, he lived in the heart of the city. Wertheimer's *palais*, where, protected by the ten imperial soldiers, he practised his renowned hospitality, was in the Kärntnerbastei. Arnsteiner's residence was more modest, though in proximity to that of his patron. Like Wertheimer and all other Jews, despite all his usefulness to the court of the widowed Empress, he was still in constant danger of banishment. Through

substantial contributions to the war-loan fund, which were collected at intervals from the Jewry of Vienna, he contrived to have
his privileges renewed from time to time.

In about 1717, together with Wolf and Samson Wertheimer, he
raised the sum of 500,000 gulden, whereupon he was granted
residence with his wife and children until further notice, although
they were not granted the status of a specifically tolerated family, as
some others had been. Four years later, an imperial command,
occasioned by a new regulation relating to the Jews, was addressed
to the 'Lord Chamberlain', 'that, insofar as *praeliminariter* the complaints made by Simon (Samson) Wertheimer are concerned,
namely that his servant Isaac Arnsteiner has been assured of residence only for the period of three years, the matter should rest with
the gracious resolution created on the 31st of May of this year'.
And so it dragged on from one case to the next. The last extension
was granted in 1736, when Charles VI again attempted to expel the
Jews, but rested content with higher contributions to the state
coffers. This time Arnsteiner actually succeeded in having his
decree of protection extended to his elder son, who was aged fifteen
at the time, bearing in mind the possibility of the latter's deciding
to marry.

Having begun as a clerk at the turn of the century, within a few
decades Isaac Arnsteiner, with Samson's help and through his own
industry, became a rich man. His supplies to the court of the
widowed Empress and for the requirements of Charles VI's army
must have brought in substantial profits. As the Vienna court
chancery wrote in a report, the Jews, 'because of their thrift and
their retired way of life, were able to supply more cheaply than
Christians'. In any case, by 1725 Arnsteiner was in a position to
endow his daughter, on the occasion of her marriage to a son of the
great Oppenheimer, with 22,000 gulden, jewels to the value of
5,000 gulden and further gifts towards the acquisition of the right
of residence and for investment in favour of their children. He
himself, after the death of his first wife, a woman from Prague, had
a short time before married a stepdaughter of Samson Wertheimer.
She was a granddaughter of that same *Liebmannin* who even at her
advanced age had been able to ensnare the hunchbacked King
Frederick of Prussia. So entangled were the fates of those few
families, in Berlin and Vienna just as in the other cities of the Holy
Roman Empire!

After his father's death, Adam Isaac, Arnsteiner's son from his first marriage, grew up in a matriarchal household. His stepmother Eleonore had eleven children of her own to care for as well as him. Even after some of these had already married or moved away, the members of her family, her employees and servants still numbered fifty persons altogether. Among her staff, according to a list drawn up in 1753, nine years after her husband's death, were numerous cashiers, bookkeepers, scribes, auctioneers, accountants, tutors, amanuenses, nursemaids and kitchenmaids, valets, chambermaids and butlers. Although these domestics may not all have been in the widow Arnsteiner's employ, but may have carried on their own businesses under the protection of her privileges, this retinue was commensurate with a great mansion in Maria Theresa's Vienna. Three years later the matriarch followed her husband into the grave, deeply mourned for her goodness and beneficence, like him who was called in the inscription on his tombstone 'a man of pure heart and clean hands', who 'helped the poor and the unjustly persecuted, and spared no means to dry the tears of the oppressed'. Whoever of her followers remained behind in her house, Adam and his family exerted themselves to leave it.

A beginning was made in 1762, when he received a magnanimous imperial document in which the office of court agent to Francis I was transferred to him. This amiable monarch, who despite his well-known high spirits was a skilful and conscientious steward of the finances of the houses of Habsburg and Lorraine, did not share his wife Maria Theresa's inimical disposition towards her Jewish subjects. As a true follower of her ancestors she resolved soon after her accession to expel the Jews, and in Prague had already made this a reality. In Vienna she contented herself with further restricting their rights through a series of stringent decrees, and excluding them from any of the reforms which Van Swieten and Sonnenfels had succeeded in carrying through. So great was the hate for the Jews of this woman, who was otherwise so warm-hearted, but in this alone hard and narrow-minded, that they were not even allowed to appear in her sight, but had to convey their requests at imperial audiences to a screen behind which the Empress was concealed.

Francis of Lorraine, later Holy Roman Emperor, who became her husband in 1736, liked to live and let live; he had no hesitation in securing for himself the assistance of such an astute and experienced businessman as the second Arnsteiner had become. This high office was bestowed by virtue not only of his father's good reputation, but quite expressly of his own 'diligent zeal, particular skill and also his honest and worthy character'. Now he might 'come and go with his servants in safety and without escort, free of tolls, duties and taxes of all and every kind', and use arms, daggers and pistols, and was not obliged to wear 'the customary yellow badge of the Jews'. Moreover, as we have seen, he was permitted to set up his household, 'for a suitable payment', and in any place, 'wherever it should appear safest to him'. In order to translate this verbal permission into fact, all that was still lacking was a word from the Empress. Even this he was finally able to obtain. When it was granted, he exchanged the Jewish residence in the Dorotheergasse for an elegant and extensive house on the Graben, in the midst of those Viennese citizens from whom he could still be distinguished by his religious customs and his appearance, but whose way of life was no longer markedly different from his own.

It was, to be sure, his appearance which gave continued occasion for their mockery. In this clean-shaven century Adam Isaac wore the beard of the prophets and patriarchs. At this time of knee-breeches and well-formed, silk-stockinged calves, he went about in a black gown that reached to his ankles, just as 'those of the male sort' had gone about in the Lower Werd, 'some in long gowns of black velvet and others in silk', and just as Samuel Oppenheimer had appeared before the Emperor who had expelled them. Thus, Samson Wertheimer, in his clothing 'like to a Polack with long white beard', had resided in his mansion on the Kärntnerbastei, and thus had Isaac Arnsteiner approached the widowed Empress Amelia. For Adam Isaac there was as little reason to lay aside this garment and this facial adornment as there was necessity for him to blow out his own candles on a Saturday. His wife Sibilla, a wise and pious woman of the house of Gompertz, would probably have taken amiss such a departure from the customs of their fathers. The sons of the next generation thought differently.

In May 1764 there were renewed deliberations in the Lower Austrian government as to how the arrogance of the Jews of Vienna could be controlled by a particular regulation. Two high officials, the privy councillors von Eger and von der Marck, referred indignantly in their reports to the fact that the adult bachelor sons of the privileged Jewish family heads not only frequented 'the coffee-houses and inns of the city, but also certain gardens and even dance-halls in the suburbs', but did so dressed just like other gentlemen of quality, for which reason they recommended that 'the married ones should grow their beards as before, but the unmarried ones should wear large bows of broad yellow ribbon in their hats'.

Such a return to practices which had long been recognised as unjust was not, to be sure, carried out in the new order for the Jews. Nevertheless, over the next years, up to the death of Maria Theresa, voices continued to be heard, complaining that 'Jewish young fellows go about openly, against all normal custom, in clothing edged with braid and in other ways not to be distinguished from that of Christians, and moreover, which was never before the case, with hair-bag or pigtail and some even with side-arms'. And finally the government announced that in order to prevent 'persons dressed in such unseemly fashion from further attending regularly the inns, dance-halls and play-houses among the Christians to be found there' it would not introduce any distinctive marks 'which should make them despised in the eyes of the world', but would 'direct the Jewish folk back into the precise bounds in which they had been kept at all times previously, and from which they had emerged only through unsanctioned innovation, to the annoyance of Christians and even of reasonable Jews themselves'.

Young Nathan Adam Arnsteiner undoubtedly gave occasion for such annoyance. The middle one of five children, protectively enclosed by two older sisters and two younger brothers, he grew up no less cheerfully and hopefully than did his bride-to-be in Berlin. Of easy-going temperament, not without inherited shrewdness in matters of business and finance, but all his life a man of simple good nature, with a childlike sense of humour, he took pleasure in all the privileges which had been grudgingly granted him, and fretted after none that was still denied him. A certain leaning towards idleness and ostentation, sometimes found in the third generation of an aspiring family, was unmistakable in him. Yet he was a long way off from that refinement which more than a hundred years later was characteristic of Hugo von Hofmannsthal, a descendant of the silk-merchant Isaac Löw Hofmann, or the later heirs of Samson Wertheimer – the von Wertheimsteins – and of the house of Gompertz. Nathan was and remained a man of plain, practical pleasures, even when the intellectual nobility of Europe met in his drawing-room. There is no question that as a 'young fellow' he was already wearing the 'clothing edged with braid', with 'hair-bag or pigtail', that he needlessly and unlawfully buckled to his side the dagger whose use was permitted to his father as a protection when travelling, and ventured to 'attend regularly the inns, dance-halls and play-houses among the Christians to be found there'.

At the same time he practised, in his father's counting-house, the management of business appropriate for a court agent and high financier, as Adam Isaac had done in the employ of his own father. Like Isaac before him, Adam Arnsteiner supplied the Emperor with horses and equipment for his regiments. His annual tax amounted to 1,500 gulden. On the other hand his privileges had been increased, so that, for example, ordinances concerning the Jews were delivered specifically to him by the authorities. And yet he was dissatisfied. In 1768 he made a formal request to the Empress that he should at last be allowed to live apart from the Jews and not to have to take financial responsibility for any crime committed by them. He even dared to threaten Maria Theresa with the warning that if these favours were not granted to him he would depart to Holland, his wife's native land. The Empress thereupon decreed: 'The court agent is by no means to be included in the ordinance which has been issued in respect of the other Jews here resident.' In her own hand she added: 'On condition that he shall no longer desire the remission of 1,500 gulden but shall continue to pay this, Hatzfeld [the minister for home affairs] to be reminded.'

If the services of the Arnsteiner family had not appeared indispensable to her, the Empress would certainly have punished such audacity instead of giving way to it. Nor did Adam Isaac, whose reputation and self-confidence were considerably enhanced thereafter, hesitate to use equally forcible language to the government of Saxony. In 1776 he complained about the high tolls which had to be paid when travelling through Dresden, and threatened not to set foot in the city again if such treatment were not discontinued. Thereupon he was issued with a passport, which he used that year on his journey to attend his son's wedding in Berlin. It was thanks to this passport that Nathan Adam and his young bride were finally excused the personal toll which the guards at Dresden had demanded with such insolence.

So the Arnsteiners, ever more manifestly, took up a privileged position among the tolerated Jews of Vienna, a community which meanwhile had increased to twenty-five families. The Jewish prince of Berlin had given his daughter to no unworthy man. Nevertheless, when she exchanged the royal Prussian capital for the seat of the imperial residence, Franziska became aware for the first time of the deep, even heart-rending contempt with which her people were regarded from the monarch's throne. Shortly before her death, Maria Theresa wrote with her own hand on a report from her court chancery recommending the granting of a three-year *Toleranz* for a Jew who had rendered a service by disclosing the fraud committed by one of his own people: 'In future no Jews, whatever their name, are to be allowed to be here without my written permission. I know no worse plague to the state than this nation, for bringing people to a state of beggary through their deceit, usury and financial dealings, for practising all the misdeeds which another, honest man would despise; consequently, as far as possible, they are to be kept away from here and their numbers are to be decreased.'

These cruel words were written in the autumn of 1777, when Franziska was not yet nineteen and had been married a year. They were such words as no Hohenzollern had spoken for centuries. Was it surprising that they offended her young and sensitive spirit so deeply that for ever after she nursed a resentment or mistrust of the ruling house of Austria, that to the end of her days she thought longingly of her youth in the more enlightened city of Berlin, that all her life she remained at heart a Prussian?

-3-

Baptism or Tolerance

Franziska's early years in Vienna are veiled in mist. Her image is wavering and pale, as if reflected in a troubled pool.

The child playing in the garden near the Schlesisches Tor, the bride under the canopy, tall and slim at the side of her plumper groom, the traveller in the carriage, vivacious by comparison with his more relaxed cheerfulness – these can all be imagined, can be worked out from her descent and her circumstances. How the young woman adapted herself to a new world, to a strange family, how she bore her totally changed existence, can only be surmised. After the closing behind her of that gate on the Graben, while she enters the multifarious rooms and tortuous corridors of the Contrini house, she disappears from our sight for a considerable time.

There must have been no lack of disputes and quarrels, sorrow and anger. Her heart filled with homesickness, she looked out from the alcoves on the first floor onto sombre cobblestones, fountains, the statue of a saint and the pillar of the Trinity. To bend to the will of the imperious Adam Arnsteiner, to submit to the gentle but firm direction of the pious Sibilla, may have been harder for her than to accommodate herself to their son by holding him under her spell. Throughout his life this good-natured man was delighted and alarmed in equal measure by her quick wit, her cleverness and her scintillating charm. Frequently he took refuge in silence and occasionally in flight from her predominance. But as long as his father was alive, he stood poised between the two powers which each sought by love and capricious behaviour to win him to their sides.

Only one report bears witness to the vexations of the time that Fanny spent under the same roof as her parents-in-law. Shortly before the feast of Passover, as related by a Hebrew chronicler, a learned scholar travelled to Vienna with his pupil, on his way to his native city of Frankfurt. On his journey he visited Adam Arnsteiner, with the intention of celebrating the feast in the latter's house. He sent his pupil to market to buy the things that were necessary for the feast. On his return, the pupil, mistaking the door, entered a room in which sat Herr Arnsteiner's daughter-in-law, combing her hair.

> The pupil reprimanded her: was it right for wedded daughters of Israel to behave thus? Then she said to her father-in-law that if both guests did not leave immediately, she would without further ado return to her father's house in Berlin. And Herr Arnsteiner went into the scholar's chamber and thanked the pupil for reprimanding his daughter-in-law. Nevertheless he entreated the wise man to find another lodging, so that his daughter-in-law should not desecrate the feast [by making a journey]. And now, open your eyes and see whether there are yet descendants of the Arnsteiners! Thus it happens when women uncover their heads.

She was not only self-willed, this young daughter-in-law from Berlin, in her refusal to tolerate these dictatorial and perhaps not particularly attractive guests in her home over the feast. She also resisted the precept of her religion which instructed women to cut their hair on marriage and to cover it with a wig. Hence the reproaches of the Talmudic student, who must have been astonished by such sacrilege; hence too the mockery of the chronicler at the rebellious daughters of Israel whose punishment was that they should bear no sons! But between the moment when Franziska threatened to depart, and the one when Adam Arnsteiner thanked the two scholars and at the same time asked them to leave his house, what anger and wrangling, what entreaties and adjurations filled the air can only be guessed. Nathan – who was no more pious than his young wife, but an inconspicuous freethinker, who in later years was to be numbered by the Vienna police among the unorthodox members of his community – must have had great difficulty in pacifying his deeply religious father and persuading him to act as he did, for fear that Franziska should really return to Berlin.

But with this momentary image, this scene in a room accidentally entered by the pupil – sitting in front of the mirror and combing her dark hair in defiance of the religious law, her large, finely prominent eyes full of tears of resentment – Franziska disappears once more into the obscurity that surrounds those years.

She emerges again in a different guise, at an indeterminate time and in an unexpected place.

Among the high officials of the court and state chancery in Vienna there was a certain Johann Georg Obermayer, who took it into his head one day to marry a very young girl. Caton von Preissing had married for the first time at fourteen years of age and six months later was already a widow. Her stepfather Herr von Rath, master of ceremonies to the Princess Dietrichstein, introduced her to his friend Obermayer, and without demur she obeyed the much older man. The wedding took place in 1776. The married couple entered upon a companionable existence in fashionable society. As was still frequently the custom among the nobility and upper bourgeoisie, they spoke to each other only in Spanish, addressed each other as Señor and Señora, and referred to each other as Doña Caterina and Don Jorge. The court secretary and later imperial councillor enjoyed having people around him, and invited gentlemen of his acquaintance, mostly diplomats and scholars, to his house after the theatre. Caton, as she was known to her friends, had guests nearly every evening. She herself received more intimate friends while still in bed or getting dressed. She lunched at about three. Then her day began in earnest.

Emilie, a daughter of the oddly-matched but evidently happy couple, was to depict this scene of the fashions of Maria Theresa's age for posterity. As an old woman, the wife of Lieutenant-General von Weckbecker, she described the life of her parents, which was in many ways an example of the usages of the time. The ladies, it seems, spent all their time at their elaborate toilet, in flirtations and gossip, visits to the theatre and informal or formal social gatherings. Caton, to be sure, as her daughter relates:

> went only to the grandest parties; the smaller ones, at which the women arrived as early as four or five and stayed till eight or nine, were not to her taste. Fanny Arnstein did the same. The two women often met in society and soon became intimate friends, but in the winter they could not meet on three evenings of the week, because Fanny Arnstein too received guests after the theatre. She was rich, and every evening there was a supper at her house, but not at my parents'; we had only water with crushed sugar and – oh miracle – tea!

When and where the two newly-wed women, who had entered the married state in the same year, first met, is unknown. At some time in those last years of the Empress's reign, the wife of the tolerated Jew Arnsteiner must have found entry to a house which had not previously granted admission to her kind. At some time she slipped nimbly over a threshold that had earlier been barred to her, began to associate with women of her own age, from whom she was distinguished by no noticeable blemish, and turned, in this lively, frivolous, easy-going circle, from a Prussian Franziska to a Viennese Fanny. She forgot the prejudice directed against her and by her to the world around her, she made friends with one or other of the light-hearted young ladies, she dared one day to invite this one or that one to her house and realised to her delighted astonishment that they did not deny her the honour of a visit; finally she even invited their husbands, whom she had met with them at the theatre, to supper after the performance, began to hold such receptions on a regular basis, and so gradually, without being fully aware of what she was doing, bridged over the abyss of millennia of separation.

This sort of thing was possible in Vienna, as it was not in the Prussian capital, without some special purpose and without causing a great sensation. Here conventions were overturned without ceremony, here social differences were effaced, national and religious frontiers were dissolved, without their disappearance being noted on the map of public life. This was, to be sure, no pre-planned retractation; it was rather the tacit, though at the same time noncommittal, surrender of long-preserved inaccessibility, it was a dropping of barriers which could be re-erected at any time. While in Berlin men like Lessing, like Dohm, like Nicolai had arisen to battle for the civic advancement of the Jews and attempted to carry it through with vigour, in the imperial capital the reservations held until now were being voluntarily abandoned. Of similar disposition, with gentler and more tractable natures, the Viennese were at the same time not disposed to raise such concessions to the status of a principle. As a favour, not as of right, their Jewish fellow-citizens were allowed entry to their circles. How far this should go was left to individual discretion.

It was not least in the name of music that members of all ranks and classes were able to unite in Vienna. When, in January of 1780, the year in which the Empress died, the Cologne lawyer Johann Baptist Fuchs arrived in the city, he found the most disparate people assembled in harmony at the private concerts of the nobility. At a soirée at the house of Frau von Hochstedten, a minister's wife, 'a Frau von Arenstein played the piano charmingly, and Mlle Weberin enchanted those present with her singing'. Thus, in that town mansion which gave Fanny – on whom, out of courtesy, the honorific *von* was prematurely bestowed – the opportunity to shine in public with the utmost gracefulness at the side of Mozart's former beloved and future sister-in-law Aloysia Weber, a transformation had taken place of which the Empress, certainly, was unaware. She, who had not long before uttered those evil words, nourished up to her last breath her hatred and loathing of any Jew who had not renounced his faith and had himself christened. If he did so, he could become her favourite overnight – just as if the holy water had the power to wash away from one moment to the next the imaginary filth with which, in her eyes, this 'worst plague' of a state was covered.

It was thus, under the rule of Maria Theresa, that the family of a certain Alois Wiener, who had entered the capital in her father's lifetime, came to high honour. This man, originally named Liebmann Berlin, had, with his two little boys, converted to Christianity and taken the Viennese innkeeper's daughter Maria Ruttenstock as his second wife. His studies in alchemy came to the notice of Francis of Lorraine, who was devoted with heart and soul to this 'secret art'. Wiener was created teacher of Oriental languages at the university and in 1747 published a book written half in Hebrew, half in German, entitled *Or Noga, Splendor lucis or splendour of light, containing a short physico-cabbalistic exposition of the greatest secret of nature, privily called Lapis Philosophorum*.

A year earlier, the Empress, to please her husband, had given Wiener a hereditary title. Now he was called Alois Wiener von Sonnenfels. His elder son Joseph, who had been born in the old faith, rose to become a professor of 'studies in police and public finance matters' and an influential reformer, who helped to abolish torture in Austria and replace the crude *Kasperl* show with the great dramatic works of Germany. In his urge 'to eradicate the prejudices and stupidities with which the people of Vienna were still burdened' Joseph von Sonnenfels even dared to offer resistance to the narrow-minded exercise of authority of Cardinal Migazzi. After succeeding, as he once wrote, in removing 'the green hat, the *Hanswurst* [clown]' from the theatre, he now hoped 'to dislodge the red hat, the Roman Cardinal and nuncio, right speedily from the cabinet'. When this remark reached the Empress's ears, she wanted to expel him from the country, but in the end she forgave him, demonstrating a mildness which she was capable of showing to all but unbaptised Jews. Joseph's brother Franz too enjoyed the sunshine of her favour, became a councillor at the treasury, and in 1797 was granted the rank of *Freiherr* (baron) of the realm by his imperial namesake, Maria Theresa's grandson.

Alois Wiener was only the first of a series of men who converted to Christianity in Maria Theresa's Vienna. They, whose forefathers 'would rather let themselves be burned alive than waver by the point of a needle from their faith', were now prepared to give up this faith altogether – not always because they expected more certain salvation from their new religion, but sometimes because, while this was guaranteed to them by neither, baptism seemed to render at least their earthly welfare more secure. The ideas of the Enlightenment had penetrated from France even to a naïvely pious Vienna. Many a one heard the message, though he might prefer to turn a deaf ear. The quick-witted Jews drew their own conclusions. If there were no God, neither wrathful Jehovah nor gentle Jesus, there could be no reason to live precariously, in perpetual trouble and anxiety, in the service of the one, when one could achieve peace and prosperity under the other's wing.

By degrees, whether out of such considerations as these or through genuine desire for redemption, a number of Jewish families had ended up in the bosom of the Catholic Church. While fathers often set themselves against the apostasy of their sons, there were also wives of these belated candidates for baptism who at times refused to change their faith. When Karl Abraham Wetzlar, whose power and influence surpassed even those of Adam Arnsteiner, converted with his ten children in 1777, causing a great stir, and was elevated to the rank of '*Panier- und Reichsfreiherr*' (banneret and baron of the realm) von Plankenstern, his wife, Eleonore, remained faithful to Judaism. One of her sons, Raimund, who married a Baroness de Pignini, became a patron of the arts and the 'generous, good and true, honest' friend of Mozart. Even if certain members of those families, and even the great majority of tolerated Jews, still resisted conversion, the baptism of Viennese Jews continued in the later days of Maria Theresa. Among others, Maria Josepha Königsberger, the daughter of a court agent, had turned away from Judaism when she married Freiherr, later Lieutenant-General, von Sebottendorf. 'Pepi' Sebottendorf had become Fanny's best friend in Vienna. Her attempt to secure her social position through baptism tempted Fanny to follow her example. But a recent an example in her husband's family had shown that neither Fanny nor her young husband was of a mind to carry their latitudinarianism so far as to abandon their religion.

Nathan Arnsteiner, as we have seen, passed his childhood in the company of his four brothers and sisters. A younger brother had moved to Fürth. The youngest son, Joseph, led his own life in Vienna, although he remained in business with his father. He was, as we know from his own account, his parents' favourite. But according to the strict old custom, Nathan, the first-born son, shared his father's home and could expect one day to take over his business alone, while his brothers were forced sooner or later to found their own households and businesses. It can be surmised that Joseph was more attractive, more talented and intelligent than the slow-moving, portly Nathan. At the same time he harboured a wilfulness that impelled him to renounce utterly the faith of his parents who, true to tradition, then drove him from their house, so that he lost them forever.

A year after they had travelled to Berlin for the wedding of their eldest son, Adam and Sibilla repeated their journey to attend the nuptials of their youngest. Joseph was then still quite the obedient child of his father and had agreed to a marriage with Johanna Strelitz, the daughter of the Berlin merchant Abraham Markus Strelitz, Moses Mendelssohn's well-beloved friend. He brought his wife back to Vienna where a baby daughter was born to him. Whether Johanna died in childbirth or succumbed to an illness is not known. In any case she was already dead when the *Wiener Diarium* of 10 October 1778 carried the following report:

> On the 28th of last month, September, we had yet another touching example of zeal for the Christian religion, when Joseph Adam Arnsteiner, youngest son of Adam Isak Arnsteiner, one of the most respected Jews of this city, received the holy sacrament of baptism from the honourable and right reverend Precentor of the cathedral, and the prelate of the Metropolitan church, as well as from his Excellency the archiepiscopal secretary of the consistory, Councillor de Terme. Not only has the newly baptised gentleman, of whose philanthropic heart, when still a Jew, we have already spoken in terms of much praise in our pages of the 25th of April of this year, through his well-conducted behaviour at all times earned the approval of one of the greatest scholars among the Jewish rabbis, but all the Christians and Jews who have associated with him give him the character of a capable and upright man, and just as his intentions towards the Christian religion have been pure and unselfish, so too we wish that this example may serve those of his brethren still left in darkness, and may bring them also in time to this happy resolution.

Four days later the journal added that 'on the 30th of this month his only child, a little daughter, likewise received the holy sacrament of baptism'.

Perhaps Joseph had not suspected, or had deceived himself into avoiding the suspicion, that this step would mean a break with his parental home. When it came to this, he was startled and distressed, but unflinchingly pursued his intention of making himself entirely at home in the Christian world. He married again; his new wife was the well-born Baroness Barbara von Albrechtsburg. Their children were to mingle not only with the old-established aristocracy, but also with descendants of Freiherr Wetzlar, who had also been baptised. Five years after his conversion Joseph applied to the Bohemian and Austrian court chancery to be raised to the rank of knight. The chancery document by which his request was forwarded to the Emperor contains the following information:

> For his own person, the applicant, since his conversion to the Catholic faith, has no further income, and previously, as a Jew, he did not carry on his own business, but worked only under the direction of his father. However it is also the case that if he is to acquire his own property here in order to farm his land, the rank of knight is necessary to him; and the request is therefore submitted to the imperial mercy, that the rank of *Ritter* [knight] should be accorded to him.

The answer was that 'assent should be granted to Arnsteiner, that when he has bought his property, the rank of *Ritter* will be granted to him on payment of the usual taxes'. In May 1783 he had purchased the estate of Weinwarts near Müggendorf and was accordingly knighted by the Emperor in the name of Joseph Michael, Edler (nobleman) von Arnstein.

He needed the title if he was to become a man of property, but after cutting himself off from his father's business he could not afford to be idle. The Weinwarts estate yielded too little profit to keep him and Baroness Albrechtsburg in the manner appropriate to their ranks, and so, 'on his own account', he conducted a banking business in the Kohlmarkt. He had, to be sure, already acquired these premises with the help of a sum furnished by his father a year after his conversion. Through the mediation of the prebendary de Terme, who had christened him in St Stephen's Cathedral, an agreement had been concluded with his parents, by which the disowned son was to receive a lump payment of 50,000 gulden in compensation for the loss of his inheritance. Cut off from his father's wealth and property as from his love, Joseph, spurred on by filial affection as much as by practical considerations, repeatedly tried to bring about a reconciliation. By chance, a letter written by him shortly before his father's death has been preserved. It speaks for all those who, in those times of change, dared to renounce the commandments and laws that had endured for thousands of years, and is one of the liveliest and most instructive documents of the era of emancipation. Here is an extract:

> Certainly, dearest parents, I know what is commonly the result of the influence of education and of misunderstood religion, but is it possible that you could hate your son because he harbours other principles of

faith than yours? in these times of enlightenment, under the government of our most gracious monarch, who exhibits his tolerance and general forbearance in all his dealings as an example to all his subjects, who allows each one to *believe* that which he will, if he only *behaves* as he should; under such a government, under which you, subject to Jewish law, enjoy the same protection, the same rights as any of your fellow-citizens, where you have gathered your treasures and may consume them in peace, without fear of any pressure or compulsion; under such a tolerant government, should you hate an innocent, irreproachable son, cast him aside, who implores only to be received by his parents and to have their blessing, because he does not share your theoretical principles? and banish from your sight forever your innocent grandchild, not yet of age, who did no other, could do no other, than to obey the well-intentioned will of her father! Herein I appeal to my brother, who is still Jewish, and to his wife my sister-in-law, who go so often into the great world, and see from their own experience that among the numerous members of the established religion they are received with love and respect, at the same time as you, out of religious hatred, banish from your sight a once beloved son! Your religion itself, dearest parents! damns nobody for eternity, and yet you would be relentlessly severe even in this temporal life!

Accordingly, once more, most worthy parents, I beseech you, hear my request, which has no selfish or ulterior motive, allow me and my dear child, your grandchild, to approach you, even to visit you daily, to kiss your hands and receive your blessing. We are human, dearest parents! Human beings who flourish today and fade tomorrow – what a terrible thought is this not for me, and I may add, must it be for you too, if one of us should be snatched away from this earthly life without a full and heartfelt reconciliation and reunion.

Appoint the hour for myself and my child at which we may betake ourselves to our parents, and believe me, to the last breath in my body,
your dearest son
Michael Joseph Edler von Arnsteiner

Whether his parents gave way to his request and restored him to their favour with his little daughter Caroline is not known. But it is to be doubted that his touching and certainly deeply felt self-vindication softened their hearts, for he is not mentioned in the wills made by Adam and Sibilla in 1785 and 1787. They were true descendants of the women and men who had run to the burning at Erdberg dancing and leaping, as if going to a wedding, who 'persevered in their wickedness and obstinacy even up to their ears' like 'accursed martyrs of the devil'. What seemed natural to their eldest son was unthinkable for them. The gulf that had earlier lain between them and the whole of Christendom now lay between them and their child, dividing a family, separating one generation from the other. But Joseph's Jewish brother and his wife, who went so often into the great world and saw from their own experience how they were received there with love and respect, did not find it necessary to take that decisive step. To the end of their days, even when they had laid aside all forms and customs of their religion, they remained members of a community whose equality of rights had by no means been achieved, whose complete freedom was still withheld long after the deaths of Nathan and Fanny.

Their friendly reception by the great world might have appeared miraculous if their era had not quite generally offered the spectacle of conflicting opinions and movements. The revolt against rationalism had begun, in France with Rousseau, in Germany with Herder. Emotion and reason had declared war on each other, poetic rapture and dry abstraction fought for precedence in people's spirits. Yet the two great opposing movements of the time demanded in equal measure, before all else, magnanimity and generosity towards all fellow-humans. While it had become 'insupportable for the awakened consciences of the Enlightenment to know that there were any among them who were without rights', the sentimental enthusiasm with which the predecessors of romanticism enclosed the whole world in their arms comprehended even those mortals who had previously been despised. The only ones to hold fast to old prejudices were certain dignitaries of that same church whose founder had taught and enjoined charity, and the practising agents of an absolutist government which admitted neither the rule of liberal reason nor romantic idealism. Viennese society, touched if not shaken by the breath of the new spirit and universal sympathy, had relaxed its conventions. The ruling powers and the clergy in Maria Theresa's last years held on to their own with a grip of iron.

The precept of physical separation of Jews from Christians had so far been suspended only in individual cases. In 1772, a Jewish family, having been evicted from their home, could find no shelter, till Franz von Sonnenfels, who had not adopted the intolerance of his new co-religionists with his baptism, made over to them one of his own houses as a residence. But repeated attempts were made, whether by the narrow-minded Archbishop of Vienna, Cardinal Migazzi, or the councillors Loehr and Count Hatzfeld of the government of Lower Austria, to restrict the few and hard-won rights of the Jews. At about the time when Fanny was already on intimate terms with Caton, the young wife of the court secretary Obermayer, Loehr remarked censoriously on the fact that 'Jewish females should be seen in such dress as is little different from that of a lady, with and among Christian people in public places, in their company and society'.

Certainly, the Bohemian–Austrian court and state chancellery, in which Obermayer was secretary and the progressive Hofrat (councillor) von Greiner adviser for Lower Austria, was not on the best of terms with the Lower Austrian government. It even opposed a new, oppressive measure concerning the Jews, which the latter planned to introduce as late as 1778, in accordance with the Empress's views. 'The closer association with Christians,' the chancellery observed, 'of which in fact no particular complaints or evil consequences have so far been brought to public notice, cannot be otherwise abolished but by Christians themselves, who alone must determine to whom they wish to allow entry into their houses. And indeed one does not after all see what great evil is to be found in it, to cause such alarm and make necessary such extraordinary arrangements.'

There was only one high official in the Lower Austrian government, Hofrat von Gebler, an immigrant from a German principality, in whom the chancellery found an ally. He remarked that 'representations might be made on the part of the rich Jewish houses, which after all deserve some consideration, such as the Arnsteiners, also bearing in mind the foreign marriages which otherwise could not be brought about, and the example of other Catholic countries, particularly of France and of the grand duchy of Tuscany. If meanwhile despite this a new and more severe measure against the Jews is to be promulgated, then the admonitions of the Bohemian–Austrian chancellery appear to me worthy of all consideration.' Whereupon an imperial resolution of December of that year ordained that no new measure concerning the Jews should be announced, 'but it should be seen to that the regulation of 1764 should be most scrupulously observed'.

And so, shortly before her death, Maria Theresa was still intent on 'reducing the numbers of the Jews here, and by no means, on any pretext, increasing them further'. At that time there were ninety-nine families in Vienna, among whom were twenty-five tolerated ones, with children and servants amounting to not more than 520 persons in all. They had much to expect from the demise of the Empress and the accession of Joseph. Yet they uttered no word of complaint or of hope, but knuckled under and kept their counsel, while the dissension of officials raged over their heads. From their ranks no request or petition penetrated to the ears of the government. On the other hand they took part, as far as they were allowed, in the destiny of their country and the rise of their city.

They sighed when another quarrel with Frederick sprang up over the Bavarian succession, and breathed again when peace was declared after ten months' bloodless war. They strolled in the Augarten which had been opened to the public, and visited the playhouse recently raised to the rank of 'Imperial and Royal Theatre' (the Hofburgtheater). They admired the new paving, in tessellated granite, on both sides, of the most important streets in Vienna; they enjoyed the splendid festivals that were held so frequently both in winter and summer, the sleigh-rides of the nobility, the solemn processions, the fireworks in the Prater; they flocked to the column of the Trinity in the Graben for the centenary commemoration of the end of the Great Plague; and they were frightened out of their wits when, a few days later, the great powder-magazine on the outskirts of the city blew up and destroyed a number of houses. Vienna was their home; they knew no other and professed their loyalty to her, even if their love was only seldom returned.

The Empress meanwhile had grown fat and sluggish, could hardly walk and had to be carried by machinery on a green morocco-leather couch to her apartments in the Hofburg and to the balcony of the Gloriette at Schönbrunn. In the autumn of 1780 she contracted catarrh of the chest. Her faith, which had made her as good and happy as she was intolerant, helped her to endure the pain and contemplate her death with dignity. She sat in her arm-chair, surrounded by her family, patiently waiting for eternal bliss. About nine o'clock on the evening of 29 November she breathed her last.

On the same day, in Berlin, whither she had travelled for her confinement, Fanny gave birth to a daughter.

It was presumably on the first, if certainly not the last, of her visits to her parental home, that little Henriette was born to her. Whenever she lost her taste for the mild air of Vienna, the soft tones of its conversation, its leisurely way of thinking, Fanny betook herself to Berlin, to enjoy its brisk wind, sharp outlines, cutting wit and agile comprehension. She refreshed herself in the circle of her clever sisters, two of whom, Cäcilie and Rebecca, were later drawn into her circle and settled in homes near hers. And she enjoyed her reunions with her brothers, although they did not possess in the same measure the circumspection and farsightedness of her father. Her eldest brother Isaac, like his brothers Benjamin and Jacob, had married a cousin from the house of Wulff, just as Cäcilie had taken a maternal cousin for her first husband. With these and numerous other in-laws Fanny had a widely ramified family, which flocked around her whenever she visited the Prussian capital. Moreover, she found in Berlin what she herself was hoping to establish in Vienna: the beginnings of the literary salon.

Under Frederick the Great, court and society had become highly Francophile. Their teachers were Parisian philosophers; Frenchmen had set up the new grammar school, and the King had appointed Maupertuis as president of the Berlin Academy that had been founded by his grandfather. The example of a constant social interchange of thought, of the cultivation of learned conversation, had come from Paris and had incited imitation. The assemblies at the houses of the Marquise du Deffand, the Marquise d'Epinay, Madame Geoffrin and Mademoiselle d'Espinasse were beginning to find followers among the Prussians. The nobility, to be sure, still hesitated to give up its formal receptions, and the bourgeoisie, lacking a feeling for higher culture, held fast to 'the simplicity of the household according to German custom'. It was, therefore, left principally to Jewish circles to unite art and society according to the Parisian model. They possessed gifts which allowed them to con-form to French culture more speedily than their compatriots – 'true intellect, wit and taste, the refined expression of refined concepts, a mocking tone and a speedy perception of the ridiculous, and finally the instinct of a certain practical rationalism in their way of life'. With their growing prosperity they were able to gratify their aspirations towards knowledge and wisdom, to recognition of what was true and possession of what was beautiful, and it was at their gatherings that liberal people of noble birth, whose families and usual social contacts offered them little stimulation, were beginning to assemble. And so, as a later observer expressed it, there developed 'a quite original intellectual atmosphere in Berlin, a mixture of Jewry, of the "enlightened ones", as our ancestors called them, and a kind of Gallic Atticism'.

One of the first houses in which such circles developed was that of the councillor Benjamin Ephraim, who, as the youngest son of the mint-master, raised his controversial name to deserved honour. As early as 1761 he had gone to Amsterdam to set up a business house in association with his father's firm, had there married a rich heiress and shortly afterwards returned with her to Berlin. Now he was establishing an art collection in his city mansion which was in no way inferior to that of Daniel Itzig and included paintings by Caravaggio, Poussin and Roland Davery. His splendidly decorated apartments were visited, if not yet by persons of rank, at least by some who were noteworthy. In the 1780s his nieces Sophie and

Marianne Meyer, later to become respectively Frau von Grotthuss and Frau von Eybenberg, introduced young sons of old families into his house, after first gaining entry to the upper social circles through their early conversion to Christianity.

But Benjamin Ephraim, like Daniel Itzig and the far poorer, though considerably more highly honoured Moses Mendelssohn, in whose houses the beginnings of an 'intellectual Berlin' had likewise formed, was by no means able to unite the higher reaches of society with those of poetry, politics and science, as a series of talented women succeeded in doing one or two decades later. When Fanny visited her native city for the first time since her marriage, Henriette Herz was sixteen and newly married, Dorothea Mendelssohn a little younger and Rahel Levin a child of nine. Before the Berlin salon came into its prime, Fanny had already founded her own in Vienna.

The Empress was dead, her world had passed away with her, and her old adversary Frederick rightly exclaimed: 'Voilà un nouvel ordre de choses!' And indeed, Joseph II forthwith set about translating all the reforms he had planned into reality. In so doing, as his mocking observer on the Prussian throne remarked, he was putting the cart before the horse, hurrying ahead of his time and the wishes of his subjects, and trying to coerce the latter into their own prosperity. Like others who have sought to set the world to rights, of whom, certainly, there were not many in his amiably sceptical country, he was convinced of his own infallibility; believed himself, since he wanted what was good and just, to be good and just in all circumstances; meted out high-handed justice and practised favouritism; vented his disappointment over misplaced trust on innocent parties; possessed little sense of humour and was not inclined to allow people to be content in their own way. *Suaviter in re, fortiter in modo*, he wielded a benevolent authority with an iron hand. The idea of 'Josephinismus' was thus more valuable than anything that Joseph himself achieved. Many of his measures fell into disuse as soon as a reaction set in under his nephew Francis; others soon turned out to be inadequate or misguided. Without question his brother Leopold, that unhandsome and self-indulgent man, was able to bring more insight and statesmanlike wisdom to bear in his short reign. But Joseph became a symbol; it was around him that legend formed. Whatever thereafter was liberal in Austria was attributed to him, who decreed freedom from the throne like a principle of absolutism.

He carried out his most important acts in the first year of his undivided sovereignty, as if he suspected how soon foreign affairs would hinder further internal reforms, and how short a span was allotted him for his work. As early as the winter of 1780 personal records were introduced among his officials by his orders, in order to separate the top intellects from the mediocre ones. In the following February he cancelled the court's authority to demand free lodging for officials in the home of every citizen; in June he approved a more lenient law of censorship as well as a new charter of tolerance with reference to non-Catholics, while a second one regarding the toleration of Jews was in preparation; in November 1781 he entirely abolished serfdom in Bohemia, Moravia and Galicia, where its practice had already been moderated; and in December he endorsed a plan for the secularisation of a number of monasteries and convents. At the same time, a new, practical system of finance administration and new methods of legal procedure and the practice of bankruptcy law were introduced, while long overdue improvements were undertaken in the fields of public education, the church and agriculture.

A fresh wind of optimism was blowing through the land. When Fanny returned to Vienna with her infant daughter, she was immediately swept along by the hope and confidence which possessed all intelligent souls. Not that Joseph's accession had been accompanied by outward splendour. On the contrary, since the Empress's death much of the ceremonious pageantry which had marked the imperial, ecclesiastical and military festivals had disappeared. Joseph continued to live in a style of marked simplicity, and it was only at his summer palace of Laxenburg that he received select members of Viennese society, landed gentry and foreign diplomats in some style, with operas, comedies and entertainments of all sorts. But the consciousness of having shuffled off the burden of a seemingly immutable past, of experiencing a turning-point in history, of being 'modern', to use a word that had recently become current, seemed better to the wiser among his subjects than the sight of magnificent processions, behind which were concealed the inflexible rule of feudal power and bureaucracy.

Joseph had in fact initiated the reform of public life during his mother's lifetime, and despite her opposition. He had introduced new regulations for schools, appointed progressive teachers at the University of Vienna, and approved the formation of a 'German society', which was to promote art and science and purify the language. Nicolai had long since expressed the hope that, once the 'philosophical manner of thinking' had been disseminated in

Austria, writers of the first importance would arise there. Klopstock had dedicated his drama *Hermannsschlacht* to the Emperor who wished to bring this about. But it was only now, after Joseph had moderated the severity of censorship, that the writers were daring to emerge from their cautious restraint.

The result was at first disappointing, even embarrassing. A swarm of inferior pamphlets, so-called *Sechskreuzerhefte* (sixpenny booklets), flooded the capital. The *Büchelschreiber* (scribblers), still using a language combining 'monastery German, provincial dialect and clumsy officialese', released a torrent of the flattest effusions on any subject to their liking, 'from the chambermaid to the Pope, and from the dogs and cats in Vienna to the Archbishop'. There was self-mockery in their own ranks. 'Now of course we have freedom of the press. Everyone scribbles away as best he can,' sighed the anonymous author of a *Lamentation of the Gracious Ladies of the Present Time*. It continues:

> My God! These people just write for money, impossible that they should do so for the sake of honour; for all the rigmarole that is dashed off these days cannot possibly, so people say, all be good healthy common sense. The writers slop everything in together, higgledy-piggledy. One rushes into print with a little pamphlet about something or other, another opposes him. The third abuses both of them; then follows a whole legion of critics who scold at each other in writing like riff-raff, and would pitch each other straight into hell; if only the general public took more care how they spend their cash!

There was a long way to go before the emergence of 'writers of the first importance', who could be measured against Herder, Lessing or Klopstock, or even Wieland or Gottsched. But not all authors were verbally incontinent, as the indignant Johann Friedel called it, in Austria. There were poets and scholars who, closely conforming to their German models, clung to the wings of true creative writers if their own moderate talent was incapable of reaching such heights. Under Maria Theresa the two Jesuits Michael Denis and Karl Mastalier had achieved some fame as imitators of the odes of Klopstock and the nature studies of Albrecht von Haller. Beside them, the lyricist Lorenz Leopold Haschka, formerly also a Jesuit, sunned himself in the approval of his contemporaries and the protection of his landlady, the wife of Hofrat von Greiner, who 'every week held sundry learned assemblies'. Of him the anonymous author of the *Lamentation* reported that he had once written to Goethe 'that he, Haschka, was exactly the same age as Goethe, so that Germany had produced two great geniuses on the same day', but had received no reply. Now he contented himself with wearing his hair and clothing *à la* Goethe.

Meanwhile this Haschka encouraged a high-thinking young nobleman, Johann Baptist von Alxinger, to dedicate himself to the art of poetry, whereupon the latter began to compose odes in the manner of Wieland. The worthy Alxinger also wrote well-meant and moralistic verse such as the 'Song of an Old Jew', a plea for tolerance which reminds one of Blake's 'The Little Black Boy' in its touching simplicity.

Among the minor talents a few others stood out, the dramatist Ayrenhoff, a lieutenant-general who wrote in the French style, the malicious polemicist Blumauer and the worthy poet Ratschky – three authors whose reputations, like that of Alxinger, succeeded in spreading beyond the Austrian borders. But of all the adherents of literature in Joseph's Vienna, hardly one is known to posterity, and it is only thanks to the circumstance that Johann Friedel, himself scarcely better remembered, told his friend in Berlin of them, that they are mentioned here at all.

Nevertheless, among many bad writers there were a few good scholars. There was the vain and eclectic, but deserving Sonnenfels, whose diction was based on that of Lessing. There were men like Jacquin, Petrasch, Birkenstock and Born, who in their respective fields were of service to the movement of enlightenment. Finally, there were aesthetes in the political world such as Gerhart van Swieten's son Gottfried, Baron Spielmann or Count Pergen. If literature and science were not elevated to the same heights in Vienna as music, if they had not as yet brought forth a figure of European standing, the Viennese possessed enough sensitivity, taste and true admiration for the greatness of contemporary German writing for a salon after the French model to be formed from among their circles, so long as a common focus could be found.

Was Fanny, in those first years of Joseph's reign, already achieving her aim of making her house a meeting-place of distinguished connoisseurs? It would seem so. Nathan was well enough known in 1781 to appear, in lace jabot and tie-wig, his good-humoured face already boasting a slight double chin, among other personalities of public life in a collection of silhouettes published by François Gonord. Franz Gräffer – the famous bookseller, journalist and anecdotist, 'ein Mann von Kopf' (a man of intelligence), as one used to say in the Rococo era, a co-author of the *Austrian National Encyclopaedia*, and, in his easy-going, butterfly-like way an Austrian counterpart to the serious Nicolai – in a *Vision of the Augarten* of the early 1780s, describes Fanny as a greatly admired lady, whose opinion was authoritative in the great world:

Everyone was flocking to the Augarten. The firework-maker Girandolini wished to provide a particularly impressive entertainment today, in defiance of Stuwer, his hot-headed rival in the Prater. The weather was delightful, as was the continuous airy concert of a chorus of those nightingales which the Emperor procured from time to time, to let them fly about and make themselves at home there.

Much of the *beau monde* had already assembled. Not a few families had already taken their midday meal at the restaurant kept by the Emperor's own caterer in the Augarten. Pleasing music from wind instruments, known as *Harmonie*, rang out. The avenues began to fill with people. In the shady walk, close to the little house, still standing, which the Emperor often occupied during the season of fine weather, Frau von Arnstein, resplendent with youthful charm, grace, culture and intellect, strolled with her husband. Among their party were the remarkable royal Negro, Angelo Soliman, in his Turkish costume of pure white, and General Ayrenhoff in uniform.

The conversation concerned the play given the day before, *The Great Battery*. Angelo heaped praise on the author. 'It pleased us,' he said, 'and no less my princely friend (he meant the then ruler of Liechtenstein) far better even than your *Mail Train*, however much the great Frederick may patronise it. The piece has some very effective scenes, and the characters are admirably drawn.'

Gräffer then describes how Ayrenhoff complacently listens to this flattery and how Angelo goes so far as to remark that the work was worthy of a Voltaire.

Frau von Arnstein smiled and cooled her goddess-like visage with a costly fan. She refrained from speech. Ayrenhoff waited anxiously for the pronouncement of this highly cultured lady whose judgement rightly counted for so much, even more than that of a whole academy.

As an indirect demand or polite invitation to express her opinion, Ayrenhoff, turning towards the lady, again removed his hat. She however continued to smile gently and sweetly. The poet, in torment, studied this smile; but he discovered there not the remotest expression of a critical nature, neither of approval nor censure. This circumstance soon plunged him into desperation. The fate of *The Great Battery* depended on the words of Frau von Arnstein.

This crisis did not go unobserved by Herr von Arnstein or Angelo Soliman. They began to feel uneasy. But Fanny possessed mercy and generosity. In order to put an end to the embarrassing situation of the three men, she was just opening her charming, rosy lips to speak, when a giant of a man, in a major's uniform, his hand on his sword-hilt, stormed up from the side towards General Ayrenhoff.

Now the writer describes how Baron Friedrich von der Trenck – for this was none other than the well-known adventurer, military man and writer of memoirs – apostrophises Ayrenhoff '*coram publico*: "Intellect is what I demand – intellect and power and life, not flat, feeble Frenchified imitation."'' The two gentlemen are at each other's throats, Arnstein tries to withdraw, but Trenck promises to moderate his behaviour. He falls in with Ayrenhoff, obliging him to take his arm, 'and so the two sons of Mars strode along behind the satin dress, in "Emperor's-eyes blue", of Frau von Arnstein, on whose right Angelo was proceeding.' Trenck asks Ayrenhoff how, as a soldier, he could write such stuff; the latter tries to bid him farewell, saying that he must speak urgently with Herr von Arnstein on business matters. 'Nothing of the kind!' cries Trenck, becoming heated again. 'Your friends are intriguing against me with the military councillor to the court.' Gräffer continues:

Meanwhile, the Emperor had returned from a ride on horseback. According to his habit, he had mingled with the strollers. Among them he noticed Fanny von Arnstein. As was his wont whenever he caught sight of her taking a walk or at a ball, he singled her out by saluting and addressing her.

He walked along with her, close at her side. 'Girandolini will put on a fine show,' he remarked. 'He has offered all sorts of attractions, for he knew that you would be an observer. And you are wearing my colour,' he added, with a glance at her gown. 'I love this colour above all others,' answered the lady. 'May that which it expresses, cheerfulness and gaiety of mind, always be granted to Your Majesty.'

Joseph replied, slightly raising his hat and with a bowing motion: 'That, unfortunately, is not possible, because you, the representative of these desirable qualities, cannot always be near me.' Fanny cast down her eyes. In a deferential, gentle tone, she said: 'I must count myself all the more fortunate, when chance sometimes brings me to your presence.'

'Oh, chance,' remarked Joseph, in happy excitement, 'is, thanks to the blue heavens, often wiser and cleverer than intention and premeditated plan. Herr von Arnstein, are you not of my opinion? And you, dear Soliman? What have you done with our Liechtenstein?'

At this moment the clash of swords was heard from the bushes nearby. People rushed up to the spot. An unseemly scuffle ensued. 'A duel,' the people cried, 'a duel!' In the confusion, Angelo Soliman tried to make room for the Emperor. But the latter was much quicker and more energetic. Respectfully the crowd moved aside. It was but twenty steps to the Emperor's little house. He offered temporary refuge there to the lady and her escorts. Frau von Arnstein, however, seemed to hesitate.

Then Joseph said: 'Have no misgivings; beauty is queen everywhere.'

This little story is only one of the 'historical novellas, genre scenes, frescoes, sketches, personages and facts, anecdotes and *curiosa*, visions and notes' published by the zealous Franz Gräffer towards the end of his life, in the last years of the so-called *Vormärz* (the period immediately before the revolution of 1848). One should not, however, make the mistake of taking him literally, as so many historians and encyclopaedists have done. One should neither believe that Fanny's judgement, at that time or at any other, could have outweighed that of a whole academy, nor conclude from his description that Emperor Joseph had bestowed his affections on her as well as on all the middle-class girls and stationmasters' daughters with whom posterity has linked his name. Indeed, it might be worth asking whether a scene such as he describes could ever actually have taken place.

Gräffer gives no date for the encounter. But Ayrenhoff's comedy *The Great Battery* was given its first performance on 1 September 1783, in the Fasantheater, and Frederick the Great, whose preference for the same author's *Mail Train* is mentioned, was still alive in that year. The fireworks of Stuwer and Girandolini in the Prater and Augarten fall into the same period which saw the black prince Soliman being taken up by Viennese society. As for the improbable supposition that Joseph could have been susceptible to the charms of a Jewess, this too finds support in history. This unusual man, who could be described by a biographer as 'cold and passionless, looking at women as though they were statues', was too much a son of his time to shun all adventures. Without question he had genuinely loved his first wife. But popular gossip was right in ascribing to him a number of secret liaisons. He was for many years the affectionate friend of Princess Eleonore Liechtenstein, whom we shall meet again later. Many 'natural' offspring, among them the 'toll-collector's wife' Anna Maria Wewerka, might serve as proofs of the favours which Joseph bestowed on certain of his female subjects. Among these was the daughter of a Jewish cantor from Schlosshof, to whom a son was born, who grew up under the name of Joseph Gottfried Pargfrieder, amassed a mighty fortune by means of successful speculation, and finally was buried at the side of Field-Marshal Radetzky.

In short, it is quite possible that Franz Gräffer's artificial 'vision' conceals a true story which may have come to his ears as a child. He himself had later offered Fanny, whom he here prematurely ennobles with the honorific *von*, the greatest admiration, again described her charm in glowing colours in another sketch, *At the Masked Ball*, and also commemorated her in his *National Encyclo-*

paedia. But was she really beautiful? This cannot be assumed from any of the extant portraits of her, neither her portrait as a young woman by an unknown hand, nor Kriehuber's medallion from her maturer years, nor Kininger's mezzotint, nor even the little drawing which shows her in a tall, beribboned straw hat in the 1790s; yet so it was asserted by many of her contemporaries.

'A tall, slim figure, radiant with beauty and grace' is how she is described by Karl August Varnhagen, who did not meet her face to face for the first time until after the turn of the century. She was called 'the fair Hebrew' by another memoirist, 'the beautiful, magnificent lady of the house' by a German musician who had known her since her youth. Gräffer may therefore have simply been expressing the true feeling of contemporary taste. But in his description of the way in which Arnstein retreats behind his wife and is honoured by being addressed only with a sidelong glance, there is concealed a very exact knowledge of the couple.

Finally, that Fanny achieved access to the Emperor, and at such an early stage, is confirmed by a more reliable witness. In a letter of April 1819 to his friend Benzenberg, the Prussian councillor of state Stägemann – a frequent guest at the Arnstein house during the Congress of Vienna – had the following anecdote to relate, from the weeks before the issuing of the edict of tolerance: 'When Frau von Arnstein in Vienna at that time, like Esther before Ahasuerus, begged the Emperor Joseph for benevolence towards her people, he answered her: "I will do everything for them that I can; but I cannot like them; just look at them! Can you like them?"' Stägemann's story, which undoubtedly he heard from her own mouth, does not relate Fanny's reply to the Emperor. Perhaps she, who possessed intelligence above all else, was disarmed by the confidential sincerity of his words. Indeed, perhaps she even shared the antipathy of the Emperor, who had condescended as low as to a cantor's daughter, towards some excessively ill-favoured and unprepossessing children of the Old Testament.

How she attained her proximity to the throne in the first place is easy to imagine. There was more than one link between her world and that of the court. One, which was to bring both joy and sorrow, was the infatuation of the imperial cabinet secretary Günther for the Jewess Eleonore Eskeles.

The Eskeles family was a very old one, which came from Worms and had travelled through Poland and Moravia to settle in Vienna. As early as the fourteenth century their ancestor, the wise Löwa the

Elder, was living in the Rhineland city of Worms. His descendants produced scholars of importance in every generation, among them the 'high Rabbi Löw' in Prague, to whom legend has attributed miraculous powers, thanks to his astronomical and probably also astrological studies. From his brother's son there descended, at the turn of the seventeenth century, the highly respected Gabriel Eskeles, whose wisdom and knowledge were so extraordinary that he had to be given a double title of rabbi. The great Samson Wertheimer gave Gabriel's son Bernhard the hand of one of his daughters, without however taking him into his international business, for this young adept of the sacred books also had 'the gold-trimmed mantle spread over him at a tender age' and he had been made the spiritual guardian of two Moravian Jewish communities: he inherited his father's country rabbinate in Moravia and also that of his father-in-law Samson in Hungary (honorary offices, which he discharged from Vienna). After his wife's death, he was married again, this time to Wertheimer's niece, who bore him a son and a daughter. The daughter, Eleonore or Lea, was born in 1752. Bernhard did not live to see the birth of another son in the following year.

Eleonore married young. Her marriage brought her to Berlin. There she must already have come to know Fanny's family, for her husband's name was Fliess, like that of the doctor who had married Hanna, the eldest Itzig daughter. But the young wife, who sensed in herself the heritage of centuries of spiritual refinement, did not languish for long at the side of the merchant Fliess. She left him to go to Vienna, where her brother Bernhard had lived since coming of age. In her native city she was known as the Prussian, just as, with greater justification, Fanny's origins in Berlin were never forgotten, but like Fanny she was immediately accepted with warmth in society. She was as learned as her ancestors. But she must also have possessed unusual charm, otherwise she would not, as a thirty-year-old, have bewitched the court official Valentin Günther, who was only a little older.

Not only did Günther find his love for Eleonore reciprocated (as early as 1779 they were already linked by a tender relationship), at about this time he also won favour with the Emperor. As a former officer and military commissioner in Transylvania, he had been taken into Joseph's cabinet to make copies of the most secret and important despatches and letters. Joseph had soon become so used to the cheerful, intelligent and handsome young man that the latter became his constant companion. He drove out with him, in a simple green barouche with two greys, holding the reins himself, with Günther at his side on the left. They would walk together in the Augarten and sat *tête-à-tête* at a reserved table in the court caterer's restaurant among other people. They were always dressed alike, in long dark-blue greatcoats, with buckskin breeches and gloves of the same, their boots fitted with spurs, and three-cornered hats on their heads. 'Günther,' writes Emilie Weckbecker, 'was most often at my parents' house. He divided the evenings which he did not spend with his imperial friend between Fanny Arnstein and them. My father always called him (as it were, in anticipation of what was to come) *l'aimable imprudent*. He loved him greatly, as he adored everything that came from Emperor Joseph.'

Günther was able to appear openly at Fanny's receptions. His affair with Eleonore Eskeles was conducted in private; at least it is not established that Joseph, while he spent his days with his favourite, was aware with whom the latter spent his nights. Günther, who was frequently invited to Fanny Arnstein's, could easily have introduced her to the Emperor, so that the good Gräffer's claim that Joseph always honoured her with a greeting when he met her walking or at a ball seems well founded. While Fanny, as she told Stägemann, had once gone to the Emperor to plead for his benevolence towards her people, her friend Günther, Eleonore's lover, had done not a little towards the issuing of the edict of tolerance in the first winter of Joseph's reign.

The reforms that the Emperor intended to undertake included a charter for the Jews. That this people within his state, from whom so many duties as well as rights were withheld, must profitably be incorporated into the community, was clearer to his eyes than to those of his officials. On this point too the latter praised his 'wise intentions, which would bring fame to the age and to his government', but advised deliberation, to which Joseph was as little disposed as in any other matter. He intended to free the Jews in his own way. True, he had it in mind neither to increase their privileges nor to recognise them as citizens with equal rights. But he was determined to abolish most of the degrading laws then in force, even at the price of the restriction of Jewish community life and religious worship, their ancient tradition. Here, too, he was ahead of his time. One hundred years later, when their religious ties had loosened, a high proportion of the Viennese Jewish community were ready for complete emancipation. However, in an age when enlightened spirits were to be found only in a small section of the upper classes, the majority of them, despite their manifest gratitude, found Joseph's concessions to them too dearly bought.

It was Günther, however, in those winter weeks, who gave a special impetus to the Emperor's decision to issue as speedily as possible a charter for the Jews which should be appropriate to the spirit of the age. He delivered an anonymous document which originated from the circle of his Jewish friends, probably from the pen of the shrewd Bernhard Eskeles. On 13 May, the Emperor announced his 'highest intentions' with regard to a new charter for the Jews and demanded that the Lower Austrian government should deliver its report on the 'future better clarification and use of the Jewish nation for the state in all the German hereditary lands'. 'Likewise,' the imperial document continued, 'we are communicating to the aforesaid government the anonymous observations concerning the Jews' charter of 1764, which have reached this most loyal place with the Emperor's most gracious signature in his own hand, in order to obtain its exhaustive opinion on the matter, point by point.' The document does not survive. But its contents may be reconstructed from the government's report of September 1781, which indeed referred to it point by point.

The anonymous correspondent cited religious intolerance as the main cause of the various oppressions and limitations suffered by the Jews. This, according to the government report, was not true; rather, the Jews for their part had 'political defects'. The first sentence of the anonymous document referred to the excessive restrictions on the Jews' ability to earn their livelihoods; the government agreed with these remarks. In the second sentence, the writer declaimed against the denial of respect to the Jews by their fellow-citizens and considered it contrary to the natural law that they should be obliged to wear beards, to live only in certain houses, to lodge only in their own inns, to give neither food nor paid employment to Christians, and not to go out before twelve on Sundays and holidays; to which the government replied that it was they themselves who chose to wear beards, that they should be allowed to go out on Sundays, but that the regulations regarding inns and servants could hardly be moderated. 'An exception could always be made for particularly well-known and accredited persons.' In the third sentence, certain requests regarding Jewish servants were made, which the government was prepared partially to grant. To the complaint of the fourth sentence, that privileged Jews were obliged to make contributions 'under a number of categories', the reply was that they could by all means pay a higher tolerance tax in exchange for exemption from other taxes.

Under the pretext of making an impartial statement in reply to these anonymous requests, the government had in fact rejected all the most crucial points. Enclosed with their report, however, was a separate statement by the adviser to the court chancery, von Greiner, in which this freethinking and progressive man expressed himself, with necessary caution, but unmistakably in favour of total equality for the Jews. In contrast to his colleagues of the Lower Austrian government he touched on the root of the matter: 'The question is this, whether the Jews in Lower Austria and in Vienna, despite their circumstances which are to be changed so radically, should nevertheless in future, as before, be only suffered or tolerated, or whether, like other religious sects, to whom only the most secret acts of worship are permitted, they should, as they are in Poland and in Holland, actually be received and accepted among other subjects, with those limitations which that other religion makes necessary for itself.'

The government, wrote Greiner, believe that it would be better to retain the existing system of tolerance. He, however, was of the opinion that from time immemorial the only mainsprings of all human conduct had been ambition and hope. When these languished, the result was nothing but total inactivity or, at the best, a very small measure of co-operation, within the state as in the case of local Jews.

> Deprived of their livelihoods by the present manner of administration on their account, degraded to the status of cattle or at least of slaves both by tolerance payments and by personal taxation [*Leibmaut*], everywhere singled out and always cast out of the community of righteous people, they could be of little use to the state, and, in fact, could not even wish to be of use; indeed, it would have been better for them and for other subjects if they had not been settled here at all, rather than to be tolerated in the way that they have been.

Greiner knew very well that the Lower Austrian government, the overwhelming majority of his colleagues and even the Emperor himself were opposed to the idea of 'reception', a total inclusion of the Jews in the middle-class community. He did not make such a demand, but he did make it sufficiently clear that he himself saw this as the only possibility for healing the present ills. The next step was an imperial resolution which was proclaimed in October. It began with the ceremonious declaration that the Emperor by no means intended 'to diffuse the Jewish nation further into the hereditary lands, or to introduce it newly where it is not tolerated, but only to make it useful to the state where it is, and to the extent that it is now tolerated', and decreed that 'the Jews' charter *de anno* 1764 shall be entirely discarded' and a new charter was to be drawn up.

An original draft by the Lower Austrian government failed to be approved because of numerous errors in form, and Sonnenfels, who was highly esteemed for his style of composition, was enlisted to re-draft it. No representative of the Jews was consulted, although the anonymous document was taken into account; the opinions of the various court and state councillors were combined into a single form, the possibility of 'reception' was disavowed and the Emperor's demand for the utilisation as far as possible of the Jewish community was translated into fact. The result was the charter of tolerance which had been awaited for so long and so ardently by the Jews, and which was announced on 2 January 1782.

With amazement, wonder and much shaking of heads the Austrians received the news of Joseph's latest reform. Freethinking spirits throughout Europe instantly united in praise of the monarch who had taken the first and decisive step towards the emancipation of the Jews and, if he had not at a stroke corrected their dishonoured and outlawed state, had substantially relieved it. Klopstock, in a poetic rapture, wrote:

Du lösest ihnen, Retter, die rostige,
Engangelegte Fessel vom wunden Arm!
Sie fühlen's, glauben's kaum. So lange
Hat's um die Elenden hergeklirret.

[You, their saviour, release the rusty fetters / Tightly bound about their injured limbs! / They hardly feel, hardly believe it. So long / Have the poor wretches lived amid the rattling chains.]

There was jubilation too among the Jews, above all those progressive members of the community who saw no harshness in the Emperor's intention to wean them away from the age-old precepts of their religion and a 'religious authority transplanted hither from the East'. They all wished to believe that their servitude was entirely over because from now on the Emperor was to allow them 'to learn all manner of handicrafts and trades here and elsewhere from Christian masters', and practise these as well as 'painting, sculpture and the liberal arts'. They were also to be permitted to turn their hands to all 'non-civic branches of business', to set up 'factories and workshops', 'to keep as many Jewish and also Christian servants as their business demand[ed], not to be obliged to wear beards, not to pay *Leibmaut* [personal tax], but on the other hand, as wholesale merchants or their sons, or as people of rank, to wear swords, to visit 'places of public entertainment', to go out before noon on Sundays and holidays, and finally 'to rent their own dwellings both in the city and in the suburbs'.

A cornucopia of favours had been emptied at their feet. What was still denied them seemed so little. It was no more than that in future, as in the past, they still might not form an 'actual community', hold public religious services, own a synagogue or a printing-press for their Hebrew books, purchase houses or land; no one could live in the capital without a certificate of tolerance, or come to Vienna from the hereditary dominions without special permission; and they were still barred from civic rights and the guild masterships. No more than the difference between toleration and 'reception', between residence subject to revocation – an existence dependent on official caprice and the current level of protection money, without civic rights although with numerous civic duties – and complete equality with their Catholic, Protestant, Greek Orthodox and Muhammadan compatriots in Austria. A small difference, which did not, however, prevent the world from seeing Joseph as the noblest benefactor of Jewry, since in other parts, except perhaps for Holland and Poland, people were so reactionary that this charter of tolerance had the effect of a fanfare of liberty, and it was only reluctantly and after long hesitation that the German states, particularly Prussia, began to follow the Austrian example.

In Vienna, however, a few weeks after the proclamation of the edict, a scandal blew up that seriously undermined the goodwill of the Emperor.

Valentin Günther, *l'aimable imprudent*, had, after his more or less successful intercession on behalf of the Jews, continued his amorous double-dealing. Occupied during the day with cabinet business or attendant on imperial entertainment, at night he relaxed from the burden of work and of constantly displaying amiability. Instead, however, of '*regis ad exemplum*', as Gräffer writes, 'going from one to another, he came to a halt with Madame Eskeles and spent his hours of rest with her. This Jewess was regarded as a Berliner in Vienna, where it was said, as once of Nazareth: can there any good thing come out of Berlin? Moreover, she loved to read books, and was known as a learned woman; which epithet in Vienna is subject to very equivocal interpretations.' It seems, therefore, that in the circles of the police, who undoubtedly observed Günther's private movements, without revealing them to the Emperor as long as they were not requested to do so, there was constant suspicion regarding the favourite's connection with the

'lady from Berlin'. This connection had meanwhile been strengthened by the fact that Eleonore had borne him two children, at that
time the almost inevitable consequence of such affairs.

In March 1782, misfortune overtook the two lovers. The manner
of this has taken the shape in popular legend of a single fantastic
occurrence. The memoirists declare that Günther visited his mistress one evening with a sheaf of important correspondence concerning Prussia in his pocket, spent the night there and next
morning, having returned to his apartments, realised to his horror
that the official documents were no longer about his person. The
lady from Berlin, with her servants, had absconded to Prussian soil
in two post-chaises, and Günther had been relieved of his post by
the Emperor. The truth is that Günther's fall and his separation
from Eleonore had taken place in a less dramatic manner, but a
more disastrous one as far as his innocent mistress was concerned.

Two years earlier a Jew from Breslau called Philipp Joras had
turned up in Vienna and, being a skilled engraver, found work with
the seal-engraver Philipp Abraham. There he made friends with
Abraham's business partner, Isaak David from Lorraine, who
occasionally visited Eleonore's house to seek recommendations to
clients. At one time or another Joras accompanied David and was
introduced to Eleonore as a writer. The two engravers, both
dubious characters, now began to hatch a plot to extract money
from the royal Prussian envoy in Breslau, Herr von Hoym, under
the pretext of spurious espionage. Joras was to settle in Breslau
again and David, under the name of Müller, was to send him
presumptive secret information, which he would pass on to the
minister for an annual salary of 1,000 thalers.

Joras returned to Berlin, and they began to put their prearranged
plan into action. After half a year had passed, the ingenious Joras
had taken on a new task which was to bring him back to Vienna
and into possession of a substantial commission. A government
minister named Görne in Berlin had a financial claim on the
Austrian exchequer and was having difficulty in collecting the sum
in question. Joras, remembering the relationship between Eleonore
Eskeles and the cabinet secretary, promised Görne's middleman, a
certain Kiewe, to obtain the minister's money from the exchequer
with Günther's help. In the course of proceedings however he
quarrelled with Kiewe as well as with his own subordinate. Kiewe
denounced him, and one day in March David and Joras were
arrested.

What these complex machinations of Prussian ministers and
Jewish pseudo-spies, and all this business of Hoym, Görne and

Kiewe, Joras, David and Abraham had to do with the Viennese lovers, nobody knew. The two arrested miscreants did not know either, in fact they explicitly denied having involved the cabinet secretary Günther in their grubby dealings. But the connection of his name with the demand for money, and the circumstance that the family doctor not only of Günther and Eleonore but also of Isaak David bore the name of Joseph Ferdinand Müller, were enough to persuade the police to accuse these four as well as those already under arrest of criminal conspiracy. It was at this point that the case was brought to the Emperor's attention.

Joseph, who had until now shown Günther only his gentlest, mildest, most communicative and tenderest side, became hard as steel in his wrath. Whether it was really not until that moment that he learnt of Eleonore's existence, or whether he just wanted to revenge a long-nourished jealousy on the mistress of his favourite – at any rate, he would have nothing to do with a private interrogation of Günther. He responded to the report from the police authorities with a handwritten note, in which he ordered that Günther should be removed from the cabinet and that an investigation into his activities should immediately begin. The same measures should be taken against the Jewess Eskeles and the medico Müller, if necessary Günther's servants should be questioned 'and altogether the whole brood is to be exposed or else the opportunity shall be provided for them to cleanse themselves of all suspicion'.

On 28 June, Eleonore was summoned to the inquiry and taken into police custody. Under questioning, records of which were later discovered, she insisted that she had had no understanding of any kind with Joras and David. Moreover Günther had never trusted her with any confidential matters, just as 'it would never have occurred to her to question him on such things, for she knew well that this would have been the surest method of banishing him from her company forever'. The two pseudo-spies, however – who were held to be genuine ones for purposes of state – had never been seen by Günther at all.

Her evidence tallied with the statements of the other accused persons, except that Joras claimed to have met Günther at her house. When he was confronted with the latter, it turned out that he had mistaken Müller, the doctor, for Günther. The total innocence of the two lovers thus seemed to have been proved, or rather it would have been so if the Emperor had decided to accept it as such. But his anger, which was considered by his contemporaries to arise from 'love gone sour', would not be dispelled. Perhaps Gräffer is right in saying that 'Madame Eskeles, intimidated by the interrogator, who sought to persuade her that Günther had already confessed all, had related a few little stories of His Majesty's amorous intrigues which Günther had conveyed to her in confidence'. In this case, Joseph's obduracy would have been understandable. It would still not have been forgivable.

Joras and David received a sentence of twice-thirty strokes and several years' penal servitude. 'The Jewess,' read the imperial verdict, 'as serving no purpose here and as a Berliner, because of her suspicious association with two notorious Prussian spies shall be removed from here without delay in the usual manner by means of a police inspector who shall accompany her to the utmost border, with the warning that should she ever set foot again in His Majesty's hereditary lands she would render herself liable to the severest penalties, and this shall be made known by order in the usual manner in all of the German and Hungarian hereditary lands.'

So Eleonore was declared guilty before all the world and banished from Austria. The Emperor, having ordered Günther to return his sword to him, summoned him to appear before him once more at three in the afternoon in the Augarten. After this conversation the *aimable imprudent* was transferred to Hermannstadt, where he became draughtsman to the imperial war council and married a young, blonde, gentle Transylvanian lady. He and Eleonore, whose banishment was by no means to be permanent, never met again.

Fanny, who had been Eleonore's confidante, whose house Günther had so often visited, must have been shattered by the whole affair. Her sorrow for her unjustly treated friend must have been mingled with shame over the fact that the latter – in the very year of the edict of tolerance – had given occasion for new prejudice against the Jews. It was for this reason that Eleonore's name was never mentioned in the Arnstein house throughout the years that she spent abroad. This deep silence was also preserved towards posterity. Not one remark of Fanny's, no sign of the despair into which the case must have plunged her, has survived.

On the other hand, another friend of Valentin Günther's expressed his feelings in a document which tells us more about him than about the case in question. Wolfgang Amadeus Mozart, in his earliest Vienna years, had grown fond of the cabinet secretary, a member of the Freemasons' lodge known as 'The Crowned Hope', which he himself was to join some time later, and Günther was a frequent visitor to his house. 'His house' was as much as to say

'Fanny's house', for at the beginning of September 1781, having given up his lodging at the house called 'The Eye of God', in the Tuchlauben, of his future mother-in-law, Maria Cäcilie Weber, Mozart moved into a room on the third floor of 1175, Graben. For more than eight months, until his marriage to Constanze, he lodged among the Arnsteins' coachmen, valets and kitchenmaids. Here he wrote his *Entführung aus dem Serail*, his Haffner Symphony, three concertos and two sonatas. Here he began to compose fugues, after acquiring a thorough knowledge of 'Händl and Sebastian Bach' at the private concerts in the house of Baron van Swieten. From here he daily visited Constanze, who lived but a stone's throw away from him, occasionally went to court to play for the Emperor, called to pay his respects at many houses of the nobility, and, on 16 July 1782, went to attend the first performance of his 'German operetta' in the Turkish style. From here, finally, he rushed with Constanze to St Stephen's Cathedral on 4 August, to marry her behind his father's back.

The sound of his piano rang out above Fanny's head by day – 'for until that is standing in the room, I cannot live in it'. Perhaps, like his friend Günther, he was occasionally invited to her apartments in the evening. The name 'd'Arnsteiner' certainly turns up on the list of high nobility for his subscription concert of 1 April 1782, among a few patrons of similar origin such as the two Barons Wetzlar, the merchants Bienenfeld and Hönickstein and the court councillor Sonnenfels. Raimund, the younger Baron Wetzlar, whom Mozart knew very well as a converted Jew, soon became his protector and was godfather to his first, short-lived child. None of this prevented Mozart from expressing himself to his father after the Günther scandal in the coarsest tones about the 'Jewess Escules':

The Jewess Escules must indeed have been a very good and useful instrument in the breakdown of friendship between the Emperor and the Russian court – for she was actually *taken to Berlin* the day before yesterday to give the King the pleasure of her company; – well, she is a sow of the first order – for she was the only cause of Günther's misfortune – if it be a misfortune to be under arrest for two months in a fine room (while retaining all his books and his fortepiano, etc.), to lose his former post, but then to be installed in another at a salary of 1,200 gulden; for he departed yesterday for *Hermannstadt*. – Yet – such a matter always causes pain to an honest man, and nothing in the world can replace that sort of thing. – Only you should realise from this that it was not such a great crime that he committed. – His only crime is – *étourderie* – indiscretion – as a result – not sufficiently strict silence – which of course is a great fault in a cabinet member. – Albeit he confided nothing of importance to anyone, yet his enemies, of whom the first is the former *Statthalter* [lieutenant-governor] Count von Herberstein, knew how to arrange it so well and finely that the Emperor, who had had such strong confidence in him that he would walk up and down the room arm in arm with him for hours on end, conceived all the greater a distrust of him. – To all this there came the sow Escules (a former *amantia* of Günther) and accused him most vigorously – but at the investigation of the affair it did not turn out too well for the gentlemen – the great noise caused by the matter had already been made – the great gentlemen always want to be in the right – and so poor Günther's fate [was sealed], whom I pity from my heart, for he was a very good friend of mine, and (if things had remained as they were) could have rendered me good service with the Emperor. – Imagine how strange and unexpected it was for me, and how it affected me. Stephani – Adamberger – and I supped with him one evening and the next day he was arrested.

Günther must indeed have been a fascinating person. How else could he have aroused not only in the Emperor, but also in Mozart, feelings which filled them with such violent wrath against his presumed destroyer? For the rest, this letter casts a little light on those weaknesses of character which may be found even in an exceptionally good-hearted genius. We see how Mozart, like any other Viennese scandal-monger, unthinkingly parrots what he has heard from gossiping tongues. We see how he unquestioningly believes the rumour that Eleonore had 'accused [Günther] most vigorously', and gives further circulation to another, that the supposed espionage had destroyed the Emperor's friendship with Catherine the Great, although he knows that Günther 'confided nothing of importance to anyone'. We see how he bears a particular grudge against Eleonore because as a result of this scandal he has lost an advocate with the Emperor. And we see finally how in spite of multiple Jewish patronage he falls to abusing the 'Jewish sow' as soon as the occasion is offered. In short, we notice not without a certain sadness how bound to their times are even the most immortal geniuses, how little they differ from their everyday surroundings.

From his letter, as from the communication of a correspondent of the *Frankfurter Zeitung* that 'the Jewish nation has few friends here', it can be recognised what damage the Günther affair had done. David and Joras, the two good-for-nothings, bore a burden of guilt in this that was heavier even than the Emperor's highhanded justice. The Emperor's attitude to the Jews, to be sure, remained unchanged after his wrath had cooled. He liked them neither better nor worse than before, but continued in his determination to use them as advantageously as possible in his state. He bore no grudge against the Arnsteins, who in the course of his reign entered into a close business relationship with Eleonore's brother. For in the very year of these happenings, if we can believe Gräffer's vision in the Augarten, he behaved with the utmost graciousness to Fanny and her husband. About the same time the latter's brother became the first of his family to enter the Austrian nobility. And three years later Nathan himself succeeded in achieving a small but significant victory. He had complained that the Viennese magistrate, in summonses addressed to him, used the word *Jud* (Jew) and omitted the word *Herr* (gentleman). Thereafter the court chancery issued a decree to the Lower Austrian government that Jewish merchants, except where no specific exceptions were made by the 1782 charter, should be put on the same level as Christian ones and the word *Jud* should be omitted from judicial summonses and other communications.

Not even Samson Wertheimer with his ten imperial soldiers standing guard over him had achieved as much. The Emperor's minions were becoming human beings, even 'gentlemen'.

−4−

Joseph's Decade

In the Berlin of Frederick the Great, which had noted Joseph's reforms with admiring or ironic amazement, a new era was likewise imminent. The King, who saw freedom as his spiritual possession, but handed it out as negligently and arbitrarily as alms to the poor; who had never taken anything in his life seriously except the greatness of Prussia, and who gave to this abstract concept, rather than to the living people of whom Prussia consisted, his meagre measure of love and sympathy – the King sat, old, alone and ill-tempered, in his palace at Potsdam and felt his powers waning. There is no doubt about the feelings which accompanied his amazement at the Emperor's latest rulings. That 'nouvel ordre de choses' that he had prophesied filled him with derisive doubt. Years ago he had made the epigrammatic remark that he wanted to make people happy in their own fashion. Joseph seemed to be forcing them to be happy in his own fashion. He, Frederick, cared not in the slightest whether they were happy or not.

Nor did he feel much inclination to apply to his Jewish subjects those progressive principles which he had so often professed. To Itzig and Ephraim, who had arrived some time earlier with a petition requesting leniency towards the Jews of Breslau, he sent a royal adjudication: 'Whatever has to do with their trade they may keep. But as for their bringing whole tribes of Jews to Breslau and making it into another Jerusalem, that cannot be.' For the rest, he stood by the ruling of 1750, which still upheld the oppressive precepts of his ancestors. When Mirabeau visited Berlin in the last year of Frederick's reign, he called this law 'une loi digne d'un cannibale'.

In any case it was difficult to know which of the two monarchs who occupied the thrones of Prussia and of the Holy Roman Empire was to be preferred. With the same conviction of his absolutist power one introduced his idealistic innovations, while the other in his scepticism left everything as it was. If one tended sometimes to prefer the Prussian misanthrope to the Austrian philanthropist, then perhaps it was because one could get along better with a freedom-loving despot than with a despotic liberator. And it could not take long for a woman like Fanny to notice – after the first upsurge of enthusiasm over Joseph's edict of tolerance had ebbed – that she and her kind could live in a more peaceful and even a more dignified manner in Berlin.

Even before the death of the old King and the changes that were gaining ground with the accession of his nephew Frederick William, the climate of opinion had become decidedly more favourable towards the Jews. The amused or contemptuous indifference manifested by Frederick towards most of his subjects – indeed towards the whole of humanity – certainly included the entire Jewish community. But his disdain was first and foremost for those fanatical champions of their old teaching and way of life who expected a degree of tolerance from him that they themselves did not extend to their own fellow-believers. It was not the 'illuminated' and emancipated spirits among them that he rejected, but those obstinately pious Talmudists who sought to frustrate with all the powers at their disposal any innovation in their religion, any attempt at integration with their environment. Above all, however, he conceded to them a right which Joseph denied them: the formation and management of their own religious community.

This, after all, was the king who had written in his *History of Brandenburg* that false religious zeal was the tyrant which depopulated nations, while the spirit of toleration was the mother who tended them and made them bloom. In his *What is Enlightenment?*, Kant had praised this king in these terms: 'A prince who finds it within his dignity to say that he considers it his duty not to dictate to his people in matters of religion, but to give them total freedom in these matters, who therefore himself refuses the arrogant label of tolerance, is very enlightened and deserves to be praised by the grateful world and by posterity.' Indeed, to such an extent had this greatest of German philosophers seen the harbinger of enlightenment in this king, who allowed the freedom 'to make public use of reason in all things', that he called this era 'the century of Frederick'. Under this king, who refused to use the word tolerance and did not always practise this virtue himself, but allowed everyone to be tolerant who wished to be so, countless men of understanding, morality and integrity came together, whose actions and aspirations were directed at raising their fellow human beings out of their spiritual immaturity.

Nicolai, the 'wandering preacher of the Enlightenment', its pedantic fighting cock, a personality who ranged from the sublime to the ridiculous, was from the first the driving force of this movement in Berlin. As a friend of the same Gotthold Ephraim Lessing, one of Germany's earliest dramatists, critics, thinkers and educators of the highest rank, who at the age of twenty had already written his first appeal for tolerance, a little play called *The Jews*; as a friend of Moses Mendelssohn, the prototype for the eponymous hero of Lessing's far more influential drama *Nathan the Wise*, he created the platform from which the spirit of toleration could be proclaimed: a periodical called *Literaturbriefe (Literary Letters)*, Germany's first mouthpiece of fearless and independent criticism.

In *Literary Letters*, in 1760, Mendelssohn could even find fault with two poems by the King and condemn them as imitations of Lucretius, as 'badly rhymed attacks on the concept of immortality'. Summoned to Sanssouci and questioned as to whether he was the author of the derogatory review, he replied: 'He who writes verses is playing at ninepins, and whoever plays at ninepins, whether king or peasant, must accept the marker's decision.' The retort was well received, and *Literary Letters*, which had been threatened with suppression, was reprieved. Nevertheless, the King, who appreciated his critic's honesty and his flair for a telling metaphor, took a mischievous pleasure in delaying his privilege of protection for a little longer. It was not until three years later that Frederick, at the urging of his companion in philosophy, the Marquis d'Argens, allowed Mendelssohn the privilege of regular residence in Berlin.

The triumvirate of Lessing, Nicolai and Mendelssohn did not last long. After his departure for Leipzig, Lessing took part only by letter in the doings of his friends, and Nicolai became the actual leader of the Enlightenment movement in Berlin. That the King would not allow Nicolai and other like-minded persons to enter his Academy was another matter altogether. He, the admirer of French intellect, who himself confessed that he spoke German 'comme un cocher', had no objection to the opinions of the spokesmen of the Berlin Enlightenment. What he set his face against, the reason why time and time again he refused their requests for admission, was the sluggish, ponderous or otherwise insipid manner of their polemic; it was not their excess of tolerance, but their deficiency in talent.

The strength of the Enlightenment might lie in Wolfenbüttel and in Königsberg, not in Berlin. But in Berlin, where the laws of a new charitable approach to one's fellow human were being proclaimed, not from the throne, but from the circles of the bourgeoisie, as it were in the still centre of this movement of a programmed morality, lived the man in whom all Germany, indeed all of Europe, saw the embodiment of emancipation. Moses Mendelssohn had arrived in Prussia as a ragged, misshapen boy, who could speak only the language of his fathers, that garbled version of Middle High German which was so unpleasing to German ears. By industry and thirst for knowledge he had in a short time absorbed the culture of centuries; he had studied German, French, Greek and Latin, had taken his reasoning powers from philosophy and mathematics, modelled his style on Lessing's, and finally, after 'enlarging himself from a metaphysician into a *bel esprit*', on equal terms with a Kant, superior to a Lavater, appeared in the public eye as the critic of a Frederick. In a single generation he realised the whole potential evolution of his people and became the symbol of a development which led in one glorious leap out of the torpor of the commonplace into that pure, rarefied sphere in which kindred spirits encounter one another *in abstracto*.

For Fanny von Arnstein this man was more than a symbol. He was at the same time closer to her and in an exalted sense further removed from her than from her fellow-believers – family friend and household god in one person. Mendelssohn's first tutor in Berlin, the Polish schoolmaster Israel Samosz, was already under Daniel Itzig's protection; without a doubt this was sooner or later extended to his pupil. In a community which had traditionally valued scholarship more highly than any external possessions, the growing reputation of the philosopher in time procured him equal status with the 'Jewish prince'. Numerous bonds were to link the two families. Fanny's elder sister Bella gave her daughter Lea's hand in marriage to Moses Mendelssohn's son, Abraham. A younger sister of Fanny's, Blümchen, was married to David Friedländer, 'Mendelssohn's ape' and his spiritual heir. More important was the influence that Moses Mendelssohn's thinking exerted on his contemporaries. We can assume that to some extent the Itzig parents, and even more their children, shared his theory of life, his religious ideas, his views on state and society, morality and decency. Fanny certainly did so. Her notebook, which contains many of the philosopher's sayings, bears witness to this. So does the whole course of her life.

But what was this theory of life which she adopted so unresistingly? Above all it consisted in an unconditional belief in God, in providence, in immortality, which was altogether different from the basic principles of the enlighteners. That treatise in the German language with which in 1763 Moses Mendelssohn had emerged victorious in the contest for the prize of the Prussian Academy had answered with an unreserved 'yes' the question as to whether metaphysics was capable of the same demonstrative power as mathematics. His fellow candidate, Kant, had maintained the opposite with the greatest logical acuteness. Mendelssohn's intellectual stance corresponded to that of the currently dominant school; but his structure of thought, to which he clung throughout his life, had already been refuted by that of Kant.

When the *Critique of Pure Reason* came out in 1782 and 1783, Mendelssohn candidly admitted that, 'used to the gentle light of the philosophy of Wolf, Baumgarten and Leibniz', he felt 'unable to follow the great philosopher of Königsberg'. In *Phaedon*, his famous work about the immortality of the soul, he continued to support the transcendental proof of the existence of God. And his last great work, *Morning Hours*, deals with the 'truths of natural religion'. It was, in Kant's words, 'the last legacy of dogmatising metaphysics and at the same time its most perfect product'.

Thus, in the midst of the debate about one of the most important propositions of the Enlightenment, this man confronted its basic postulate without understanding, in fact with hostility. Frederick, who was not so much at the still centre, but rather in the path of the spiritual searchlight beam of this movement, recognising this fact, had already for this reason withheld his favour from the critic of his 'rhymed attacks on immortality'. That short span of time – a rare one in Germany – during which German philosophy turned its back on metaphysics and allowed itself to be led by the clear and consistent reasoning of science, the time of Kant, of Lessing and of Frederick was one in which Moses Mendelssohn had no part. He had less in common with the true Illuminati who, following Diderot and Voltaire, had made a clean sweep of the obscure heritage of scholasticism, than with his daughter Dorothea, that apostate who after his death had embraced the religious mysticism of the romantic period.

Had the Enlightenment been no more than a declaration of war against dogmatic religion, Mendelssohn – like those dignitaries of the Christian church who had joined its ranks – would have appeared out of place among its adherents. But it was far more than this. It was a humanitarian revolution, a 'crisis of world and cultural history penetrating into all spheres of life'. 'In the place of authority it set autonomy, in the place of subjection and dependency, maturity; in the place of the church as the greatest power, the state; in the place of moral constraint, freedom of conscience; in the place of collective power, the rights of the individual; in the place of dogma, reason, and in the place of oppression, tolerance.' On almost all these points Mendelssohn, and thus all his followers, agreed with it.

Not only to preach tolerance, but also to reinforce it with theory was his most keenly pursued aim. In this he demonstrated the courage, possessed by the true enlighteners, to forsake well-worn paths. He wrote to the Crown Prince of Brunswick: 'As all humans must be destined by their Creator for eternal bliss, an exclusive religion cannot be the true one.' By means of a transcendental argument which would have been dismissed by his more progressive friends, he was underpinning a doctrine which nevertheless was conclusive to them. It was the doctrine that Lessing later put into the mouth of his character Nathan, that 'tolerance did not mean the uniting of faiths, "the merging of faiths", the mixing of religions, but that every creed, and particularly every creed confirmed by reason and by historic revelation, should be seen as justified'.

With the help of this doctrine he confronted Lavater, who had demanded of him the decision either to refute the – equally metaphysical – *Proofs of Christianity* advanced by the Swiss philosopher Charles Bonnet or to assent to them. With its help he evaded a similar attempt by the Protestant provost and church councillor Teller to lead him away from his own religion. This wrangle was echoed by a jocular conversation in verse which, admittedly, was driven close to the bounds of good taste by Teller as much as by Mendelssohn. Teller had called out to him:

An Gott den Vater glaubt ihr schon,
So glaubt doch auch an seinen Sohn,
Ihr pflegt doch sonst bei Vaters Leben
Dem Sohne gern Credit zu geben!

[Since you believe in God the Father, / Why not believe, then, in his Son? / Your custom is in father's lifetime / Gladly to grant credit to the son.]

To which Mendelssohn replied:

Wie könnten wir Credit ihm geben?
Der Vater wird ja ewig leben.

[How could a son be given credit / Whose Father has eternal life?]

Because of his conviction that there were several revealed

religions, each of which was equally binding and decisive, Mendelssohn kept away from dogmatists as from atheists to the end of his days. In the earliest days of their friendship he had written to Lessing: 'Your believers always show great deference to revealed religion, which seems like cunning to me, and your sceptics and so-called free spirits are absolutely not to be endured.' And he added gloomily: 'I had quite another idea of the world when I knew it only from books and from the character of a Lessing. I am astonished when I think of the power that prejudice has over people's dispositions.'

It was prejudice in the minds of well-meaning people or of his spiritual kin that saddened and agitated him. And so he conducted his battles, not against the malicious adversaries of the Jews, leaving this altercation to Lessing and Nicolai, but against those of his own mind and religion: against the Prussian military adviser Christian Wilhelm Dohm, who had published a work *On the Civic Improvement of the Jews*, and against the leader of his own religious community in Berlin.

Dohm's work, one of the most important documents of Enlightenment literature, had appeared towards the end of 1781. It contained the most exact and best substantiated demands for emancipation, disposed the great minds of the time, such as Count Mirabeau, in favour of the cause of the Jews, and was probably not without influence on the Emperor Joseph's edict of tolerance, which followed close on its heels. Mendelssohn, however, who had given the impetus to its composition and welcomed it as a philanthropic act, disagreed with it on a number of points. Above all he was infuriated by Dohm's exaggerated demand for autonomous Jewish communities, whose administrators were to be granted the right of discipline and exclusion from worship over their followers.

Mendelssohn expounded his well-considered principles two years later in his essay *Jerusalem, or On Religious Power and Judaism*, in which he dealt with the question of true tolerance even within each religious community. The church, he concluded, like the state, had no unlimited claim on its members. Just as the state was not empowered to practise restraints on faith or conscience, neither might the church exercise any force against individual adherents or their opinions. Whoever demanded tolerance for himself and his church in a mixed state should be no less tolerant within his own community.

One would think that such an admonition should hardly have been necessary, that a conclusion from such a compelling analogy should go without saying. But the leaders of the Jewish community in the German provinces, many of them from the East and almost without exception fanatical Talmudists, obstinately opposed any attack on their ancient rights. Sighing under the yoke of the powerful, they exerted the same pressure on their fellow Jews. Anyone who dared to think independently was uncompromisingly rejected by them. Moses Mendelssohn had long ago fallen into disfavour with them and his every utterance conjured up their wrath. When this Jewish Luther had completed his annotated translation of the Pentateuch, the rabbis of Prague, Fürth and Altona condemned the work without having set eyes on it.

In Vienna, influential people – among them Fanny and Nathan Arnstein – as well as the imperial library had long since subscribed to it. The King of Denmark and a number of German princes had also demanded its progress. Only members of Mendelssohn's own faith were to be denied it. Sonnenfels, it is true, had with the help of the court made the stubborn rabbis see reason and brought about the abrogation of the ban, but Mendelssohn himself restrained his Viennese friends from taking such action on his behalf. It was only when another person's work was at stake – Hartwig Wessely's defence of the Emperor's edict of tolerance – that he marshalled all his forces in offering resistance.

Mendelssohn, who personified emancipation, was among the Berliners who had received the news of that edict with some caution. 'It may perhaps be a passing fancy without lasting effect,' he had been heard to say, 'or, as some fear, it may turn out to be based on a financial consideration.' Above all he was unhappy with the spirit of Joseph's reform, directed as it was entirely at the union of faiths, because he himself had visions of a higher tolerance, that of true freedom of religion.

Wessely, a Jewish scholar and Mendelssohn's close friend and collaborator on his version of the Pentateuch, was of another opinion. To him the Emperor's reforms appeared to emanate from the most disinterested motives. He even welcomed the compulsion by which a people who had been segregated from others through the ages were suddenly to be torn, as it were, out of their eccentric way of life and made to conform with the world around them. Those very precepts which had aroused dismay among the Austrian Jews – that they should from now on use the language of the country in which they lived, should train their children in previously unaccustomed trades and educate them in new schools which would no longer be dedicated mainly to the study of the Talmud – all these he held to be worthy of obedience. He therefore composed a letter addressed to the Jewish communities in the Austrian provinces, in which he sought to dispel their misgivings, drafted an educational curriculum for them and admonished them to comply unconditionally with the Emperor's commands.

His text, in Hebrew, bore the title *Words of Peace and Truth*. The product of genuine feeling, it found an audience among judicious people. But the strict guardians of tradition accused him, as they did his friend Moses Mendelssohn, of heresy. Once again it was the chief rabbi of Prague who was the first to put him under proscription. Wessely took this calmly. But when his own religious leader in Berlin showed signs of taking measures against him, he summoned his friends to help him. Mendelssohn immediately intervened. He went to the minister von Zedlitz, submitting a complaint against the intended censorship. Zedlitz at once sent a note to Daniel Itzig, the head of the community, asking him who or what institution was putting pressure on Wessely. 'It would not be a good thing for a man to be driven out of the city because of a well-written book, and I do not understand how a consistory can interfere in such a matter.'

There is a historical irony in seeing a Prussian minister appealing to a Jewish dignitary for tolerance towards another Jew. So differently were roles distributed in those days! Itzig having proved slow in pursuing the matter, Mendelssohn then rallied all his forces to prevent Wessely's proscription, without, however, going directly to the rabbi, as he feared 'getting into too deep waters with him'. And finally he succeeded, with the help of his friend Friedländer and the latter's brother-in-law Isaac Daniel Itzig, in averting Wessely's persecution.

Meanwhile the Jewish community at Trieste had become the first in the imperial provinces to apply themselves joyfully to the execution of the new regulations. On the advice of the governor of the province, Count Zinzendorf, they had approached Mendelssohn on the subject of textbooks that were to be introduced, and had requested a list of all his writings that had appeared in print. Mendelssohn recommended Wessely's works to them among others, and sent as a sample his *Words of Peace and Truth*. The enthusiastic gratitude of the Triestines encouraged Wessely to bring out another 'open letter', as a result of which the most highly respected rabbis of Italy openly took his part. In all these transmissions of letters and books from Berlin to Trieste the young Arnsteins acted as intermediaries. Whether or not her father had been indecisive or dilatory in the 'Wessely dispute', Fanny championed the cause of Mendelssohn and his friend with all the fire of which she was capable.

The fine example of religious tolerance which Mendelssohn offered despite all his loyalty to the faith of his fathers finally induced even his philosophic adversary, 'the all-crushing Kant', to express admiration of him. 'You have managed,' the latter wrote to him in August 1783, 'to combine your religion with a degree of freedom of conscience of which one would not have thought it capable, and of which no other can boast. At the same time you have demonstrated the necessity for unlimited freedom of conscience to every religion with such profundity and such clarity that our own church too will have to consider how she can share everything that may be burdensome and oppressive to her conscience, which should at last unify her in the ultimate points of religion.'

Faith combined with freedom of conscience, equal status for the religion of the Old Testament with all others – for those who had made Mendelssohn's teaching their own, there was no need to undergo a change of faith. How fully Fanny von Arnstein lived out the spirit of this teaching can be concluded from the fact that she herself never converted to Christianity. Certainly she understood its essence, which is made clear in the fable of the rings in Lessing's *Nathan the Wise*. It concerns a father who bequeathed three rings, only one of which was genuine, to his sons. However, the rings were interchanged, so that it would never be clear which was the true one. The rings symbolised the three religions, Christianity, Islam and Judaism. Fanny's belief in the message of this parable can be measured by her unquestioning acceptance of her daughter's conversion, while she found her own unnecessary, and was prepared with equanimity or even goodwill to see her whole family enter into the Christian world.

Her native city might have afforded a more dignified existence, but in Vienna Fanny led a more agreeable life. That 'douceur de la vie' which Talleyrand bemoaned after the fall of the *ancien régime* – here, in the imperial city, it lay on everything like sugar icing, permeated the air and turned every day into a delicious joy. However excessive the thirst for enjoyment, however shallow the amusements of the Viennese might appear, anyone who had lingered among them was swept along by their inclination towards earthly pleasures. Despite all the curtailments that had been made to the sumptuous splendour of Maria Theresa's day, there was no lack of sociable receptions, of private concerts or even imperial banquets. The great

New Year's Day levées were still held at court, and in his palace theatre, as in the orangery at Schönbrunn, Joseph arranged for performances of the latest operas and comedies to be put on with the utmost pomp.

The position of court poet was of the highest importance to him. Almost daily he summoned his theatre director Count von Rosenberg, his composer and librettist to an audience, in order to enter into their wishes, plans and intrigues. Like his ancestors Leopold I, Joseph I and Charles VI, and very much in contrast to his mother, he had a penchant for the dramatic arts. When still co-regent he had transformed the imperial court theatre into a national theatre, and later made it his personal business to ensure that Vienna was never at any time without an Italian opera. Giambattista Martini was his favourite composer; he particularly esteemed Salieri and Paisiello; and he had much respect for Mozart, although it was his instrumental music above all that pleased him. He denied neither his time nor his money to the guardians of the arts. If his Viennese missed the public pageantry of the old days, if the winter balls, the sleigh-rides and processions had lost much of their brilliance, the footlights shone all the more brightly.

To allow to the world of illusion what he denied to reality not only bespoke Joseph's own inclinations, it was also quite in the Austrian manner. As everything here was in a state of flux, as the boundaries between simulated and genuine festivity were continually blurred, the cause of the general high spirits was after all a matter of indifference. Moreover nature, as everywhere in those days, had been made into a work of art, a public performance, a delightful illusion. The gardens with their bowers, statues and fountains, the parks with their summer-houses and avenues served as backdrops which gave every encounter, every conversation a certain theatricality. The glorious surroundings of Vienna played their part. On the gentle, wooded hills, in the charming valleys the Viennese went about on foot or in their carriages, and lived in their summer retreats in a delightfully heightened style – in harmony with the landscape whose grace they knew how to imitate.

Social life, after all, was to them only a play which was performed in different places from day to day, but with the same cast and hardly any change in the dialogue. Madame de Staël's remark of two decades later holds good for this time: 'Precise adherence to good manners has led in Vienna to the most tedious practices. Three or four times a week all the good people proceed from one salon to another . . . and it is impossible in all these numerous assemblies to hear anything which rises above conventional phrases.' She missed any expression of intellect in this society; nothing, she wrote, remained in one's head except noise or emptiness, in spite of the security, the elegance and distinguished manners which reigned here, there was a lack of 'something to say, something to do, an interest, an aim in life'.

The monotony of the great world in Vienna, to Madame de Staël's mind, was insupportable. But what she did not realise was that it was precisely the monotony of these social pleasures that constituted their particular charm. Their very repetitiousness was soothing to a circle which was fearful of change of any kind. People met in a timeless space, in the illusion of a duration disturbed by no unforeseen events of any kind, in a calm windless place, a protected corner as far away as possible from revolution or even death – as it were, in a terrestrial eternity. And those meaningless encounters which drove Madame de Staël to desperation were spiced by a particular kind of mischievousness. In reality one seldom found oneself in the position of being bored by Viennese society. Then as today, wit was replaced by malice.

Fanny, who in Joseph's decade was more and more favoured in taking part in the gatherings of polite society, was able to display the charming malice indispensable in that world, but she also possessed considerable *esprit*. So effortlessly was she able to decant her learning into sparkling phials, so swiftly did she lend polished form to her observations, so neatly did she avoid the slippery surface of platitudes, that these, of all her talents, won her the admiration of her contemporaries. The small change of real slander, of spiteful arrows and pointed remarks tossed around in the Vienna salons was seldom, if ever, used by her. When she rejected or even hated, she was immoderate in her speech, a very Prussian characteristic, refusing to swallow chalk, like the wolf in the fable, in order to lend a feigned gentleness to her voice.

Her German compatriots, the Silesian Gentz and the Rhinelander Varnhagen, two supple and two-faced characters whose pens dripped with as much extravagant praise as vicious censure of Fanny von Arnstein, were to take offence at the openness with which she expressed her feelings. Her Viennese friends found little reason to do so in those days. Full of respect for the grace of form with which they managed to compensate for their imaginative shortcomings, full of understanding for their non-committal yet intricate social game, Fanny moved at ease among the ladies and gentlemen of the nobility, the military men, diplomats and dilettanti who constituted her circle. Few of them were able entirely to live up to her intellectual demands. Hardly one could have served as her ideal, as did Moses Mendelssohn. There was only one man in Vienna who, as it were, spoke her own language – the statesman and scholar Joseph von Sonnenfels.

In Austria, this man had become the national symbol of the Enlightenment, just as Mendelssohn epitomised the Enlightenment in Berlin. There were, to be sure, profound differences, not to be explained by their varying temperaments and characters alone, in which the contrast between the Prussian capital and the imperial city also became evident. Their origins had led from the same tenebrous depths into the light. But whereas Mendelssohn's father had been a little community scribe in Dessau, Sonnenfels was descended from one of the most powerful German Jewish families; indeed he was a great-grandson of Jost Liebmann and his beautiful, quarrelsome wife, who had ensnared Frederick I even in his advanced years.

Sonnenfels had not had to overcome the problem of emancipation; it had solved itself for him while he was still at his mother's knee. His father's conversion and ennoblement, his own military service, a Christian stepmother and later a Christian wife smoothed his way to high position at court. Maria Theresa was most favourably disposed towards the man who combined a true spirit of reform with the most subservient reverence for throne and nobility. That his enemies sometimes dubbed him 'the Nikolsburg Jew' was a flaw which could not detract from the smoothness of his rococo visage.

While it has been said that baptised Jews take on the whole historical past of Christianity, and on laying aside Judaism even adopt the hereditary anti-Semitism of Christians, Sonnenfels bears witness against this theory. In this his merit is no less than that of Moses Mendelssohn, who had realised the potential ascent of his people in the life of one man. On the one hand, a despised beggar boy had become a highly honoured philosopher. On the other, a Jewish child developed in the course of his life into a protector of the Jews, who – like his father and brother – defended their cause, like every progressive cause, without disavowing his own past. He was, in the words of the title of one of his own publications, a 'man without prejudice', who could present his ideas in a flexible manner and, if necessary, was prepared to take a stand even against men in the camp of the Enlightenment.

Thus, as spokesman for Austria, in one of his earliest publications Sonnenfels had rejected Nicolai's reproach that this country had not yet produced a writer of general importance. With equal lack of inhibition he had polemicised against Cardinal Migazzi, that bulwark of reactionary thinking in Maria Theresa's Vienna. At the end of his days he sat on a committee for the establishment of the entire administration law with as much matter-of-factness as on a committee for the expurgation of the Talmud. A man who 'did not stay where the blind accident of his birth had cast him' but casually leaped over his own shadow, without seeking henceforth to wipe it away or destroy it, was a new thing in the history of Jewry.

Like everyone else, he was not without contradictions. Like all people of many-sided talent, all extrovert spirits, all zealous go-getters, he had his share of unpleasant qualities and not a few enemies ready to pillory them. Undoubtedly he was vain, tactless, overbearing, irritable and talkative, a speechifier and snob, who almost expired with reverence in the presence of high nobility. At the same time he was never afraid of unpopularity, which grew as a result of his insistence on necessary reforms. Such Janus-headedness could not but confuse his contemporaries. When Lessing, disillusioned with Friedrich and Berlin, was thinking of founding a 'colony of scholars' in Vienna, he challenged Nicolai: 'Just let someone try in Berlin to write as freely about certain things as Sonnenfels has done in Vienna; let him try to tell the truth to the distinguished rabble at court as he has told it.' Nicolai replied: 'I am happy to believe anything good of Vienna; but do not give Sonnenfels as your example! For every few words of truth that he speaks to the lower nobility, he bows the more deeply to the higher ones, and to everything that the Empress does.'

This exchange of letters took place in August 1769, and typifies the unsettled nature of Sonnenfels' public image at that time. To the Empress, meanwhile, he showed only his most amiable side. She looked on him with the same cordial favour that Queen Victoria bestowed a hundred years later on her Jewish Prime Minister, Disraeli. And even if Nicolai's angry declaration that 'Sonnenfels, in his once famous book *Police Science*, defended all Maria Theresa's laws, from the soul-destroying censorship of the time to the chastity commission' is an exaggeration, he took care never to go further in his proposals for reform than the Empress appeared willing to follow him.

When Fanny arrived in Vienna, Sonnenfels was at the height of his power. On Joseph's accession his public influence shrank. This was certainly not due to any reservations about his origins, for Joseph showed the utmost graciousness to another baptised Jew, his court poet Da Ponte. It might have been rather his loquacity, his courtly attitudes, his all too portentous bearing which displeased the frugal and laconic Emperor. Above all, Joseph's plan was to reform the administration of the state alone, without the advice or help of some Enlightenment philosopher or other, but relying only on the expert recommendations of his officials. Sonnenfels, who among others had prepared the way for him, had now become an obstacle. This still middle-aged man, without whom he could not so easily have persuaded his mother into accepting a whole series of innovations, already seemed old to the Emperor, a remnant of the past. Sonnenfels was, in fact, to a greater extent than he himself suspected or would have admitted, conditioned by the times of Maria Theresa, indeed deeply rooted in that reactionary tradition against which he had struggled so obstinately and courageously. And yet, though driven back by the Emperor into the restricted sphere of purification of the language and drawing up of statutes, he still remained the model herald of enlightened absolutism and indeed of that 'Josephinismus' for which he had been allowed to prepare the way, even if he could no longer help to carry it through.

As Mendelssohn had been a household friend and household god to the Itzig family, so Sonnenfels was revered by the Arnsteins. At what time Fanny became part of his circle cannot be established, but it must have been very soon after her entry into society. The earliest evidence of their friendship is found in a little collection of portraits which was presented to Fanny in 1793 by her closest confidants. Here, among the names of those who fell at her feet 'pénétrés d'amitié et de reconnaissance', is that of the sixty-one-year-old councillor Sonnenfels. The bond between them seems to have been an enduring one, for in the new century the name of Sonnenfels is to be found on every document which bears witness to the conversion of a member of her family to Christianity.

At the same time, we must not overestimate his influence on Fanny. While she saw in Sonnenfels the man of brains, the meritorious constitutional lawyer, the reformer of the administration, it was Mendelssohn who remained her oracle, the model of her philosophy of life. Beside the power of this pure personality, the sight of this almost saintly walk through life, beside the example of this character of Biblical dignity and irreproachable morality, an equivocal, all too human apparition such as that of Sonnenfels must have faded into comparative insignificance. If Sonnenfels was the result of an exceptionally successful assimilation, Mendelssohn had given the concept of emancipation a higher and more evident meaning. It is only when one compares the two men, who had become the symbols of the spirit of the age in Vienna and Berlin, that it becomes quite clear what moved Fanny to refrain from a change of faith and to content herself with an exercise of charitable feeling transcending all religions.

Her intellectual profile in those years is easier to outline than the course of her everyday life, the thousand expressions of a strong and self-willed temperament. Of the goodness of her heart, as of her anger which flared up as swiftly as it was mollified, she has herself given evidence in her wills. What she did and experienced, whom she visited and received, what public occasions she attended and what journeys she made, can only be presumed.

We may imagine her, languishing and shivering, with the other Viennese, in the 'unusual heat, the frequent storms and downpours' of the summer of 1781. We may fancy her among the curious crowds who had assembled in the streets on the occasion of the Pope's visit in the following spring, about whom Johann Friedel reports: 'That in our eagerness to see, we forgot to fall on our knees, as I suppose the Italians are accustomed to do, no one will take amiss; and that we did not stone the Jews who crowded in among the observers may, I hope, serve as the surest proof of how advanced we are beyond all other nations in the matter of tolerance, even if we write less about it.' In July she certainly attended the première of *Die Entführung aus dem Serail*, as she did all Mozart's subscription concerts, her name being on the list. And perhaps in that year she also became one of the 30,000 victims of the illness which had befallen Vienna and was generally known as the 'Russian catarrh' or influenza.

The trade agreement with the Ottoman Empire concluded by Austria the following March, which gave a strong boost to trade with the Levant, may, although it increased the wealth of the Arnsteins, have been of less concern to her than the splendid procession of the Augustinian order to St Stephen's Cathedral to mark the centenary of the Turkish siege and the relief of Vienna. The bitter cold of the winter of 1784, the dreadful build-up of ice which made the Danube overflow its banks, tore apart bridges and flooded the city's market streets and the suburbs, gave her the opportunity to practise her later much-praised benevolence. By this time her position in society was already secure, although her social circle was not yet as brilliant as it was to become by the end of the century.

The young woman, 'resplendent in grace, culture and *esprit*', to whom even the Emperor behaved benevolently, was, in the words of her brother-in-law Joseph Michael, 'received in the great world with love and respect'. But of what did that great world consist? First of all, of high officials and the lower nobility, the friends of Caton Obermayer and of Frau von Hochstedten, whose husband was a government minister, as well as the baptised or merely tolerated families of Sonnenfels, Wetzlar and Schönfeld, Wertheimer, Hofmann, Hönickstein, Todesco, Bienenfeld, Liebenberg and Leidesdorf. Her following among the distinguished young people who adorned her salon so abundantly under Emperor Francis must certainly have already begun. In an unmistakable reference to Fanny, Johann Pezzl, a memoirist who despised the poor Jews and followed the social ascent of the richer ones with mixed feelings, observed in 1783:

> And the fair Hebrew xx! is she not still today the Aspasia of our young cavaliers and elegant gentlemen? Do not the followers of the Pope, of Luther, Calvin and the English church vie with each other to kneel before her Ark of the Covenant? . . . It is true that they say the manners in these houses would not indeed satisfy an orthodox rabbi, but in such circumstances who cares for the shaggy-bearded pedant chewing at his Pentateuch and Talmud?

Nevertheless, just such a pedant was Fanny's father-in-law, still master of the house in which the young cavaliers knelt before Fanny's Ark of the Covenant. Another pedantic reader of the Pentateuch was her mother-in-law Sibilla, and yet another was Fanny herself, the subscriber to the works of Mendelssohn. It would, therefore, be a mistake to presume a continuing conflict between the 'fair Hebrew' and her God-fearing family. Rather, in the last years of Nathan's parents there was considerably greater concord between them and the young woman, who did not intend to sacrifice her religion to her social ambition.

She had borne a grandchild, if not an heir, for the old Arnsteiners. She had procured help for Mendelssohn and Wessely. She had succeeded in spreading the ideas of the Berlin Enlightenment in her circle, especially since these in no way gave preference over general religious liberty to the assimilation and conversion which were advocated in Vienna, and for whose sake Joseph Michael had been driven out. Adam Arnsteiner, who kept his own house rabbi, might only a little reluctantly have taken Wessely's part against the orthodox scholar, just as in that squabble between Fanny and the sage from Frankfurt he must certainly have decided only with difficulty to send not her, but her antagonist, away from his house.

Sibilla however, although pious, was capable of open-minded views. A true 'Gompertz scion', from a family whose ancient scholarship has survived to our own day, and which had belonged since time immemorial to the Jewish intellectual elite, she had with the years converted to Fanny's modern way of thinking. In the end it cannot have been difficult for Fanny to come to an understanding with her mother-in-law.

Moreover, she was given her freedom and allowed to travel; her zest for life was in no way restricted. She had not been forbidden to choose her parental home as the birthplace of her little daughter. In March 1785 she was away from Austria with her child, for in the last will and testament which Adam Arnsteiner drew up about this time he bequeathed 5,000 gulden as dowry to 'my granddaughter Judith, a daughter of my elder son Nathan, at present in Frankfurt'. Judith, or Henriette, as she was called after her grandfather's death, was only one of the many heirs among whom the wealthy Adam's estate was divided.

When Adam drew up his will, he had imagined himself sound in mind and body. But before the year was out, he had already departed this life in which he had come to such prosperity. The newspaper *Wiener Zeitung* commented on his decease in respectful terms:

> Here, on the 21st of this month, occurred the death of Herr Adam Isak Arnsteiner, of the Jewish religion, merchant and money-changer under imperial privilege, in his sixty-fourth year. He will be generally mourned as a deserving citizen of the state, an upright man and beneficent philanthropist. His last will and testament too is in accordance with his whole way of life, since he has bequeathed 1,000 fl. to the institute for the poor in Vienna as well as considerable sums to the poor of both the Christian and Jewish religions.

Now he was dead, he who had defied the Saxon and wrested from Maria Theresa the prerogative of unhindered residence. With the help of his God he had increased his paternal inheritance and left the sum of 777,568 gulden, of which 250,000 gulden had been put into his business, about 300,000 represented assets as well as interest, more than 200,000 bad debts and interest, some 500 gold, silver and valuables, hardly more than 100 gulden clothing and body linen, 'household and table linen 800 fl., porcelain 900 fl., furnishings 400 fl., kitchen equipment 40 fl., horse and carriage 242 fl.'

The total sum was considerable. The estate of Samson Wertheimer, the richest Jew in the Holy Roman Empire, had come to less than three times that amount – 1,830,660 gulden. Certainly, after the deduction of other bequests the residuary legatee, Sibilla, received only 110,000 gulden, a little more than her eldest son. However, she was now the head of the family and the mistress of the house in the Graben, where the young couple could continue to reside only as long as they behaved peaceably and were at one with her. The business from now on bore the name 'Adam Isaac Arnsteiner's Widow and Son'. But the matriarch was not to survive her husband for long. Two years later she too passed away. The time of tutelage was over. A decade after coming to Vienna as a bride, Fanny took over the command of her own household.

Only now did she truly come into her own; only now did she attain her majority. First of all she extended her drawing-rooms by taking over the former quarters of her parents-in-law. Sibilla had left furnishings to the value of almost 2,500 gulden, probably including a good number of the 'faded tapestries, white-lacquered chairs with goat's feet, inlaid cupboards, curtains of Chinese chintz, bed-screens, fruit-baskets containing painted plaster fruit, Japanese vases, pagodas, stuffed birds and statues of Meissen porcelain' which corresponded to the taste of Maria Theresa's time. To these furnishings Fanny applied the 'yardstick of the fashion of Joseph's era'. Next she enlarged her circle, invited ladies and gentlemen of the higher nobility, and found that a friendly reception, enjoyable conversation and brilliant entertainment were not disdained. This was part of a development which ran counter to previous hierarchies of the strata of society and introduced into private apartments the more relaxed and mixed encounters which till now had been customary only at public concerts and at musical soirées.

The attendance list of a concert given by Mozart in April 1784 includes the following names: 'Mme de Trattner, Auersperg, Mme de Stökel, Baron van Swieten, Prince and Princess Palm, Comte de Nimptsch, Staremberg, Comte Paar, Schafgotsch, Lobkowitz, de Hönickstein, Le Comte Fries, de Puthon, D'Arensteiner, Bar. Wetzlar Père, Gebsattel, Esterhazy, Prince Louis Liechtenstein, Harrach, Dominic Kaunitz, Prince de Paar, de Born, Prince Gallitzin, Hoyos, Czernin, Neipperg, Joh. Adam Bienenfeld, Mme Türkheim, Sternberg, Zichy, Lignowski, de Sonnenfeld, Bar. Wetzlar Raimund, Comte Waldstein, Nostitz, Hofrat Müller, Prince de Schwarzenberg, Comte Bergen, de Hazfeld, Montecuculi'.

Here, not only are the three classes of the higher nobility, among them princes, counts and barons of ancient title resident in Vienna, jumbled together in a remarkable fashion, but representatives of the secondary nobility are also listed, including, according to Johann Pezzl, the 'brand-new barons, the knights and titled persons by diplomatic decree', but also those persons 'who are usually called *Honoratioren* [dignitaries]: councillors, agents, doctors, bankers and merchants'. The wife of the court printer Trattner rubbing shoulders with a prince of the ancient house of Auersperg, the ennobled Jew Hönickstein flanked by a Lobkowitz and a likewise recently elevated Swiss! If the Neippergs and Kaunitzes, the Paars and Liechtensteins wanted to listen to Mozart's music together with the Sonnenfelses, Wetzlars and Arnsteiners, then they would all visit the Arnsteiners' salon on the same day.

Fanny could not receive all these heads of Austrian society at her house. For most of them there was no hurry; not until the turn of the century did she sit at the same table as they. Nevertheless, after the deaths of Adam and Sibilla the doors of the house at 1275, Graben, were wide open at all times and guests of ever greater importance passed into its rooms. Fanny was not far from Pezzl's mind when he characterised the rise of the second rank under Joseph:

> This rank contains a core of businessmen who work hand in hand with the stars of the first magnitude in the state, and help to promote the working of the great machine. Patriotism, integrity, industriousness, expertise, understanding and diligence make them respected and popular. This class is beginning, among all professions, to be the most enlightened, which produces an excellent effect. As these persons' gatherings are not quite so rigorously barricaded against other honest, but untitled, earthly beings as those of the nobility, the enlightened way of thinking is spread abroad through them to many others, and through these again to many walks of life among the public.

Pezzl continues:

> Here it is helpful that some ladies from these houses combine the same way of thinking with feminine charm, and are thereby doubly agreeable. I would name them, if it were allowed by their modesty, which makes them only the more estimable. They are pupils of Musarion; their manner is as instructive and tasteful as it is charming; in their houses one does not yawn the evenings away with the wretched shuffling and dealing of cards. Little concerts, confidential small talk among friends, literary novelties, discussions about books, travel, works of art, the theatre; the events of the day, and interesting news related, judged and illumined with a little spice, make up the entertainment, and shorten the long winter evenings for the intimate circle. There one makes the acquaintance of most of the resident scholars as well as the foreign ones who occasionally pass through Vienna on their journeys.

And finally he finds it necessary to defend these ladies against the accusations made by some Viennese scoffers:

> Is it to be believed? These ladies have just experienced the fate which befell Mesdames Geoffrin and Necker in Paris. Some narrow-minded people tried to stir up hate against them because they held *bureaux d'esprit*. These rascals should bethink themselves that it is truly a term of praise for a lady to say that she is forming a *bureau d'esprit*, when so many other women keep *bureaux de sottise*.

Nathan Arnsteiner could increasingly at that time be counted among the 'businessmen who work hand in hand with the stars of the first magnitude in the state, and help to promote the working of the great machine'. His father had left him not only a wholesale business and office, but also a widely ramified net of official and private business connections, which, first in partnership with him, then alone, and finally with his associates, Nathan made into a transfer point for diplomatic and financial arrangements. It must be said that Nathan, who all his life stood in the shadows of more important personalities – those of his father, his wife, his friend and partner Eskeles – seems to have steered his ship very skilfully through the hazards of business life. If he himself was as good-natured, patient, humorous and harmless as he has been described, he still had the wit to surround himself with cleverer and more energetic people. And even if he liked his peace and quiet, and probably preferred to sit at the card-table rather than attempt to shine among Fanny's illustrious guests, he was no spoilsport. But above all he had courage, the quiet, persistent courage of the great financier, who knows how to deal cold-bloodedly with sums of money whose loss could at any moment bring dishonour and ruin upon his head.

Very little evidence about the activities of the house of Arnsteiner has been preserved, although the bankers' register of the exchequer already shows contracts with Isaac Arnsteiner under the years 1716, 1727, 1731 and so on. Only at the beginning of Joseph's reign do we find more precise indications in the records of creditors to the state concerning the type of business that Isaac's son and grandson had to carry out by government order. In 1779 there is mention of deliveries of hay to Hungary. In the following year Adam, together with the houses of Fries, Grosser and Puthon, obtained the tobacco concession – one of the most profitable monopolies the state could bestow. During the whole of Joseph's decade, sums between 2,000 and 15,000 gulden are regularly assigned to Arnsteiner; they represent payments for goods delivered, but also for capital loans.

That a certain degree of caprice played its part in the repayment of such monies is clear from the documents: a request in February 1788 by Nathan to the state to repay him 20,000 gulden is simply refused.

Certainly, the state coffers had need of every penny that February. On the ninth of that month, in alliance with Russia, Joseph had declared war on the Ottoman Empire. Meanwhile, Nathan's 20,000 gulden would not go very far. Millions were needed, and millions were to be procured with his help.

Nathan was not the only Viennese financier who made it his business that spring to replenish Joseph's army fund. Among others, the banking house of Dobruschka-Schönfeld was looking about for financial sources, and in fact it had first approached Isaac Daniel Itzig through its negotiator Joske. As soon as Nathan learnt of the plan, however, he intervened energetically. He proposed a lower rate of interest to the imperial finance department, swiftly set off for Berlin and carried out the transaction, as the imperial ambassador to the Prussian court, Prince Reuss, reported, 'avec toute la prudence et sagesse'. It was his first independent attempt to raise enormous sums, like his father, for the conduct of war. He did this, it is true, with the help of three brothers-in-law: Fanny's brother; the latter's agent David Ephraim, who was married to Fanny's sister Rebecca; and his own sister's husband Salomon Herz. But without paternal support or the advice of his experienced mother he was taking a great responsibility upon himself. This enormous sum, which he undertook to negotiate – in the end it came to ten million – was followed by loans of similar sums during the Napoleonic wars. It is not even certain if the transaction was a success. But Isaac Daniel Itzig would undoubtedly have raised the sum for his sister's husband, who moreover was backed by the entire credit-worthiness of Austria.

Apart from this, Nathan contented himself in Joseph's last years, as under the latter's brother Leopold and at the beginning of the reign of Francis, with smaller but more regular services to the state. He accepted bills with a considerable discount on deliveries in kind and insurance policies for the Hungarian, Bohemian, Silesian and Galician governments. In July 1791, an advance of this kind, made to the copper board, came to the sum of 200,000 gulden, which was paid back to him with the addition of 3 per cent interest. From transactions of this kind, supplemented by extensive private trading and the undoubtedly lively activity of his exchange office, he drew a growing profit – enough to enable him to consider the acquisition of real estate, the enlargement of his household and the purchase of a second and more representative residence than the narrow town house in the Graben.

But we are anticipating. Emperor Joseph was still alive, though ailing and weakened by many adversities – his quarrel with the union of German principalities, his war against the Ottoman Empire, the revolt of the Netherlands, the insurrection in Hungary and the bad news from France, where the Bastille had been stormed and his sister Marie Antoinette obliged to return to Paris – but still firmly in the saddle of the decade that was moving towards its close. The greater his failure in the field of world politics, the more profound became his influence on internal state affairs and the reorganisation of his capital. Feverishly he issued laws and charters, founded a commercial bank, built up all the monastery gardens on the city outskirts, opened new theatres and provided at least one splendid celebration for his Viennese, who had little stomach for war and were in need of entertainment: the great gala in honour of the marriage of his nephew Francis with Elisabeth of Württemberg in January 1788.

Neither was the capital – although its sky was overcast, and the fresh wind which at first had wafted from the throne more and more resembled a sandstorm, hectically whirling up and dying down again – in other respects lacking in diversions. During these years three of Mozart's greatest operas, *Figaro*, *Don Giovanni* and *Così fan tutte*, received their premières; F. L. Schröder at last brought Shakespeare's plays to the stage of the national theatre in a worthy form; and a succession of suburban theatre companies put on those countless nonsensical farces with which the Viennese loved to stuff themselves as with a surfeit of sweetmeats. On the feast of Corpus Christi, the clergy, bedecked with gold, walked through the streets under canopies, followed by the Emperor, the nobility and the military. And on St Anne's Day, Stuwer's famous fireworks were let off in the Prater.

The most delightful picture of the city in the last year of Joseph's life emerges from one of those anonymous travellers' reports of which we have already spoken. It describes a Vienna in which some 250,000 persons now live in 6,000 houses. The suburbs are built up and growing closer together; walking on the Glacis, bounded by avenues, of the ten bastions and ravelins one sees them lying around the city's core in a pleasing semi-circle, and glowing at night like a 'fiery amphitheatre'. By day the population streams in and out through the four gates; at night, between the hours of nine and twelve, they promenade along the Graben, Kohlmarkt and Hof, eat ice-cream in the refreshment tents or sip coffee in one of the hundred coffee-houses of the capital. Crystal chandeliers glitter in the homes of the wealthy. In the poor people's windows hang bird-cages full of chirping canaries, finches and nightingales, which are as beloved here as white pomeranians and spitzes. Light-footed ladies in white and blue taffeta gowns hurry along with an 'uncommonly gracious gait', for in Vienna everything moves very quickly. Chambermaids cut 'important figures' in their silk shoes, their mistresses' cast-off gowns and black Bohemian caps. In front of the inns, which, 'unlike the clean Italian ones, are very dirty', stand waiters in green coats, their hair 'dressed like an *abbé*'s', enticing guests in. A medley of people untiringly buzz through the streets, among them Turks, who can also be seen close to the Prater and Augarten, smoking their pipes on their balconies or sitting on cushions in front of their houses.

A sight which astonishes the anonymous visitor more than any other is that of the 'noble street-sweepers' – those unfortunate criminals of rank, who as a punishment for some offence are obliged to take a broom and cleanse the paving-stones of Vienna of refuse. 'In recent times,' he relates, 'the councillors Kriegel and Zetti cleaned the streets. Both died within a short time of each other and one was still alive when I was in Vienna. Their places were taken by Legisfeld (who defrauded the Emperor of 150,000 gulden) and Ettlinger.' Finally, he tells a story, of interest in this context, about Ettlinger, whom he believes to be innocent, although forced to wear a badge with the inscription '*Falsarius* and gross deceiver of the exchequer'.

> Ettlinger must clean the streets for two years, and during this time see his wife in the arms of a Jew. One has read and admired the transactions of the Jew Arnsteiner, who is a rich money-changer in Vienna, and who settled a yearly allowance of 500 gulden on Madame Ettlinger when her husband's misfortune occurred. The Jew had already made this settlement upon her in her husband's time, but now that the latter had been taken from her, he increased her allowance because he now had her to himself. Some may perhaps wonder that a Viennese female should receive an allowance from a Jew. But the Viennese beauties are not fastidious in a certain respect. Christians and Jews, Turks and *Raizen*, all are alike to them if they can but satisfy their lust or their purse. The law of tolerance is perhaps having its effect on the beauties of Vienna.

Should one assume that Fanny's husband was Madame Ettlinger's protector? We can neither confirm nor deny this with certainty. There was more than one money-changer of this name in

Vienna. The anonymous report might refer to Joseph Michael, who all his life was less talked of than his elder brother and was less well off, despite having been ennobled before him. A few years later Joseph was involved in a night brawl which allows one to speculate about some secret transaction or other.

If nevertheless the idea of Nathan in the arms of Madame Ettlinger is not easily dismissed from the mind, then it is because of that hardly conclusive but still compulsive instinct which in time biographers acquire for their subject. A mild and good-humoured, cheerful and pleasure-loving man, who has lived for thirteen years at the side of a much admired, clever, but occasionally forceful or even domineering wife, may not without reason seek the consolation of one of those Viennese females of rounded figure, 'pretty, dainty little face, graceful gait' and flirtatious charm, who know how to love so submissively and devotedly.

So much for this episode, which casts an uncertain light, but in no way a shadow, over Fanny's unquestionably happy marriage! After all, people still had one foot in the Rococo era, a time in which such dallying was not taken too seriously; they were in Vienna, a city in which marital fidelity was not considered part of *bon ton*. 'Every decent man must have his mistress,' wrote our anonymous commentator, who held against Madame Ettlinger only the fact that she received her allowance from a Jew. Yet the Jews had infiltrated all walks of life. In this year of 1789 they were even to be seen emerging in the Viennese townscape as recruits in the army. The charter of tolerance had granted them the right, or the duty, to do military service in wartime. Now the campaign against the Ottoman Empire gave them their first opportunity to do so. It was, to begin with, not their lot to cut a good figure in uniform. They provoked caricature; and so Löschenkohl, the silhouettist, engraver, publisher, inventor and the most important visual recorder of the Vienna of Maria Theresa, of Joseph and of Francis, immortalised them in a matching pair of engravings. He depicted in these 'the Jews fighting for Joseph II, the Holy Roman Emperor, against the Turks' – in one complaining about the drill, in the second proudly loading their guns and standing at attention. In both cases he completed the picture with a rhymed explanation. The second poem portrays them in martial mood:

Allo dann frisch voran, nun wollen Flinten laden
Und zeigen jetzt der Welt der Juden Heldenthaten.
Macht fertig euch zum Schuß, der Türk reit wirklich an,
Gebt Feuer unverzagt, Joseph reit selbst voran.

[Forward then briskly, let us load our guns / And show the world how Jews can be heroic; / Make ready to fire, the Turk truly advances, / Shoot without fear, Joseph rides at our head.]

But Joseph no longer rode at their head. Only last June he had given 'a shining example to the last musketeer' in the plague swamps of Semlin. He had returned from this summer campaign in a shattered state, and had been in poor health all winter. Since early spring he had no longer believed that he would recover and, as he said, 'awaited death without desire or fear'. So in this second campaign of 1789 he could no longer serve as an example of 'old Roman military discipline' but, partially bedridden, had to observe from Vienna how his field-marshal Laudon marched with all his forces towards Belgrade. Fifty years after its conquest by Prince Eugene of Savoy the fortress was that autumn recaptured. The ceremonial *Te Deum* that was held in St Stephen's Cathedral was attended by Joseph, once more 'radiant with his old liveliness'. The winter was mild, trees and shrubs began to flower prematurely, yet Joseph was declining. His long-standing lung disease which had erupted anew in the swampland of the river Save, was consuming him. He had already commissioned his epitaph from an Italian abbot. It contained the sentence: 'Here lies a prince who, with the best of intentions, was unable to carry out any of his plans.'

By February 1790 it was all over. His last letter had been addressed to his old friend, Princess Eleonore Liechtenstein, to whom he had been cordially devoted for many years. During the night before his death he had restless dreams, fantasising about the Netherlands, about Hungary and the Tyrol, about the Turks and Prussians. The apparitions of these insurgents and antagonists stood about his bed like Richard III's enemies at his encampment at Bosworth. He died at the break of day. Few mourned him. Greeted at his accession with loud acclaim as a harbinger of liberty, he now went to his grave accompanied by an embarrassed silence. His Viennese, embittered by the high war-taxes and rising cost of living, pursued him even after his death with their mockery: 'After the Turkish campaign Joseph gave his officers the small cross and his citizens the great one.' Another cruel saying was circulating: '*Imperando et revocando vixi* [I lived giving commands and then revoking them]'. He had finally summed up his own existence to a minister of state: 'I feel at peace, only a little aggrieved, after all the troubles of my life, to have made so few people happy and so many ungrateful.' It was the most damning verdict on this frustrated attempt to enforce justice from the throne. Yet of Joseph's reforms, which had brought down upon him the wrath of the Dutch and Hungarians and had either been rescinded by himself or allowed to lapse by his successors, there still remained that spark among the ashes which was to kindle the liberalism of the next century. Yet his world ended with the beginning of the final decade of the last one, and with it the belief in tolerance and the spirit of progress which had given it wings. However much the 'enlightened circles' among his subjects, including Fanny, may have sighed over the capricious and despotic manner of his policies, it now seemed to them that the light of their future had been extinguished. They deplored not so much the passing of the man on whom they had pinned their hope, but rather the total loss of that hope which could no longer be pinned on anyone. Fanny's notebook contains some verses of unknown origin – not in her handwriting, but presumably copied at her request – which illustrate Joseph's broken existence in the last weeks of his life:

Conversation de Joseph avec l'Echo

JOSEPH	L'ECHO
Je suis seul en ces lieux et personne ne m'écoute	Ecoute
Qui ose me répondre? et qui est avec moi?	Moi
J'entends c'est l'Echo qui répond a ma demande!	Demande
Peux-tu prognostiquer si le Brabant me resistera?	Resistera
Ce peuple en courroux me resistera-t-il encore?	Encore
A me contrarier sera-t-il dompté?	Dompté
Voilà donc mes projets réduits en fumée?	Fumée
Dieu! que dois-je attendre après tant de malheur?	Malheur
A composer avec mes sujets serois-je donc réduit?	Réduit
Les Belges sont fiers, comment donc l'entreprendre?	Rendre
Rendre ce que j'ai acquis par des faits inouïs?	Oui
Qu'aurai-je donc gagné pour ma gloire et peines?	Peines
Mais qu'auront donc mes sujets, et les Belges surtout?	Tout
Que veux-tu que je fasse après tant d'injustice?	Justice
Et que deviendrois-je et mon peuple malheureux?	Heureux
Et qui suis-je donc qu'on tient pour immortel?	Mortel
Tous ces peuples soumis ne me craindrons plus!	Plus
Autrefois mon nom seul inspiroit le terreur . . .	Erreur
Laisse-moi, je te prie, et souffre que je pleure	Pleure!

Pleure! With this dreadful command, echoing down the corridors of time, Joseph and his unfulfilled promise pass into history.

–5–

Enlightenment and Transition

Ideas do not die with, and like, those to whom they owe their life. They may be carried to the grave with them, but they go on moving in the dark earth, to come to the light of day once more in a transformed state. Nevertheless it can be said that with Joseph's death the Enlightenment was over in Austria.

In Prussia it had been for some time on the point of extinction. When Lessing, its guiding spirit, had passed away, its long illness began. Five years later Moses Mendelssohn died, not least as a result of one of those paradoxes which the enlightened were having to resolve among themselves; the realisation that Lessing had in the end become a follower of Spinoza was like 'a lance piercing his heart'. He hated pantheism, believed in a personal God, and would probably have understood total godlessness more easily than this belief, inconceivable to him, in an insubstantial omnipresence. While working on a letter 'To the Friends of Lessing', in which he was seeking to refute Jacobi's theory of Lessing's apostasy, excitement overcame him to such an extent that he collapsed. It was January. Soon after him, in August of 1786, the King ended his days at Sanssouci.

The most attentive follower of the Enlightenment, though not its most zealous prophet, Frederick had taken with him its age, which had also been his own. Few tears were shed for him either. Joseph, whom he had praised in calmer times, but described in old age as 'an evil demon, a possessed man and accursed Viennese tyrant', composed the most merciless obituary. As a soldier, the Emperor wrote to Kaunitz, he mourned the loss of the great man who would have a place for all time in the history of military science, but as a private citizen he regretted that death had come to him too late. Not much more friendly, indeed as indifferent as were the Viennese to his own death, did the people of Berlin prove to the memory of Frederick. Mirabeau described the atmosphere in the city on the passing of the King. He wrote two years later:

> I still tremble, and my spirit is indignant at the sight which Berlin offered to my astounded gaze when it heard the news of the death of the

hero who had made the universe fall silent in amazement, or speak out in wonder. All was muted; none was sad; all were busy; none was sorrowful – no grief, no sighs, no praise! So this was the end of so many battles won, of such great fame, of almost half a century's dominion full of brilliance and greatness! People were sick of it, sick almost to the point of hate . . . The only general who wept was Möllendorf . . . Why this unsociable ingratitude?

Why? Because, like his antagonist Joseph, this monarch lacked one quality without which the best prince is despised, with whose help the worst seducer of the people becomes the darling of the masses: human warmth. His subjects had done homage to him, had heaped gifts upon him – shortly before his death Daniel Itzig had sent him grapes from his garden – but none, save perhaps his dogs, had loved him. More was now awaited from his nephew, an inept but well-meaning weakling, than had been expected of Frederick, who had been of strong character and an admirer of reason. Even the 'thinking heads of the Jewish nation' who had found the opportunity under the old King's 'philosophical rule' to 'show off their talents in public and meet with approval', were hoping for more immediate signs of favour, such as the abolition of the troublesome personal tax, the unequal jurisdiction, the financial extortion and the law of the so-called 'Jews' porcelain' – a law by which they were forced to buy a certain number of products of the state manufacture, usually the ugliest. As early as four days after Frederick's death their community commended itself to the grace and favour of His Majesty of Prussia, Frederick William II, and in October their deputies, led by the chief elders in the country, Daniel Itzig and Jacob Moses, as well as the elders Veitel Ephraim, Isaac Benjamin Wulff and the chief court banker, Isaac Daniel Itzig, presented a poem of homage to the King. In the same month Frederick William confirmed by order of his cabinet a judgment of the supreme court which had been passed in a 'curious Jewish lawsuit'.

The banker Moses Isaac had died in Berlin in May 1776. His will, deposited at the Berlin city court, stated explicitly that only those of his five children who had remained faithful to the Jewish religion should have a share in the sum total of his entail or the interest upon it. After his death two of his daughters who had converted to Christianity contested the will. Frederick had upheld it without much ceremony. Now Isaac's daughters renewed their complaints to his nephew, but were refused a second time. The words in which Frederick William rejected their appeal were designed to open up to the Jewish community the prospect of far-reaching relief of their condition:

In the matter of Moses Isaac the tribunal's decision must stand immutable; the Lord High Chancellor shall convey my satisfaction therewith to the tribunal in my name, and let this serve as encouragement to the tribunal, hereafter as heretofore, to dispense justice without respect of person, as I expect from all conscientious judges in my states; for I shall never permit the course of the strictest justice to be obstructed or the law to be bent, but each and every subject, whether Jew or Christian, must be able to enjoy the protection of the law.

Three of these words should indeed have warned them not to expect too much. 'Hereafter as heretofore!' So though this king might be more human, that is to say gentler and less inflexible than his uncle, no new, less stringent regulations were to be expected from him. The *loi cannibale* of 1750 remained in force. Of all the demands put to him by the Jewish elders, he approved only the suspension of the personal tax and the end of the forced purchase of porcelain – this last, admittedly, only against a forfeit of 4,000 thalers. For the rest, he began to bestow far-reaching signs of patronage, which he denied to the Jewish community in general, upon certain favoured members. Above all it was on Daniel Itzig's eldest son Isaac – a brilliantly talented man, ambitious and thus ideally placed, who, however, lacked the sober solidity of his father – that he bestowed his confidence in great measure. Soon after his accession to the throne he appointed him chief banker to the court, repaid through him the debts he had incurred when crown prince, and allowed other very large sums to pass directly through Isaac's hands, which were used in part to bribe Russian and French diplomats. In short, Fanny's brother had access not only to the King, but also to his purse. It now becomes clear with what justification Nathan Arnsteiner applied to him at about that time to solicit a loan for Austria!

When the King finally put in hand the building of a public highway from Berlin to Potsdam, he appointed young Itzig supervisor of the work. In the first year of his reign he had already authorised him to acquire landed property. Like his father, Isaac settled on the outskirts of the city of Berlin as it existed at the time. He bought the freehold property of Schöneberg, enlarged it by adding some adjacent properties, built accommodation for day-labourers on his own land and, with the help of the building contractor Zelter, later a friend of Goethe's, he built a small hunting lodge adorned with elegant reliefs and stags' antlers. He enlarged the park in which it stood as far as the Tempelhofsche Weg and established a tree-nursery in it; he also donated a clock for the church tower of the village, whose most important local landowner he had become.

Daniel Itzig's son had, apart from his official duties, taken over his father's banking business and from the first conducted it with success and energy. His growing status, above all as building adviser to the court, was symptomatic of the changing mood in the country. Frederick William, simultaneously a freethinker, pietist and rake, wanted to live as well as let live. He had nothing against the Jews, as long as they did not offend his squeamish aesthetic sensibility, guided by the taste of Louis XVI. Among the frivolous, high-spirited society that soon grouped itself around his throne, witty and talented or elegant and charming members of the Jewish faith, insofar as there were already such persons, had no difficulty in finding a place. After all, they had for some time been given a friendly welcome by the 'enlightened' circles of the bourgeoisie.

A prologue recited by the actor Fleck in August 1788 before a performance of *The Merchant of Venice* at the Berlin National Theatre, to take the sting out of the mockery of Shylock, indicated the new attitude:

Nun das kluge Berlin die Glaubensgenossen des weisen
Mendelssohn höher zu schätzen anfängt: nun wir bei diesem
Volke (dessen Propheten und erste Gesetze wir ehren)
Männer sehen, gleich groß in Wissenschaft und Künsten;
Wollen wir nun dieses Volk durch Spott betrüben? Dem alten
Ungerechten Haß mehr Nahrung geben? Und Röthe
denen ins Antlitz jagen, die menschenfreundlich gesinnet,
Gegen arme Christen und Juden gleich gütig sich zeigen? –
Nein, dies wollen wir nicht. Wir schildern auch bübische Christen
Schildern (mit Abscheu) verfolgende Christen; wir tadeln der Klöster
Zwang und Grausamkeit an den eigenen Glaubensverwandten.
Unser Schauspiel zeigt das Lächerliche, das Laster
An dem entarteten Adel und an den Tyrannen der Erde,
Höhnet den schlechten Arzt, beschimpft den bestochnen Richter,
Straft den geizigen Diener des Altars. – In Nathan den Weisen
Spielen die Christen die schlechtere Rolle, im Kaufmann Venedigs
Thun es die Juden. – Nur wen es jücket, der kratze sich! so sagt
Unser Hamlet. Wir sagen: Wer heile Haut hat, – der lacht!

[Now the sage Mendelssohn's fellow-believers
Are prized at higher rate by wise Berlin;
Now that great men in sciences and arts
Are seen among this people, to whose laws
And prophets we do honour; shall we distress
Such people by our mockery? Shall we give
More nourishment to ancient, unjust hate?

And bring a blush to those philanthropists
Who seek to show themselves equally kind
To Christians and to Jews? No, we will not.
We show (with loathing) Christians who are rogues;
Christians who persecute; we censure too
The monasteries' constraint and cruelty
Towards our own companions in religion.
Our play shows the ridiculous, the vices
Of tyrants and degenerate nobility,
It mocks the quack, accuses the bribed judge,
Rebukes the miserly priest. In *Nathan the Wise*
Christians come off the worst, as here the Jews.
What says our Hamlet? 'Let the galled jade wince',
And if your hands be clean, say we – then laugh!]

It cannot be denied, however, that this speech aroused resentment among some of the audience and could not be repeated at subsequent performances of the play. People grumbled, writes the worthy Johann Balthasar König, 'and rightly so, that the Jews wanted exemption from being shown in the theatre, whereas all classes and conditions of the public, the nobility, the military, the clerics, citizens and peasants, had to be on parade, each according to his ridiculous or more serious character'. He did not take account in his verdict of their hypersensitivity, their constant mistrust, for which allowances could perhaps have been made after all the bitter experiences of their past, and from which they are still less free today, after much more cruel strokes of fate. This, too, is typical of the times. If a chronicler of 1790 thought nothing of lumping the Jews together with 'all other classes and conditions', the nobility, the military, clerics, citizens and peasants, then this means that their incorporation into society had already progressed to a considerable degree.

It had progressed so far, in fact, that something happened in May 1791 which had never before been known in the whole of the Holy Roman Empire; a Berlin family of the Jewish faith became naturalised. The man who, with his kindred, entered the human community as a member with equal rights, was Fanny's father, Daniel Itzig. The preamble to his 'certificate of naturalisation' describes how this pioneering event came about:

We, Frederick William, by God's grace King of Prussia, make known that at the most humble and obedient request of our chief court banker and supervisor of road-building, Isaak Daniel Itzig, in consideration of his faithful services previously rendered to us, and further to be rendered, and also in order to bestow a deserved token of our highest favour to his father Daniel Itzig, banker of this city, on account of his well-known constant good conduct and unselfish behaviour, we have most graciously resolved to naturalise the said Daniel Itzig and his descendants of both sexes by marriage, thereby conferring on them all the rights of Christian citizens in our sundry states and dominions. This we do in this fashion, and by these letters patent, in order that the aforesaid Daniel Itzig and his descendants of both sexes by marriage shall be regarded and treated everywhere as an actual Christian family of citizens, without being subject to those restrictions to which until now the generally privileged Jews have had to conform.

It was the first document of its kind, a model for those that were to follow, and thus significant in each of its enactments. Above all, it conferred civic rights on all the issue of Daniel Itzig and their spouses, on the female side, admittedly, only as far as the grand-children. From now on they were 'to be admitted to all civic functions, honours, trades, crafts and professions', to be allowed to set up their households wherever they liked, 'according to the same laws, to the same extent, and in general on the same footing as is the right and duty of Christian citizens'. In their legal dealings they should be treated and judged by all courts and authorities in the same way as Christian citizens, were not required 'to seek any concessions in respect of their applications, marriages and acqui-sition of property' and were 'freed absolutely of such taxes and duties to which Jews are subject as Jews'. They were relieved of joint liability with the protected Jews as they were of the jurisdic-tion of their rabbis, the discipline of ritual and synagogue and generally of their dependence on the elders of the Jewish com-munity, while it was open to them to remain voluntarily bound by it. In fact, this document took their special position into considera-tion to such an extent that they were subject to Christian law for all civic purposes, but to Jewish law in religious and ritual matters.

Together with these rights the Itzigs were indeed also charged with 'performing unquestioningly all judicial and personal duties which our Christian subjects are pledged to carry out toward us and the state, with life and property, in civil and military services, according to the same laws and in the same manner at all times'. And finally Daniel's family were admonished

that they and their issue should exert themselves to the utmost to bring up their children as true, upright citizens and subjects, useful to their vocations in all cases, since if contrary to expectations any of them or their issue should fall into the Jewish petty dealing that is still common among a great part of the Jewish nation and linked with deceitful frauds, or should even have anything to do with usurious practices, such a person shall be deprived of the benefit of naturalisation and the rights bound up therewith in this document, and consequently return into the state of a common Jew.

The document ends with an admonition to all governments, law councils, chambers of war and of crown land, magistrates, officials and judicial authorities, to 'respect most conscientiously' the new status of the Itzig family.

Fanny's parents and relatives had thus attained an objective from which she herself was still excluded in Vienna by Joseph's edict of tolerance. They stood at the end of a development which had begun with the fall of Jerusalem and their forced move to Germany. Without giving up their faith, they had become Prussian citizens. Indeed, this right explicitly extended to Fanny herself, her husband and daughter. They who in Vienna were only tolerated, who according to the letter were expressly excluded from the possession of landed property and above all from civic rights, could in Berlin regard themselves as subjects of the King having equal status. At a later time, Fanny would be described as 'scandaleusement prussienne'. From 1791 onwards, she considered herself 'honorablement prussienne'.

Joseph, however, who had wanted to do so much and had achieved so little, who took away with one hand what he had given with the other, Joseph was dead, and Fanny was alive. Indeed, after the first pain of losing the hope that had been bound up in him had passed, she even revived after the death of the monarch, whose misfortune in the end had hung over the capital like a dark cloud. The new Emperor, Leopold, like the new King of Prussia, Frederick William, a believer in living and letting live, was not only a clever and circumspect statesman, but also a genial, pleasure-loving gentleman. He brought his mistress, Madeleine Bianchi, who was both the Empress's lady's maid and her confidante, from Tuscany to the Hofburg, where he also conducted minor amours, manifested his pleasure in all earthly enjoyments and during his short reign was unstinting with entertainments and public show.

In a Vienna which, freed from its perpetually bad conscience, was sinking back with relief into its old, unfettered *joie de vivre*, Fanny's first great epoch began. She was a little over thirty, but at the height of her powers of attraction. A certain sharpness and awkwardness which may have clung to her in her youth had been softened by the gentle air of her new home, veiled by the arts of the Viennese *marchands d'modes* and polished by the emollient nature of her surroundings. She was considered a beautiful woman, and was certainly a fascinating one. Alxinger, the amiable poet, once sang her praise in those years when she had been taken ill, probably by some harbinger of her later, fatal illness:

Wohlthätig, reitzend, klug und ohne jene Mängel
Die sonst als Gegengift der Schönheit Abbruch thun
Ist Fanny, ruft der Neid; wohlan, sie kränkle nun!
Damit die Welt doch seh', sie sey nicht ganz ein Engel.

[Kind, charming, witty, Fanny lacks those flaws / That oftentimes of beauty make a mock; / Let her fall ill, cries Envy, then we'll see / She is not wholly of angelic stock.]

Karl August Varnhagen, too, whom however she met only in later life, praised her appearance to the highest degree. Although other, less friendly verdicts on Fanny from his pen have survived, which will in no way be glossed over in these pages, the image of her recorded in his *Denkwürdigkeiten* (*Memorable Occurrences*) remained imprinted longest in his memory and may serve as a valid description of her person, her character and her sphere of activity. Varnhagen praises her house, in which 'the most distinguished foreigners, reigning lords and princes, ambassadors, high military officials, clergymen, merchants, artists, scholars and all classes of society found a pleasant reception, cultured entertainment, brilliant sociability'. But no smaller was the number, he wrote, of 'those who, less favoured through their position in the world, sought not only enjoyment, but rather protection and support in this circle, and were here encouraged with magnanimous sympathy and generosity'. It was to Vienna's gain that Fanny had come from Berlin, where she had grown up in prosperity and with a liberal education. However:

It was certainly not her imported wealth which allowed Frau von Arnstein to shine in Vienna, she found greater means in every respect both in her own and in the surrounding conditions. Only her being early accustomed to move in plenty and radiance, and the emphasis which outward resources lend to all personal presence and manners, doubtless gave her a great advantage in her entry into a new circle of life. She had need of this advantage in order to assert greater ones. Of tall, slim stature, radiant with beauty and grace, of distinguished manner and behaviour, spirited and fiery expression, combining acute intelligence and wit with a cheerful temper, not without learning, and mistress of foreign languages as well as her own, she was a most striking and notable phenomenon in Vienna; the qualities which belong in general to only a few women of the highest position were observed wondrously shining forth in a Jewess, whose freedom of thought and culture, which had flourished under the blessed influences of the reign of Frederick the Great, could only have a more powerful effect in a city where these last advantages were scarcely widespread, but had already begun to be appreciated and desired. The activity of Emperor Joseph II was already bearing fruit in Vienna and was still infiltrating ever more deeply in all conditions. A more favourable time could not have presented itself!

Varnhagen continues:

A pleasant house, open every day to numerous guests of all classes, the most tasteful surroundings, the richest hospitality, the confluence of distinguished foreigners, the combination of noble standards and customs with a middle-class, no, not even middle-class, but quite exceptional position, the undisputed rule of a charming, active woman who animates and kindles everything around her; all this in a sumptuous capital, the hub of many states and peoples, where the greatest luxury, the most comfortable living, are in full swing, united with proud superiority and harsh prejudice, but also with light-hearted simplicity and good humour; imagine these two elements in daily contact, in perpetual reciprocation, and it will not be found excessive to maintain that Frau von Arnstein's house has throughout many years performed the function of a mission-house, whose directress bears the credit for establishing contacts without which it could not have been achieved, and whose consequences have passed unfathomably into the stream of ordinary life! For a long time Frau von Arnstein's house in Vienna was simply the only one of its kind, and if later many others, but surely none like hers, have come into being, then this too is to the credit of this excellent woman, by whom this passage was first opened and made viable for her successors. The free, respected position, removed from the constraint of prejudice, which the adherents of the Mosaic faith have enjoyed and now enjoy in Vienna was quite undeniably first won with and through the influence and activity of Frau von Arnstein.

The richest brilliance of her salon, as Varnhagen describes it here, was not to unfold until the time of the Congress of Vienna. The reigning princes, the ambassadors and high military officials of whom he speaks were still only sparsely represented in earlier decades. Nevertheless Rahel Levin wrote from Breslau in August 1794 to her brother M. T. Robert in Berlin that she had met the privy councillor Levaux in a public garden restaurant, 'who had come from Vienna, and related wonderful things of Frau von Arnstein, about her house, princes, ministers, counts, ambassadors, gardens, late suppers, and everything that we already know of Vienna'. For the past three years two sons of the high nobility, young Prince Carl of Liechtenstein and his brother Wenzel, had frequented Fanny's house. Other heirs of ancient names were soon to be counted among her intimates.

A little album, bound in green silk, presented to Fanny by her friends in 1793, comprises in two dozen pencil drawings by Johann Fischer the closer circle of her friends. It consisted, apart from the handsome, manly Carl Liechtenstein, of Prince Paar (depicted once *en négligé*, once in wig and pigtail), the Russian Prince Grégoire Czernitscheff, Counts Pergen, Gattenberg, Marschall, Nolten, Anton Appony, Wrtby and the exceedingly ugly Künigl, a Marquis Gallo, Councillor von Sonnenfels, a Herr von Schalk from Berlin, a Dr Sallaba, a certain Reinhardt Wernegk and two clerical gentlemen, the Abbé von Collenbach and the '*sous-abbé*' of the papal nuncio. It will surprise no-one that Fanny's circle included more men than women. But her best female friend, the enchanting Pepi Sebottendorf, is here too – 'ever amiable', as she was called by Councillor Levaux – and with her a Countess d'Alton, a Frau von Luerwald, a Frau von Sowek and a Demoiselle Julie Degelmann. They all prostrated themselves at her feet with the well-meant, if ill-rhymed, dedication:

En contemplant tous ces Portrait
Qui, dans la plus foible Nuance
Nous retracent la Ressemblance;
On éprouve de viff Regress,
Que la main qui traça ces traits
Nous les présentes tous muets
Si l'Art eut pu créer la voix
Ces bouches diroient à la fois,
Pénétrés d'Amitié & de Reconnaissance
Chacun de Nous, Fanny, vous aime & vous encense.

She herself, the hostess, was also depicted by Fischer. Here Fanny does indeed, as a Weimar lady was later to remark, bear 'quite the stamp of the women of the Old Testament', but then again she also resembles other beautiful women of her time – the early Romantic era – with her sparkling eye, the charming and intelligent mouth, the mixture of sensibility and wit, of grace and capriciousness. What this little portrait already reveals is even more evident from her notebook, mentioned earlier, which has survived for posterity together with the album. It is impossible to say when she began to write in it. If we knew this, if we could date the many and varied entries in her own handwriting and that of others, the poems and aphorisms, the quotations and maxims that appear in it, we might be able to solve the puzzle of Fanny's inner development, her changes of mood, even the secret of her most overwhelming experience.

None of this is revealed by the book. We must satisfy ourselves with knowing that it was only in Vienna, at the end of Joseph's decade and perhaps as much as five years afterwards, that it served her as a notebook; that within this period of time which cannot be more precisely determined she poured her ideas and feelings into this little receptacle; that she made it the mirror of her reading and her favourite diversions, and, at times, even of her philosophy of life; and finally that she allowed privileged friends and family members to enter in it verses and anecdotes of their own choice.

Fanny's commonplace book reveals an impulsive person, a woman filled with noble as well as passionate feelings, a moralist and thinker, who nevertheless a moment later finds pleasure in the most insipid puns, charades and rebuses. She writes and reads English, French, Italian and Slavic texts apparently with as much ease as German ones. Her own models, whom she quotes most frequently, are principally Pope, together with Addison, Pascal and Wilhelm Heinse's Renaissance drama *Ardinghello*. For the rest, the names of Voltaire, Lessing, Wieland, Mendelssohn, d'Alembert, the poor Jewish poet Moses Ephraim Kuh, and finally of Shakespeare and Milton, crop up, copied by other hands at her request or spontaneously contributed. The sum of the wisdom of these and other, unknown writers ought to produce a well-rounded view of life. But the longer one leafs through Fanny's notebook, the more inconsistent appears the image of her world.

Fanny strives after a moral standard of life: Pascal's saying 'Les belles actions cachées sont les plus estimables' comes to mind. Fanny doubts whether it is possible to lead a blameless life: 'La durée de nos passions ne dépend pas plus de nous que la durée de notre vie.' Fanny suffers from immaturity: 'La jeunesse est une ivresse continuelle, c'est la fièvre de la raison.' Fanny feels old age approaching: 'En vieillissant on devient plus fou et plus sage.' She admires wit: 'Chacun dit du bien de son Coeur, et personne n'en ose dire de son esprit', or Pope's (slightly misquoted): 'True wit is nature to advantage drest / what is often thought but never so well exprest.' But she recognises the superior strength of emotion: 'Destroy love and friendship / what remains in the World Worth accepting?'

The two moods which she expresses most frequently are zeal for virtue and scepticism. A modest existence, patience, contentment, tender friendship, simultaneous fear and abhorrence of vice – 'To vice only one step is needed / If once you stumble, one false step follows another'– appear her ideals. Nevertheless she discovers again and again the questionableness of all things, the worm at the core of even the best-regulated lives. Her emotion impels her to strive after the high, the good, the beautiful. Her reason reminds her repeatedly that it is unattainable.

Does true virtue exist? 'La vertu n'iroit pas si loin, si la vanité ne luis tenoit compagnie.' Does one resist vice voluntarily? 'Quand les vices nous quittent, nous nous flattons de la Créance que c'est nous qui les quittons.' Is there such a thing as reliable friendship? 'He who would find a friend without faults, let him leave this world, or return into himself.' Is perfection possible? 'In this world perfection appears only momentarily, and these moments alone are our enjoyment', or Pope's (again slightly altered): 'Whoever thinks a faultless piece to see / thinks what never was nor is nor ever shall be.' Has constancy true value? 'La persévérance n'est digne ni de blâme ni de louange parcequ'elle n'est que la durée des goûts et des sentiments, qu'on ne s'ôte et qu'on ne se donne point.' Is it possible to be natural? 'Rien n'empêche tant d'être naturel que l'envie de le paroitre.' Is there profit in becoming wise? 'Qui vit sans folie, n'est pas si sage qu'il le croit.' Does not philosophy help, at least? 'La philosophie triomphe aisément de maux passés et de maux à venir; mais les maux présens triomphent d'elle.'

Dark thoughts! Yet they never overpowered her cheerful disposition for long. In the end it was always a happy, not a bitter scepticism that filled her. With patience one could come to terms with anything: 'Even the best must own Patience and Resignation are the pilars [*sic*] of human peace on earth.' In spite of everything her disposition was basically serene, her mind was sensible and unprejudiced. She held certain principles to be immovable, for example, the equality of all religions, the love of humanity as a substitute for any religion, the free position of man in the universe. An unknown hand penned two lines in her little book: 'If you honour not God in man / how will you honour him in the temple?' She herself follows this with a little anecdote which reads like a mocking postscript to Mendelssohn's teaching: 'Le Cardinal de Polignac ayant demandé à Bayle de quelle Religion il étoit, celui-ci lui répondit, qu'il étoit Protestant: Mais le mot est bien vague, reprit le Cardinal, êtes-vous Luthérien, Calviniste, Anglican? . . . non, répondit Bayle, je suis Protestant, parceque je proteste contre toutes les Religions.' And finally, a true child of the Enlightenment, she transcribes a version of Pope's famous epitaph on Newton, which mirrors her belief in the empirical perceptibility of the universe:

All nature and her law
lay hid in night
God Say'd let Newton be
and all was light.

In the face of emotional disturbance she is, certainly, more helpless. If her understanding is schooled by the model of the 'illuminated ones', her feelings rise in the high waves of the Romantic period. 'L'absence diminue les mediocres passions,' she quotes, 'il augmente les grandes, comme le vent éteint les bougies et allume le feu.' And below this she writes, 'Je trouve ceci plus jolie que vrai, F.' What experience is hidden behind this opinion? Perhaps a passion of which she repents with Pope's:

Constraint in all things makes the pleasure less
Sweet is the love that comes with willingness.
Men some to business some to pleasure take
But every woman is at heart a rake.

The passion which may have taken hold of Fanny at a time when her salon was filling with the young nobility of Austria remained concealed. How far this experience went is not disclosed even by its tragic outcome. The misfortune of which she was the innocent author in her middle years was not to come to pass until the reign of Emperor Francis II which began in 1792. Leopold was upon the throne, that unpromising monarch who promised so much, who tried to correct his brother Joseph's gravest errors in a brief space of time, and forthwith made peace with the Ottoman Empire, brought about an agreement with Prussia, won back the Netherlands, at first offered no resistance to the French Revolution and moreover found time to give Frankfurt once more 'the masquerade of an imperial coronation parading in its tattered rags'.

It was Carl Liechtenstein, Fanny's young friend, who made the ceremonial announcement to Marie Antoinette of her brother's accession to the throne in 1790. The Queen wept bitterly in his presence, but was as far from demanding Austrian support from him as she was in her well-known letter to the Emperor of November 1791, which included an exact description of conditions in France. And only with hesitation and reluctance did Leopold prepare himself to lend her such support. For this intelligent man, who spoke little of freedom but practised it the more frequently, found justice in the demands of the French people for a constitution, would undoubtedly in time have given one to the Austrians and, had he been granted a longer life, would have brought to his realm a government of enlightened liberalism.

Friedrich Gentz, the Prussian military adviser and future Austrian privy councillor, was the author of the most telling description of this emperor, whose 'disposition receptive to hope, slowness in decision, circumspection in execution, [and] decided preference for the business of internal administration of the state nourished in him those peaceable principles and leanings on which all his plans were built and all his steps were based.' Leopold's sense of justice is not mentioned here. But it was this very virtue which led him to revoke the arbitrary decisions made under the capricious administration of justice during his brother's reign. A case in point was that of Eleonore Eskeles, who had been deported at Joseph's command. On 7 December 1791, in expressing the wish 'that no one should be sentenced purely on the assertion by infamous witnesses of suspicions which not only have not been proved true, but have not even been judicially examined', Leopold ordained the end of her banishment.

Nevertheless the banished woman possessed the tact not to return to Vienna for another ten years. To her brother Bernhard Eskeles, who had taken the case to Leopold and brought it to a successful conclusion, her decision could not have been unwelcome. This man, as learned as he was efficient in business, had recently formed a connection with Nathan Arnsteiner and the latter's brother-in-law Salomon Herz, had put his exceptional intelligence at the service of the Arnsteiner business and begun to lead the enterprise to previously unattained heights. Since June of that year it had already been entered in the list of creditors of the finance department. State commissions, even if they were minor ones in these predominantly peaceful times, were continually being carried out, and Nathan's new partner must have been thankful not to have a scandal which involved his name revived in the public's memory.

During the short period of Leopold's reign in Vienna, and Frederick William's in Berlin, the same breeze wafted from the throne in each capital. Admittedly, one ruler was shrewd and responsible, the other dissolute and idle; one carried on state business with circumspection, while the other left all-important decisions to his ministers. But in their philosophy of life, which united indulgence towards their own inclinations with a corresponding measure of forbearance with the shortcomings of others, the two monarchs, in other respects hardly kindred spirits, resembled each other. Neither considered that revolutionary changes were called for. So it was that they felt bound to take up similar positions in the matter of the Jews.

Two days before its dissolution in September 1791 the French
National Assembly had drawn up a decree whose effect was to repeal
all special enactments respecting the Jews. Neither Leopold nor
Frederick William would have dreamed of doing likewise. What was
said about a dispensation of the Emperor's of August 1790 was true of
both of them: his tone was 'strict towards the poor, mild towards the
wealthy foreign Jews, favourable to the tolerated ones'. Both rulers
were prepared to acknowledge the emancipated, cultured and socially
acceptable adherents to this faith. The great mass of Jews, who still
lived in a state of poverty, misery and limited intellectual horizons, they
regarded with an abhorrence which excluded them as much as before
from human society in general.

But this miserable mass, this grey and ill-favoured army of the
disinherited, moved on steadfastly in the rear of its stately and
richly adorned vanguard. Weighed down by the suffering of the
centuries, their backs had become crooked and their pace heavy and
dragging. They had the restless look of the persecuted and the
greed of a starving man forcing his way through to the bread-
platter. Finding support only within their own families and community, they had only indifference or even hate to offer to the rest
of society. In their narrow, dirty lodgings they lived in a constant
state of siege. By being constantly prepared for them, they positively called down ever more blows of fate upon their own heads.
Had there not been those among them who had freed themselves
from this vicious circle and given an example to the world of how a
dehumanised Jew could be transformed into a Jewish human being,
their condition would have been held to be unalterable. But such
examples were multiplying. The public was forced to take notice of
them. 'As is well known,' wrote Count Sauer, the Austrian district
governor, 'a great part of the Jewish nation is low-minded, their
manners are rough and uncouth. The better part of the nation
desires that their spirit may be transformed and gladly offers to lend
a helping hand.'

It was not, to be sure, the Jews who had already taken up
Christianity who were offering this helping hand. They had cut
themselves off from their community and shaken off their fate with
their religion. Thus a Freiherr von Wetzlar, whose sons-in-law
came from the families of the Counts Triangi, Festetics and Clary,
was already separated by a gulf from the 'rough and uncouth' part
of his nation. His example might seem worthy of aspiration to
some, reprehensible to others. The more indistinctly it melted into
the background of Austrian society, the more it lost in symbolistic

power. It was their own upper stratum, it was the men and women who had remained within their community and had attained honour and esteem, who daily bore new witness that the rise of the Jews was a possibility. They were the visible end result of a development which, then as now, if it had been allowed to proceed in peace, would have removed the Jewish problem from the face of the earth within a predictable span of time. Fanny was one of these. She was a living symbol, whether or not she was aware of it.

The army of the disinherited not only followed hopefully those who marched at its head. Its ranks were in addition constantly swollen by those coming from the East who hungered for education and self-improvement. The Jews in Poland had reached those regions through repeated expulsions from Germany. They had huddled together there in dense settlements in which at least they could be secure from exile. They regularly fell victim to pogroms which were crueller than anything they had experienced in the Holy Roman Empire. But they preferred, in the frequently long intervals, to live undisturbed in their pious community, to speak their own archaic language, a transmogrified Middle High German, to study their old Hebrew texts and, without pretension or ambition, to carry on their retail businesses or humble crafts or to work the land. At the top of their hierarchy stood, not power or money, but intellect, but it was an unfruitful, useless mode of thought which was pursued here. Boys of lively understanding were instructed solely in the Talmud, their powers of invention and imagination directed only at anachronistic mysticism or the long worn-out paths of Jewish folklore.

From these Polish settlements young people were continually setting off to the West, to unfold their talents in other ways. Such a one was the poet Isachar Falkensohn Behr, who turned up in Daniel Itzig's house in about 1770, praised his daughter in verse, won Lessing's confidence and finally, under the title of *Poems of a Polish Jew*, published naïve and mischievous Rococo verses in the old German manner; these were reviewed in the *Notes of Frankfurt Scholars* by a slightly embarrassed Goethe, who had expected something more extraordinary. Another was Salomon Maimon, whom the Berlin philosopher Markus Herz recommended to his friend Kant twenty years later with the moving words:

Herr Salomon Maimon, heretofore one of the plainest of Polish Jews, has for several years worked his way up in almost all of the higher sciences in an exceptional manner through his genius, his sagacity and diligence, and in particular has in recent times made your philosophy, or at least your manner of philosophising, so much his own that I dare claim with confidence that he is one of the very few of the present inhabitants of the earth who so completely understand and comprehend you. He leads a very wretched existence here, supported by a few friends, entirely on speculation. He is also my friend, and I love and esteem him uncommonly.

Maimon, the truly enlightened Jew, the man who 'took the first step towards the further development of critical philosophy by exposing the problematic character of the concept of the "thing in itself" and thus paved the way for Fichte's idealism', found acceptance in a salon which was the Berlin counterpart of, and in a certain sense the model for, Fanny's hospitable house in Vienna. Here the rear-guard stragglers of the Enlightenment rubbed shoulders with the harbingers of the Romantic period. Here one stood on that threshold in time of which Maimon's transition from Kant to Fichte seemed the very symbol. A combination of beauty and reason had created this salon. Markus Herz was the head of the household – 'a deep, clear, cool, positively thinking intellect', a student of Kant and a follower of Lessing, whose abhorrence of Goethe's *Werther* and the 'damned sentimentality that the novel aroused, if it did not actually create it' he entirely shared. His wife, however, was Henriette Lemos, the 'tragic Muse' of the young Romantics of Berlin.

Henriette was born in 1764, the daughter of a doctor of Portuguese descent and a Frenchwoman, and had been brought up in the strictest Sephardic tradition. At the age of twelve-and-a-half she was already engaged, and at fifteen married to Dr Markus Herz, who was twice her age. Her beauty was extraordinary. The oval face with the lustrous eyes, the nose with its perfectly straight line from forehead to tip, the mouth at once full and finely drawn, the exceedingly delicate complexion and luxuriant hair put one in mind of the statue of a Greek goddess. Her figure, too, was classical, nestling voluptuously in the folds of the Empire fashion which was just coming in. That her head seemed a little small in proportion to her body, that her tall stature required a majestic carriage, was indeed sometimes the occasion for mockery. 'One should have looked at her through a diminishing glass,' commented Caroline, the daughter of the Austrian privy councillor Greiner.

In her youth Henriette was mocked far less than she was loved, even if this was, as Prince Louis Ferdinand remarked in her presence to the Duchess of Courland, and she herself found to her chagrin, 'never as much as she deserved'. Perhaps it was she who loved herself best. Nevertheless, all her friends and admirers – who included men such as Mirabeau, Laroche, the Humboldt brothers, Counts Dohna and Bernstorff, Gentz and Brinckmann, Schlegel and Schleiermacher, Jean Paul and finally the young Ludwig Börne, a noted political writer – with one voice praised her wit. But, in conformity with her general grave and tragic demeanour, she appears to have possessed more gushing sentimentality than true wit and intellect.

The deep knowledge, the pure reason for whose sake the youth of Berlin at first sought out her house were those of the doctor of medicine, district medical officer and philosopher, Markus Herz. He had gathered around himself a group of voluntary students to whom he gave lectures on philosophy and experimental physics. This 'very select audience' was joined by the younger brothers of the King of Prussia and the Humboldt brothers, who had been introduced to Dr Herz in the spring of 1786 by their tutor, Christian Knuth. From her husband's circle of students Henriette chose a few individuals whom she brought together more closely in a reading circle, her so-called 'Tuesday club'. Some Enlightenment figures such as Nicolai and the military adviser Dohm also formed part of this nucleus of her salon. But among the younger visitors who crowded around the beautiful Henriette and her friend, the clever Dorothea Mendelssohn, among the Humboldts and others such as Carl von Laroche and Friedrich Schlegel, a leaning towards mysticism, an exaggerated 'sentimentalising' that Johann Friedel had smiled at in the compatriots of his 'friend in Berlin' was already in vogue. Dr Herz, too, 'smiled at the extravagances of the league of virtue which Henriette had founded and which became a prelude to Romantic folly. Young Wilhelm von Humboldt played a leading part in it. They addressed each other as *du*, wrote each other long letters in Hebrew characters, exchanged rings and silhouettes and cared nothing for the constraints of conventional propriety.'

In those years of transition an odd mixture and marriage of German and Jewish pathos was taking place. The urge towards transcendental cognition was and is common to these two peoples. In one historic moment it took hold of both with the same vehemence. After decades of rationalistic enlightenment the pendulum had swung back. Rousseau's example had moved Herder, Herder's had moved the youth of Germany, to seek truth in their feelings and not in their minds, in the original virtues of man and not in calculated science. The throne itself, after Frederick the enlightener had closed his eyes in death, provided an example of a 'mysticism steeped in sensuality'. Even in the Jews, who – as we have seen with Mendelssohn – had turned only reluctantly towards the religion of reason, the ancient tendency towards mysticism reawakened with new force.

A wild doctrine, which had been founded some hundred years earlier by the visionary and adventurer Sabbatai Z'vi from Smyrna, was again gaining ground. Z'vi had given himself out to be the true Messiah, and achieved recognition in many Jewish communities in Europe and Asia Minor. The cabbalistic enthusiasm, the belief in miracles and superstitions that attended his person, were propagated in Poland among the pupils of Juda Chassid, 'The Pious'. After Chassid's death in 1700, the delusion seemed to have died away. Now, however, the time was again ripe for its revival. A sect calling itself the New Chassidists formed among the eastern Jews and spread to the western ones. Their leaders, the Zaddiks, wanted to be seen as holy men and miracle-workers. They called their supporters to religious raptures, to wild frenzies like those of the dervishes or the American Shakers, and believed that the true way to God was to be found in fervent rejoicing.

It was far from Henriette Herz's thoughts to adopt the doctrine of the Chassidists. Probably she knew hardly anything of them. But there was an internal connection in her descent from the Sephardic strain, that imaginative Jewish nobility which had also produced Sabbatai Z'vi. One chord of her being, which tended by nature towards mystical high-flying, vibrated in resonance when the young German enthusiasts sought to enhance everyday life with poetry, and blur the boundaries between life and dream, between truth and fiction. They read Shakespeare together, as well as the first English novels of sentiment – 'I must confess,' said Henriette later, 'that we all felt a certain longing to be heroines of novels' – they took on the persona of Goethe's young Werther or those of the guilty couples in his *Elective Affinities*, and had just enough of the rebel in them to put into practice what the fictional characters only aspired to.

Here one committed adultery not with the flirtatious frivolity of the Rococo, but out of defiant conviction. It was not, however, committed in every case. The nineteen-year-old Wilhelm von Humboldt's relationship with Henriette, some three years his senior, remained unconsummated, although even after his marriage to Caroline von Dachröden he loved her tenderly, even 'childishly'. But presumably Schleiermacher, the Romantic theorist and translator of Plato, evoked a more than Platonic response in Henriette. And finally, in 1798, Dorothea Mendelssohn, who, a year before Henriette's marriage, had herself become the wife of the merchant Simon Veit, left him in order to live with Friedrich Schlegel, the 'Titan with the fists of a child', reversing the title of the 'League of Virtue'. Soon afterwards Schlegel published his *Lucinde*, the credo of this ostensibly revolutionary movement, which, however, was to create a reaction in every sphere, from the religious to the political, except in that of social morality.

The real revolution was taking place in France. The great writing was being produced at the small princely courts of central Germany. In Berlin, however, all was seething and bubbling in society, literature, art and philosophy, old standards were being overthrown and transmitted wisdom was being abrogated, to make room for all sorts of 'artificial systems, useless experiments, improvised dogmas'. 'A foolish generation,' writes the social critic Hillebrand, 'was wandering around in the wreckage.' Anyone who, like him, dismisses the delusions of the Romantic period because, in continuing to procreate, they were to give birth to the deranged notions of German politics, with their momentous consequences, must indeed condemn those Prussian decades. The greatness of a state which arises from such dark and troubled origins must seem all too dearly bought.

It was a creatively fruitful epoch, but a philosophically pernicious one, in which this internal contradiction within the German character came to light. The deeply divided figure of a Friedrich von Schlegel, who was at once 'critical and devout, Protestant and Catholic, wicked and pious', is one of its embodiments. Another is Gentz, the dubious genius, the first continental personification of the reactionary intellectual. A third is Schleiermacher, who threw once more into metaphysical confusion the minds of those who had already been won over to the clear, scientific observation of mankind in the universe. But what an abundance of talent had been necessary to set up these artificial and improvised dogmas! What powerful, even if dangerous, imagination, what visionary force it had taken to call to life a new creativity from long dammed-up springs and forgotten myths!

In those very years of political weakness and military powerlessness, before Prussia's patriotism awoke, the ground was being prepared for its subsequent highly intensified and belligerent national spirit. The country in which the greatest as well as the most ominous ideas were ripening, which was to save Germany more than once and finally to unite her, came forth from that process of fermentation. The grapes of nationalism as well as of romanticism were being trodden in the press, at first in separate vessels, whose contents, however, soon flowed together. The Jews of Berlin participated directly in what was happening there. It was in Henriette Herz's salon that Schlegel and Schleiermacher met for the first time, that Gentz and Wilhelm von Humboldt cordially shook hands. In their 'League of Virtue' lay one of the origins of the anti-Napoleonic resistance.

The new, more relaxed and mixed society whose unifying ideas was that of their Prussianness also met at the houses of the mint-master Ephraim's granddaughters, the Meyer sisters – Sophie, who had married Baron Grotthuss, from the Baltic province of Livonia, and Marianne, now called von Eybenberg, the morganatic wife of the Austrian ambassador, Prince Reuss. Both women had been christened and thus had access to several houses whose doors were closed to Henriette Herz. Marianne von Eybenberg, whose charms had ensnared Goethe, Gentz and Count Christian Bernstorff, later associated on an equal basis in Vienna, if not with all the top nobility, at least with the Princesses of Courland, the Lignes and Clarys. But her star was already on the wane when that of a small, unhandsome individual was beginning to rise: shortly before the close of the century Rahel, the daughter of the jeweller Levin, had taken up her place in the centre of intellectual Berlin.

'I was a Jewess, not pretty, ignorant, without *grâce, sans talents et sans instruction*'; thus she described herself in an attack of the blues. Her contemporaries found her intelligent and clever – a female genius – and posterity has agreed with them. Among all the women of the emancipation, of whom she was the most outstanding, she suffered the most from her Jewishness – it turned her life into a continual 'bleeding to death' and any attempt to arrest this into a 'new death'. Nevertheless she constantly made such attempts, entered the world of Christians with a fearful heart, loved handsome counts and diplomats, told Prince Louis Ferdinand 'attic truths' to his face in her Berlin garret, admired his mistress, the loose-living Pauline Wiesel, married the upstart Varnhagen, had herself christened and all the while walked as if on hot coals, like the little mermaid who grew feet instead of a tail for the love of a human and whose every step cut her like knives.

Rahel was indeed an exceptional case. What she did, what she thought, how she lived, carried the stamp of her individuality. Whoever thought he could judge her sisters in religion in Berlin by her standard, or even tried to ascribe the same convictions to them, would then as now be on the wrong track. The universalism to which she adhered, her contempt of war as a crude, uncultured business, distinguish her from her time and her contemporaries. But this much is important here: that she indeed considered

Henriette's 'League of Virtue' to be a 'childish freemasonry', rejected her Berlin friends' francophobia and saw Napoleon as the founder of a united Europe, in which she herself could one day be truly at home – but that in the end, in the high wind of the wars of independence, she did slip into that nationalism which was to bring with it new threats to her and her kin. Yes, she too, the cosmopolitan, joined this movement, although, of sharper understanding than her sisters, she recognised its profound danger.

But certain things – the Prussian patriotism of the Jewish salons, the estrangement from a France which, after all, had been the first and only European country to welcome their Jews as citizens, the romantic glorification of Germany as conjured up by old myths and fairy-tales – were drifting over from Berlin to Vienna. There sat Fanny, proud of her Prussianness, surrounded by friends in her house which was open at all times, but which somehow lacked the right meaning and content. The conversations in her house, polished as they were, had so far served merely as aesthetic entertainment, had been elegant declamations, idle verbal altercations, with no other aim than to create a lively and animated atmosphere. Now, about the middle of the last decade, a purpose was evolving. Fanny travelled to Berlin, visited Henriette Herz, Marianne von Eybenberg and Rahel Levin, met the men of the new era, made the acquaintance of the first French emigrants at the salon of her own sister Sara Levy, who had formerly often entertained the Comte de Mirabeau, and returned to her house in the Graben filled with enthusiasm.

At last it had become possible to unite Prussian and Austrian feelings in one breast, for shortly before Leopold's death the two countries had formed an alliance and were now indeed ranged together against France, which had declared war on them. It was true that the National Assembly had freed the French Jews, but Fanny had been granted civic rights by Frederick William. Her two homes had a common enemy, who became hers. She hated the French and continued to hate them even when the King of Prussia made peace with them. She believed in Prussia even when it lay prostrate, and had doubts about Austria, which, so it seemed to her, was conducting the war in too lukewarm and indecisive a manner. She rejoiced when, years later, another Prussian ultimatum was issued to France, wept over Napoleon's victories and, to the annoyance of the Viennese court, continued to conspire against him after he had already become the Emperor's son-in-law. In short, she was more Prussian than the Prussians – one of the first, but not the last of her stock to carry this unrequited love to the extreme. The tragedy of German Jewry was anticipated in her.

She herself, to be sure, was very far from being a tragic figure. Rahel might be cleverer, Henriette more beautiful, but neither possessed what had been bestowed on Fanny: a happy disposition. Undoubtedly she was irritable and could flare up savagely if something went against her grain. But she was just as quickly appeased, would become kindly and mild, give particularly generous presents to all those she had offended and make amends with her playful, even though sincerely felt, expressions of remorse for the vexations caused by her ill temper. Fickle, forgetful, tempestuous, always as ready to laugh as to weep, unaccountable and yet lovable in the extreme – this is how we must picture her. She possessed the manner of great ladies, for she had been spoilt by fate. Yet she was – as we also learn from Rahel Varnhagen's letters – just as capable of lively and querulous confidentiality with servants, ladies' maids and the rest of her 'people' as of social intercourse with princes, prelates and diplomats. If towards the end of her life she was enfeebled, bad-tempered and restless, her deep inner serenity and real sense of humour had not forsaken her. All this and more is already recognisable in her first will, a hasty draft, parts of which are quoted here:

I request my husband to dispose as follows:
I would wish to be able to give to my family in Berlin the capital of 10,000 gulden held for me by my husband . . . my pearls, as my favourite pieces of jewellery, I ask to be divided into necklaces for each of my sisters, and whichever of them shall first be snatched away from this life/ which God forbid should happen for a long time/ let her bequeath this necklace which has been made her portion to another sister, so that these pearls, as a cherished present from my husband, shall never pass out of my family – – – my jewellery I give as a present to my daughter, and of my trinkets, as well as of part of the jewellery, if the trinkets should not suffice, she shall make a choice to give as keepsakes to her male and female cousins on her mother's side, according to her own judgement . . .
For what concerns my remaining disposable possessions, . . . let my husband leave a small pension to our remaining domestic servants, or indeed give them a present, at the same time assuring them that if I had been richer I would gladly have done more for them and the services they have rendered . . .
What can I leave to my husband but boundless gratitude for his love and consideration which he has given me from the hour in which we were united by fate, if he needs a trifle to revive my memory in him, then let him be the first to choose, everything in any case is his – and the

right to dispose of these things is mine only through his kindness, with which, as I live, he has never denied me anything, and therefore he will certainly not refuse me at this moment

I request that Pepi as my tenth sister shall be given a tenth string of pearls with the same proviso that she shall bequeath it after her death to one of my sisters, moreover all my necklaces, hair rings and keepsakes of my sisters shall be her portion, because she certainly rates them at double their worth, moreover all my Wedgwood, and porcelain cups as well as the furniture embroidered by my sister Wulff – for this she shall take over all my papers, and if my family request it shall supply to them all the letters addressed to me by them, . . . let her forgive me this last heavy charge as well as the ill-humour which she has had to suffer from me from time to time, and which were certainly not the consequence of an ill-natured heart . . .

Finally, I request my husband, if it should please God to let me end my life before the education of my daughter should be complete, to entrust her to the care of my sisters in Berlin, and when she has reached a riper age, to marry her only to the man she has chosen, if it is otherwise according to her wish, yet not to allow her to take this step either in the heat of passion, or against her will, should my husband grant me this last request, to entrust my daughter to my sisters, he will heap up my gratitude, and if it is permitted for the blessed in heaven to pray for those left behind, and to care for their well-being, then he will never be lacking in the happiness for which my grateful soul will entreat on his behalf –

Fanny Arnstein
née Itzig

5th August 1793

From my daughter's attachment to her father as well as to me I promise myself a blind obedience to his will, as he will certainly demand nothing of her but what will be for her own good, and I also request her to support me towards him in the request to entrust her to my Berlin family, and to be obedient to them as to her parents, and also to remain true to the laws of her forefathers, as one can have no good opinion of the manner of thinking of a person who changes the religion into which chance has allowed her to be born. It is not prejudice that allows me to make this request to her, but rather the intention that she should not lose the esteem of the thinking world.

Fanny

This rough draft is not to be taken literally. It was evidently dashed off in haste and not deposited at the Lower Austrian government offices as were Fanny's later wills. All the other testamentary arrangements put in writing by her, as well as the contents of her notebook, are much more elegantly formulated. But the document may give rise to certain conclusions. It demonstrates Fanny's fear of a disorder towards which she undoubtedly tended, her great love for her sisters and the whole family in Berlin, her grateful attachment to the good Nathan and finally her attitude towards religion. That she here disapproves of a change of faith on her daughter's part on the grounds of firmness of character is no less significant than her wish not to be charged with prejudice on this account. After all, Pepi, her best friend and 'tenth sister', the wife of Lieutenant-General von Sebottendorf, had been a member of the Christian church for more than fourteen years.

What may seem surprising in this first draft of a will is Fanny's attitude to her personal fortune. Despite the 10,000 gulden which were in Nathan's safe-keeping, she did not consider herself wealthy, indeed she wished herself richer in order to be able to do more for her domestic staff. When we consider that the expenses of Goethe's upper-middle-class household were furnished at that time by 2,400 gulden a year, and that the annual income of the house of Rothschild was a comparable amount, we cannot agree with Fanny's low opinion of her fortune. But the daughter of the Jewish prince was not accustomed to applying middle-class standards; she had brought 70,000 thalers – some 133,000 gulden – as her dowry and with some justification compared herself to the aristocracy in her way of life and expenditure. As far as the Rothschilds were concerned, their prosperity was still in its infancy, and their father, the court agent for Hesse and Hanau, Meyer Amschel, could not compare with the Bethmanns for influence and importance in Frankfurt. Nathan Arnstein, meanwhile – he had some time ago abbreviated his name to a more distinguished-sounding form – was on the point of becoming the most important financier in Vienna. Indeed, until the Rothschilds outstripped him in the years before 1848, Nathan, together with his partner Eskeles, was considered the first banker of the new Austrian Empire.

At the beginning of the reign of Francis, Fanny was perhaps not as rich as she would have liked to be, but certainly richer than most of her compatriots. Certainly, it had once again become more difficult to realise larger sums of money, for the war demanded funds, and money was in short supply. At his unexpected and premature passing, the statesmanlike Leopold had left behind a kingdom pacified only with difficulty. His son had been scarcely two weeks on the throne when a new dispute between nations was in motion. The first year of young Francis's reign, 1792, was no doubt enough to instil in him for all time a horror of revolution and Jacobinism.

In March he had become King of Hungary and Bohemia, in August the last Holy Roman Emperor; but before his arrival back in Vienna after the coronation in Frankfurt, his unfortunate aunt, Marie Antoinette, had been imprisoned with her family and, in the following January, she was guillotined. The Emperor's first twelve months were not yet over when the reign of terror began in Paris. The pallid young man who took a childish pleasure in legal subtleties, secret-police machinations, cosy court intrigues, masked balls and fancy-dress fêtes, found the whole business had suddenly become too much for him.

At the end of 1792, Alxinger wrote to his revered friend and master Wieland to give his opinion of the new monarch:

> The Emperor has the best of hearts and the most upright of characters. But steadfastness and lasting love of his work are not to be expected of him at his age. Our ministers, however, are heartily disgusted with the Enlightenment and have not progressed with the century. They would like to rule according to the fashion of a hundred years ago, call everything Jacobin which disapproves of the old fashion and are determined to carry their point in their own way, let it cost what it may. The freedom of the press and publicity are detested in the extreme, and whoever has spoken in your favour at any time is certain never to gain preference. *Censorship is worse than ever* and Joseph's great spirit has entirely retreated from us.

The long and reactionary era of the 'good Emperor Francis' had begun. In his subjects' minds, although the disturbances of the Napoleonic wars, two occupations of Vienna and a turbulent Congress still lay ahead of them, that attitude was still to be found which was to characterise the Biedermeier period – a twilight state like that after a heavy meal, when the body is satiated and the mind has sunk into a half-sleep. All resistance was broken down by the long-faced man who was outwardly paternal, inwardly intimidated. Intellectuals and aesthetes who showed libertarian tendencies or belonged to the Freemasons, who had been encouraged by Joseph, were silenced.

As early as August 1794 Count Saurau, the lord lieutenant of the city and most important prop of the secret police, had set up a criminal court to which the leaders of the so-called 'Viennese Jacobins', among them some totally harmless persons, fell victim. Lieutenant Hebenstreit was hanged in public in the following winter and the other 'conspirators', since the death penalty had been abolished for civilians under Joseph, sentenced to appalling terms in prison which few of them survived. A Hungarian rising too was punished in the most severe manner and no fewer than five political criminals executed. It took such acts of infamy to arouse the Austrians, not a rebellious people, to indignation.

From now on they grumbled wordlessly, while the middle classes sighed, and the former Illuminati resigned themselves under Francis's rule to the weak hand in the iron glove. Nor was Fanny, the daughter of the Enlightenment, well-disposed towards this Emperor. Informers were continually reporting to the court that she had been guilty of disrespectful remarks. Here began the first differences of opinion with her husband. For Nathan – whose brother Joseph had been elevated to the rank of *Freiherr* soon after the change of government, who himself was to be ennobled by Francis and whose association with the nobility, like his fidelity to Austria, where his grandfather had made his home, had inspired in him only the most loyal feelings – was faithful to the Emperor through thick and thin.

He had more reasons than these to be so. His house had, in these warlike times, taken on significant new responsibilities; it was procuring money and military supplies, drumming up contributions to challenge Napoleon's victories, paying Austria's ambassadors abroad, discounting on English bills going into millions, and was, in brief, one of the most important financial props of the government, indeed of the whole coalition.

His daughter Henriette too, still in her tender years, was contributing her mite. When, in April 1793, little Josepha von Sugalla, 'urged on by love for my gracious sovereign', took up a collection among her friends and laid 317 gulden at his Majesty's feet, Henriette's name was among those on the accompanying list of subscribers. The great-granddaughter both of Wertheimer's counting-house assistant and of the supplier of horses from Grätz was already taking her place quite unselfconsciously among all the noble offspring. The young ladies of the families of von Suttner, von Eichenfeld, von Ehrenburg and von Quirinzenstein, von Born, von Störck, von Fastwitz, von Mannagutta and the like, belonged, if not to the first, at least to the second ranks of society. The children of the merchants von Puthon and von Natorp, an Anna von Sonnenfels and an Elisabeth von Henikstein were also among them, and if Nathan's daughter still lacked the handle of 'von' to her name, her cousins Marianne and Theresya von Arnstein already sported the desirable prefix. The thirteen-year-old Henriette was probably the only little girl of the Jewish faith in the whole circle, which had been joined by middle-class children such as the daughters of her landlord, Contrini. But between her 4 gulden and 30 kreuzers and the coins contributed by the other young donors there was not a hair's difference.

Henriette's mother, although not filled with 'love for her gracious sovereign', was still a patriot – if not on behalf of Austria, at least against France, which was the decisive point at this time. Moreover, she really had little personal occasion to bear a grudge against the regime. However tyrannically it might behave towards a section of the populace, however much it persecuted the poor members of her own kindred, however intolerant it was in general, to herself it showed only its better side. Fanny had total freedom of movement, could travel as often as she pleased to Berlin, where the old Baltic Count Nesselrode claimed to have seen her frequently during those years, and at home continually increased the brilliance of her salon and widened the circle of her friends.

One of that circle of intimate friends who had dedicated their portraits and poetic tributes to her in 1793 had been Count Pergen, the chief of police. She could have no better advocate at court. Two years later Fanny was again presented with silhouettes by some of the guests in her house, including Count Neipperg, later the husband of Empress Marie-Louise, Counts Maruzzi, Wilohursky and Rosenberg, and the very rich councillor Braun, who was raised to the nobility soon afterwards and had lately become vice-director of the Hofburgtheater. Braun possessed the most beautiful pleasure gardens in the capital and ruined himself by his sumptuous festivities in honour of the Empress. This time, too, a dedication accompanied the present: 'Tout ce qui est fait par les mains des hommes est périssable, il n'y a que ces caractres [*sic*], que la main de l'Amitié trace dans un coeur reconnaissant, que les temps ne sauront pas détruire. Vienne, Octobre 10, 1795.'

The financier of the coalition, the amiable hostess were not in the end denied the privilege granted to every prosperous family: a house and garden on the outskirts of the city. Although the 'juifs de Frédéric le Grand', despite the prohibition in the old general regulation, were allowed to call such rural establishments their own – and not just the wealthy Daniel Itzig, but also a bookkeeper and philosopher like Moses Mendelssohn – the Jews in Vienna were most strictly forbidden to own any landed property. Since 1764 this very prohibition had been several times confirmed. Only indirectly, *mandatario nomine*, had such purchases been accomplished or rights of temporary possession established through tenancy contracts of many years' standing. Until her death Fanny resided in a rented mansion in the centre of the city. But, in 1794, outside the gates of Vienna, on the way to Schönbrunn, she and Nathan were able to acquire a property which extended from the height of the present Mariahilferstrasse as far as the river Wien, at that time not yet built up.

In the old land register it appears under the description 'About one-third vineyard', lying on the Braunhirschengrund 'behind, that is, under dwelling no. 1'. This house, a former summer palace of Archduchess Maria Christine, and its garden were extended in magnificent style by Fanny, in memory of her father's property at the Schlesisches Tor. Here she dwelt during the long, hot summers. Here, during the fine season, she received her friends and visiting foreign celebrities – such as, at the turn of the century, Lady Hamilton and Lord Nelson, then at the height of his fame.

Thus softly bedded in the most pleasant social life, the wife of a prosperous and influential man, the mother of a promising daughter, the intimate friend of many persons of nobility and intellect, mistress of the house in the Graben and of that in the Braunhirschengrund, she was struck by the first blow of fate: Prussia, to which she was devoted, in which she believed, withdrew from the coalition. When, on 5 April 1795, the – in her eyes – ignominious peace of Basle was concluded, she was for the first time ashamed of the country whose proud citizen she had become. The year was not yet over when a tragedy occurred which affected her even more deeply. A brilliant young man, her friend, perhaps her lover, was killed for her sake in a duel. It was the only truly shattering experience in an existence which, despite all inherited adversities, not yet overcome, seemed blessed with happiness.

-6-

The Third Solution

Dynasties change – the nobility survives. In the heyday of the monarchies in Europe there was hardly a state whose ruling house was not younger than the most distinguished of its subjects. When Francis of Lorraine came to Austria to unite in marriage with the daughter of the last German Habsburg, the Liechtensteins had been resident in Vienna for more than a thousand years. Faithful servants of the Babenbergs, they had, like the Trautmannsdorfs and Auerspergs, been ennobled. But the true ancestors of these 'Joinvilles and Montmorencys of Austria' were the brothers Heinrich and Ulrich Liechtenstein of the days of Frederick the Warlike. Heinrich had covered himself with glory in battle against the heathen Prussians, the Mongols and Hungarians for his Duke, had then ridden once more against the Hungarian King Bela for his royal ruler Przemysl Ottokar, and as an old man had won a victory over King Ottokar in the service of Rudolph of Habsburg – when no fewer than fourteen Trautmannsdorffs had fallen at his side.

On the death of Hartmann von Liechtenstein, about the middle of the sixteenth century, the third of his three sons, Gundacker, was given the rank of *Fürst* (prince), and became head of the house. Whether the Prince Liechtenstein who, together with Prince Eugene and the British ambassador of the time, was a frequent guest of Wolf Wertheimer – the son of Samson, who had rendered services to the court with the first Arnsteiner – was a descendant of Gundacker's line, is not known. If this were to be the case, it would have a certain historical piquancy. For young Carl Borromäus Johann Nepomuk, Prince Liechtenstein, who visited Fanny's house at the end of the same century, was a direct scion of Gundacker – a son of the brave Field-Marshal Carl Borromäus Joseph and of Princess Eleonore, née Öttingen-Spielberg, Emperor Joseph's beloved of long standing and a beautiful, proud woman, accustomed to commanding respect.

Eleonore, who had inherited a fortune from her maternal aunt, a Duchess of Guastalla, spent the first years of her marriage to the young Major-General Liechtenstein on her estates in Moravia and those of her husband in Lower Austria. Emperor Joseph, at that time already a sorrowing widower, noticed her for the first time when she went to his coronation in Frankfurt in 1764 as a lady-in-waiting. Brought up in a Strasburg convent, she had had a more thorough education than most of the titled young ladies of Austria and combined genuine charm with a lively, if conventional intelligence. In Maria Theresa's Vienna, favoured by the Empress as by her son, she immediately took up a privileged position in society. Her martial husband often left her on her own when the army required his services abroad. But Eleonore Liechtenstein was no Marschallin from Hofmannsthal's *Rosenkavalier*, consoling herself with noble boy-cousins. If she returned anyone's affections, it was those of the Emperor, although even this is by no means certain. In any case she was and remained his intimate friend, although she was unable to share Joseph's reforming spirit, but rather clung to the traditional, feudal-federalist forms of government and was prejudiced against the Enlightenment, against all unbelief as well as all excess of sensibility. 'I thank God,' she said in 1806, 'that I have never read the works of the seductive author [Rousseau]; my *abbé* always prevented me from doing so, he would sooner have allowed me Voltaire.'

Her son Carl, born in 1765, she enveloped in jealous love. An attractive young man of impressive stature, at eighteen he towered over his father by half a head and was at this age already becoming entangled in affairs with women. His first mistress was some eight years older than he, Anna Baldauf, whose father and brother were both hackney-coachmen and who was known as 'the lovely Nandel' and made famous by the painter Liotard as 'la belle chocolatière'. With his friend Carl Dietrichstein he used to visit her at her house in the suburbs; it was only when, urged by his parents, he broke off the relationship that the lovely Nandel turned to Dietrichstein. At nineteen Carl had already fought a duel, incurred debts and begun to lead the carefree life of the young nobility described around 1784 by the anonymous Berliner to his friend. 'Head and heart in the right place,' his mother lamented, 'but a weak character, a merry, happy-go-lucky fellow, irregular in his duties!' His father had destined him for a military career; Eleonore wanted him to dedicate himself to study and a civil career. As usual, she had her way. The young prince travelled with a tutor to Leipzig and Göttingen, attended lectures by famous scholars and then continued his educational tour through Germany and Holland and finally England. He returned a more manly, serious and quiet person. Emperor Joseph appointed him to an administrative post in Brussels, under the command of a Trautmannsdorff, between whose family and the Liechtensteins there was, of course, a long-standing connection. In November 1788 his father's serious illness finally recalled him to Vienna.

In those last years of Joseph's life, when the Emperor had recognised the fruitlessness of his efforts and was sinking more and more into melancholy, his only recreation was the society of five ladies of the highest nobility, whose small circle met three or four times a week. Around Eleonore there were gathered her own sister, Leopoldine, who was daughter-in-law to the chancellor, Kaunitz; two other sisters, Princesses Clary and Kinsky; and a relative, Princess Leopoldine Liechtenstein. In their simple everyday clothes they would sit at a round table, sewing and chatting, for all card games were outlawed. Apart from the Emperor, hardly any men were received; only Field-Marshal Lascy and the lord chamberlain Rosenberg were sometimes admitted. Here Joseph spent his happiest hours, occasionally expounding his already shattered plans for reform or expatiating in self-defence on newly issued laws. In doing so he would frequently encounter opposition to his enlightened regime. Nevertheless the five ladies were the comfort of his saddest days, and the words of farewell that he wrote to Eleonore from his deathbed were addressed to their whole circle.

With Joseph's death, Eleonore's star too was extinguished. Her own husband, by then a field-marshal, had already been snatched away in the spring by a putrid fever which had taken hold of him during the Turkish campaign. In January 1790, a month before she lost her imperial friend as well, young Carl had caused her an unexpected sorrow. Against her will he married Countess Anna Khevenhüller, a delicate, sensitive, but spiritless young creature. The wedding had shaken his mother so severely that she became ill and kept to her room. She had prevailed only in one respect: Carl and his wife were to continue for a while to live in her town mansion, which had devolved upon herself and the field-marshal, as the younger son of the reigning Prince Emmanuel von Liechtenstein. In October of the same year, young Princess 'Nani' gave birth to a son, who was also named Carl. Her pleasing manner had meanwhile won her Eleonore's sympathy. But to the same degree that the inclination between her and his mother was growing, Prince Carl had begun to turn away from his amiable, but slightly tedious wife.

The date of Carl's first appearance at Fanny's salon is unknown. His name is associated with hers as early as the summer of 1790, about the time that Emperor Leopold had announced a new edict concerning the Jews which was more favourable to the tolerated individuals. It seems that it was a 'Prince Liechtenstein, an acquaintance of Baron Arnstein' who had conveyed the preceding petition of the community for more lenient provisions 'directly to His Majesty, in the name of the local Jewry'. If this was the case, then history again repeats itself here. For, just like the *'aimable imprudent'* who had interceded on behalf of the Jews under Joseph, their new spokesman occupied a post in the imperial cabinet office, indeed he had been appointed its director by Joseph. As Joseph did with Günther, Leopold went for walks with young Carl, confided secret plans to him and in every way expressed his favour towards him. Eleonore, his mother, was also invited to court again, but she was resentful because she no longer enjoyed any special privileges, but was 'treated like any other princess'. The other four ladies of her circle were no less indignant over the same neglect.

Carl and his younger brother Wenzel, an intelligent but frivolous person who had been destined for holy orders, must already have been making frequent visits to Fanny that summer, for in July Eleonore wrote complainingly to her daughter Josephine: 'Carl and Wenzel often visit the Arnstein house and it seems that that is where they acquire the abominable principles, the dandyism and self-importance that I loathe so much.' The abominable principles or exaggerated marks of honour which were conferred upon them at the Arnsteins' were probably not the only motives that persuaded the sons of ancient houses to seek out their company. Here one could listen to free speech and good music, converse about writers – including those with rebellious or progressive leanings – without being prevented by an *abbé*, meet interesting foreigners, artists and scholars, such as were never admitted among the high nobility, and pass one's time in a far more exciting manner than in the stiff and silent atmosphere at home.

Like others of their class in Berlin, the young aristocrats of Vienna found this kind of salon simply irresistible. Wilhelm von Humboldt had sometimes headed his letters from his parents' house 'Schloss Langeweile' (Castle Boredom). There were such castles in Austria too. Above all, however, they were received by a hostess who, though no longer in her first bloom of youth, was at the height of her powers of attraction, spoke fluently and stylishly, 'played the piano charmingly', sang delightfully, was well-read and well-travelled and was always opening new windows to a world which one had never known or with which one had not maintained any connection.

Had anything more than a friendly flirtation taken place between Fanny and Carl Liechtenstein? Viennese society might not have been of that opinion, otherwise it would not have behaved with such tolerance towards Fanny after the tragic end of this relationship. The biographer of his mother Eleonore who, two generations later, relied on family correspondence and documents, also decisively rejected this notion. And yet we are forced to believe in a more intimate relationship. It was not a time when tender inclinations were wont to be nipped in the bud. People had not learned to exercise restraint when they felt a powerful attraction. In Vienna, the manners that had prevailed since the days of Aeneas Silvius, the fifteenth-century scholar who became Pope under the name of Pius II, had become more refined by the graceful amorality of the Rococo era, but had by no means improved. In the more prudish Prussia, long-preserved inhibitions were now giving way to that impulse towards free love which the Romantics were beginning to preach and practise. Fanny could not regard as forbidden what was happening around her every day. Moreover her marriage, though happy, was not sustained by passion, Henriette was and remained her only child, and the portly, cheerful Nathan had probably for some years been seeking respite from the high tone of his wife's salon in the arms of Madame Ettlinger, or of some other equally well-rounded and intellectually unpretentious Viennese beauty.

We seek what we ourselves are not or do not possess: clever wives wish for handsome young men, their husbands a pliant, undemanding female, and young gentlemen from old, exclusive families an unprejudiced lady-love. Carl, whose first mistress, the lovely Nandel, had been eight years older than he and who lived in a constantly changing relationship of admiration and rebellion with that impressive lady, his mother, with his tendency towards charming recklessness and amiable weakness, found his counterpart not in the gentle little Nani Khevenhüller, but in women of greater impact and maturity.

And how, if some violent emotion had not erupted into her world of noble thoughts, moralising phrases and playful epigrams, are we to explain the presence of a poem in Fanny's notebook, transcribed in English, that has the effect of a sudden cry of pain?

My life my soul my all that
heaven can give
Death is life with thee, and
without thee 'tis Death to
Live.

How, finally, are we to interpret those long and burning verses
of love which appear a page earlier, in an unknown handwriting –
verses of such a revealing and prophetic nature that one cannot but
quote them here?

D'une volupté pure
tes yeux sont le tableau
Non, jamais la nature
N'a rien fait de si beau

Cette nuit, dans un songe
caressant tes appas
Heureux par ce mensonge
Je mourois dans tes bras.

Toi que mon coeur adore!
ah! Reviens sur ce coeur!
Viens, jouissons encore,
Mourons d'un vrai bonheur.

Ce rêve, cette ivresse
c'est le feu du désir;
O ma belle Maitresse!
C'est l'instant du plaisir.

A ta bouche charmante
Ma bouche veut s'unir;
Et mon âme brulante
N'a plus qu'un seul désir:

Te voir, t'aimer, te plaire,
T'adorer, t'attendrir;
A l'ombre du mystère
Être heureux – puis mourir.

Around 1791, Carl von Liechtenstein had been a frequent guest
at the Arnsteins'. Four years later came the disaster whose innocent
and involuntary originator was his hostess.

A certain young Baron Weichs, the Canon of Osnabrück, had
become one of the circle of her admirers. One evening, as related in
a report published in Fanny's lifetime, the Canon wished to escort
her to the Italian opera, when Prince Carl, who was 'not only
highly esteemed, but also loved' by her, entered her house.

Prince Carl tried to force Herr von Weichs away from the beautiful
woman's side. There followed a short but violent exchange of words,
which von Weichs brought to a conclusion by a blow to the face. This

action passed almost unobserved, and Prince Carl would have suffered it in silence in order not to attract more attention. On the following morning Baron von Weichs sent him a note offering to shake his hand in reconciliation. The Canon could not be accused of cowardice, for, like his father, he was a bold and fearless hunter and at the same time an excellent swordsman. In this respect he had the advantage of his opponent. Prince Carl asked his brother, Canon Moriz [*sic!*] von Liechtenstein, for advice. The latter, a man compounded of rashness and lack of foresight, suggested that his brother should invite von Weichs to breakfast at the young Count Rosenberg's and settle the matter there.

Von Weichs accordingly received an invitation from Count Rosenberg. The two gentlemen made their appearance, and with them Moriz von Liechtenstein. After breakfast had been taken, the parties stated their positions. Moriz was pressing in demanding a duel, to take place immediately in the rooms of Count Rosenberg. In vain Canon von Weichs argued that the place was too cramped; after breakfast one was not in the mood for a duel, and with a full stomach the slightest wound could be fatal. He added that the Prince should choose pistols, for with the sword he was superior to him in both strength and skill. Prince Carl seemed to agree. Meanwhile the Baron once more offered him his hand in reconciliation. But the two seconds, Moriz von Liechtenstein and Count Rosenberg, insisted on an immediate duel. The Canon was really not a little embarrassed; he was a stranger in the salon of the Count, who wanted to be his second, and yet was a near relative of his opponent. Moriz von Liechtenstein was to be his brother's second – how easily could treachery occur! This thought was indeed bound to weigh on his mind, since nothing had been said in the note about a duel.

What should he, what must he do? The seconds were making preparations on the spot. The light was evenly placed, and now they stepped to the combatants' sides. The Canon kept his head, and although Prince Liechtenstein swiftly thrust at him, he parried with cold presence of mind, and gave him a slight wound on the arm. 'That is nothing!' cried the second, and against the rules of duelling demanded a second bout. Prince Liechtenstein made another, very animated attack. At the second thrust, in quarte over the arm, the Canon parried in tierce, and again in tierce he pierced at the same time through the heart of the unfortunate Prince. He sank to the ground, for his lung had been hit. In haste he was carried home. What a sight for his wife, who although neglected by him, nevertheless loved him deeply.

It was Wenzel, 'l'Abbé Monstre' as he was known, whose foolish urging had put his brother in this mortal danger. But if the unknown writer has erred over his name, his account corresponds in all other respects with a document of 9 December 1795 in which the Prussian ambassador in Vienna, Marquis Lucchesini, reported the matter to Frederick William II:

Prince Carl von Liechtenstein, whom Your Majesty knew at Pillnitz, in the entourage of the late Emperor Leopold, came into dispute over an affair of the heart with a young canon of Osnabrück, Baron von Weichs, son of the chief master of hounds of the Elector of Cologne. The matter was managed with no great prudence by the Prince's brother and a young Count von Rosenberg, who had knowledge of it, and yesterday, towards eleven in the morning, a duel with sabres took place in the rooms of the said Count Rosenberg. Prince von Liechtenstein, violently excited, had the misfortune to receive a wound between the fifth and sixth ribs, which forthwith was seen to be fatal, since his opponent's dagger had penetrated four or five inches into his body toward the lungs . . . The misfortune has become a subject of regret for all classes of the population of Vienna, who are very willing to make allowances for the Prince's affairs of the heart. His opponent has been arrested this morning, quite nearby, and the two seconds, whose imprudence is partly to blame for the misfortune, Canon Wenzel von Liechtenstein and Count Rosenberg, have likewise been taken into custody.

The guilty men escaped heavy sentences. The Elector of Cologne immediately interceded with the Emperor on behalf of the son of his chief master of hounds, entreating him to moderate the sentence of confinement in a fortress imposed upon Weichs by the Austrian appeal court. After all, Weichs had already been punished enough for his 'misdeed arising from youthful indiscretion and impetuousness through the loss of his benefice and the execution of a severe verdict'. It was above all for his father's sake that the Elector hoped for Francis's indulgence. In October 1796 the Canon's sentence was reduced from eight to two years. Count von Rosenberg had to remain only another six months in the fortress and Prince Wenzel was banished to Graz for a year. Thereafter, the monstrous *abbé*, in the words of a memoirist of the time:

> after he had proved his remorse, was taken back into favour. He resigned from his order, became a Knight of Malta and finally died as an Austrian lieutenant-general. He possessed the cross of the order of Maria Theresa, and despite the hardly commendable start to his career, despite his renown as a *roué*, he died a good Christian after all at the age of eighty-two, mourned by his friends and by many others. It was his aged mistress who converted him. In the mode of expression peculiar to him, he once asked his cousin: 'Have you not confessed your sins for a long time? Believe me, confess, for it is a great pleasure to do so.'

Carl von Liechtenstein, however, was beyond help. He died sixteen days after the duel, and on 24 December the register of deaths for the city of Vienna recorded as follows: 'Deceased, His Princely Grace the Honourable Carl, Prince of the Holy Roman Empire *von und zu* Liechtenstein von Nikolspurg, Duke of Troppau, imperial and royal chamberlain, then lord of the Moravian estate of Krumau, and so forth, in Vienna, thirty years of age, in the house of Carl Baron von Wetzlar, at number 82 Teinfaltstrasse, of a wound.' How Fanny received the tragedy is described in detail by Varnhagen:

> The incident caused an uproar throughout Vienna; the most distinguished and powerful families took an interest in it. But the woman who had quite innocently become the occasion for this misfortune, and was deeply affected by it, encountered on all sides the profoundest sympathy and consolation; court and city vied to pay their respects to her; the most unequivocal tributes were paid to the magnanimity, high-mindedness and self-denial with which she had conducted the whole relationship. She could therefore surrender wholeheartedly and without misgivings to the tragic experience from which, it is said, she never recovered for the rest of her life. Everyone found her sorrow just and beautiful, and she could grieve without shame for the man who had sacrificed his life as her knight. We remember having read in the travel memoirs of an Englishman, whose book, however, is not to hand, that Frau von Arnstein always commemorated the day of Prince von Liechtenstein's death by silent mourning, and that she locked herself into a black cabinet which was entirely dedicated to the memory of the deceased, and in which, at other times too, it was her habit to spend many an hour in meditative contemplation and retirement. No one has ever been able to boast of having seen this cabinet; but the story was, to be sure, very widespread, and was generally taken to be well-founded.

It was left to Eleonore Liechtenstein's biographer to cast an ugly shadow over this romance of medieval melancholy. Following a letter from the dowager Princess, which, however, is not quoted verbatim, Nathan is said to have demanded of Carl's widow the redemption of bills to the value of 40,000 gulden, although he had advanced him only 10,000. The Emperor himself is said to have summoned Arnstein to his presence and rebuked him in the severest manner on account of his usury. This assertion, however – like the decisively expressed view that 'there had been no question of a love affair' – is neither believable nor historically authenticated.

The biographer, it is true, did not dare to tarnish Fanny's reputation. No one, he expressly writes, had uttered even the mildest suggestion of guilt against her, indeed, she 'continued to be the object of respect from all sides'. But his, or the Princess's, complaint against Nathan appears no less unthinkable. Not only is there no record of any similar behaviour on Nathan's part, not only, bearing in mind his well-known good nature, would it have been quite uncharacteristic for him to have revenged himself on a deceased rival in such a base and transparent manner – but the Emperor, had such an act of infamy reached his ears, would certainly not have ennobled its author within the year. And on no account, only a few months after this expression of his favour, would he, 'in consideration of the truly noble manners, understanding, virtues and many praiseworthy qualities for the possession of which our dear and faithful wholesale merchant Nathan Adam Arnsteiner is commended', have made him a *Freiherr* of his hereditary lands and of the Holy Roman Empire.

To the private sorrow to which all those concerned in the misfortune abandoned themselves during that winter was added the general anxiety about the disturbing progress of the war. In Paris, Robespierre's despotic rule had broken down, the men of Thermidor had triumphed, and the Directory had been founded. But the French fought on, indeed, after an invasion of England had been considered and abandoned, they threw themselves with all their might into conflict with Austria. In northern Italy, still distant from Vienna, but within the Emperor's administrative domain in Lombardy, the two armies clashed. Young General Bonaparte, who was now for the first time being talked about outside France, was victorious at Lodi. Meanwhile the Austrian supreme command had devolved upon the brave Archduke Karl. He found himself ranged against a hostile and superior strength, in the face of which, in the current state of armaments, he was a helpless victim.

The French had been able to set up eleven divisions, and, while Napoleon stood firm in Italy, had allowed two Rhine armies under Generals Jourdan and Moreau to advance towards Bohemia and Bavaria. In order to oppose to these massed troops even an approximately equal military force, volunteers from all sections of the population were needed. While still in the reign of Leopold, Carl Liechtenstein, as the leader of his cabinet, in collaboration with the appeal judge von Fillenbaum and three patriotic citizens, had established such a corps, which had distinguished itself in the first Rhine campaigns under the name of Österreichisch-Wurmsersches Freycorps. In this spring of 1796 the Jewry of Vienna too played their part in supporting this corps. Further volunteer corps were now recruited in great numbers by Counts Wenzel Paar and Franz Hugo von Salm. From the state they received only their weapons, while all necessary funds were provided by the citizenry.

All this anti-French activity, in which the tolerated Jews of Vienna eagerly took part, was, to Fanny's distress and shame, alien to her family in Berlin. There it had become the correct thing to resign oneself to the King's conclusion of peace with the revolutionary army. Indeed, after the agreement of Basle, her own brother, Isaac Daniel, with the approval of Frederick William, had been responsible for substantial deliveries to the army in France, including 10,000 horses for the army of Sambre and Maas. But the continual devaluation of currency under the Directory not only destroyed Isaac's expected profit, but plunged him into ruin. We can guess with what feelings Fanny, in March of that year, learnt of the insolvency of Itzig and Co. Anger and distress over her brother's irresponsibility were mingled with the painful satisfaction of knowing that his help towards the enemy had received such a poor reward. Her old father, who had already retired from business, immediately waived all his claims against Isaac and his younger brother Benjamin, who shared his responsibility, and, moreover, made available to them a sufficient sum to pay off their staff and minor creditors. Fanny, in the prevailing circumstances, was not prepared to make similar sacrifices.

Isaac Daniel's liabilities, at the unfavourable moment when he was obliged to declare himself bankrupt, came to some 900,000 thalers, of which 620,000 represented his French debt. Also among his major creditors was the firm of Arnsteiner & Compagnie with some 130,000 thalers. That Nathan totally rejected a settlement, indeed that he impounded his brother-in-law's French claims, must at first appear strange. Certainly he was at this point no longer entirely his own master, but had to submit to the advice of his partners, above all that of the shrewd and circumspect Eskeles. On the other hand, if it had suited him to spare his wife's brother, he would undoubtedly have got his own way. The truth is that it did not suit him. The good-natured man, who was in other respects not to be reproached for a lack of family feeling, had other reasons for his action than simply ruthless business sense. A true servant of Austria, he considered his brother-in-law's dealings with France to be contemptible. Eight years earlier Isaac had joined with him in raising a war loan for the battle against the Turks. This time he had supported the enemy. Loyalty to the state was now loosening even the closest family bonds. Even Fanny raised no objection – she declined to use her power over her usually submissive spouse and gave her unfortunate sibling no comfort in his desperate situation.

Isaac's bankruptcy proceedings were protracted; by 1811 they had still not been concluded. Napoleon, to whom an appeal was later made for an appropriate payment of the French debt, roundly dismissed the request. This may have been a further reason for

Fanny's burning hatred of the prospective Consul and Emperor. For gradually, when her anger against Isaac Daniel had died down, pity for him began to take the upper hand. In her next wills she again referred to her 'beloved elder brother'. In Berlin, incidentally, no punitive action had been taken against the bankrupt. He had, as was recognised, become a victim of the 'fallen rate of exchange which was to be considered as a *force majeure*', and his collapse was looked upon as a misfortune, rather than as his own fault.

Isaac, the *Hofbaurat* (building adviser by royal appointment), who had flung his whole business and private income into the bankrupt estate, became totally impoverished, lost his house and land and died, a broken man, in 1806. After his death, his three sons were brought up in Berlin in the house of their aunt, Madame Levy. The eldest, Moritz, was a pupil of the philosopher Fichte, who took a personal interest in his education in philosophy and political science. When, in 1812, a seminary on Pestalozzian lines was founded on Fichte's initiative, Moritz was its most zealous pupil. Soon afterwards, with his younger brother, he joined the first Prussian volunteers as a fusilier in the third battalion of the second regiment of Guards. On 2 May 1813, at Lützen, where his brother was also wounded, his right leg was shattered by canister-shot. He died eleven days later. Whatever mistakes could be charged to his father's account, this young freedom-fighter had atoned for them.

However feverishly the Austrians were arming, the great decisions were not to be made until the following year of 1797. But by the winter the situation was already becoming dangerous. Mantua fell in February, and the first Viennese volunteer corps put up a good show in all its futile attempts to relieve the city. Now Napoleon, against the Directory's instructions, decided not to march on Rome, but first to make peace with the Pope, and advanced northwards, across the rivers Piave and Tagliamento. Archduke Karl, who had defeated Moreau's army at Würzburg in the spring, had hastened to the Italian front from the Rhine, but he found only the debris of an Austrian army. 'Until now,' said Bonaparte to his soldiers, 'I have always met armies without commanders, but now I meet a commander without an army.' The general won a swift and easy victory. He crossed the Alpine passes and marched as far as Judenburg and Leoben.

Vienna was up in arms. Schools and banks were closed and some, more faint-hearted than others, left the city. All foreigners

were 'got rid of'. Even some of the imperial family betook themselves to Prague. Count Saurau, now prime minister, and Duke
Ferdinand of Württemberg, the new lord lieutenant of the city,
called the populace to a levy *en masse*. On 11 April 1,000 students
and over 7,000 volunteers were mustered in brightly coloured
uniforms in front of the imperial couple. Two days later 730,000
men had already reported, but there were nowhere near enough
weapons for them all. On 17 April, a date which henceforth
became a public holiday, the ceremonial presentation of colours of
the citizens' regiments took place all along the bastions of the city,
from the Schottentor to the Stubentor. They swore the oath of
allegiance, a military mass was held and they then proceeded in
splendid formation to the outskirts of Nussdorf. The citizens of
Vienna, normally not particularly belligerent, shouted themselves
hoarse. It was as if they were swimming in a sea of patriotic
emotion.

Nor did the tolerated Jews remain in the background. Three days
before the volunteers' parade on the Glacis with banners brandished
aloft, their representatives and committee members, among them
Nathan Arnstein, had gone to Count Saurau and given guarantees
of their assistance in supporting the levy. The total levy fund had
been fixed at 300,000 gulden. No less than 90,000 gulden, a tenth of
which was personally supplied by Nathan alone, had been raised by
the tolerated Jews. In the engraving by Ignaz Joseph Wertheim
which immortalises the *Rivalry of the Viennese Jewry*, Eskeles, and
behind him Arnstein, can be recognised to the right of the scribe.
One individual member of this deputation is still depicted with a
beard and long caftan. All the others appear quite assimilated to
their compatriots in their outer clothing.

The students and young citizens were marching, the people
rejoicing, the Jews bearing the cost, colours were brandished,
uniforms glittered – and next day, it was all over! Napoleon, three
days' march away from Vienna, had decided to break off his
triumphal procession there. 'I was playing vingt-et-un and stopped
at twenty,' he later remarked to Madame de Rémusat. On 18 April
he signed a preliminary peace treaty at Leoben. Two weeks later
the levy of eighteen battalions and two squadrons returned to
Vienna, giving occasion for yet another brilliant parade, commem-
orative medals for all the volunteers and the ceremonial bestowal of
the freedom of the city on Count Saurau and the Duke of
Württemberg. The Viennese were well pleased with such a bloodless but honourable way of conducting a war. They greeted peace
with a similar sense of relief. It was not yet clear at what price it

would be granted them, but they wanted it at any price.

'My despair is complete,' wrote Thugut, the Austrian minister for foreign affairs, 'at the insane rejoicing of the Viennese over the simple word peace. No one asks whether the conditions are good or bad. No one cares about the honour of the monarchy and what has become of it in the course of ten years. They only think of dashing off to a ball or eating roast chicken. In this mood, how can one offer any resistance to the energy of a Bonaparte, who undertakes any hazard with cheerfulness? Only peace, peace.'

The summer was hot. It would be a good year for wine. In the autumn, when the longed-for peace agreement was signed at the castle of Campo Formio near Udine, the Viennese had long been ensconced in their *Heurigen* taverns, caring but little for its actual content. All Belgium and Lombardy were lost to Austria, in exchange for which she acquired Venice as far as the river Adige, Dalmatia and Albania. But more than this, she agreed to the final transfer of the region on the left bank of the Rhine to France, which Prussia had already conceded.

When the foundation of the 'cisrhenian' republic was celebrated in Bonn at the end of the year, the triumphal procession marched to the Jewish quarter and the wooden gate, which had been left ostentatiously closed, was broken down by carpenters with axes. The crowd shouted in acclamation and 'kissed the female members of the subjugated people, insofar as they were young and beautiful'. This symbolic liberation made not the slightest impression on the tolerated Jews of Vienna. In concert with their fellow-citizens they sang the words of the new hymn written by Haschka and set to music by Haydn: 'Gott erhalte Franz den Kaiser' (God preserve Francis the Emperor). And some, the most prosperous and powerful among them, were rewarded by the Emperor for their loyalty.

In November 1797, Francis wrote to Count Lazansky that he wished, 'in order to give a sufficient token of my favour and satisfaction to N. Arnsteiner and his two partners Salomon Herz and Bernhard Eskeles for their zealous services rendered to my exchequer with such great exertions in these troubled times, to raise them all to the nobility of my hereditary lands, with remission of taxes.' Herz and Eskeles received their patents of nobility; Nathan's was not made out until four months later. In April 1798, as the Emperor had recently informed Lazansky, he had, 'out of patriotic feelings, donated to the superannuation fund a four-percent promissory note for 10,000 gulden' and 'for this praiseworthy action' he was now to receive the title of *Freiherr* or baron.

The three partners in the firm of Arnsteiner were not the first unbaptised Jews to be elevated to the nobility. Two of the three Hönig brothers had converted and were now known as von Bienenfeld and von Hönickstein or Henikstein; the third retained his faith, despite which Joseph made him a privy councillor and in 1789 graced him with the title of von Hönigsberg. Three grandsons of Samson Wertheimer's were also, without changing their religion, allowed to call themselves von Wertheimer or von Wertheimstein. Further cases followed. But all these men had at best been given the rank of *Edler* (nobleman). Nathan Arnstein was the first Jewish baron in Austria.

When, six years earlier, his long-converted brother had applied for the same honour, Hofrat Greiner had stressed in a letter to the privy state chancery 'that Joseph Michael . . . for his own person possesses no special credit, but his father has rendered many beneficial services as court agent to the imperial house, and his brother Nathan Arnsteiner, as a partner in the contracting company continues them in a praiseworthy manner; in consideration of which no further objection will be made to the above-mentioned request'. Joseph Michael, then, had, as it were, obtained the title of *Freiherr* through Nathan's good graces. Nathan himself was granted it on the grounds of his special achievements. His patent of nobility is too splendidly redolent of the atmosphere of that time and of the last breath of the dying Holy Roman Empire for us to refrain from quoting large portions of it here:

We Francis II, by God's grace elected Holy Roman Emperor, at all times augmenter of the realm, King in Germany, of Hungary, Bohemia, Dalmatia, Croatia, Slavonia, Galicia, Lodomeria and Jerusalem, Archduke of Austria, Duke of Burgundy, Lorraine, of Styria, of Carinthia and Carniola, Grand Duke of Tuscany, Grand Duke of Transylvania, Margrave of Moravia, Duke of Brabant, of Limburg, of Lutzenburg [Luxembourg] and of Guelderland, of Württemberg, of Upper and Lower Silesia, of Milan, of Mantua, of Parma, Florence, Guastalla, Auschwitz and Zator, of Calabria, of Bar, of Montferrat and of Teschen, Prince of Swabia and of Charleville, Princely Count of Habsburg, of Flanders, of Tyrol, of Hainault, of Kiburg, of Gorizia and of Gradiska, Margrave of the Holy Roman Empire, of Burgau, of Upper and Lower Lusatia, of Pont-à-Mousson and of Nomeny, Count of Namur, of Provence, of Vaudemont, of Blankenburg, of Zütpfen, of Saarwerden, of Salm and of Falkenstein, of the Wendish Mark and of Mechlin;
Acknowledge publicly by this letter, and make known to all men: Albeit we, in our royal and archducal majesty and honour, in which the

Almighty according to His divine will has placed and established us, and out of our own inborn kindness and benevolence, are inclined at all times to consider and to encourage the honour and usefulness of each and every one of Our loyal and well-conducted subjects, and to bestow upon them and furnish the same with particular favours, advantages and privileges, yet our mind is in justice more inclined and desirous to impart Our royal and archducal favour, and to bestow more numerous honours and privileges, to and upon those whose forebears and they themselves, besides their worthy descent, conduct themselves virtuously and laudably, and have proved themselves loyal and zealous at all times toward Us and Our royal and archducal house in steadfast and submissive devotion and untiring service.

Having now graciously considered, observed and contemplated the truly noble manners, understanding, virtues, skill and the many praiseworthy qualities with which Our dear and loyal merchant Nathan Adam Arnsteiner is renowned to be gifted, and particularly having taken into consideration that from his youth he has devoted himself to business, and thereby, by means of his established wholesale house, supported the manufactories of the hereditary dominions, promoted export trade, and thereby sedulously endeavoured to diminish the outflow of money abroad and to increase the influx of foreign money, indeed often, by sacrificing a part of his own income, to afford assistance to the common good, for which zealous and excellent services which he rendered with so much exertion to Our most noble exchequer in the troublesome times of war, We had already resolved to raise him to the nobility, while he continued further in his patriotic sympathies, and many times rendered particularly excellent services to Our most noble exchequer as well as to the state, and made sacrifices, and thereby heaped up such deserts as give him just claims upon the gratitude of the state: . . .

Therefore We, on account of these considerations and reasons here given, have been moved spontaneously, in confirmation of Our highest goodwill, after mature reflection, on good advice and right knowledge, and also on royal and archducal authority, graciously to raise and to honour the said Nathan Adam von Arnsteiner together with all his legitimate heirs and their heirs and heirs' heirs of the male and female sexes, for ever and ever, as long as any of their descendants shall be in existence or still living, to the rank, honour and dignity of *Freiherren* and *Freiinnen* of our hereditary kingdom, principality and dominions, and also to add, associate and reconcile those persons of the rank of *Freiherr* of our hereditary kingdom, principality and dominions to the company and community of others of the Holy Roman Empire.

Nathan and his heirs are then granted the right 'to be honoured, described and considered as *wohlgeboren* [esquires] in such a manner as though they, like others of the Holy Roman Empire, had also issued and descended from *Freiherren* and *Freiinnen*, of paternal or maternal stock, of our hereditary kingdom, principality and dominions'. In other respects they shall be 'capable of partaking in each and every favour, freedom, privilege, old tradition and custom, right and justice, and likewise honourable appointments', and everywhere 'have a residence befitting the rank of a lord'. The document goes on to permit the arms of the Freiherren von Arnstein to include on the shield, half gold and half blue – apart from an anchor, two buffalo horns and the coronet of a *Freiherr* surmounted by three golden jousting-helmets – the imperial eagle, and these arms from now on they

> can and may use and enjoy at all future times, in each and every affair, business and dealing, [. . .] in attacks, battles, disputes, conflicts, tournaments, jousting, fencing, tilting, campaigns, banners, facings of tents, seals, signets, jewels, burials, paintings and otherwise in all places and for all purposes according to their honour, necessity, will and good pleasure.

Anyone, however, who did not recognise this new dignity of the Arnsteins' was to encounter 'Our heavy sentence and disfavour and thereto a penalty of one hundred marks of gold in full weight'. Given in Vienna, 'on the fourteenth day of the month of April in the seventeen-hundred-and-ninety-sixth year after the gracious birth of Christ, our dear Lord and Saviour, the sixth of our Holy Roman Empire and the seventh of our hereditary lands. Francis.'

With due formality the Arnsteins were not merely incorporated into the bourgeoisie as in Prussia, but received into the *Freiherren*. They had thereby gained more, and at the same time fewer rights than their relatives in Berlin. All possible favours, freedoms and privileges had become theirs, yet, as with their fellow-believers, they were still subject to the special laws relating to tolerated Jews. They were allowed to display their arms on their tents in attacks and battles, in jousts and tournaments, but they were still forbidden to own a house in the inner city. How the contradictory ordinances overlapped and interlocked, what was granted in one place and forbidden in another, what one was here commanded to do and there excused from doing, can now hardly be established. Probably it was never clear, and in each case left to the benevolent or malicious discretion with which officialdom translates imprecise instructions into reality. The Arnsteins probably knew how to employ a degree of tact in staying within their limits, by not claiming any privileges for themselves that were incompatible with the situation of the other tolerated Jews, and by not demanding a fine of 'one hundred marks of gold in full weight' every time a butcher's boy shouted abuse at them.

Shortly before his elevation to the nobility, the office in charge of Jewish affairs, as was usual at certain intervals, had drawn up an official account of Nathan's household. It is to this list that we owe the information available about Nathan's family and domestic servants at the turn of the century. Fifty years earlier Eleonore Arnsteiner had kept a staff of eighteen domestics, quite apart from the business staff in the house. Nathan had need of only thirteen, nine of whom lived under his own roof. But even with only a valet, lady's maid, housekeeper, cook, English governess, two house-maids, a kitchenmaid, two footmen, two coachmen and a stable-boy called Lazarus Abraham, one could run quite a grand house. At the time of that census it was still in the Graben. Soon afterwards Nathan and Fanny seem to have transferred their city residence, for in the business almanac for 1799 his address is given as 34, Herren-gasse – the Palais Wilczek. In any case, the interval before the next war could be passed pleasantly enough. The Congress which was to determine the peace of the realm was meeting in Rastatt. This peace was already being called a 'proclamation of the new war'. But as long as the Congress was sitting, no shots were being fired, and as long as there was no shooting, the situation was not serious. The Viennese saw no reason to restrict their entertainments. In the Arnstein house, as a traveller remarked in 1798, there was a ball every two weeks, where 'the guests were too many for the place'.

A reception of this period is described in the memoirs of Emilie Weckbecker. Her mother Caton, one of Fanny's first women friends in Vienna, had already died. But the imperial councillor Obermayer took his twelve-year-old daughter to an evening en-tertainment given by the Duke of Württemberg together with the banker Bienenfeld. The prologue to this reception is noteworthy. The Duke, who was still lord lieutenant of Vienna, was continually in debt. In order to return the compliment to the Turkish ambassa-dor extraordinary, who had been his host on a previous occasion, he sent an adjutant to his friend Adam von Bienenfeld to request the use of 'your house, your rooms, your servants'. When the banker responded by placing the first floor of his house in the Obere Bräunerstrasse at his disposal, the Duke invited all the generals of the army and the *corps diplomatique* to the soirée. In addition, Bienenfeld invited several gentlemen from the state chancery and the eight pupils of the Academy for Oriental Lan-guages, and his daughter Therese invited the ladies – including Countesses Lodron, Wratislaw and Petrasch and Baroness Wetzlar.

Some appeared in Turkish costume; even little Emilie had been dressed up in white trousers, a caftan in dark blue silk and a fez with a diamond-trimmed aigrette. The Pasha, glittering in Oriental splendour, played chess with the Duke. Emilie was allowed to pass him his *chibouk*, a Turkish pipe. Then the entertainments began.

> Countess Petrasch danced a shawl dance, and I was to have danced Alcina's solo; but before this, when the Duke made a clumsy move at chess, the ambassador intentionally gave the chess table a push, so that all the pieces were knocked out of place; he rose, and so everyone rose with him. Now refreshments were served in crystal cups and gold and silver dishes, and the event ended in everyone's driving to Fanny Arnstein's, where a late soirée was being held for the ambassador.

The haste with which the Viennese had returned to their dancing and feasting, to the festivities of more peaceful days, again infuriated the other visitors from the German states whose hopes of redress against French supremacy in Europe depended on an all-German moral–political purge. Prussia and her north German allies had, it is true, been the first to lay down their weapons. But these Viennese were so loud in their pleasures that they did not hear the hidden trumpets calling them to a patriotic uprising. To his annoyance, Ernst Moritz Arndt, who visited the capital in 1798, made these observations: 'Everyone enjoys lavishly whatever his income and his stomach can bear, cares neither for his neighbour nor for the whole world, and is hardly to be distracted from his glass of wine, roast chicken or capon when an unexpected uproar breaks out.' Like the worthy Nicolai, he was shaken by Protestant disgust against the soft, sugary way of life in this city, where even *abbés* 'paraded in petticoats, with beautifully dressed hair and red stockings', where thousands idolatrously knelt before an image 'that would startle the very swine', and where censorship and police wielded such unquestioned power that a general 'pasting-over of the eyes' and 'boarding-up of the forehead' had taken place.

In his vigorous language, reminiscent of Luther's, Arndt lamented Vienna's relapse into her old indolence. Joseph had been on the road to 'doing something good', and even if not everything could be wonderful under him, there was still much under way; but with him, most of it sank back into nothing and night. His successors did not wish to 'renew the battle with the Hydra to which he succumbed', and the repressive influence of Cardinal Migazzi, censorship and the Pope came into their own again: 'Perhaps they have frightened the Regent with ghosts of the revolution and the overthrow of all the old systems. Certainly there are many who, moved by the spirit of the time and illuminated by that spark of light that was spread abroad by Joseph, think more freely and boldly, but they may not speak freely and boldly.' So nothing remained but 'to see revealed before all eyes the most monstrous superstition, the most childish foolery in the capital city of Germany, and at the end of the eighteenth century.'

C. G. Küttner, who travelled to Vienna at the same time, was more kindly in his disposition towards Vienna. In spite of everything, one could now buy *Phaedon*, which was not to be had eighteen years ago, with as little difficulty as Mendelssohn's other philosophical writings, or Kant's *Critique of Pure Reason*. As for Francis's rule, which according to Arndt sees its task only as 'a clever leading by the nose', a 'lulling to sleep of the noblest powers', Küttner has little objection to it. The Emperor was 'exceptionally popular, while the bitterness of the Viennese against the French and even against the Prussians is great'. Although in recent years 'the aristocracy and the clergy, two institutions against which Joseph battled with all his might, are noticeably in power again', at least non-Catholics are not excluded from any civic rights. For example, a man called Meissner, a Protestant and a foreigner, is a professor in Prague, 'Baron von Arnsteiner, a Jew, occupies a public office [?], and another Jew is a cabinet councillor. A few years ago, they very nearly made the Jew Henik into an Austrian landed gentleman (for this too is permitted by law), because he is a considerable and at the same time highly esteemed lord of a manor.'

If Küttner errs in some respects, his description of balls and masquerades, of dancing entertainments in the dance-halls known as *Zur Mehlgrube* and 'New World', of sleigh-rides and receptions in great houses, which took place between and, indeed, probably during the coalition wars, corresponds to reality. The treasury's deficit, which had stood at 100 million gulden two years earlier, had been reduced by one-third during this brief period of peace. There was still inflation and a currency shortage. In spite of this, the Viennese indulged in riotous living. 'If a foreigner comes to Vienna,' Küttner reports,

> his minister sends out forty to fifty cards in his and his own name and escorts him to the public evenings given by Prince Colloredo and Counts Kollowrat, Lazansky, Trautmannsdorf and other noblemen. He is invited to balls, concerts, grand banquets, and for this at certain times he pays his respects to his hosts on days when guests are again received. . . . A foreigner in this situation will generally have little

difficulty in being introduced to the houses of Arnsteiner, Eichelburg, Button [Puthon], Henikstein and others. In these and the above-mentioned he finds the highest nobility of Vienna, and also the so-called second nobility; in these houses he meets more or less all the foreigners who can lay a claim through their rank or their position to an invitation to these parties. But if this foreigner is an observer, he will soon discover that all these parties – are not Viennese parties at all. He can see the Viennese princes and great ones there, but they do not draw him into their narrow circle, do not invite him to the small parties that they hold with their acquaintances and closest relatives. In the houses of the second nobility it is another matter, and here, or at least in some of them, he can make himself at home.

If Küttner's conversation was no more elegant than his style, his hosts may not have taken much pleasure in his company. All the same, it is to him that we owe the best contemporary description of Fanny's salon at the turn of the century. He does not, it is true, specify it as hers, but everything points to the Arnstein house as being the one of which he writes – not least the fact that its name, according to him, is at the head of the 'second' society:

Among these various houses there is one in particular, where, in the course of a winter, one can see more society than perhaps in any other in this city. It is the house I have visited most frequently, and I would name it, if I had not resolved to avoid all names as soon as I enter into a subject in detail. If these letters should fall into the hands of the amiable ladies of this house they will recognise themselves in the description, and receive my thanks for the many pleasant hours I have spent with them the more willingly, because I offer them with discretion. – In this house guests are received daily, I might almost say at all hours. It is, from the social point of view, the greatest in Vienna, if one can call that house the greatest that is open at all times, or begins entertaining at any time. One finds there every rank, every station – I had almost added, every religion; but this never makes any difference in Vienna, and in social life is in no way considered. Here I see princes, both Austrian and those from other ruling German houses, archbishops, bishops, prelates, foreign ambassadors, scholars, officers, merchants, artists, bourgeois, people of all nations and all classes.

One talks, one plays, one dines, one stays, one goes. Every taste is catered for here, and everyone finds some form of entertainment, provided that he is capable of one. Whoever seeks witty conversation will for the most part find it here, without its being anxiously pursued, or anyone's undertaking to entertain the rest of the company with his wit or knowledge. But even this house is only half a Viennese house: and as soon as I gradually began to inquire after the people I met there, I discovered that the real, that is, the native Viennese formed only a small part of the company.

It was only half a Viennese house because Fanny came from Prussia. But in the shape of the second of those amiable ladies to whom Küttner's thanks were due for so many pleasant hours, Henriette now enters the scene for the first time. The little girl who added her name in her childish handwriting to the list of young ladies of the nobility had grown up in the midst of all the public disturbances and private misfortunes. At eighteen that autumn, she was of marriageable age. In her person the characteristics of her parents were united in a remarkable way. Prettier in the conventional sense, and certainly more emotional than her mother, she nevertheless did not possess Fanny's compelling presence.

Henriette was to find many admirers, surround herself with famous men, indeed conduct a sort of salon herself, at a time when the great age of the salon was already over. But as long as her mother lived she stood in Fanny's shadow, and after Fanny's death it was a reflected splendour from earlier days, rather than her own inner radiance, that attracted people to her side. She combined Fanny's charm and culture with that Viennese good temper which was prefigured in Nathan's softness and complaisance, so that she bore with sweet resignation a disappointing marriage and the gradual fading of the social glory that had surrounded her in her youth. Not that Fanny had deliberately tried to outshine her daughter! She adored the pretty, good-natured child, had no other wish but to make her happy, and still kept Henriette by her side after the latter had married and left the parental home. But Fanny was, if not the most interesting, at least one of the most unusual women in Europe. Henriette was both less and more: she was entirely lovable.

Imperceptibly, in these turbulent years, Fanny entered upon a new phase of her life. With the death of Carl von Liechtenstein, which had put a sudden end to her only *amitié amoureuse*, the days of her youth were over. For more than a decade, in a certain sense perhaps to the very end, she retained her girlish fervour, a mental and physical agility which prevented her from ever really becoming old. When in good spirits and lively company, on festive occasions, she managed time and again to sparkle, succeeding as of old in making up for the lack of proportion in her features by wit, brilliance and vivacity, and transforming it into a kind of beauty. But the first traces of the passage of time were beginning to show. Count Nesselrode, who had first met her a year before the duel, found her shockingly changed by the turn of the century. Gentz and later Varnhagen were able to find her on one occasion exceedingly engaging, on the next 'not at all charming'. Like so many women whose attraction is stimulated by their moods and inclinations, she was *journalière*, could enchant one day and repel the next, depending on whether she was seeking to please or speaking her mind. In anger or sorrow she was now more and more inclined to let herself go. And before the year of the Congress lifted her once again to heights of euphoria and influence, she was to experience still more in the way of anger and sorrow.

Her own effectiveness gradually became uncertain and changeable; but in her daughter she had found a perfect companion and advantageous foil, who henceforth stood by her side. If Fanny became agitated over Napoleonic victories, the Emperor's stumbling politics or a person who displeased her for one reason or another, Henriette's charm had the power of softening and smoothing over her own acerbity. To herself and to others, this child very often seemed more like the youngest of her sisters; Henriette was included in the extravagant love Fanny felt for her 'Berlin *famille*'. This family, meanwhile, had begun to thin out. Her mother, the kindly Mariane with the sea-blue eyes like her own, that model of an Old Testament spouse, who all her life had stood in her husband's shadow, had preceded him in death. Now, in the last May of the century, Daniel followed her. Together with her, surrounded by his many descendants, they had celebrated his seventieth birthday in 1794. A coffee-cup from the Prussian porcelain factory, gold-rimmed and delicately painted, on which, beside the names of Daniel and Mariane, are inscribed those of their children and grandchildren on fifteen scrolls, is preserved from this festive occasion. It is moving to find among them the deceased members of this clan in grey, rather than black lettering: Daniel had seen the passing of a son, a daughter, four grandsons and three granddaughters before his own end drew near.

The modest inscriptions on this porcelain cup give evidence of figures to whom clings a whole glittering web of future history, like the threads of a silkworm. Here is the eldest daughter, Hannchen, married to a Dr Fliess, the ancestor of a well-known physician of our own day, the friend of Sigmund Freud. The second, Bella Salomon, whose daughter Lea was to marry the son of Mendelssohn the philosopher and become the mother of Mendelssohn the composer, while her brother Jakob entered the service of the Prussian court under the name of Bartholdy. Isaac Daniel, the poor supervisor of road-building to the court whose wife, Edel Wulff, had borne him ten children, including the later hero of

Lützen. Blümchen Friedländer, here already renamed Flora, the wife of the spokesman for emancipation in Germany. Elias, an official in the Potsdam municipal government, whose son, the 'exceedingly Christian' Julius Eduard Hitzig, later became the friend of the writers Brentano, Chamisso and E. T. A. Hoffmann. Benjamin, husband of another Wulff daughter, who also lost his son Jacob on the battlefield of the war of independence. Fanny with Henriette. Her favourite sister Cäcilie, at that time still unhappily married to a Wulff. Sara Levy, the childless one. Rebecca Ephraim, whose son Julius Schmidt became a Prussian consul-general. Jacob Daniel, presented by a third Wulff daughter with only one son, the later Benjamin Barnheim. Rachel, who was blind. And finally Jettchen Oppenheim, whose daughter married a country nobleman and was murdered on her estate in 1882, and whose son was ennobled as a Herr von Oppenfeld.

They all stood around Daniel Itzig's grave when he was buried in the Jewish cemetery in Berlin according to the ancient funeral rites of his faith. Not one of them had dared in the patriarch's lifetime to leave the religious community of which he was the chief elder in the land. A family closely bound together, related by intermarriage many times over, they seemed to have marched in closed ranks out of the dark Middle Ages into modern times. Still huddled together one last time, before they dispersed in all directions, they listened, on 7 June 1799, to the reading of Daniel's will. The wise old man had divided his estate and, apart from a large sum of money, had 'with due consideration' left a family fund whose proceeds were to benefit his grandchildren. The net sum of his fortune came to 400,000 thalers in *Friedrichsdor* (as the Prussian currency was known) – almost twice as much in gulden – and its beneficiaries were his thirteen living children and the daughter of his deceased son Moses. To Fanny, as to the other married daughters – including Cäcilie, who had meanwhile separated from her husband – fell the sum of 20,000 thalers, or 38,000 gulden.

But the true range of his possessions emerges only from the document concerning the family fund which was made public on that same day in June. To this Daniel Itzig assigned the entire proceeds of his 'furniture, possessions in silver, gold, paintings, jewels, timepieces, porcelain, mirrors, glass chandeliers and wine, in short all those things known as movables', such amounts of cash and shares as remained after the apportionment to his children, as well as his city mansion, which was to be 'conserved unsold for twenty years from today' and rented out. Moreover the fund received the 'so-called *Meyerey* [dairy-farm] at the Schlesisches

Thor with all its outbuildings, gardens, fields, meadows, cattle and farm implements, and likewise the so-called Bartholdy's *Meyerey* at the Schlesisches Thor with all its buildings, gardens, fields and meadows, as well as the outhouses belonging thereto including the mill and mill-house at the Schlesisches Thor.' After twenty years they too would be sold for the inclusive price of 60,000 thalers. Finally there were the annual payments from the royal department of works for the iron-foundry, Sorge und Voigtsfelde, sold in 1782, 'my houses behind the new warehouse called von Horstsche, the house in Spandauerstrasse known as Neuruppin, the house near Monbijoux, formerly Mohrsche' as well as the inheritance expected from his sister Hanne.

It was a mighty estate which had been gathered together and was about to be dispersed once more. In that tradition of the Biblical people which had been alive with its last powers in Daniel Itzig, his earthly goods were scattered to the winds by the next generation. 'Madame Levy', his only truly faithful daughter, lived until 1854 in the warehouse on the site of the present National Gallery in Berlin. Bella Salomon remained for a time at the Bartholdy dairy-farm where she had brought up her children. The other properties and estates were lost one by one. Only the garden in Köpenicker Strasse, that one testimonial to his aesthetic taste, served for a few decades longer as a reminder of the paterfamilias in the brown velvet coat, the Prussian prince of the Jews. Then the columns and statues, the towers and pavilions, the arbours and avenues fell, to become one with the same sand-brown Berlin soil under which their creator lay at rest.

Daniel Itzig, the servant of the great Frederick, had passed away three years after yet another change of sovereign. Not long before, he had addressed to Frederick William II a request for the alleviation of certain laws affecting the Jews. The response to this was issued in the name of the young King who called himself Frederick William III, but who seemed as unlike his father as it was possible to be.

'A well-meaning, but awkward and shy young man', he had every intention of driving off the vapours, a mingling of Pythian fumes and the perfume of the *ancien régime*, which for a decade had hung about the throne. Politically at first entirely subject to the pressure of Francophile cabinet ministers, he dedicated himself, together with his good and beautiful consort from the house of Mecklenburg, Luise, to a return to social morality. This was to include fair and just treatment of those of his subjects who were not yet recognised as citizens and disadvantaged by certain oppressive ordinances. Frederick William III had every intention of lending them his ear, and in the later years of his rule the Jews were finally freed from the discriminatory laws. In the meantime he took a lively interest in all proposals for the improvement of their situation. But it was only at this time of moral and religious upheaval that the true difficulties of the Jewish question had become apparent. What forces were still at work against their solution is clear from the last important communication on this subject – one of the most remarkable documents of the emancipation. On 2 April 1798, the following resolution was imparted

to the Jewish elder Daniel Itzig and his associates in reply to their representations submitted on the 22nd of May, 1795:

that their request for the abolition or alleviation of various laws against the Jews has been given mature consideration and the opinion of the law commission has been sought upon it. It is certainly not to be denied that in the laws whose abolition is sought by the applicants there exists a certain harshness and a prejudicial distinction between Jewish subjects of the state and the others; and it is to be desired as much for the honour of humanity as for the good of the citizenship that these laws should be abolished. However, these same laws form only a part of the general legislation affecting Jewish matters, whose purpose is to secure the other subjects of the state against the inconveniences which the reception of the Jewish nation among them involves, by virtue of the peculiar character of this nation.

As long, therefore, as the latter continues to segregate itself, not only in speculative religious opinions, but also in practical principles, customs, usages and dispositions, from the rest of the inhabitants of the state, and to nourish a certain national hatred against the latter; as long as it, by virtue of its inner constitution and hierarchy, forms as it were a distinct state within a state; as long as education among its masses is arranged in such a perverse manner, running counter to the purposes of the state; as long as no thorough and general improvement takes place in all these matters, which only the nation itself can bring about; as long, therefore, as the grounds exist which have motivated the laws which are the subject of the present complaint, as a means of security for the remainder of the state's citizens; so long will it be impossible to abolish these laws, and even less so since, on the one hand, experience has not taught them that such disadvantages have truly resulted therefrom for the innocent members of the nation, and, on the other hand, the continued existence of these laws is yet another motivating reason to work towards such a solid reform as is described above, thus rendering themselves qualified for complete equality with the other citizens of the state.

The reason, thousands of years old, for that special position within the rest of the community, the reason for the formation of their own congregations, their own jurisdiction, own dietary regulations and matrimonial laws, was anchored in their religion. The pious people of earlier days had understood if not approved it, and all the more zealously sought to persuade this stubborn sect towards baptism. Now that religious zeal was beginning to dwindle not only among Christians, but also among Jews, now that the Enlightenment had swept away dogmas of all kinds and thus had an increasing effect even on men such as Mendelssohn and Wessely, Markus Herz and Salomon Maimon, the original justification for such archaic, exclusive and sometimes even aggressive special practices was disappearing. Whoever wished to persist in them, without recognising their ritual importance, made himself guilty of the same rigid intolerance with which he charged the Christian world around him. The religious community had become a national group, that 'distinct state within a state', which society saw with more justification than ever before as an unnecessary foreign body. In these gentler days, the humility of their faith might have gained for them concessions which were withheld with unaltered sternness from the arrogance of their self-imposed isolation.

To the enlightened Jews of Berlin this contradiction had become clear. In order to escape it, they now took refuge in great numbers – to their civic advantage, though not without a similar contradiction – in the bosom of that other doctrinaire ruler: the Church. Around the turn of the century, apostasy from the beliefs of the Old Testament, which had begun in the last two decades, had become an everyday matter. Over half of the Berlin community, Rahel Levin later wrote to her brother Ludwig Robert, had converted during the past three decades. As long as Daniel Itzig lived, none of his children or grandchildren had taken this step. Nevertheless 'it had been said for some time' of Elias, his second son, 'that he would convert to Christianity with his whole family immediately upon the death of his nearly eighty-year-old father, who was a zealous Jew'. As soon as the patriarch was in his grave, not only Elias, but also other descendants of Itzig hastened to have themselves baptised. One of the first was Jakob, the son of his daughter Bella Salomon, who changed his faith as early as that same year of 1799 and at the same time took the name of the estate where he had spent his youth. When his brother-in-law Abraham Mendelssohn later led his children Felix and Fanny to the baptismal font, after his sisters Dorothea and Henriette had already become Christians, Jakob Bartholdy had dispelled his last scruples:

You say you owe it to the memory of your father – do you then think you have done something wrong by giving your children that religion which you think the better for them? It is positively a tribute which you and all of us are paying to your father's efforts towards true enlightenment in general, and he would have dealt as you do for your children, perhaps like myself for my own person. One can remain faithful to an oppressed, persecuted religion; one can force it upon one's children as an expectancy of a martyrdom prolonging itself throughout one's life – as long as one believes it to be the one that alone confers bliss. But as soon as one no longer believes this, it is barbarism.

It was barbarism to continue to cling to a faith which had lost its meaning. But what was it to accept a new one, if one were already convinced of the error of all religious dogma? To many, what Heine later described as the 'entrance ticket to European culture' seemed worth a Mass. Other, more sincere sons of the Enlightenment sought to replace their old, inflexible religion with a free, general doctrine which no longer conflicted with reason. It was this spirit that produced the anonymous 'Open Letter to his Reverence the Chief Ecclesiastical Commissioner and Provost Teller at Berlin from several family heads of the Jewish religion', which David Friedländer had sent in the year of his father-in-law Itzig's death to the most enlightened and humane theologian of the Prussian capital.

A motto from St Paul's First Epistle to the Corinthians was placed at its head: 'But when that which is perfect is come, then that which is in part shall be done away. When I was a child, I spoke as a child, I understood as a child, I thought as a child: but when I became a man, I put away childish things.' The request to Teller, in the form of an entreaty for 'instruction, counsel and support in the greatest and most sacred concern of mankind, in religion', consisted of the question as to how conversion was possible while renouncing the new 'ceremonial laws': 'Instruct us, noble friend of virtue: if we should resolve to choose the great, Christian Protestant community as our place of refuge, what public avowal would you, would the men who sit with you on the revered council, demand from us?'

Not without numerous concessions to the attitude of the Christian world, Friedländer dares to make special conditions for a change of faith. He mentions the 'doctrines of the system presently in force among the Jews which run counter to common sense', their persistence in that 'idea of a Messiah, which completely obscured their minds and made all free thought impossible', the formulas of prayer full of eternally repeated lamentations and sighs for the return to their lost land. He admits that the Christians of the

Protestant religion had progressed far ahead of himself and his kindred. This, however, was true only of the development of the spiritual powers, of the acquisition of scholarly knowledge, not of morality. In order now to be able to conform to the more progressive Christian philosophy of life, the Jews must be sure that they would commit themselves only to certain basic truths, which he explicitly names: 'a) There is a God. b) The soul of man is incorporeal. c) The purpose of man on this earth is the striving after a higher perfection and therewith after the possession of eternal bliss. d) The soul of man is immortal. e) God created man for eternal bliss.' The pupil and spiritual heir of the metaphysician Mendelssohn is unreservedly prepared to become one with Christianity in the spirit of these propositions. He must resist acquiescence in new dogmas:

> If furthermore the Protestant religion prescribes certain ceremonies, then we can well acquiesce in these as mere forms, which are necessary for the admission of a member into a society. But let it be well understood that we make a precondition, with good reason, that these ceremonies shall be required only as observances and customs [. . .], but not as signs that he who undergoes them is silently confessing that he accepts the dogmas of the church of this society as a believer.

It was, with all its respect for the 'venerable philanthropist' Teller, a bold, embarrassing and unacceptable offer. How could even the most enlightened theologian have agreed to a compromise which seemed to demand a new and even more drastic reform of the already reformed church? Teller's way out lay in declaring the conversion of such rational and morally superior men of the Mosaic faith as had turned to him in this open letter to be superfluous. 'Why,' he asked, 'do you not remain satisfied for the present with having separated the pure gold of your original Israelite creed from the ignoble parts later added to it?' Although himself no proselytiser, Teller would with all his heart have given his hand and voice to those who converted to Christianity. But he would lay upon them no other yoke but that mentioned in the words of Christ, 'My yoke is easy and my burden light', and believed that in this he was acting entirely in the spirit of Christ and his chosen apostles. It was a shrewd admonition to demand even from the most purified religion no more than it was capable of giving.

The well-meant, but hopeless plan was abandoned. Friedländer, to whom Teller's advice made sense, remained a Jew and opposed to the end of his days the unconditional conversion of so many of his faith. Since even the progressive churchman who had designated Christianity as 'the best doctrine of wisdom' in his essay *The Religion of the More Perfect* seemed unable to offer him such a one, he preferred to 'bear those ills we have / Than fly to others that we know not of'. But the failure of his serious and sincere efforts was a sign that a compromise over the Jewish question was not possible.

The universal tendency was towards lapidary decisions, to a separation in two directions. One led unconditionally to Christianity. The other was indicated in a train of thought of Prince de Ligne's concerning the fate of the Jews, in the course of which this diplomat, man of the world and *bel esprit* sketched out a 'Project for a Jewish State' as early as 1797, in a letter to Sophie von Grotthuss:

> If the Christians have neither the wit nor the kindness to free [the Jews] from their present condition and make something sensible out of them, then I could wish for them that one of the Jews living in Turkey were efficient enough to win that influence with the Grand Seignior that would reclaim for them the kingdom of Judea, where they would certainly behave themselves better than in the past. . . . When I speak of a return to Palestine, I am referring only to the poor devils and the class between the rich and the poor.

Total assimilation or the construction of a new national state in their ancient land! At the turn of the eighteenth century it had already become clear that there was fundamentally no other solution. The general religious liberty whose realisation was near at hand had become worthless even before it was guaranteed. While the progressive leaders of the state were still at work to establish the civic equality of Jews firmly by law, society had already rejected it out of other than merely religious prejudice. From racial hatred, that concept which was at that time beginning to emerge from its shell and was to take such dreadful shapes in the course of time, there was no other escape but disguise or flight.

Which one wanted to choose, which one could choose, was at that time not certain. It would have taken a very long period of leisure, a time of reflective consideration in one's own camp and peaceable patience in the other, for every person of Jewish origin to put this question of conscience to himself and to answer it. Then again, the assimilation of an individual was not the end of the matter. Generations would have had to pass away, an unconstrained mingling and intermarrying with the people in whose country one had made one's home would have to take place. One did not have to join forces with the Christian religion, one could equally well adopt free-thinking philosophies of life. The important thing was not what was accepted, but what was given up: no more and no less than the national character. Whoever was not prepared for this sacrifice was rebuilding with his own hands the ghetto walls which had been broken down with such difficulty. And whoever was not prepared for it must also, as soon as a return to the land of his fathers became possible, not only preach in favour of such a return, but actually perform it in person.

A long period of leisure, during which these two attitudes might be allowed to crystallise unhindered, was, as it turned out, not granted to the Jews. But in the years of emancipation, when with the goodwill of the most open minds, and by means of a gradually developing assimilation into society, all the pros and cons of their situation became evident, they had at least a breathing-space. The majority of those surrounding them were well-disposed towards them, or at least not constantly on the point of denouncing them as scapegoats for every kind of war, plague, conflagration, ruined harvest and shortage of money, and punishing them in the cruellest manner. The air around them was no longer, and not yet, poisoned. They were allowed leisure to think about themselves, indeed they were even helped to do so.

At this moment, even what in the long run proved impermanent seemed possible. A woman like Fanny von Arnstein, who refused to take up one of the two positions, who moved half in the Jewish and half in the Christian world, was at home in both and looked with the serenity of a true daughter of the Enlightenment upon the orthodox as well as the converted among her fellow-believers – such a woman was, for all that, the symbol of a third solution of the Jewish question, which would have been so perfect that it could not be carried out: like every other idea since the beginning of time.

−7−

The High Priest's Blessing

The peace that had seemed like a call to arms had turned into war again with no period of transition. No one had announced it. A landing in England, the only warring power to have continued the battle against the Directory, had not taken place. Instead, Napoleon set sail across the Mediterranean. He defeated the Mameluke Beys at the Pyramids; soon afterwards, Nelson sank the French squadron at Aboukir. At the same time Russia, enraged by the attack on Turkish Egypt, began to march. In Austria the scent of victory was in the air. Swept along by the enthusiasm of the younger Pitt, to whom a new united advance gave promise of the certain end of the Republic, for the first time in history she formed an alliance with her old enemy, the Ottoman Empire. Bavaria, Naples, Portugal were ready to join them. In the course of the summer of 1799 the second coalition was formed.

Young Frederick William, meanwhile, advised by Count Haug-witz, whom the Abbé Sieyès called the 'Minister of Doing Nothing, or for the Prevention of Foreign Affairs', was sitting on the fence, bending now to one side, now to another. Not only Sieyès, the go-between for France, but also the ambassadors for England and Russia found a hearing in Berlin. Gentz, who was in the pay of the British secret service, pressed for participation in the war by means of intrigues and brilliantly argued documents. None of this helped. Prussia persisted in her neutrality, even when the predicted victories of the allies actually took place − victories in Switzerland and northern Italy, a stalemate in Egypt, Napoleon's return without his army. And then, a few weeks before the turn of the century, came the *coup d'état* of 18 Brumaire.

Napoleon was now first consul, the man of the new century, heir and conqueror of the Revolution. His first act was to make offers of peace to Vienna and London. 'Shall the war that has devastated the four corners of the earth last for eternity?' he wrote to George III. And: 'I dare to assert that the fate of all civilised nations is bound up with the end of a war that affects the whole world.' As he had calculated in advance, his plea for reconciliation had a more convincing effect upon France than in the capitals of the coalition. So

the fighting went on, with genius and good fortune. Russia had by
now become war-weary once again, and retreated. The Vendée,
the last centre of resistance in France itself, submitted. With tried
and trusted troops, Napoleon crossed the St Bernard in May,
surrounded the Austrian army at the Po, attacked in the rear and
destroyed it at Marengo. In December, Archduke Johann yielded at
Hohenlinden to the troops of his old enemy, Moreau.

Austria found herself forced to convert the false peace of Campo
Formio into a real one at Lunéville. The French possession of the
left bank of the Rhine, and the Italian daughter republics, were
ceremonially recognised. Under Napoleon's protection, Prussia
occupied British Hanover. England found herself isolated; at the
same time, Pitt fell from power over the question of the Irish
Catholics, the supporters of peace gained the upper hand, and in
March 1802 Napoleon was able to greet the representatives of his
most implacable enemy at the conference table of Amiens. The
following spring, to be sure, this enemy once again declared war
against him, and two years later Austria too had broken that 'true
peace' which after all had proved no more than a resentful armistice.

Far away, against a constantly changing heaven, lightning flashed
and thunder rumbled, while every moment of delusive brightness
was soon banished by the threatening dark. In the foreground,
bathed in sunlight or gently shaded by rosy baroque clouds, lay
Vienna.

Elsewhere the cannons might roar. Here one was outside the
danger zone. Marengo, Hohenlinden – where were they? As far as
the palace of Lunéville, where four years of peace had been negotiated! Be it war or peace: the life of the capital went on confidently
as before. The men in black or blue tail-coats after the English
fashion, their unpowdered hair falling over their foreheads, the
women in the flowing, high-waisted robes of the Republic, moved
in a pleasantly languid rhythm through the day. One saw to one's
business, drove out, took a refreshing little siesta in the afternoon,
changed one's clothes and in the evening met one's friends at
parties, at the opera, at the theatre. The more violently the tides of
world history crashed at the borders of nations, the securer one felt
in the midst of uneventfulness. It might be that the people were tied
to the Emperor's apron-strings. They followed him willingly, as
long as it was not forward into a threatening future, but merely
circling in an eternal, cosy round.

No loud words disturbed the civic slumber. No writer or statesman attempted to quicken the pulse of the times. Alxinger and
Blumauer were dead. The gentler Haschka and Ratschky were still
alive. A German traveller and follower of Kant, J. W. Fischer, had
nothing to report of the literary Vienna of 1801 but that 'Caroline
von Greiner, now Pichler, was writing charming heartfelt poetry
under the name of *Gleichnisse* [*Parables*]'. Otherwise one read Johann Andreas Cramer and La Fontaine. Things were, as usual,
better where music was concerned. Haydn had recently composed
his most beautiful works, *The Creation* and *The Seasons*. The unique
genius of Mozart was beginning to be recognised, nearly a decade
after his death. But the present was less easily grasped. 'In compositions for the piano,' Fischer reports, 'Beethoven and Anton Eberl
are now probably the strongest. Both have originality, fire and
power; both overflow with ideas, and the works of both are fairly
difficult to execute . . . Both are distinguished by very great genius, but then again also by many peculiarities, for which genius
must be forgiven. Eberl's power shows itself more in the general
than in the particular.'

Be that as it may, the controversial question of whether Beethoven or Eberl were the greater master was permissible in society
conversation. More delicate subjects were better avoided: 'If anyone, somehow or other, tries to steer the conversation away from
the tiresome weather, the theatre, and at a pinch from the city's
news, which has already been recounted a hundred times, a noticeable unease suddenly becomes visible in all faces, and it may even
happen that the lady of the house changes the subject with a polite
phrase such as, "Let us not talk for ever about these learned
matters!"'

Whatever houses the good J. W. Fischer frequented, Fanny's
could not have been one of them. It was the very things he found
fault with that were excluded from her sphere of influence. Indeed,
the task she now had to fulfil was a greater one than in the more
open-hearted days of Joseph. Henriette Mendelssohn, who spent
those days in Vienna, wrote to Rahel Levin: 'Her house is the only
one of its kind, just as she is; it is almost the only vantage-point
from which one can really appreciate and enjoy Vienna; there one is
in good company, quite without constraint, as *comfortable* as one
can be even in one's own house, and from there one sees the doings
of the Viennese, and their jokes and earnest, as in a deceitfully
painted peepshow, without being crowded and pushed, or offended in every point of feeling by their unspeakable bad taste and
coarse frivolity.'

And if this verdict, originating from Fanny's more intimate circle, should seem to have been a prejudiced one, there are enough impartial reports extant which can confirm it. Around that time there is an accumulation of accounts from which her image, her house and her circle come alive to us.

An English lady, for example, the widow of a Captain St George, née Chenevix, who, provided with excellent references, went the rounds of the Viennese families of the nobility in the spring of 1800, wrote in her journal in April: 'I have met likewise with a very amiable woman to whom the Countess Münster recommended me. She is a *Berlinoise*, and the widow of Prince Reuss [Marianne von Eybenberg], but is received in very few of the first circles here, on account of her birth, her father having been a merchant. She was originally a Jewess. I went to Mad. Arnstein's with her, which I fear was a breach of etiquette, Mad. Arnstein being a banker's wife, and of the second class of *noblesse*. However, I found there a pleasant society, and an easier *ton* than in most houses at Vienna. She keeps open house every evening to a few women, and all the best company in Vienna as to men. She is a pretty woman with an excellent address.'

With that snobbery which allows English visitors to seek the company of the highest strata of society when abroad, even if they themselves are not of the best stock, Mrs St George had succeeded in being received, by way of the British ambassador Lord Minto, by the Esterhazys, the Schwarzenbergs, the Colloredos, the Starhembergs, the Cobenzls and finally even at court. Nevertheless she retained the sober viewpoint of the northern Protestant, on whom the opulence of southern hospitality does not make all that much impression.

Mrs St George found much to criticise in Vienna. At Lord Minto's one saw far fewer handsome and elegant people than in London. Prince de Ligne disappointed her, being by no means the 'aimable roué, plein d'esprit et de talents' she had expected. The Emperor, much to her astonishment, was fond of his wife, 'which in Germany is a singular thing, as a mistress is almost considered here as a necessary part of the establishment of a married man'. Neither was the horticulture to be compared to that in England. Prince Starhemberg's great park 'is much admired here, and would be thought tasteless in England'.

A barbarous custom, not to be reconciled with human dignity, was to send runners ahead of all distinguished carriages: 'It is so cruel and so unnecessary. These unhappy people . . . seldom live above three or four years [in their trade], and generally die of consumption.' The fact that the top aristocracy here did not disdain to concern itself with financial transactions also caused her raised eyebrows: 'Prince Staremberg, Marechal Kinski and the Prince de . . . are the chief usurers.' The young Austrians displeased her by their deficient lifestyle. 'Classical knowledge is not thought essential to the education of a gentleman; study, in general, not a favourite pursuit, and reading scarcely considered an amusement. Consequently the young Austrians do not excel in the art of conversation. They have little grace, and scarcely any beauty.' Not excessively taken by the brilliance of Vienna under Francis, although she found the landscape pleasing, Mrs St George set off on her travels again, this time to honour the court and nobility of Berlin with her presence. Before leaving she visited Fanny once more: 'I dined also again with the Arnsteins, who I see hate the Austrian government. She is a Prussian, and, according to the latest cant phrase, "that accounts for it".'

Whether or not Fanny hated the government, it was to her and not to Nathan that those imprudent words of censure from which the English widow drew her conclusions should be ascribed. It is certain that she did not allow herself to be deceived by the favour of the Emperor who had ennobled her husband, but recognised and deplored his petty, mistrustful, reactionary manner of conducting the state. To make her house into an island where the vestiges of the spirit of Joseph and of Leopold survived – this was her aim. Besides, she was pursuing her own policy of unconditional resistance against Republican and later Napoleonic France. Whoever appeared lacking in energy in this respect – whether it were Thugut, his successor Cobenzl or even the fearless, but not always victorious Archduke Karl – became the object of her displeasure. So much the happier was she to be able to receive at her home the hero of Aboukir. The delightfully ironic account of this visit is by Caroline Jagemann, the Weimar singer and acknowledged mistress of Duke August Wilhelm, who gave a guest performance in the capital in 1800:

> Among the most pleasant of my circle of acquaintances in Vienna were the house of Arnstein and the physician Frank with his young wife . . . The Arnstein family had a garden residence near the city, received me with great civility and redoubled this after my successful debut . . . In their very pretty domicile one could daily see foreigners from every country, and even Lord Nelson was expected, together with Lady Hamilton, known for her airs. After many hours of uncertainty as to

whether these illustrious people would accept the invitation, at last they arrived: Nelson, a thin little man with one eye and one arm, who did not look like a hero, Lady Hamilton, a tall stately figure with the head of a Pallas, following him with his hat under her arm. They stayed the whole evening and left their hosts in a state of the greatest satisfaction over the honour done to them.

Not only Fanny and her daughter Henriette are mentioned in Caroline Jagemann's memoirs. It is here too that 'Baroness Eskeles, her sister' is mentioned for the first time, who, like her, 'outwardly bore quite the stamp of the women of the Old Testament' and also had 'not quite overcome the peculiar dialect of her nation', but who understood 'how to make up for what was striking in her features by elegance in form and deportment'. The German singer and the British naval hero had been guests at the Braunhirschengrund in the summer. A few months earlier Fanny had experienced the pleasure of welcoming her 'beloved sister Wulff' to Vienna for good. Cäcilie, the nearest to her in age and temperament, had separated from her husband and since then remained unmarried. Now, through Fanny's good offices, a marriage had taken place between her forty-year-old sister and Bernhard von Eskeles, seven years her senior, a match which gave promise of mature happiness to the couple.

Eskeles, a man of good sense and integrity, had in the course of his industrious life so far neglected to marry. He had long been known as Vienna's most skilful financier, who incidentally had saved the exchequer a great deal of money by discovering a bank-note forgery. At the height of his success, he began to regret his bachelorhood. Thus he had paid court to Henriette Mendelssohn, the amiable and rather shy governess, on her visit to Vienna, but she had returned to Paris still unwed. Soon afterwards, Cäcilie Wulff appeared at her sister's house and won his heart. It was his marriage to the beautiful Itzig daughter which brought him the fulfilment of his life. As early as the following year she gave him a daughter, Marianne, and soon afterwards a son. A part of her 'Berlin *famille*' had, to Fanny's joy, been transplanted to Berlin.

Not to Henriette Mendelssohn, nor to Mrs St George, nor to Caroline Jagemann, but to an unknown young Bavarian do we owe the most vivid portrayal of Fanny at the beginning of the nineteenth century. In his letters from Vienna to a 'woman of quality' he indulged in extravagant praise of everything that concerned and surrounded her. While his style at times resembled an affected imitation of *Werther*, however, one must not dismiss him as an easily impressed person seeing through rose-coloured spectacles. He speaks somewhat contemptuously, for example, of the 'baronised Israelite ladies' of the house of Wetzlar, who were married to Counts Clary and Triangi:

> I have never been able to resolve – by all means call it prejudice, if you will – to enter into even the remotest acquaintance with a member of their family. Only yesterday I was told that one of these daughters of Jerusalem, while still in a state of maidenhood, was commonly known in Vienna, not unwittily, as the *golden calf*, because of her wealth and the simplicity of her heart.

In view of such resistance or prejudice, as he himself calls it, against the Israelite nobility, what he says about Fanny carries all the more weight:

> Baroness von Arnsteiner, or Fanny, as she is generally called here, is a woman of several-and-thirty years, and by birth a Berliner. She is a daughter of the Jewish businessman Itzig, known for his wealth, his philanthropy and honest disposition; he was an enlightened man, in the good sense of the word; evidence of his clear-sightedness, which lifted him above the great prejudices of his people and their, at that time, still meagre culture, are the education and upbringing that he gave his children. Each of the Itzig daughters was educated with so much care, and enjoyed such abundant instruction in all branches of languages and sciences, that, had it been the will of fate, they would not have disgraced the rank of princesses. Judge from this how pleasant it must be in this house, whose mistress unites in herself good breeding and the virtues associated with this social advantage. She has good sense and character and is only seldom enslaved by her moods as are others of her sex.

We have already heard Fanny's hospitality sufficiently praised. Nevertheless it is permissible to quote the young Bavarian on this subject, because he adds some light to the familiar picture:

> Towards every stranger she is almost equally civil, and knows how to create a pleasant relationship with him immediately. Her elegant house is open to any traveller recommended to her. From midday about twelve until well after midnight one here meets the most select company, to whom one has daily access, without special invitation. In order to do the honours at her own house without interruption, she never or seldom goes out, probably no small sacrifice, whose weight the visitor cannot acknowledge with sufficient gratitude. One comes without great ceremony and goes without taking formal leave; all the tiresome etiquette of the higher circles is banned; the spirit, freed from the restraining fetters of propriety, breathes more freely here. For these

reasons, too, the conversation never languishes or becomes trivial, but is at all times lively and interesting, and generously spiced with Attic salt.

As uncritical as is his attitude to Fanny, the young Bavarian has not quite lost all his powers of judgement in her circle. 'A certain Generalin von S., who is a relative of Frau von Arenstein, and generally represents her when she is prevented by ill-health or other hindrances from presiding in her house', comes off much less well. Pepi Sebottendorf – for it can only be she to whom he refers:

is a woman of some thirty years of the race of Israel, has good sense and is well read, yet is so infected by sensibility that one can place her with a good conscience in the class of those persons whom Salzmann in his *Karl von Karlsberg* is wont to call *angel souls*. It is certainly fine to have a soul, but also very unfortunate to have too much.

Poor Pepi obviously has far too much, for:

our lady, for instance, does not walk like one of us, she positively floats, she lisps and affects the accents of natural speech, her glances are filled with longing, and a certain languishing character is cast over her whole figure, which cannot but force a smile from the man in question; in short, this oddity simply does not meet with my approval, for I love nothing that transgresses the bounds of nature, and she goes far beyond that line of demarcation. Let us then wipe her off our canvas!

In his description of the young Henriette, however, he seems stirred by the same exaggerated sensibility which he cannot forgive in the lisping Generalin:

You must, however, consent to visit with me once more that temple of good fellowship into which I have only recently introduced you, and in which Fanny Arenstein is the queen of every feast. If you already know this lady and have grown fond of her, we must now observe the fair scion of this parent stem, I mean her only daughter Henriette. Like the gently radiant Orion on the fair forehead of the nightly sky, so Henriette von Arenstein shines through her grace, beauty and wit on the social horizon of her paternal house. This metaphor is by no means too strong, it entirely corresponds to its subject, and if her mother did not possess her own merit, a glance at the perfect development of this seventeen-year-old daughter of hers would be a eulogy to her.

If, according to the ideas of connoisseurs of art, noble simplicity is the true character of beauty, then it is certainly personified in Henriette von Arenstein. Free of all constraint, her whole being breathes that charming ingenuousness, that nameless something in words, expressions, features, etc. that secures for her sex the victory over the heart of every man of feeling. This young lady unites what can in every respect be counted among the rare gifts of heaven, talent and beauty, and nobility of the heart with riches. But what increases the value of these good qualities in her, and whereby she proves herself worthy of the same, is the low value that she sets upon these things. It seems she is unaware of possessing the same, in her heart there reigns a solemnly guarded sense of virtue, and in her countenance there beams constantly that gentle smile that Homer ascribes to his gods. Cheerfulness, the foster-brother of Cupid, is her constant companion. This ever gladsome disposition, this modesty, this remoteness from would-be wit, all this makes her the pleasantest companion and the most amiable of girls.

The enraptured Bavarian was clearly blindly infatuated with her. 'But how comes it', he cries:

> that so many qualities have not stirred the heart of a young man, that a worthy spouse has not yet fallen to the lot of this Grace; would not then those only half-developed buds, inspired by the rays of a new, beneficent spirit, unfold into the most beautiful religion? . . . This time will only come when a young man proves himself worthy of the possession of such a treasure. There have indeed been several who have aspired to the hand of this Cupidess, but of them all there was only one whom her heart chose; a closer connection with him, for unknown reasons, did not take place, but it is now said that a young Portuguese is seeking her hand and indeed already has the approval of the parents. To what extent Rumour of the thousand tongues speaks truly in this, all-disclosing Time will teach us. Meanwhile this much is certain, that to whatever man's share this sweet girl may fall, she will make him happy.

What unhappy love-affair had Henriette experienced in her early years? We do not know. But there was indeed a 'young Portuguese' – he was to become her husband. For the time being he remained in the background. In the late summer of 1801 Fanny left with her daughter for Berlin, to stay for several months at the house of her aunt Levy. Indeed, she stayed until far into the winter, which in this year of European peace was to prove particularly cheerful and stimulating. Masquerades, sleigh-rides, evenings at the theatre alternated with long nightly conversations at the salons of Rahel Levin and of Henriette Herz.

In Vienna Fanny had once again drawn up her last will and testament, 'as I consider it necessary to put everything I leave behind in order before my departure'. This time she specified that all her jewellery and money should go to her daughter Jette; but provision was also made for 'needy persons of all kinds and all religions'. Once again she thanked everyone 'for the faithful attachment, love and *consideration* shown to me for so many years for my excitability, which has often given them great offence, and was the product rather of my mind than of my heart', and declared that she died, 'although not willingly, yet with the comfort and knowledge that so far as has been in my power, I have fulfilled the duties of a wife, of a good mother and certainly also a good daughter'. Despite such thoughts of death, soon afterwards she was, with Henriette, taking pleasure in the stimulating social life of Berlin.

Nor did it take long before the 'most amiable of girls' whose praises had been sung by the young Bavarian had turned the head of a Swede. Karl Gustav Freiherr von Brinckmann, educated, together with Schleiermacher, at the school of the Moravian brethren at Barby, had for nearly ten years been secretary to the embassy in Berlin. This small, infirm man whose constant state of enthusiasm had won him the reputation of an eccentric, frequented the Herz salon with Humboldt, Schlegel and Tieck, Rahel Levin and later with Fichte, in short with the most interesting people in town. He had visited Goethe in Weimar and had also called on Schiller. Chamisso and Rahel's brother Ludwig Robert laughed at him. But his friendship with Friedrich Gentz was genuine. He shared with him not only an aversion from 'decadent Berlin "enlightenment-ism"', instilled in him first by the Moravians, then by the philosopher F. H. Jacobi, but also the love of ladies and the love of oneself. Like Gentz, he complacently observed himself in all his ecstasies. 'Brinckmann is really divine,' wrote Prince Louis Ferdinand to his mistress Pauline Wiesel, after alienating her affections from Brinckmann, 'lovers write for the sake of love, but he loves for the sake of writing.'

Having lost Pauline, Brinckmann immediately consoled himself with a number of ladies. But it was Henriette whom he awaited most longingly at a soirée of Rahel's, where Gentz, Louis Ferdinand and his sister Princess Radziwill were present. Whether she actually arrived, the report by Count S., who recalled the occasion in his memoirs, does not reveal. In any case the Arnstein ladies had met Gentz several times that autumn. On 21 October the latter mentioned in a little note to Brinckmann: 'Mlle d'Arnsteiner recently promised to lend you and myself [Schiller's] *Maid of Orleans*. Can you not bring about the realisation of this promise?' Brinckmann's love for the 'glorious *Freiin* von A. from Vienna' had been as little concealed from his friend Gentz as from Henriette herself. Perhaps her mother, before Henriette finally decided to bestow her hand upon the 'young Portuguese', had brought her to Berlin one last time in order to find her an even worthier consort? Many admirers, including the Danish embassy secretary Baron Selby, had in fact presented themselves. But none of them, and least of all Brinckmann with his sickly appearance and his numerous amours, seemed worthy of her aspirations, and so, towards the end of the year, they resolved to return to Vienna.

Before this took place, Fanny and her daughter had undertaken the reconnaissance expedition of which Varnhagen speaks in his *Denkwürdigkeiten*: 'During Bonaparte's consulship she made a journey to Paris. She returned from France with very unfavourable impressions. The later wars and hostile invasions suffered by Austria filled her with a burning hatred for Napoleon and the French, she passionately expressed this hatred even in the presence of the enemy, and one could not flatter her more agreeably than by disclosing a similar disposition.' Whether it was the memory of the criminal courts of the Terror, the resumption of of an absolutist system or the arrogant, swaggering manner of the French public, flushed as they were with victory, that made such an unfavourable impression on Fanny, is not revealed. She certainly did not stay long enough in Paris to sample its more engaging features, for by the middle of November she was back in Frankfurt, where the great banker Bethmann, a business friend of her husband's, gave a ball for her and Henriette. From there, the Baltic Count Wilhelm von Nesselrode wrote to his son Carl, a young diplomat in Berlin, who had evidently questioned him regarding the two ladies:

> Mme Arnsteiner, que j'ai beaucoup vu à Berlin, il y a six ou sept ans, joint à beaucoup d'esprit une très grande amabilité. Sa fille, je crois, avait alors douze ou treize ans, et annonçait déjà par ses premiers progrès les plus heureux résultats d'une éducation très soignée. Je ne les ai revue qu'un instant (car elles ne s'y ont arrêtées que deux jours, en venant en dernier lieu de Paris pour se rendre à Berlin) à un bal que Maurice Bethmann leur a donné. J'ai trouvé la mère extrêmement vieillie de figure, la fille dansant à merveille et d'une manière distinguée; on la dit ici promise à un comte de Degenfeld, attaché à la mission prussienne à Londres. J'ignore si ce bruit est fondé.

He then praised the great progress that had been made by the Berlin Jews in recent times, above all since 'un nommé Mendelssohn' had brought them particular honour. He, Nesselrode, had in fact considered his book on immortality a 'galimatias métaphysique qui n'expliquait rien', but this was 'une maladie assez commune chez nos savants allemands'. As always – 'mon dernier mot sera, que Mlle Arnsteiner étant fort aimable, sa mère ayant beaucoup d'esprit et à coup sur un plus grand savoir-vivre que les trois quarts et demi des dames de Berlin, vous ferez bien de voir et la mère et la fille, le plus souvent que vous pourrez'.

Should one assume Degenfeld to be the man who was the object of Henriette's unhappy love? Only this incidental remark in a casual acquaintance's letter, itself based merely on an unconfirmed rumour, suggests that this was the case. After her return to Berlin, young Nesselrode, encouraged by his father, must in fact have visited her several times. 'L'amabilité de Mme et de Mlle Arnsteiner a fait naître chez moi le désir de fréquenter les juifs; s'il y en a beaucoup qui leur ressemblent, leur société vaut bien la peine d'être cultivée', he informed Count Wilhelm. But at the beginning of the new year the ladies departed. And 'on the first day of the week, on the 22nd day of the month of Ellul, in the year 5562 from the creation of the world, by the Viennese reckoning of time Sunday the 19th of February 1802', Henriette's engagement to the 'young Portuguese' was celebrated.

Fanny's daughter, as an informant assures us, 'had been brought up quite in a kind of natural religion'. Nevertheless, when she was to be united with the son of the landowner Eliseus Pereira from Holland, no ritual but the Jewish one could be considered.

It was a strangely archaic document, of almost Biblical simplicity, by which these children of two refined families were promised to each other:

> Herr Ahron, son of Herr Elisah Pereire, has said to his bride, *Freiin* Henriette, daughter of Herr Nattan Baron v. Arrnstein: Be my wife after the law of Moyses and of Israel, and I will hold thee in honour, feed and nourish thee after the manner of Israelitish men, who justly do their duty by their wives, feed them and nourish them. I will also give thee thy bridal gift which belongs to thee according to law, namely one hundred times three-score of shekels, and thereto also all female necessities. The bride *Freiin* Henriette also agrees to be his spouse. Her dowry from the house of her father, as well as money, gold, silver, jewels, all these the bridegroom accepts for one hundred pieces of silver. Against these the bridegroom will add from his own property another one hundred times three-score of shekels, so that the whole sum comes to two hundred times three-score shekels . . . All these conditions the bridegroom undertakes to fulfil without opposition in the presence of his bride according to the best law and usage which are common among the daughters of Moyses and of Israel. In witness whereof two auricular witnesses have signed without prejudice by request.

The young man's origins are uncertain and the only evidence for them is found in family legend. Here and there they are linked with those of Baron Diego d'Aguilar – a brilliant and romantic figure from the Marrano clan of Pereira – who lived in Vienna between 1750 and 1755 and was there the head of the Sephardic community. A kinship with him has not been verified. On the other hand, the tradition exists among Henriette's descendants that their paternal ancestors had emigrated from Palestine to Portugal by way of Salonica and had there become persons of rank under the name of de Pereira. A certain David Chevalier de Pereira, who after the manner of the Marranos – who had been forcibly converted to Christianity but continued secretly to practise Jewish rites – had accepted and retained the 'Portuguese' religion, is said to have fled to Holland before the Inquisition. He had left a substantial fortune to his son Eliseus. This Eliseus, who was married to a Chana Machado, had by virtue of his services to the house of Orange acquired the Dutch title of Baron and together with it considerable properties, including the castle of Luxenburg near Utrecht and estates by the Zuyder Zee, near Rotterdam and Haarlem. His son Aaron was born in 1773, a fourth child, at the same palace of Luxenburg. Before the end of the century he travelled to Austria, where as a rich young man with good references he soon gained access to Viennese society.

The Sephardim had long been regarded as the natural nobility of the Jews. A marriage between their daughter and the son of such a distinguished and well-to-do house no doubt appeared desirable to Nathan and Fanny. It might be thought that they had persuaded the gentle girl to accept Pereira's courtship. It was Henriette herself, however, who decided in his favour for not quite comprehensible reasons. Gentz, who came to Vienna the summer after the engagement, informed Brinckmann in a long letter about the atmosphere in the Arnstein house:

> You will certainly be curious to know what I think of Henriette's marriage, which by the way will certainly take place at the end of this month. Here you have it. Pereyra is quite an ordinary individual, ugly rather than handsome, stupid rather than intelligent, and without any outstanding quality either of his person, his conversation or his character. On the other hand he is rich, extremely respectable and *gentlemanlike* in his bearing, in his conduct, in his whole way of life, has by no means anything Jewish in his speech or manner (but indeed in his face), and possesses, as I am thoroughly convinced, a very great good nature and gentleness and equanimity and friendliness on closer acquaintance.
>
> In fact the whole family seems to be dissatisfied with this match, which is based entirely on Henriette's free choice; for I have heard it positively attacked by many persons, and not yet positively defended by any. I believe, however, that Henriette must have had her good reasons

for this choice; it was not passion that prompted it; a person of so much understanding and of so much good sense certainly knows, as long as no passion is involved, what she wants and what she is doing; and therefore I have unconditionally declared myself for Pereyra, who by the way does not displease me at all, among the common suitors for this jewel, certainly one of the best, and at all events much better than Selby. – But I have made the acquaintance of another, of whom it is more difficult for me to understand how she could refuse him; of him I will tell you by word of mouth.

Whether he did so or not, this suitor of Henriette's, too, will remain unknown to us. On 19 September she was married to Pereira, in the marriage contract already referred to as Heinrich Pereira. Nathan gave his daughter a promissory note for 100,000 gulden, on which he was prepared to pay running interest, while the capital was not to be made over to her for six years. Fanny, who shortly before her daughter's wedding, this 'most important *époque* of my life', had once again made her will, left everything to Henriette, nothing to Pereira. He was not to 'reckon it as coldness, or lack of affection, not to have thought of him here in particular, yet I still know him too little to count him already so completely as one of my family'. After the wedding she went yet again on a long journey, while the young couple moved into the Neuling house in Krugerstrasse.

Gentz did not attend the ceremony, although it might have provided him with as much amusement as that in 1772 had done to Frederick the Great's sister Queen Ulrica of Sweden. He had left for England, and was not to settle in Vienna until March 1803. By the end of that year he had already 'fallen out for ever with the Arnsteiner woman'.

The brief and abruptly terminated friendship between Fanny and Gentz deserves consideration, because it illustrates, not only the sufficiently well-known, complex character of this statesman, but much more the contradictory attitude of that time towards the Jews. Gentz, who admired Rahel Levin and had had an affectionate relationship with Marianne von Eybenberg, when in his own private circle expressed himself very coarsely against them. 'In the first place,' he had written to Brinckmann in June 1801, 'just leave the cursed Jews out of the question: I do not fear the scholars; for they are so sober that you will soon lose your appetite for those rogues. But if fate so wills that you should fall in love with some Jewess – then indeed I am lost . . . The warning of little Levy sounds awfully in my ears: I oppose to her my own: *Fuge, o fuge Judaeos.*' He becomes enraged, too, at Humboldt's friendship with them: 'It is after all scandalous that one cannot see Humboldt's name mentioned any more unless it is linked with that of a Frenchman or a Jew . . . And who is this scholar Friedländer, so well known in Germany? Certainly some dreadful dog, who wanted to take the Berlin Enlightenment for a walk among the Parisian philosophers?' In the same letter in which Gentz reminds Brinckmann of Henriette's promise to lend him *The Maid of Orleans*, he informs him: 'Perhaps you do not know that I have become the first member of the newly established censorship commission over all Jews. The Arnsteiners shall soon feel my hand.'

To persuade a man of such power and such malice that, as a Jewess, one was nevertheless, in Nesselrode's words, 'fort aimable', was no mean achievement. In December of the same year two short sentences indicate that Fanny, whom he had recently met, had made an impression even on Gentz: 'The news of [Madame von] Arnstein pleases me greatly. I find her, indeed, so interesting that I wish to please her.' In January he hopes to see her again before her departure for Vienna: 'Please let me know, dearest friend, if the Arnsteiners do not leave until tomorrow, and if one can still visit them this evening. If both are the case, I would suggest to you that we should meet between seven and eight at Humboldt's, and from there go on together to Levi's.' Her outward appearance, too, produces its effect. In March, Gentz writes facetiously about the agreement of Amiens: 'Peace is certain. It also passes, if not all understanding, at least mine. More beautiful than the neck of Fr. Arnstein – for thus one must express oneself for the sake of propriety – in very truth it is not.' And as soon as he arrives in Vienna, magically attracted by a few representatives of that people which in general he rejects, mocks and even hates, he betakes himself to the Arnstein house, which helps him to bear for a few weeks the deadly tedium of the capital in summer. He warns Brinckmann:

Do not go to Vienna in the summer. It is the most unpleasant place of residence that can exist anywhere . . . Anyone not fettered with iron bands to the city has gone to stay in the country . . . Those who stay behind keep their houses hermetically sealed, and see every visit, or rather attempt at a visit, made by a stranger as null and void. In short, you are left, with the oppressive heat in this narrow, monastically constructed city, with its permanent stink, with its unparalleled dust, with its bad, inedible food, with its 800 hackney-coachmen, and its 30,000 *badauds*, with the – anything but amusing – Prater and its roast chickens, with three or four mediocre theatres, coffee-houses detestable to the point of nausea, and several thousand trivial, thoroughly stupid, frigid, completely useless *filles de joie* – alone.

That this picture is far from exaggerated may be guaranteed you – first, by the extremely favourable prejudice with which I came to Vienna – further, by the special and extraordinary good fortune which procured me (before a thousand others) a clean, elegant and very comfortable apartment in the best district of the city, the constant use of a very good carriage, and many other little domestic comforts – by the no less exceptional good fortune which allowed me to become acquainted without difficulty at least with whatever interesting men are to be found here (for the art of approaching the women I have not yet been able to discover); finally, and above all things, by the advantage, which cannot sufficiently be praised, of my connection with the house of Arnstein.

There now follows an often-quoted passage, which lost none of its significance even after a trifling argument had alienated Fanny from him for ever:

The Arnstein house – for here, and only here, is concentrated quite simply everything which to a certain extent counterbalances the disagreeableness of Vienna – the Arnstein house is the greatest, and in a sense the only resource of all foreigners arriving here, and an inestimable one for those who, like myself, through old acquaintance, connections with Berlin, and those very relationships with Jewish families which we, my dear B., have so often despised, and which daily I now grovellingly revere, acquire a stronger claim to personal favours and the attestations of friendship.

How happy I felt, when here, at the same moment, apart from your amiable friend Henriette, and her excellent mother, I found in addition Mad. Levi, whom I always loved and esteemed, Md. Ephraim, whom I – to my eternal shame be it said – never deemed worthy of one glance, and in whom I now recognise one of the most interesting women I have ever seen. – Mad. Eskeles, about whom I often used to mock you, and whom I have now learnt to esteem, – Frau von Eibenberg, who is my comfort here, my friend, my support, when I found beside all these witty, good-natured, in every respect praiseworthy women, everything which Vienna may contain that is alive, sociable and bearable, united together! This house is in more than one sense of the word a little world. Without it, I would already be far away from Vienna again; with it, no matter how disagreeable everything else may be, one cannot easily lose heart or perish completely.

In the spring, after his stay in England, things already looked different. On his journey home, Gentz had questioned Brinckmann from Brussels about his hostesses: 'Have you heard nothing of the Arnsteiners? I have nowhere heard a word about them. How is the little one [Rahel], how are Mad. Levy and Ephraim, those incomparable and unforgettable friends of mine?' In Vienna, satisfactorily lodged in the Kohlmarkt, he at once began to frequent the great houses of the nobility. They were no longer hermetically sealed to the stranger who called on them at a pleasanter time of year and with more impressive recommendations than before. The head of the imperial cabinet, Count Colloredo, his superior – whom, to be sure, he loved as little as he did the foreign minister, Count Cobenzl – had introduced him to the first families of the land, the Liechtensteins, the Lobkowitzes, the Schwarzenbergs, the Esterhazys and the Auerspergs. It no longer seemed necessary to seek refuge at Fanny's. In any case, at the end of the summer she had gone to Holland with Henriette and Pereira to visit the latter's family. Meanwhile Gentz had had sight of a document which, after decades of clemency and human decency over the Jewish question, introduced a new, evil and ominous note into the debate.

K. W. Fr. Grattenauer, a Berlin lawyer and Gentz's legal representative, had some time earlier published an anonymous pamphlet entitled *Against the Jews: A Word of Warning to our Christian Fellow-Citizens*. Just as if Lessing had never lived or his *Nathan* had never been written, this man once more brought out the already rusty poisoned arrows and mud-slings from the arsenal of ancient anti-Semitism. But more than this, he poured scorn on the aesthetic Jewesses who had won such esteem in Berlin:

> They read many books, speak several languages, propose many arguments, draw in various manners, paint in all colours, dance in all styles and possess everything individually, but not the art of uniting all the particulars as a whole into a beautiful femininity. The refined tact of the great world they learn neither in Paris, nor in Berlin, nor in Vienna, let them keep company as long as they will with princes, counts and gentlemen.

The ladies who were under attack offered no resistance. But the protests of others resulted in a police prohibition in Berlin of all broadsheets for or against the Jews. Nevertheless, further scurrilous pamphlets followed. Suddenly it was once more socially acceptable in the salons to question the equality, which had been born in the salons, of one's Jewish fellow-citizens. National anti-Semitism, that unlovely child of the awakening national sentiment in Prussia, had come into the world. Gentz learnt of this from Berlin newspapers and from Brinckmann's letters.

His first impulse was one of rejection:

> What struck me unpleasantly about your letter is what you say about Grattenauer. With what deep displeasure, disgust and revulsion I beheld those accursed headlines in the *Berliner Zeitung*, I am incapable of describing to you . . . Unfortunately, I happen to be in touch with this damned person . . . But the suspicion of participating to the remotest degree in his trashy writings is one which I cannot endure.

A month later he had read the pamphlet. Thereupon the brief interlude during which he had 'daily grovellingly revered' his relationships with Jews was already over. Above all his latent satirical streak, which permitted him to betray his best friends – not to mention his second-best ones – for the sake of a *bon mot*, was awakened by Grattenauer's unexpectedly well-aimed polemic: 'One could not easily be less favourably disposed for the judgement of a document,' he declared to Brinckmann, 'but to pay due respect to truth, and in just praise of the incorruptible ingenuousness of my nature, I must say – that I . . . read it with exceptional pleasure.' It was, he continued, 'written almost throughout in an excellent, indeed masterly way'. Its style reminded him of Lessing, 'to whom many passages have an unmistakable and yet unaffected similarity'. Further, there reigned here 'such a complete knowledge of the subject, such erudition' and so forth, 'that no Jew or patron of the Jews in Germany will easily believe himself capable of inflicting palpable blows upon an enemy who appears so well armed (*armé de toutes pièces*).'

> But the most striking thing of all to me, and what makes me necessarily believe that you had not yet read the last two pieces when you wrote about the matter, was the true, rich and inexhaustible wit with which this beast goes into battle. This cannot be further demonstrated: every page speaks for itself. The investigations into the title of Jew, into the Jewish stink, into Jewish quackery, into the *Appretur* [superficial varnish] of Jewish women (the word *Appretur* is itself worthy of immortality, and will certainly not be forgotten again, as long as there are Jews) – all these chapters would have done honour to the greatest writer, if ever need and not mischievousness had moved him to write against the Jews. It is quite simply impossible that what is truly witty and endlessly amusing in these passages should have escaped you. I would like to send a courier to Rome in order to prepare this great feast for Humboldt, for which the deepest sorrow cannot have made him unreceptive. I at least can assure you that I have not laughed for years, quite alone and by myself, as I have done over this pamphlet. Laughter to the point of tears! I cannot say more in praise of a work whose very existence, only an hour before my closer acquaintance with it, aroused nothing but indignation in me . . . But now, my dear Brinckmann, I adjure you not to allow this judgement of mine to become known.

The echo of his own immoderate laughter about the reviled 'Jewish beauties' still ringing in his ears, he betook himself to Fanny, who had returned to Vienna at the beginning of October. On the same day on which he reports the effect of Grattenauer's pamphlet upon his lachrymal glands, he writes to Brinckmann:

> The Arnsteiner woman has been here again for about eight days, but without Henriette, whose arrival is still very uncertain. She charged me today with giving you endless kind messages. I ate with her at midday, and we talked long and much of you . . . It had been going very well for some time, till suddenly a fatal discord was introduced, when one of the last, the very last of creatures, a certain Chevalier Rongé (a friend of Fanny's!!!), who always calls you 'his good Brinckmann', even '*mon cher* Brinckmann', joined in the conversation. As I had firmly resolved, from the first day that I saw this villain, never to speak to him, I had to stop speaking of you, because the danger of having to reply to him was becoming ever more urgent. – The Eskeles woman is in childbed again. – The company in these two houses, as much as I honour the two sisters, really always verges far too much on *mauvaise société*. Now that I have orientated myself in Vienna in order to find better, it costs me an effort every time I go there; but it would be crass ingratitude if I neglected them; and of this I will never be guilty.

Nevertheless, Grattenauer's poison has taken possession of him. Two weeks later – and he seeks to recognise the reason for his altered attitude to Fanny in herself: 'The Arnsteiner woman has noticeably declined since her last journey (not physically, for, thank God, she is in very good health), her house becomes worse every day; Sonnenfels and the Chevalier Rongé (otherwise known as Runge) are her daily heroes.' Not long after he repeats his opinion:

> Do not forget, when you write, to touch on two points. 1. what is the position with Müller; 2. what you think of Rongé. – a few days ago Madame von Arnstein (who has inexplicably declined since her return from Holland) declared that you worship this rascal; I believe she said this only to take revenge on me; for in the course of a somewhat lively exchange of words I had made it very clear that I regarded this favourite of hers as simply one of the last of mankind.

Not only the Chevalier Rongé, about whose objectionable personality nothing further is known to us, but every other occasion is now enough for him to attack the Jews.

> The Jewish Almanac of the Muses I do not yet know, but otherwise I have seen more or less all of this year's almanacs, including that of Schlegel, of which you give me a sample. One can indeed only sigh over

this aberration. If the bunglers who have long since been condemned, the Kotzebues and his like, the enlighteners in Berlin etc. continue in their mischief, we observe them in contemptuous silence.

And finally:

> Your last letter but one was a real masterpiece of wit and persiflage, I read it out to several people. But the heavenly passage about Rongé I kept for myself alone. I have quite fallen out with the Arnsteiner woman. The D. take the Jews!

What had happened? Convinced by the arguments of the Gratte-nauer pamphlet, Gentz had hastened to Fanny's side only to find confirmation of his new aversion to the Jewish salons. The wretched Rongé seemed a welcome excuse for avoiding her now. But his bad conscience – the oppressive doubt as to whether he might not after all be guilty of 'crass ingratitude' to her – was still stirring in him. It was only through a childish quarrel concerning his beloved Pauline Wiesel that he obtained the satisfaction of henceforth renouncing, with good reason, this company which had become so irksome to him. Pauline, the bewitching courtesan of several great men and friend of many a woman of importance in Berlin, and at the same time a positive bundle of vices, had at various times granted her favours to Counts Shuvalov and Hatz-feld, to Prince Louis Ferdinand and to Brinckmann, and possibly to Gentz himself, who was not otherwise known to have a taste for ladies. Rahel adored her heavenly wantonness. Madame de Staël declared that she would have given all her literary fame for one of Pauline's honeymoons. Fanny alone had no wish to join in the fashionable infatuation with this foolish beauty, and, as usual, did not mince her words. She perhaps suspected, but fearlessly took the risk, that her attitude would release a flood of malice on Gentz's part:

> Now I can and will also tell you that the first (not the only) occasion for my *brouillerie* with the Arnsteiner woman, which has now, thank God! become a total and, I hope, everlasting separation, was a spirited quarrel over Pauline. The A. woman spoke of her as, I suppose, befits and becomes a common Jewish creature; in her temerity she went so far as to attempt to deny me the right to defend 'such a person!'; I, however, afire with rage, set forth to her, perhaps rather too plainly, how and why she should not presume even to think, much less to speak, of 'such a person'. – From this day her hatred for me began to develop, later progressing to full ripeness through her long-nourished anger over my good reception into the great world which was closed to her, and which

she envied me with true Jewish fury – through the quarrel with Rongé, whom I had to her face declared the last of all beings – and through the accusation that I had said *que je n'aimais ni les bâteaux plats ni les platitudes.* You cannot imagine how happy I am about it. My time is so precious to me that, although part of it does indeed belong to society, I prefer at least not to fritter away this time in the worst society; and how bad the A. woman's society has now become (since it now includes neither Henriette nor [Mesdames] Levy and Ephraim from Berlin), you cannot possibly imagine.

Sonnenfels and his wife, the most dreadful of earthly beings, Rongé, a certain lawyer called Ankerström (some still call him Ankerberg), Count Salmour from Dresden, for whom no gallows is high enough, Dlle. Schmalz and her sister, a certain Mad. de Brevilly [Brévillier], who is approximately *en femme* what Rongé is *en homme*, Count Keller, a most miserable picture of simplicity, and a few (actual) mistresses of great gentlemen – these are the *habitués* and *habituées* of this house. I regret that I must almost also number Baron Reutersvärd among them. On days when dinners and suppers are held it is indeed somewhat better; but the company at Buisson's in Berlin (for that is about the nature of the Arnstein house) would still appear a paradise by comparison. – Mariane [von Eybenberg] is another who no longer sets foot in this house and, like me, is totally out of favour. She too has several times most valiantly reproached the Arnst. woman for her vile utterances about Pauline; but all is wasted on such an inveterate Jewess as the A. woman.

It is seldom that such a document so clearly writes its own commentary between the lines! That Gentz can accuse Fanny of nothing more than calling Pauline Wiesel a 'person', that he picks out only the less reputable names among her circle, but is forced to admit that things are 'somewhat better' at her dinners and suppers, that his impotent and forcibly exaggerated rage discharges itself in phrases such as 'Jewish creature', 'Jewish fury' and 'inveterate Jewess', and that he finally admits that both he and Marianne von Eybenberg are 'out of favour', that is, have themselves fallen from grace with Fanny, speaks volumes for or rather against him. With the uncompromising nature that she shared with her north-German compatriots, and whose less pleasant effects had sent Gentz, among others, to settle in the more conciliatory atmosphere of Austria, where compromise was always a possibility, she had dismissed him from her house. The 'great world' which she 'envied' him – insofar as it was still closed to her – a decade later was passing through her doors in full strength. The name of Gentz, however, never again appeared on her list of guests. On the Tuesday evenings of the period of the Congress, when all Vienna was making its appearance at Fanny's, Gentz often 'went to bed at nine'. For the time being, however, he continued to supply Brinckmann for a whole year with derogatory accounts of the Arnstein family, which perhaps shows that he was still suffering from the pangs of conscience.

'Your idol, Jette Arnstein,' he reports in June 1804, 'is also here again; but she is said to have changed to the point of being unrecognisable. I do not see her, for my breach with her house is irreparable. In general, despite being fond of Jette, I am glad of it; why should one, in the midst of so many terrors, see Jews as well!' In August the indeed rather dubious Chevalier Rongé appears to have travelled to Berlin and announced himself at Brinckmann's. His speeches in praise of Fanny and lamentations over Henriette annoyed Brinckmann. When the latter complained of him in writing to Gentz, his correspondent unexpectedly took sides with Rongé and against Fanny's daughter:

> To begin with, everything he has said about the outward changes in the much admired lady is literally true. *Voûtée, composée sans grâce, sans tournure* – on this question there is but one voice in Vienna; and everyone who has eyes must recognise the truth of the matter. What is sadder – and note well that I am here relying on data provided by her best friends – what is sadder is that she has totally lost her former amiability, is no longer interested in anything, manifests in her expressions and her manners a certain deadly indifference and complete enervation, just plays with a changeling of a Jew-child, and even extracts tears daily from her mother. – How all this has come about, I know not how to explain, although I had already clearly seen the germ of all this in her marriage to that infamous Jew; only I had not expected such a dreadfully swift development. Thus far, Rongé is totally right . . .
>
> As far as the *mésalliance* is concerned, my opinion on this is more or less as follows. The Arnstein barony is not highly regarded in Vienna; here R. is right again, although it was not he but Prince de Ligne who coined the very pretty *bon mot* in which A. is christened '*le premier baron du vieux testament*'. Nevertheless it is true that Henriette at the time of her blossoming was sought after and desired by quite other persons than the Jew Pereyra, whether he comes from Portugal, Holland or directly from Jerusalem. But from the moment in which Henriette fell in love with this Jew – for she did in fact love the rascal – she sank very low indeed in public opinion; and now that her amiability has completely disappeared, like a dream, together with her charms, a certain equality of rank has indeed set in between her and her husband; but as soon as one weighs Jew against Jew, then R. once again is right in saying that the Portuguese Jews are more distinguished than the Polish–German ones; and P. in fact belongs to one of the most distinguished Jewish families in the world.
>
> I am sorry that this verdict of mine will not especially agree with your great fondness for Henriette which, as I see, still continues. But believe me, dearest friend, that it is founded on the purest truth. I have not the least quarrel with Henriette, and would probably never have fallen out with her; if I did not see her on this occasion, the fault lay entirely with

her quite insufferable mother. The falsest and most ridiculous thing in Rongé's discourse is what he says of this woman. Go through all the classes of Vienna and ask every individual (excepting four or five among them, Rongé, Abbé Collenbach, and a few Frenchmen of the new regime), and you will hear the same on all sides, namely that the Arnsteiner woman, as pleasant and entertaining as she was once, has now become, *à la force de prétensions manquées, de dépit contre la première noblesse, de mauvaise humeur causée par le succès des autres et par sa propre décadence uff.*, one of the most unbearable persons to be found anywhere. Her house, too, is almost deserted; the above-named, besides Sonnenfels and his wife – two of the most dreadful creatures! – a few foreigners passing through, and a couple of old women, are all that remain to her; and it has gone so far that, *de l'aveu de toute monde*, the *premier baron* is now counted the best of the whole family.

Not even the Francophobia which he shared with her was credited by Gentz to poor Fanny! Among the few guests at her house, so he observed with the dangerous suggestiveness of the practised agent, were 'a few Frenchmen of the new regime', a remark probably designed to discredit her entirely in Brinckmann's eyes. But among his new illusory notions, nourished by Grattenauer, was the view that Jews were 'born representatives of atheism, of Jacobinism, of enlightenmentism'. He wrote to his friend in September:

Never has a Jew seriously believed in God! Never has a Jewess – I state this without exception – known true love! – all misfortune in the modern world, when one pursues it to its deepest origins, clearly comes from the Jews; they alone made Bonaparte Emperor; they alone struck the north of Germany with such shameful blindness that Villers' prize essay is taken for a book of holy scripture! – But enough of these cannibals!

One seems to hear in these words the barbaric voices of our own century. The deeply devout Moses Mendelssohn, his daughter Dorothea, utterly consumed by her love for Friedrich Schlegel, the sentimental Henriette Herz and Fanny Arnstein, apart from Gentz the most embittered enemy of Napoleon in Vienna, were not accepted by him as counter-evidence. Indeed, even Jakob Bartholdy, the brother of Lea Mendelssohn and nephew of Fanny, whose visit to the capital provoked this outburst, would have been able to correct him if he had been in his right mind. For this man, whom Gentz describes to Brinckmann as 'one of the most odious of this infamous brood', whom he calls a beast and a 'Jew-boy' unjustifiably protected by Prince de Ligne, always acted as the very embodiment of the Prussian patriot.

But Gentz was not in his right mind, nor did he wish to be so, when he made these senseless statements. His wish, as a true child of his time, was 'to escape from the sphere of reason in the narrower sense of the word'. The mixture of romanticism and cynicism in his breast was an unprecedented chemical compound, which from then on remained present in the German metabolism. Whither it led has best been expressed by himself: 'In these days of dissolution very *many*, this goes without saying, must work on the culture of the human race; but some must positively dedicate themselves entirely to the hard, the thankless, the dangerous task of combating the excess of this culture.' Excess of culture? Combating? It was the most shameless renunciation of the progress of humanity ever penned by a man of letters!

Nevertheless, when mud is thrown, some of it will stick. As crass and as infected by envy as Gentz's description of the decline in the Arnstein house might have been, there may have been some basis for it at the time. Perhaps Henriette had really changed in the first years of her marriage, although she once again aroused extravagant admiration at the time of the Wars of Liberation. Perhaps Fanny's daily acquaintanceship had indeed fallen off – the Chevalier Rongé cuts a poor figure, however one may judge him. Even her salon may have temporarily lost some of its brilliance, for what social circle remains always the same? But on one point the slanderous gossip must be totally rejected: namely the allegation that Fanny was consumed by a 'dépit contre la première noblesse'. Certainly she was socially ambitious, and wanted to draw towards herself everything that appeared interesting and important. But she well knew, and had long resigned herself to the fact, that she was neither acceptable at court nor admitted to the intimate circle of the most ancient nobility. It was enough for her that she was visited by both ruling princes and members of that ancient nobility.

For some time there had been a new venue for these visits. On St George's Day, 1804, Nathan had signed a contract with the daughter and heiress of the merchant Natorp, Baroness Bernardine von Kielmansegg, according to which he was to rent 'the whole of the first floor' of her *palais* at 582, Hoher Markt, 'together with the stables, coach-houses, attics, timber-yards and cellars', for 5,000 gulden a year. From this *bel étage* there was a view of one of the most beautiful squares of Vienna: the old forum of the Romans' provincial city of Vindobona, now the domain of the *Fratschlerinnen* (market women), the fish- and crab-sellers, *Häringern* and *Ganstern* (sellers of herrings and geese), with their booths and stalls. Fanny's eye now fell, not on the column commemorating the plague or the grey façade of the Herrengasse, but on a Biblical scene. It was the great fountain which the architect Fischer von Erlach had built in honour of Joseph I and which depicted the marriage of the Virgin Mary to Joseph, roofed over by a four-columned canopy. Four angels surrounded the group, within which the high priest, his hand raised in a strangely papal gesture, united the young couple according to the custom of the Old Testament. Fanny could not have missed the symbolism of the monument. Here, just as it happened soon afterwards in her own family, the birth of the Christian tradition was taking place from the womb of the Jewish one.

Meanwhile the inhabitants of this house were experiencing the latest and most exciting development in world events. On 10 May Napoleon had proclaimed himself Emperor of France. This confirmed the shrewd foresight of Gentz's declaration, soon after the establishment of the consulate, that Bonaparte's republicanism was no different from monarchy. In the summer, before the usurper had even found time to crown himself in the presence of Pope Pius, Francis proclaimed a 'pragmatic law' which made him the first hereditary Emperor of Austria. A few days after that singular spectacle of 2 December in Notre Dame, the Viennese were enjoying their own imperial procession – just as if they begrudged the Parisians their new dignity.

The reversion of France to a traditional form of government, however, was observed not altogether with disapproval in Austria. Gentz's appeal to Count Cobenzl, the minister of foreign affairs, not to recognise Napoleon's imperial dignity was set aside, and a document of protest from the Bourbon pretender was burnt before the eyes of the French ambassador. While Gentz boiled with rage against the government and the court, excluding only the romantic Archduke Johann, his worst enemy, Fanny, in her new salon on the Hoher Markt, raged with equal violence against the shameful forbearance with the French. She did this in their own language, as was customary. The young Arthur Schopenhauer, who had been received with his parents that summer in the 'hospitable house of Baron Arensteiner', found this habit in Viennese society, of speaking French even in wholly German company, particularly unpleasant. There was only one excuse for it, as the sixteen-year-old confided to his journal: 'That French as a language of conversation unquestionably surpasses all others and that Viennese German is so very bad.'

It was the last winter of peace before the renewed tempest that was to carry the war into the very heart of the capital, as had not happened even at the time of the Turks. Forty years later, Franz Gräffer recalled the masked balls he attended at the time. Not from hearsay, but from his own memory he conjured up the appearance of Fanny, who made an indelible impression on the young man taking his first steps in a ballroom. He may now be quoted with a better claim to authenticity than that scene in the Augarten which Gräffer had reconstructed from contemporary accounts. He describes the dancers, the entrance of Prince de Ligne. Then he and his companion notice a lady on the rostrum who is causing a stir.

> We hear whispers. 'A goddess, verily. How she is enthroned! Those eyes, a world of wit. That nobility of posture.' A few women whisper to each other: 'How can they call her beautiful, or even bewitching? She has charm, yes, a certain attraction. She has knowledge, many talents, exquisite manners, a *savoir faire, comme il faut*. But, good heavens, for all that, without her millions?' What malice, I thought, when Herr Fergar, reddening with indignation, blurted out to the speaker: 'With respect, Frau Marquise, if you yourself had all her millions, no one would take any notice of you for all that; and if Fanny Arnstein had not a penny, she would still be a millionairess.'

Gräffer continues:

> The women disappeared, allowing us room to observe the admired lady. Indeed, should one wish to paint the Graces, this woman must sit as a model. Yes, grace, everything about her is grace. That figure, that deportment, those movements, all curving lines. My Hogarth, you who discovered or christened the curving lines, here you have what you never saw in your lifetime. All is harmony; this woman's expression is music. Then there is her breath, her speech winged with liveliness and wit. All around her was enthusiasm. Everyone stared at the wondrous vision, as if under a magic spell; mute, motionless. But behold! O the magnetic power of kindred spirits! Already the Lignes and Harrachs draw near, already they are seated at her side.

She, this wondrous vision, was forty-six years old that winter – an age at which beautiful women are often already faded, while clever women are sometimes still very attractive. Surrounded by the legend of her imperishable charms, she exercised on Gräffer an effect which she had already partly lost. It was the last time that she was to give rise to such hymns of praise, but not the last that she was able to captivate in the same way. True, she already had a grandchild, little Ludwig Pereira, who had been born in Amsterdam in August 1803. But at the same time Cäcilie, who was not much younger than she, had given birth to a son. The Itzig daughters retained their youth well. What helped Cäcilie to preserve herself even longer than Fanny in good health and physical vigour was her calm, relaxed manner, which contrasted sharply with her sister's bursts of enthusiasm. Fanny, however, was consuming herself – in social life, in conversation, in everyday and in national politics. Over the next few years she had only too much opportunity to disturb herself over world affairs.

When, in March 1805, Napoleon raised himself to the title of King of Lombardy, which had been made into a republic by the peace of Lunéville, the Austrians' forbearance came to an end. Several more months passed before Cobenzl decided to advise the Emperor to join the third coalition. It was not until the autumn that the camps finally declared themselves. This time, Sweden ranged itself with England, Russia, Austria and Naples on the one hand, while first Bavaria, then Württemberg and Baden decided to take the field with the *Empereur* and his Spanish allies. Austria's 'finest and most numerous army' of 94,000 men was in Italy. But this time Napoleon wanted only Vienna – as much as five years earlier he would have liked to advance on the city. Once the south-German states had gone over to him, he was in no difficulty. At Ulm he met Mack, the 'modern' Austrian soldier, in whom the leaders of the coalition had placed so much hope. He succeeded in obtaining the general's capitulation. On 17 October Mack signed the document of surrender. Three days later 22,000 Austrians left the city to lay down their arms before Napoleon.

Vienna was in a state of the greatest agitation. It seemed cold comfort that the *Empereur*, while victorious on land, had lost his entire fleet. Where was Trafalgar? No one knew. But everyone knew Ulm! The Mediterranean was distant, but the Danube was near, flowing straight into the capital. On 1 November Murat had already reached Linz. At the same time, Davout was advancing through Styria, Mortier towards the left bank of the Danube. Everything was going so fast that there seemed no prospect of defending Vienna. The Emperor was at the river Inn to lend support to Kutuzov's relief force and his own troops. The Empress prepared to leave the city. This time when things became serious no volunteer corps, which might have been able to throw itself against the enemy at the bastions, was levied. Those, bourgeois or noble, who were ready to be called up were formed into a kind of citizens' militia, not to fight, but to be responsible for the preservation of order and security. Meanwhile, art treasures, museum collections, archives and state funds were being transferred, some to Moravia, some, by water, to Hungary. Many were already fleeing, even before the French had crossed the slopes of the Vienna woods.

On 8 November the Empress left Vienna. At the same time Gentz, convulsed with sobbing, was being driven to Brno in the carriage of a military friend. The next morning a deputation representing the city and the realm went to meet the French vanguard. Murat declared to them that 'the salvation of the city depended upon his reaching the Tabor bridge unharmed'. The bridge, which allowed the army an unobstructed path to Bohemia, had been already been prepared with slow-matches for burning, but when, at eleven on the morning of 13 November, the enemy led by Murat and Lannes marched with banners flying and drums beating, through Mariahilf, through the Burgtor, through the city, by way of the Kohlmarkt, the Graben and the Stephansplatz to the Roter Turm, the citizens' force saluted, no one thought of setting fire to the bridge, and the generals crossed the river in double-quick time. Under cover of darkness, Napoleon, who until then had stayed at Sieghartskirchen, entered the imperial city to set up his court and camp in the castle of Schönbrunn.

Fanny had stayed in Vienna – not out of pride alone, but for the sake of Henriette, the birth of whose second child was imminent. With impotent rage she observed how, when the people hearing rumours of a Russian army in the offing attacked a few officers of the French garrison, the citizens' militia called the precipitate patriots to order. We do not know whether any soldiers were billeted in her house. But it was enough that the blue coats were seen flashing in all the streets and squares and that the tricolour was hoisted upon the Hofburg. The worst for her was to know that Prussia, which at the beginning of November had demonstrated a certain willingness to join the coalition, appeared to be delaying its decision ever longer. Murat had hastened to Moravia, to force the Russians and Austrians into a decisive battle. Count Haugwitz, the Prussian foreign minister, who had promised to give the allies his answer by 15 December, hoped only that this battle would remove the necessity for this answer. Sent south by Frederick William to lay before the *Empereur* the Prussian proposals for negotiation, he travelled 'with the slowness of a dying man' via Prague to Brno.

Napoleon, who had arrived there before him, directed him to continue his journey to Vienna, to confer with Talleyrand. Scarcely had Haugwitz reached the city when the event he had been awaiting took place: Austerlitz.

Not least through the fault of Prussia, the day was lost. If Prussia had acted earlier, who knows what might still have been saved. Nothing now remained for Haugwitz but an alliance, or for Cobenzl but an armistice with Napoleon. In Vienna, on 28 December, from the balcony of the corner house of 1, Grünangergasse and 16, Schulerstrasse, the so-called Neubergerhof, in which the French marshal Oudinot had taken up his quarters, the peace which had shortly before been signed in Pressburg was announced. In later years, when she had been raised with her husband to the Austrian nobility, Henriette Pereira moved into the same Neubergerhof – it carries her coat of arms to the present day. For the time being she was still living in Krugerstrasse. There, eleven days after the entry of the French, she had given birth to a son. On 28 November there occurred an event of which Fanny von Arnstein could not have dreamed when she gave her daughter's hand to a man of an ancient Sephardic family:

> That I the undersigned, at the express request of the parents, by previously obtained permission of his Grace the Prince-Archbishop of Vienna, have in total secrecy baptised according to Christian Catholic custom the son of Herr Heinrich *Pereira* and of Frau Henriette, née Freiin von *Arnstein*, in the Neuling house No. 27, Krugerstrasse in the parish of the Augustines, and have given the child the name *Adolph Franz*, I witness with my own signature.

The document is signed: 'Josef Gotzinger, secular priest and chaplain at Rheindorf.' The second signature reads: 'J. Sonnenfels, Knight of the Order of St Stephen.' 'Approved! Sigismundus, *Archiepiscopus*.'

'In total secrecy!' Nevertheless there can be no doubt: Fanny knew of it. Her friend Joseph Sonnenfels would never have dared to sign such a document unless it corresponded to her wishes. For whatever reasons Pereira and Henriette had decided to prepare the way for their own conversion by means of this baptism – Fanny had agreed to it. Nor should one assume that this was a case of resumption of the Marrano crypto-Judaism which was traditional to the Pereiras in the male line. Everything points to the fact that Henriette and her husband, not without consideration of material advantage to themselves, but also out of conviction, had begun to strive after Christianity, so that, when in the end they, too, were baptised, the new doctrine had become more than a religious form. We need not even suspect them of that sceptical piety which Jules Lemaître has called 'piété sans foi' – a desire but inability to believe. No, just like Dorothea Mendelssohn, who rediscovered her father's faith in God, first in the Protestant, then in the Catholic creed, they too intended to subjugate their former devotion to the new denomination. And Fanny, whose eyes had been opened by the parable of the three rings in Lessing's *Nathan*, did not stand in their way.

-8-

Desperate but not Serious

Shivering with fear and cold, as though they had been troubled by ominous dreams and, under the influence of the nightmare, in their chilly bedchambers, had cast aside their warm eiderdowns, the Viennese awoke to the new year. Napoleon had departed before New Year's Eve, restoring their arsenal of weapons to them untouched, in gratitude for their 'good behaviour', their 'honour, faithfulness and decency' during the occupation. His troops, however – living proof that those terrible dreams of the enemy seated on the very edge of one's own bed had been true – remained quartered in the city, a vexation to the citizens on whom they were billeted. It was not until 13 January that the last of the French marched out of the city gates, and three days later the imperial couple were able to venture back into the capital.·

Their arrival was greeted, with however little justification, by joyful applause on the part of the population. The dome of St Stephen's Cathedral had been adorned, and all the villages through which Francis and his consort passed were transformed into forests of fir and pine. Throughout the Leopoldstadt the houses were decorated with trees, garlands of flowers and embroidered hangings. Across the Tabor bridge, which had opened the path to Austerlitz to the enemy, the festive procession now continued in the opposite direction, past the Roter Turm, through the Hoher Markt, and, describing a wide curve, to the cathedral, to end after a solemn *Te Deum* in the Hofburg. In the evening, there was free entry for everyone to the theatre and to a masked ball.

The cheering which had greeted the Emperor may have sounded a little feeble here and there – like the disillusioned *Evviva* offered to the Count in the first act of *Figaro*. Francis had, of course, no intention of behaving like Almaviva by hindering his subjects' festivities or even ordering them into the army. Quite to the contrary, his return confirmed the feeling that peace had been restored and that one should begin to enjoy life again. But this peace was more shameful than had been those of Campo Formio and Lunéville. Venice, but recently won, fell to the kingdom of Italy, Istria and Dalmatia were from now on to be subject to French rule, and the new King of Bavaria had pocketed the Tyrol and Vorarlberg. In exchange for these old hereditary lands, Salzburg and Berchtesgaden had been won, which pushed Napoleon's blue-coats a few kilometres further out of view. No more, in truth, than a few kilometres! For the French forces stopped at the Bavarian border, demonstrating that not even they had faith in this peace. 'All Austria,' writes the Viennese chronicler Hormayr, 'seemed to breathe deeply and freely again. But whoever looked out with attentive gaze onto the tempest-breeding ocean of the European world could see well enough that it was not over yet by any means, this time of trial.'

Fanny did not need to peer out onto that tempest-breeding ocean in order to surmise the destiny of the coming years. She looked down upon the monarch proceeding in his state coach along the Hoher Markt, and saw the powerlessness of Austria written in his face. It was no energetic Maria Theresa, no strong-willed Joseph, but a temporiser and a weakling who sat upon the throne, while one even stronger than the great Frederick was sweeping his way across the map of Europe. Probably either of his brothers, Karl and Johann, would have made a better emperor than this man, who was neither a circumspect diplomat and determined general nor a be-nign father of his people. Even wiser princes were unable to arrest the victorious progress of Bonaparte. But to keep the misery in his own country within limits, not to disregard for over two months an urgent request from the court chamber concerning the speedy improvement of the exchange rates, not to bring his people and officials, through distrustful hesitation and procrastination, even nearer to the verge of death by starvation than the nation's defeat was already, inevitably, doing – all this at least should have been possible.

Francis, who on his return had solemnly promised 'to dedicate every moment of My life to the enhancement of the welfare of the good and noble people, who are as dear to Me as children of My heart' – but nevertheless continued to allow money vouchers to be printed, malcontents to be spied upon, bakers' shops to be guarded by the military, and domestic servants and housewives to be driven apart with truncheons or even sabres – Francis was, in these days of terror, hardly a comfort to his Viennese. No wonder that their cheering became ever more feeble, that they grumbled where they could, and that Count Zinzendorf could speak in 1806 of the 'proverbial Viennese commandments', which were silently being broken by one and all.

The Prussian lady in her mansion on the Hoher Markt was ill at ease in this situation – probably the more so as the wretchedness of the people brought ever more income to her family. In the peaceful years before Ulm, her husband's bank, which in 1804 had taken the name of Arnstein & Eskeles, had received a number of commissions from the state, which increased its prestige even if they were not very lucrative. It had transferred their allowances to the imperial ambassadors in Paris, St Petersburg, Genoa and Christiania; it had supported the fiscal department by means of occasional loans raised from financiers of its acquaintance such as Bethmann in Frankfurt or Schubak in Hamburg. Now that the high contributions to France were added to the costs of defeat in war, the loans negotiated by the bank were again soaring to enormous heights. In January, Arnstein & Eskeles had to find 4,500,000 and in March as much as 32,000,000 gulden, in the second case jointly with the houses of Fries and Geymüller.

In handling such transactions, which combined the welfare of the state with his own advantage, Nathan may not have expended much thought on the plight of the little man who was being ruined by the inevitable devaluation and the rising cost of living. After all, even the members of the high nobility at that time saw no harm in spending 100,000 gulden annually in the leisurely enjoyment of their revenue, while a harassed little clerk or postman was forced to manage on 400, the buying power of which sank first by half, then by a third. Fanny, however, was moved to compassion by poverty. She helped where she could. The *Wiener Zeitung* repeatedly published accounts of the support she gave to the needy. In her will of July 1806 she remembered both the Christian and the Jewish almshouses, commending the 'poor of both nations to the hearts of my husband and my daughter – and these are good funds', and added the remarkable clause: 'I request my daughter, not indeed to give any priority in her gifts to any nation or religion, but on the other hand always to remember that *the poor Jew finds support only among his fellow-believers, while the poor Christian is supported and helped by both nations.* Let her impress this upon her children, though they are brought up in the Christian faith, so that when they too one day perform charitable acts, they may not turn away the poor Jew from their door unheard and without help.' She made generous provision for her own servants, including her new lady's-maid, 'Sophie, who has had great patience with me', and remarked, moreover, that 'my husband's excellent nature, and my daughter's goodness and sense of justice assure me that our faithful servants will be provided for'.

In this, as in her other wills, which deal only with general benefactions, with concern for her poor relatives and the 'memory of her unforgettable father', there speaks a humility and modesty which accord ill with Gräffer's portrait of a salon lioness heavy with her millions. When she admonishes Henriette to support her Berlin aunts and cousins after her mother's death, she hopes at the same time that God will allow her to live a little longer, making it easier for her, 'by means of my savings to enable my daughter the more easily to make all these little sacrifices'. Her expenditure on cloth-ing, too, does not seem to have been excessive, for she mentions her 'very undistinguished wardrobe and personal linen', which – with the exception of the beautiful 'lace and shawls', which are to be conveyed to her Berlin nieces and her women friends, 'among whom I number Frau von Sonnenfels' – are to be shared between Sophie and her housekeeper Oda, otherwise Sara, Epstein.

Goods and chattels, it is clear, did not mean all that much to her. If Pereira, to whom she entrusts anew 'the happiness of my good, gentle daughter', again inherits nothing, it is because she has already given him in Henriette 'the only blessing, the only treasure I have possessed'. And finally, in a touchingly childlike manner, she once again asks for forgiveness of her weaknesses: 'I was, despite my moods, and in my own fashion, a loving and good mother, a good housewife, good sister and good friend – what good deeds I failed to do were certainly not in my power, this I may say without flattering myself, the happiness of others was always closer to my heart than my own.'

The lady from Berlin felt no more at ease during the summer, as she watched from oppressed Vienna for signs from her native city. What she had hoped and prayed for all this time seemed now, when prospects appeared at their gloomiest, to be on the point of fulfil-ment. Fanny had often lamented that Frederick William III, to whose father she owed her civic rights as a Prussian, was just as much of a temporiser and a weakling as Francis. Now this 'north German variety of the Habsburger' was about to put the inheri-tance of the great Frederick at hazard, and this at a moment when the game was already lost.

Since his accession to the throne, the King, persuaded by over-anxious cabinet advisers as well as by his own democratic tend-encies, had offered no resistance to the Revolution and its offspring. As early as 1798 one of his ministers of state said to the French ambassador: 'You have only the nobility against you; the King and the people are unequivocally for France.' More progressive than, though not as foolhardy as Francis, and, like him, surrounded by more talented or at least more hot-blooded siblings – Louis Ferdinand, as high-spirited as he was dauntless in the face of death, Prince August, who loved Madame Récamier, and the beautiful, witty Princess Radziwill – Frederick William had pursued a policy of caution. Now, when Napoleon was relentlessly advancing, when half of Europe was already in the hands of the Bonapartes, when sixteen German princes had left the National Federation and formed the Confederation of the Rhine, when the Holy Roman Empire was in ruins and the crown of Charlemagne had slipped from the head of Francis – now the King made up his mind to march.

It was the peculiar tragedy of this campaign, doomed to failure from the start, that the greatest minds of the nation, men like Stein and Hardenberg, had advised in its favour, whereas its outcome retrospectively appeared to justify the wretched procrastinators who until now had successfully kept Prussia out of the war. But neither the one group nor the other had any real influence over this new turn in history. So much suppressed aversion, disappointment and humiliation had been stored up for so long, ready to explode, that any spark could set it off. Napoleon, however, during the summer put on a veritable pyrotechnic display of provocative injustices. He forced Prussia into war with England and then negotiated with the new British Prime Minister, Lord Grenville, to the latter's cost; he broke all his promises and treated the Prussian King's envoy with contemptuous mockery.

The question of Hanover, which he had made over to Frederick William and was now offering to the English, finally provoked a Prussian ultimatum. This time Austria watched sceptically and indolently as three north-German armies with no plan of action were sent into the field against six brilliantly commanded Napoleonic corps. At Jena and Auerstädt the Prussians were crushingly defeated. Eleven days later, on 25 October 1806, Napoleon was in Berlin. His entry was announced by the city commander Count Schulenburg with the words: 'Calmness is the first duty of citizens.' The royal family had fled in the direction of Russia. And the *Empereur* proceeded to Sanssouci, to taste the full sweetness of his victory in the palace of Frederick the Great.

Her native city too dishonoured, the familiar streets and squares branded with the mark of the conqueror! Fanny sat weeping in Vienna. A world had collapsed around her. She was not the only one to feel this. 'Where is our age?' lamented Rahel Varnhagen in 1818. 'It was destroyed in the year six.' More had been destroyed than at first appeared to be the case. The heroic death of Prince Louis Ferdinand, the 'Prussian Alcibiades' as Clausewitz called him, as commander of the Prussian vanguard, was symptomatic. The bond between nobility and Jewry, both of which had for so long been allowed to generate wit and a patriotic spirit, loosened or was torn. The new bearers of the Prussian idea, philosophers, firebrands, poets of the younger Romanticism, no longer frequented the salons of the 'fair Hebrew'. They crowded around officials and bourgeois, around the privy councillor Stägemann, around such literary figures as Karl Friedrich Zelter and Achim von Arnim with their glee clubs and dinner-parties.

The first lecture ever held in Berlin by Fichte on his scientific doctrine had been a private seminar in the house of Sara Levy. Now, however, though not without continuing to further the careers of Madame Levy's nephews, Fichte was deviating more and more from the basic principles of tolerance of the Enlightenment by preaching a national state with no place in it for the Jews. While the new first minister, Freiherr vom Stein, during the 'blessed years of misfortune' which followed Jena, began to introduce far-reaching reforms which – though this was not his doing – laid the foundation for the civic equality of the Jews, anti-semitic prejudice was again growing in cultured circles. The more national feeling developed, the more violently people hated anyone who, voluntarily or compulsorily, was excluded from it.

The camps had re-formed. It was only in a more narrow definition of the state, a mystical immersion in one's own past that one now expected to discover the strength to resist Napoleon. In the end it was the *Empereur*, who had coined the phrase 'Dare to know', who brought the concepts of world citizenship and materialism into all the countries usurped by him, who appeared as the true heir of the Enlightenment. That his misdeeds, his cynical arrogance, his thirst for power and obsession with expansion discredited this Enlightenment is the heaviest reproach that posterity must make against him. He might liberate the Jews in his dominions and even express sympathies for them which, however, he later abandoned – but those among them who mistrusted his ominous patronage were right to do so. One such was Fanny's brother-in-law Eskeles, who had been invited in October 1806, a few days before the Prussian defeat, to attend the assembly of Jewish notables convoked by Napoleon in Paris. This meeting, whose purpose was to clear up the last differences of opinion between the now naturalised French Jews and their fellow-citizens, had been given the title of Sanhedrin, from the name of the highest court of justice in ancient Jerusalem. The invitation to Bernhard von Eskeles, as representative of the Austrian Jewish community, was worded in the most respectful manner:

Monsieur!
J'ai pris la liberté de Vous faire adresser un paquet, contenant la procla-mation de l'assemblée des Israélites de France et d'Italie à leurs corréligionnaires, pour que Vous ayez la complaisance de le remettre aux Syndics de la Communauté Juive à Vienne. Sachant par la renommée, dont Vous jouissez tout l'interêt que vous prenez au bien de l'Humanité en general, l'assemblée est convaincu d'avance, qu'elle ne pourrait faire une acquisition plus flatteuse, que celle, qu'elle ferait en votre personne, s'il Vous était possible de prendre place parmi ses membres.
    Il lui faut des personnes qui comme vous Mr. distinguées par leurs talents, leurs vertus et leurs fortune, ayent l'influence nécessaire pour faire approuver ses décisions par l'universalité des Israélites.

Recevez Mr. etc.   *J. Rodrigue fils.*
Paris le 11 Oct 1806   *secrétaire*

The first step towards a world union of Jews, which later haunted the minds of their persecutors, seemed to have been taken here. But Napoleon's plan prospered no further. Nor did the 'flattering acquisition' of Bernhard von Eskeles take place, for the latter immediately went to the head of the police department to report the contents of the letter. On 20 October this authority was already able to report to the Emperor that the Jews of Vienna 'expected nothing from Napoleon's plans for their nation and saw in them only a financial speculation'. The Emperor's well-known mistrust was not so easily lulled in this case. He continued to have his Jewish subjects kept under surveillance. Nothing could have been further from his mind than to reward their loyalty with civic rights. From the obscurest street pedlar to the *Freiherr*, they re-mained no more than 'tolerated'.

The occupation of Vienna had had the protracted consequences which are apt to succeed a violent shock. Try as one might, true *joie de vivre* would not return, and the court, plunged into deep mourning by the sudden death of the Empress from puerperal fever, had no appetite for festivities. Foreigners who visited the capital during that spring of 1807 were affected by the melancholic mood. 'Le séjour a été un peu triste,' wrote Count Carl Nesselrode to his father. 'Il n'y est question que de morts et d'enterrements. A l'Impératrice a succédé le prince Staremberg et, pour que le moment soit bien lugubre, nous avons eu un temps réellement affreux.'

Even so, the young diplomat found some diversion in certain Russian houses, which with an easy conscience continued to hold receptions, at Princess Dolgorouki's, at Madame de Shuvalov's and at the beautiful Princess Bagration's, and also visited 'dans seconde classe très souvent les Arnsteiner, Pereira, l'oncle Gontard (qui, par parenthèse, donne très bien à diner) et les Brévilliers que j'aime beaucoup'. Gentz, who had compared a 'certain Mad. de Brévilly' to 'that most dreadful of all creatures, Chevalier Rongé', had left the country and was in Prague awaiting the recovery of the Austrian party in favour of war. Meanwhile, it was far from anyone's mind to wish to change the state of things. During this summer Napoleon concluded a peace with his last continental opponent, Alexander of Russia. Since Jena he had been at the height of his power.

Fanny, too, was living a quieter, more withdrawn life during those years. She gave no glittering receptions, but kept up her regular circle, where foreign visitors such as Nesselrode, or the *Oberprocureur* of the duchies of Schleswig and Holstein, Freiherr von Eggers, or the worthy German traveller Gottlieb Hiller, were welcome at all times. In the houses of Arnstein and Eskeles, Eggers praised, as usual, the 'most refined social behaviour, the liveliest conversation, the least constrained hospitality. At Baroness Arnsteiner's you find company every afternoon. Hardly a visitor from the cultured classes comes to Vienna without seeking out such a circle of acquaintances; and none who finds it will leave Vienna without grateful reminiscences.' Hiller reported that he had 'enjoyed the greatest public esteem so far in the house of Fanny Baron [*sic*] von Arnstein':

This house is, as it were, the artistic rendezvous for foreigners, and everyone who, as such, is to some little extent distinguished, even in other respects, is presented to the Baroness; thus one not infrequently meets Greeks, Russians, Frenchmen and Dutchmen together at her table on a *single* occasion. Since these various nations flow together, as it were, into *one* European people through a *common* French conversation, and I am not yet able to utter an occasional *mon ami* as a finished *Serviteur*, I frequently appear as a gloomily animated Pygmalion statue, until some worthy Teuton breathes a new spark of life into me with some barometric observations.

With the tireless curiosity and vitality which were so characteristic of her, Fanny constantly gathered new foreign guests around her; but she attached herself most closely at this time to her intimate friends and family. These were years of reflection, years of restraint. The breathless haste, the frenzy with which she formerly rushed into the great world, the quicksilver liveliness of spirit which she had dedicated to the instruction and bewitching of young men of noble birth, the abandonment with which she planned every guessing-game, every visit to the theatre, every evening reception of her own, had given way to a calmer mood and a more measured way of life. After all, she would be fifty this autumn, and would really have had to call herself an old woman if she were not still lovable and loved, and often asked herself when the time of maturity and of turning away from outward pleasures was to be expected. Well, that time never came, and even the restfulness of those years was only a small pause for breath. The triumph of an existence whose motivating force was a hunger for humanity which could never be assuaged, an undying wish for the reconciliation of opposites, for the mingling of elements which strained away from each other, for the brotherhood of the most varied number of persons conceivable – this triumph was still to come. Meanwhile she gave tea-parties, issued invitations to dinner, and enjoyed most of all entertainments *en petit comité*, at which she need not mince her words during political discussions.

Gentz was probably right in saying – although he found less friendly ways of expressing it – that a temporary *embourgeoisement* had taken place among Fanny's circle. Instead of Princes Liechtenstein and Paar, the house was now frequented by the good Caroline Pichler, who had also begun, in her homely, honest way, to conduct a salon in the suburbs; by the amiable Frau von Brévillier – later housekeeper to Count Fries and governess to his children; or by Johann Jakob von Gontard, '*l'oncle* Gontard', a scion of the well-known Frankfurt family, who had lived in Vienna for some time and was an old admirer of Fanny's. He was the donor of a pretty present which is still in the possession of her family – a coffee-cup, which apart from his and her names bears the charming dedication: 'A ton bonheur, je porte envie / adieu, ma coupe, souviens toi / sur les lèvres de mon amie, / de lui parler souvent de moi.' It was probably Gontard, too, who about this time advised · Fanny to buy a second country home – this time at Baden, near Vienna, where he himself owned a small mansion on the main square. Her new property, which was to be filled with particularly interesting visitors at the time of the Congress of Vienna, was at the edge of this beautiful town, in what is now 25, Theresiengasse; it is the only residence of hers to be preserved, even if substantially altered.

For the rest, her circle of acquaintances had recently grown. Eleonore Eskeles, for example – or Frau von Fliess, as she was now politely called – had been living in Vienna again for some time and had here created, in Caroline Pichler's words, 'a pleasant meeting-place for a limited but select circle of cultured people'. This clever woman, to whom, moreover, Caroline ascribes 'endless good nature', was now receiving belated satisfaction for the disgrace in which she was driven out of town in Joseph's reign. Presumably she had postponed her return for so long in order to bring up the two children who were the fruit of her relationship with Valentin Günther. Now she was free. While her former lover, after leaving the service of the state, stayed with his blonde, pale Transylvanian in Lorettom on the Hungarian border, 'in his shirt-sleeves, with a white apron tied in front, powdered and with a little pigtail *à la* Emperor Joseph', she spent the evening of her years in dignity and urbane elegance.

In addition, a second sister of Fanny's had recently settled in Vienna, though for a distressing reason. Rebecca, perhaps the wittiest of the Itzig daughters, 'who talked like a poet', had fled Berlin with her husband David Ephraim after his bankruptcy. Like Isaac, the first-born of Daniel Itzig, this second son of Veitel Ephraim had brought disgrace on his house. In Vienna he took the name of Johann Andreas Schmidt and had himself christened. Whether and when Rebecca followed him into the Christian world is unknown. And finally, Jakob Bartholdy was there again, whom to his annoyance Gentz had seen four years ago going in and out of the house of Prince de Ligne. Not only family loyalty persuaded Fanny to have her nephew about her as much as possible. He was, like her, an ardent enemy of Napoleon, who had only one thought: that of extinguishing Prussia's shame as speedily as possible. He also reminded her of her youthful surroundings, which had later become his – the dairy at the Schlesisches Tor, whose name he had adopted and which his sister Lea had once described so vividly to the painter Merkel: 'Imagine the densest, coolest shadows of venerable chestnut, lime and plane trees; friendly spots and dainty summer-houses; high, arched arbours; an abundance of the treasures of Flora and Pomona . . . and thereto a small, comfortable, country residence, on whose walls climb vines, mulberry and peach trees', all this in the middle of 'the flat countryside of Brandenburg', on its 'meagre soil', and exceedingly 'quiet, friendly and secluded'.

It was a vision which Fanny was fond of calling to mind; particularly now, when she neither could nor would visit her poor, dishonoured Berlin.

The more modest social life which had followed the occupation of Vienna regained its former glory in January 1808, following the imperial example. On the sixth of that month Francis took his cousin, Maria Ludovica d'Este, as his bride, and a few days later the entire nobility appeared, decked in gold and diamonds, in a splendid masquerade – representing the homage paid to a Hindustani sultan – at the first great general masked ball. At the same time an adventurer, the physician, mechanic and entrepreneur Siegmund Wolfsohn, opened Vienna's newest and most ornate dance-hall, the Apollosaal. In the midst of the greatest poverty, here was a flourishing place of entertainment which took 20,000 to 30,000 gulden in a single evening. All this was the prelude to renewed amusements which took place in the shadow of Napoleon in the old, carefree, sunny spirit. 'Les exploits militaires,' Madame de Staël observed sarcastically, 'devaient être l'intérêt principal d'une monarchie qui s'est illustrée par des guerres continuelles: et cependant la nation autrichienne s'était tellement livrée au repos et aux douceurs de la vie, que les événements publics eux-mêmes n'y faisaient pas grand bruit, jusqu'au moment où ils pouvaient réveiller le patriotisme: et ce sentiment est calme dans un pays où il n'y a que du bonheur.'

She, the most famous woman in Europe, had come to Vienna that winter, accompanied by her two younger children Albert and Albertine and her tame philosopher, August Wilhelm Schlegel. It is questionable whether the Viennese spoke for years afterwards of 1808 as the year in which Madame de Staël was their guest. After all, part of the pleasant slumber which allowed them to ignore important events was a certain absent-mindedness regarding persons and phenomena which occasionally passed before their eyes. All the same, this unhandsome, coarse-featured, plump-armed woman, dressed to kill, aroused more than the usual attention as she made the rounds of the first families and certain smaller houses. She displeased two such different hosts as Prince de Ligne, who found himself provoked to inner disagreement by her dogmatic statements, and Caroline Pichler – later dubbed by her 'la Muse du Faubourg' – whose cosy literary circle was abruptly and wilfully interrupted by the turbaned *femme du monde*, who was to mock it in the most amusing way on the same evening, two houses away at Countess Wrbna's.

What Caroline Pichler could endure least of all was that Germaine de Staël did not treat her elegant scholar 'with the respect and consideration which she should really have owed to a man of his talent. There often appeared to be a tone of authority, such as one would use to a subordinate, in her behaviour towards him'. To be sure, this worthy woman, in whom the 'crass sensuality' and 'impure urges' of the Romantics induced an uncomprehending disgust, knew nothing of the document by which Schlegel had bound himself to Madame de Staël as her lifelong slave. When Caroline's novel *Agathokles*, containing an attack on Edward Gibbon, a friend of Germaine's mother in her youth, was published that spring, she may have prejudiced Madame de Staël against herself. Germaine however remained 'very civil' to her and even invited her to the performances of her plays, in which she herself played the main parts, at the private theatres of Countess Zamoiska and of Prince Liechtenstein in the Herrengasse.

When and how frequently Madame de Staël met the woman who had been compared by the memoirist Pezzl to Mesdames Geoffrin and Necker is not known. Rahel Levin seems to have thought that she and Fanny were virtually inseparable, for in January 1808 she wrote from Berlin to Brinckmann: 'Frau von Staël is in Vienna, I could almost say at Frau von Arnstein's.' But she probably overestimated the attraction of another brilliant hostess for the self-obsessed *femme supérieure*. Germaine sought above all the acquaintance of the high nobility, to which, as Frau Pichler remarked testily, she 'was not entitled by birth', and preferred the apartments of Princesses Ligne, Liechtenstein and Lubomirska, of Countesses Wrbna and Zamoiska, to the salon of the wittier, but less well-born Prussian lady.

At any rate, she knew Fanny's family and had visited her sister Sara in Berlin four years earlier. Without actually pitching her tent in the Arnstein house, as Rahel thought, she unquestionably went there from time to time. She may also have called on Henriette, for there is evidence of at least one return visit. On the last day of March 1808, Count Carl von Zinzendorf, Vienna's most assiduous diarist, entered in his little book the fact that he had seen many ladies at Madame de Staël's, 'entr'autres Mme Pereyra de Haking, qui a pourtant du juif dans la physionomie, et qui est extrêmement maigre'. No further meetings with her or her mother are recorded. But when Germaine, back in Coppet, was toying with the idea of an early return to Vienna, the occasion being her affair with the young Austrian officer Maurice O'Donnell, it was Fanny and her family who were to assist her. A police report of July 1808 announces that 'Madame de Staël is thinking of arriving in October and the Arnsteiner and Eskeles ladies are making efforts to find her an apartment'.

Germaine, whose lover had brutally rejected her, did not travel to Vienna again that autumn. Nevertheless, she would not resign herself to the breach with O'Donnell, pursued him with letters and contrived plans for establishing stronger links with Austria. She wrote to Maurice in November, for instance, that she was considering the purchase of one of those 'biens ecclésiastiques qu'on met en vente en Autriche . . . Je consulte M. Arnstein par le revenu.' What she wanted to know from O'Donnell was whether he would encourage her plans in general. In the same letter she suspects that she has cause to be jealous of the young woman to whose thinness and physiognomy Count Zinzendorf took such exception: 'On dit que vous aimez beaucoup madame Pereyra, mais je ne puis me persuader, que vous ne me retrouveriez pas plus digne de votre amitié que personne, car je n'ai jamais cessé, depuis je vous connais, de prendre sous une forme ou sous une autre le plus tendre intérêt à vous.'

Nothing came of all this – neither of Germaine's church property nor of O'Donnell's return to her, still less of any amour between him and Henriette. When, however, in 1812 Madame de Staël took up residence in the capital for the second time, from now on hardly noticed by the great world in its fickleness, she was as welcome as before at the Arnsteins'. Fanny's old friend Collenbach sat next to her at dinner. A little tactlessly, he put a question to her which arose from the presence of the 'inescapable Schlegel': 'Madame, que vous est M. Schlegel?' 'Monsieur, j'avais pris M. Schlegel pour être précepteur de mon fils, mais je l'ai trouvé au-dessus de son état.'

In the spring of 1808, her tame philosopher had cultivated all those relationships which she herself had neglected in favour of the circles of the higher nobility. He had been a frequent guest of Eleonore Fliess and had also cut a good figure at Fanny's salon. The lectures on dramatic theory which Schlegel gave during Lent before no fewer than eighteen princesses and all those members of Viennese society who 'rightly or wrongly laid claim to culture and elegance', were certainly attended by Fanny. She had enough of the intellectual dandy in her nature to prevent such an event from slipping past her.

Had she followed her sister Cäcilie and the latter's sister-in-law Eleonore to Franzensbad that summer, Fanny would have taken part in an event which it would have been even more of a pity to miss than August Wilhelm Schlegel's lectures. This event – granted even to Rahel Varnhagen only fleetingly and in embarrassing circumstances – was a friendly meeting with Goethe.

The beautiful or perhaps merely clever 'Hebrew ladies' of Berlin had always been very active in helping to augment the poet's fame in Germany. He himself, it is true, like most of his contemporaries, was ambivalent in his attitude to the Jews. As a child he had fearfully confronted the strange-looking figures in the Frankfurt ghetto. As a young man he had commented benevolently on the author of the *Poems of a Polish Jew*, despite his disappointment with them: 'We wish that on the path by which we seek our ideal he may meet us again on a higher spiritual level.' In his poetic play *Fair at Plundersweilen* he had mocked a people whose members Moses Mendelssohn, Markus Herz, Friedländer and Meyerbeer he fully appreciated. When it was a question of setting Homer against the Old Testament he inveighed against 'Jewish pomp', to which one owed 'sodomising and Egyptian–Babylonian caprices'. As an old gentleman he was still fulminating against a new law for the Jews, whereby marriage to unchristened persons was to be permitted. At the same time he loved young Felix Mendelssohn, admired Sophie von Grotthuss, with whom he was linked by a long corre-spondence, and even entered into an affectionate relationship with her sister Marianne.

Since Marianne von Eybenberg had been living in Vienna, she too had corresponded with Goethe and strengthened the picture in his imagination of the Phaeacian city whose inhabitants 'day-dreamed the time away in a fool's paradise'. While she begrudged Fanny von Arnstein her brilliant sociability, the latter probably cast glances tinged with envy at her friendship with Goethe. His letters reached Marianne by way of the 'Comptoir du Baron D'Arnstein', so that the opportunity to establish a connection could easily have arisen. Clearly, however, it was far from being Fanny's way to strive strenuously towards one, as Rahel did time and again. It was her quieter, generally less ambitious sister who had allowed Marianne to give her an introduction to Goethe when she travelled to the Bohemian spa on this occasion with Frau von Fliess.

'Madame Eskeles,' Goethe reported to Marianne from Carlsbad on 12 August, 'I have seen only at the concert – and, as I fear, I have not done enough in taking up your recommendation.' He still hoped, so he wrote, to find the lady in 'Franzensbrunn' or to seek her out on her return. The connection was formed as soon as he came to Franzensbad. 'There is here a Frau v. Eskeles from Vienna,' his secretary Riemer wrote to Friedrich Johann From-mann on 4 September, 'probably already well known to you, who is daily frequented by company, from which I am able to abstract an idea of what it may be like in Vienna. One eats quite excellently there, and this might well be the greatest pleasure of all those which great society, which lives from day to day, can convey.'

Goethe's diary reveals even more clearly that it was to a great extent the seductive arts of the Viennese cook, whom Cäcilie had brought with her, to which he succumbed unresistingly. But, after all, both ladies were sufficiently well read and cultured to encourage him to read to them in the evenings from some of his minor productions – though not *Die Wahlverwandschaften* (*Elective Affinities*), which Marianne was the first to see. The pleasant encounter lasted for twelve days, during which they met continually. It began on 31 August: 'Early to take the waters with Madame E. and F. . . . In the evening to Frau v. E. for tea. Finkenstein, Count Moschynski, Englishman Smith.' On 1 September: 'Early to take the waters with . . . Frau v. E. and F. . . . Afterwards to Frau v. E. for *déjeuné*, where young Count Finkenstein & wife. When these had gone, [there was talk] about Frau von Staël. Afterwards Dr Warburton and Count Finkenstein senior . . . In the evening to Frau v. E.'s for tea and supper'.

After so short an acquaintance, to take no fewer than three meals at her house – that was quite something! Moreover, he there received reports about the visit to Vienna of Madame de Staël, whom Marianne had already described to him in May as a 'monster of genius'. On 2 September: 'at noon to Frau v. E. with Ignaz Potocki, Count Moschynski . . . After luncheon, Stories of Dispersed People . . . In the evening to Frau v. E. for tea and supper.' And so it goes on. On the fifth, sixth and seventh both meals at her house. 'In the evening [of the eighth] . . . there was a firework display. Afterwards read the new Melusine and some of my sonnets.' On the twelfth, Goethe leaves Franzensbad at about six o'clock. But the connection is a lasting one. They begin to correspond; he does not, however, write to the good hostess and housewife Cäcilie, but to Eleonore Fliess, who was poorer, but wittier.

Almost all of these letters are lost to posterity, but their despatch was faithfully noted in his diary, together with Eleonore's address, in 'Oberbräunerstrasse No. 1209 on the second floor'. The following February, Marianne mentions that 'Frau von Eskeles writes to me of you with delight, I could wish that you would say something to me of her; although I know everything about her; I would still like to hear it in your own words.' But her wish to learn something pointed, perhaps even pointedly derogatory, about Cäcilie from him was not fulfilled. Goethe had begun at about this time to estrange himself somewhat from Marianne Eybenberg; her constant 'grumbling and politicising' repelled him and reminded him distressingly of his former beloved Charlotte von Stein. The question about Frau von Eskeles was dealt with by his secretary Riemer.

The correspondence with the Viennese ladies continued. In April 1809 Eleonore sent the 'Illustrious *Herrn Geheimen Rath*' a dozen impressions of coins for his numismatic collection and at the same time mentioned Friedrich von Schlegel's having settled in Vienna. A year later she wrote: 'Baron von Retzer – Steigentesch – Frau v. Pichler, Eskeles and Pereira commend themselves to your further benevolent thoughts. The last-mentioned, who this winter had the sorrow of losing one of her sons, asks me on every occasion when I recall the happy hours spent in your company at Eger with my sister-in-law Eskeles, if she must really depart the world cheated out of Herr v. Goethe?'

Not Fanny, but her daughter Henriette was now putting out feelers in order to make the much-desired acquaintance with the great man. And finally Caroline Pichler too turned up in the circle of Viennese letter-writing ladies: 'For some time now, at the request of my kind friend Frau v. Fliess, I have been at pains to search out examples of the handwriting of notable persons for your collection.' Admittedly she had not been able to get hold of a manuscript of Mozart's, for which Goethe had expressed a wish. 'You receive therefore only the little I could get, but Frau v. Fliess will richly compensate in her package for the deficiency of mine. My sheets are: Haidn, Lord Nelson, Abbé Hell, Denis, Mastalier.' Her letter closes with the hope that her *Agathokles*, which Eleonore had sent him on her behalf, might meet with his approval. The picture of a Goethe carefully incorporating into his autograph album the handwriting of a Denis and a Mastalier – kindred spirits to that Haschka who wore his hair and clothing *à la Goethe* – is not without its comic side. History, however, dealt even more ironically when the requested Mozart autograph came into Goethe's possession, not through Caroline Pichler, but through Eleonore Fliess. In May 1812 the latter informed the poet that she had resorted to Mozart's widow, who was living in Denmark, 'married to Herr von Nissen, former *chargé d'affaires* at the court here, and I expect an answer shortly'. Soon afterwards she was in a position to fulfil Goethe's wish. Suspecting nothing of the wild insults inflicted on her thirty years earlier by Mozart in a letter to his father, 'the Jewess Escules', that 'sow of the first order, the only cause of Günther's misfortune', now sent a sample of his handwriting to Germany's greatest poet. And a few months later, as if fate had waited only for this last trump-card to end her life victoriously, she too died.

According to Metternich, it was at Jena that Napoleon's power had been at its greatest. If at that time he had refrained from destroying Prussia, and instead had added her, in her weakened condition, to the Confederation of the Rhine, his empire would have gained in stability and longevity. But the dynamic forces to which he himself was a victim drove him onwards. When, in the autumn of 1808, he met the Tsar for the second time at Erfurt, his situation had already been shaken by the Spanish uprising of the preceding spring. Even so, Alexander, to whom he offered the grand duchy of Warsaw in gratitude for his continued neutrality, seemed prepared to maintain a passive attitude towards a renewed European campaign against France.

That such a campaign was imminent was known to everyone. Encouraged by the French failures in Spain, a new warlike spirit has stirred in Austria. In August six Viennese militia battalions stood ready, adequately equipped and in full uniform, whose costs were covered by the estates of the realm. And on 1 November all the battalions which had been set up in the course of the year were able to take part in manoeuvres on the Glacis before Archduke Karl.

This time it was serious. Napoleon's defiant prophecy in the Paris senate after his return from Erfurt, that 'within three months his eagles would be placed upon the fortifications of Lisbon, the British leopard would be plunged into the sea, and within the space of a year not a single village would be in revolt throughout the whole Pyrenean peninsula', had not deceived the Austrians as to his precarious position. The mockery of French newspapers, in which it was claimed that their country had become so impoverished after the last war that the nobility had fetched all the old cannons out of their domains and presented them to the Emperor, but that the capital had become so depopulated by starvation and emigration that several persons had already been gobbled up on the Glacis by wolves roaming as far as the city gate, infuriated the Viennese even more. The din with which France blew her own trumpet finally – in Madame de Staël's words – reached their ears and awakened their patriotism. In Salzburg too, in the lands above and below the river Enns, in Bohemia, Moravia and Silesia, militia battalions were being formed. In anticipation of the now inevitable war, Count Stadion, the former ambassador to Berlin, now a minister of state, was transforming the feudal army into a people's army.

The Prussians, so much was clear, were once again not of the company. The shattering defeat of their first and only campaign had exhausted them, the loss of Warsaw rendered them totally dejected. Instead of planning new military ventures, from which they no longer expected anything, they had undertaken the reform of their urban administration, national laws and educational system. A further humiliation lay in store for them. The great Freiherr vom Stein, who followed the teachings of the French Revolution, while despising its heirs, was about to be driven out on the orders of Napoleon and to the delight of his own reactionary landed gentry.

Austria was to take him in. Austria, in this autumn of 1808, already had many Prussians who had left their own country for one reason or another. Some came because they hoped to indulge their religious–romantic sentimentality unhindered in the Catholic atmosphere of Vienna. Others, such as Varnhagen, wanted to be at the hub of resistance against Napoleon and render military services – like Jakob Bartholdy who, with the help of his aunt Fanny, had already, despite a slight deformity, entered the second Viennese battalion of militia as a first lieutenant under the popular dramatist Ernst August von Steigentesch. Others, again, such as Friedrich Schlegel, combined one motive with the other. Most of these were enthusiastically received in the Arnstein household.

One man who arrived in the capital towards the end of the year, and was to stay until shortly before the outbreak of war, was Johann Friedrich Reichardt, a composer and writer on music from Königsberg. Summoned to Berlin by Frederick the Great as a very young man, he had played a great part as *Kapellmeister* to the Prussian capital. There he had already made Fanny's acquaintance. Later, because of his growing republican tendencies, which, however, he combined with antagonism to Bonaparte, he was obliged to leave Berlin. The peace of Tilsit had made him a Westphalian subject, which he bore with composure, as Goethe – whose poems he liked to set to music – bore his allegiance to a French tributary state.

To set himself up in Vienna, the city of music, which he had visited once before in 1783, was Reichardt's only motive for his journey. He had no intention of conspiring, either with his compatriots against Napoleon, nor against Emperor Francis on behalf of Jerôme Bonaparte. Nevertheless, he was not trusted. The police records contain a note: 'Here in Vienna is *Kapellmeister* Reichardt from Berlin, about whom indeed nothing definite can be said, but who can be regarded as a very suspicious person.' Just as unsuspectingly as the good Eleonore Eskeles about what was being said behind his back, he rushed enthusiastically into society life, and years later, when his benevolent, indeed flattering *Vertraute Briefe* (*Confidential Letters*) were published, completely effaced the bad reputation of Prussian observers in Vienna, for which Nicolai was to blame.

Reichardt arrived on the afternoon of 24 November and spent his first evening at Fanny's house. He had put up at the hotel *Römischer Kaiser*, and had rushed to the Hofburgtheater to hear the opera *The Orphanage* by Joseph Weigl, where he met 'our friend from Berlin, the little Greek Bartholdy': 'He assured me that one could attend the evening *assemblée* at the Arnsteins', which he had left not long since in full swing, even in boots and travelling clothes; and I gladly hastened thither with him at once. There, too, I found quite a new Vienna; for perhaps half of the very imposing and numerous *assemblée* were indeed wearing boots. The noble, splendid lady of the house, the most interesting friend of my youth from Berlin, and her excellent sister, Frau von Eskeles, received me.'

Although most of the guests were occupied at the gaming tables which stood in several rooms, Fanny gradually introduced him to her friends. He met Fräulein von Kurzbeck, Vienna's most popular amateur pianist, who had studied with Clementi and Haydn and whose playing was, 'according to the verdict of all connoisseurs, the most similar to that of the late Mozart'. Baron von Steigentesch, Bartholdy's colonel, shook him by the hand. Among his old acquaintances, he again met Sonnenfels and the latter's wife Theresia – 'known as Aspasia because of her lively wit' – as well as Franz Pignatelli, Prince von Acerenza, who was thought to be in the service of the Russians, and a Frau von Severin, whom he had already met in St Petersburg.

Towards ten o'clock, as Reichardt reports, the company gradually departed; he himself, with Bartholdy, paid a further visit, to Cäcilie Eskeles, who had invited him to a late supper. At about eleven he was entertained by her – certainly no worse than Goethe had been – for which he was particularly grateful, since he would have got nothing to eat at the *Römischer Kaiser* at that hour. Next day he ate once again 'very agreeably at a little family party of twelve persons at Baron von Arnstein's, seated between the brilliant mother and the very gifted daughter, Frau von Pereira. The latter's delightful children joined us for the dessert. How splendid are the three boys that this delicate little woman has borne in four years! Handsome and vigorous as ever van Dyck painted. The father too is a cultured and interesting man, of an individual character.'

Soon Reichardt appears 'at a pleasant dinner at Herr von Pereira's', where he meets the Italian writer and composer Abbate Carpani and spends 'a pleasant half-hour at the fortepiano' with him. There follows a visit which touches and moves him above all else – to the 76-year-old Haydn. 'Fräulein von Kurzbeck, for whom he has a fatherly affection, and Frau von Pereira, full of enthusiasm for him as for everything great and fine, took me out to him.' In a little summer-house in the suburbs the 'splendid old man' sits at a table covered with a green cloth, his garments of grey cloth with white buttons and a curly wig delicately coiffed and powdered, 'very stiff and almost rigid, not unlike a living wax-work'. Fräulein Kurzbeck introduces him, Haydn embraces him and weeps tears of joy. 'Frau von Pereira, whom with his failing memory he did not at first recognise, reminded him in a childlike, playful manner of diverse jests, and he soon fell into the same manner with her, which he must always have loved very much. Now, however, the ladies suggested that we should leave the weak old gentleman, it was after all affecting him too much, and took their leave.' None the less Haydn calls them back again, shows them his treasures and releases them only after another hour at least.

A sociability emerges from Reichardt's reports which already seems much more unconstrained and open-minded than at the beginning of Francis's reign, and in which the boundaries between the separate circles and cliques become indistinct. Through Baroness Grotthuss, who lodged at the Arnstein house in September 1808 and is still resident there, he is invited 'to the Czernins in Wallnerstrasse'. It is unthinkable that Sophie's hostess Fanny was not also present! At a private concert in the Palais Lobkowitz, where Reichardt is exceedingly honoured and extracts from his operas *Rosamunde, L'heureux Naufrage* and *The Blue Monster* are performed, he meets the Schwarzenbergs, Fürstenbergs, Liechtensteins, Kinskys, Colloredos and other leading families. Invited to a *thé dansant* at the house of 'a rich young boyar', he recognises in the latter's wife, 'a pretty little Wallachian princess', a lady whom he has already met at the Pereiras'. 'At an elegant tea-party given by Frau von Eskeles I lately also met the beautiful gifted Lady Fitz-Gerald' – a close friend of Bartholdy's, the natural daughter of Duke Philippe Egalité of Orléans and of the French writer Madame de Genlis, who had lived in Berlin and met Fanny there.

The good cuisine of the Eskeles household continually finds favour with him. 'Thus in the last few days I have again had such a pair of highly refined dinners at the houses of Baron von Steigentesch and of Herr von Eskeles as one can find truly only in Paris, and, what is not easily found there at the same time, they were also entirely enjoyable and cheerful because of a small, very well chosen gathering.' Apart from private hospitality, trouble is taken to show Vienna's most sumptuous establishment to the honoured visitor. The Apollosaal is closed, as it is not yet *Fasching* (the carnival season). 'Baron Arnstein had, however, secured its opening for several friends, ordered carriages and had us driven out to the very distant suburb where the Apollosaal is situated. It is a quite singular, fantastic monster of splendour and variety, which must, when illuminated, have a quite dazzling, magical effect. Only such a rich, truly great city of general prosperity could create and maintain something like this.'

On 8 January, the first day of *Fasching*, Reichardt is to see the hall in all the glory of its chandeliers, admire the fountains and follies, enjoyed by up to eight thousand people simultaneously, and wonder at the buffets, confectioneries and restaurants where a mixed throng of nobles, bourgeois, peasants, and tenant farmers dissipate more than 60,000 gulden in a single night. After all he was an *homme moyen sensuel* and not a Prussian pedant, as Nicolai had been. The 'softness, love of comfort, thoughtlessness, idleness and constant dissipation' which the latter had censured in Vienna had indeed by no means been done away with. But Reichardt had no complaint to make. 'Everything here breathes cheerfulness and jollity' – that was enough for him. The critical enlightener would have questioned the expediency of such amusements in the midst of increasing misery and in the face of the threat of war. Reichardt, however, though like Nicolai he had grown up in Frederick's Berlin, was a man of the new era. He hated the 'mania for reading', that 'disease of the North', and was convinced that true salvation lay in naïve sensibility, indeed 'that with all our empty meditations and with all our joyless pursuit of art we have become very poor citizens of the state and of the world and need to become children again'.

Filled with childish pleasure, he also took part in the lighter musical enjoyments Vienna had to offer: 'There were several little Italian duets . . . which I had already heard recently at an evening party given by Frau von Pereira, where a Prince Rohan' – this was the Austrian lieutenant-general Ludwig Rohan-Guémenée – 'with a pleasant talent of his own, sang his own compositions at the fortepiano with a slight voice, but in the true Italian manner, and in a particularly lively way performed a whole series of delightful waltzes, partly singing, partly whistling, with the sole accompaniment of the fortepiano'.

The waltz had begun to supplant the other dances, and Henriette was one of the first to give it her approval, as Reichardt relates:

On one of these evenings I also attended a numerous, great *assemblée* at Baron *Arnstein*'s, which had much in common with the famous *assemblées* of Madame Récamier in Paris, including the fact that the company was after all too large for the place, as impressive as it is, and pressed to and fro like waves of the sea. Before the whole gathering had collected, Frau von *Pereira*, together with Frl. von Kurzbeck, played a very brilliant double sonata by Steibelt in a most masterly way, and then, with incredible patience and kindness, many beautiful waltzes, to which handsome young people whirled around merrily in the ever-increasing throng. As soon as the furthest room was opened for supper, I departed: it was nearly midnight. With what dignity and grace, kind and agreeable to each comer, the beautiful, radiant lady of the house played hostess, was a sight to be seen.

The New Year was approaching. It was a severe winter, with an unusual quantity of snow. The street urchins climbed up onto the backs of the sleighs, and no one told the coachmen – 'which always infallibly happens among our own people, to my great annoyance. I took a seat with Herr Schröter in his carriage, to pay a momentary visit to the *assemblée* at the Arnsteins' house, which today, in honour of the New Year, was very numerous and brilliant. Here all this sort of thing is arranged the evening before.'

Nevertheless, the receptions at which the Viennese ceremoniously congratulated each other on the entry of the fateful year of 1809 were drawn out well into the first days of January:

At a very elegant dinner of Frau von Eskeles' I had the opportunity to offer my compliments to several of my closest acquaintances. I wish I could give you a true notion of the exquisite, perfect charm of this house, how everything, down to the smallest point, harmonises into a comfortable, tasteful enjoyment. And then I'd have to be able to describe to you the noble couple, with their delightful, handsome, almost too clever pair of children. The beautiful, interesting, sensitive wife, you did indeed know in Berlin; but the husband – about him I can tell you only in a few words, as he himself expresses himself everywhere in but few words – he is a man of *esprit* and understanding and heart, a complete man. I would consider it a true prize in life to live in the same place and in close contact with him.

Not only Reichardt, but also Rahel Levin – at the time of the Congress – described Cäcilie's husband, Nathan's partner, in a captivating manner:

Eskeles: of whom I am very fond, because his wisdom oozes out of his very pores, he eats, he is silent, he laughs, all wisely: he makes all sorts of individual, original remarks! Yes! in a certain sense he amuses me better here than anyone else; because he has remained quite patriarchal, with great gifts of the mind, and a rich life has passed over him, which he has cultivated quite in his own way, and he utters many original things with the *aisance* of the most experienced of men, in the good Old Testament manner.

But Rahel's husband, as he later became, who was to visit the Arnstein, Pereira and Eskeles houses soon after Reichardt, adds a few marginal notes to this description in his *Denkwürdigkeiten*:

In order to see the last remark in its true significance, one would in fact need to be better informed, for while in Frau von Eskeles' rooms everything, in the splendour and tastefulness of the furnishings as in the distinction of the company and the tone of conversation, vied with the highest circles of Vienna, and indeed the children had not the remotest notion of their actual origins, yet Eskeles himself, after having appeared for a time in accordance with propriety and dignity in this distinguished world, used to slip off forthwith into a back room, where he received visits from his fellow-believers, old cronies and shrewd business associates, and spend the rest of the evening carelessly and cosily over tobacco and beer.

Varnhagen, whose duplicity will become evident in due course, here tosses a few of those malicious little darts, which so easily escaped both his pen and Rahel's, in the direction of the good-natured Reichardt, as well as of the families described by him:

In his letters about Vienna, which had recently been published, Reichardt had spoken openly of all these persons and family relationships, and although he wished only to praise, he did not always quite hit the mark, and I heard many complaints about him, indeed it was expected of me, since my literary side had not remained a secret, that I should set my presumably better opinion against his. My question as to whether I might speak only of the women, or must also refer to the men? all too soon betrayed the fact that I was after all not altogether to be trusted, and the matter was dropped.

He does, to be sure, make an exception of Eskeles when, in his next sentence, he writes that 'in these houses really only the women' had been taken into consideration, and there was 'practically no mention of the men'. But since Reichardt mentions only Heinrich Pereira in terms of friendly praise, while he has not a word to say about Heinrich's father-in-law, nothing can be added to the likeness so far sketched out of Nathan as a good-natured but thoroughly insignificant man.

The German musician stayed in Vienna long enough to experience the serious preparations for the new campaign. In the midst of the most high-spirited *Fasching* activities, the citizens' militia began their foot and mounted exercises, the six militia battalions of the capital were inspected and the presentation of colours was performed. Reichardt, meanwhile, seemed to weaken somewhat in the course of the winter. The incessant revelling, the balls and grand receptions overpowered him, and he asked himself, sighing, how the ladies managed to dance daily throughout the week, to attend frequent banquets and at the same time always to look fresh and be in cheerful spirits. He now gave preference to the 'little round tables', such as he could often find at the houses of the Lobkowitz, Czernin and Fries families. 'I prefer to visit even my friend and protectress of many years' standing, Baroness Arnstein, if I know her to be at the little round family table with a few friends.'

After all, it was still granted to him to enjoy Henriette's musicality in the most intimate of circles. She had inherited the talent of her mother and aunts, who had all become accomplished pianists in early youth. Fanny had not played for a long time. This had already been noted with regret in the 'Register of Virtuosi and Dilettanti of Vienna':

Frau von Arnstein: the most instructive and difficult compositions are her favourite pieces. She reads very well, has a light touch and masterly attack. She excels in pieces requiring rapidity. It is to be regretted that for some years she seems to have lost her taste for playing, for she hardly touches the fortepiano any longer. Persons of her powers should not desert their necessitous art, which already, more and more, is in need of active encouragement. She also has a very pleasant voice and fluent throat. Her little daughter likewise shows promise of many musical talents.

Henriette was now one of the best pianists among the ladies of Viennese society. The concert to which Reichardt was invited took place one Sunday morning at the home of her tutor, Streicher. This famous piano-maker had arranged the late Prince Louis Ferdinand's quartet in F minor for two fortepianos for herself and Fräulein Kurzbeck, 'these two talented ladies', 'with great art and skill . . . and had practised the very difficult passages with the two ladies at length and with the greatest conscientiousness'.

Reichardt writes, greatly moved:

Thus, on a lovely, bright morning, in Streicher's apartment, we heard that most brilliant composition performed by beautiful, accomplished hands, on two of this master's finest fortepianos, with a perfection such as one seldom encounters. The delicate artistic souls entered into the composer's sublime and beautiful thoughts and fantasies with so much imagination and feeling, and executed the most difficult passages with such precision and completeness that they truly conjured up a whole world of music about us. Only a very few, quite select connoisseurs took part in this elevated pleasure, and this increased it even further. The beautiful, sensitive Princess Kinsky, who had sent her own excellent instrument for the purpose, with her sister [a future Countess Schönborn] and her brother-in-law, Frau von Henikstein and Prince Lobkowitz made up the whole of the noble audience.

It is a scene from the Biedermeier era that is sketched for us here, a foretaste of those humbler gatherings that Henriette Pereira was wont to hold in her own house in later years. It shows that classes formerly remote from each other were now coming together even in a more intimate setting: when Henriette played the quartet of the 'Prussian Alcibiades' in the presence of the princely music-lovers, she had not yet been christened. For the rest, only one other experience of Reichardt's was to 'beautify' his stay in Vienna – the concert performance of his opera *Bradamante* on 2 March at the house of that great patron of the arts, Prince Lobkowitz. A few weeks before the declaration of war against Napoleon 'the arch-dukes, the highest nobility and the finest connoisseurs and dilettanti of all classes in Vienna, together with all the local *Kapellmeister*' met together to hear the work of the north-German visitor. Beethoven, the Prince's particular protégé, Salieri, Weigl, Clementi and many other musicians had appeared. 'Among the beautiful, sensitive ladies one saw many eyes red with weeping, the militia was marching out almost every day now, and all the officers whose battalions were in the other Austrian provinces and in Bohemia were more and more betaking themselves thither.' The patriotic enthusiasm of the whole people, according to Reichardt, was growing daily. The children of the houses of Lobkowitz and Dietrichstein had no tutors, since these had already taken up arms. And finally even the opera was robbed of its mutes.

Now even those last Viennese who were still abandoning themselves 'au repos et aux douceurs de la vie' were beginning to notice what was in the air. It did not prevent them from giving themselves once more to carnal pleasure on the last day of March, which was also that of Lent: 'Everywhere Italians stand in open booths with thick smoked sausages and all the people carry about great masses of meat until late at night.' On 3 April the Easter Monday masked ball was celebrated with pomp and a fancy-dress parade. Three days later Archduke Karl had his carriage prepared and departed for the army. At the same time the Emperor left the capital. After a final report in which he described Vienna as simply the 'most pleasant, richest and gayest resort in Europe', the *homme moyen sensuel* Johann Friedrich Reichardt also took his leave. The war could begin.

It began with a flourish and with the victorious sound of trumpets. Within a few days two imperial armies, one sent against Udine under Archduke Johann, the other against Bressanone under General Chasteler, achieved decisive successes. It went otherwise with the principal army, commanded by Archduke Karl, which had crossed the river Inn into Bavaria on 10 and 11 April. Within five days the Austrian corps were intersected, their left flank and rear threatened, and finally, at Regensburg – which had earlier been taken by Prince Johann Liechtenstein – they were forced across the Danube into the Bohemian mountains. On 23 April they suffered a devastating defeat. Instead of pursuing the vanquished army, Napoleon now began to arm for his second march on Vienna. From Regensburg, which he had taken by storm, he promised his troops that they would occupy the city within four weeks. In the capital itself there was still no news about the imminent danger. A letter of 29 April from Cäcilie Eskeles to her sisters in Berlin may best express the atmosphere in the city:

> Today is an important day – the news of a battle is awaited until late in the evening, may the Almighty grant that the outcome is a happy one for us, and that it may be as bloodless as possible – The last encounter, which was of five full days' duration, all of which proved favourable for our arms, infused the enemy with admiration for the courage of our troops. The night that followed thereupon was unfortunately unfavourable to us, yet one can still hope for the best . . . The noble Straub – the innkeeper who won the Tyrol back for us and sent his adjutant to the Emperor with the words 'there yer Majesty, you've got yer little country back' – came three or four days ago with his adjutant a saddler to the Emperor in his encampment and demanded to be admitted to the Emperor. '*Grüss di Gott*, yer Majesty' he addressed him, 'I hear things aren't going so well for you – we'll give you a hand. I'm here with 80,000 men . . . We just need a little bit of cash and a bit of powder' – both were given to him, and we hope to God that all will go well.
>
> Even if a troop from the enemy army should come here to pillage us, we should be calm – Hadik was in the Seven Years' War and after he received the contributions he demanded he quietly departed again – more than that the French could not do for the present, if they really

came, so that if the affair of which news is expected today or tomorrow should really turn out unfavourably for us, which is possible, since the goddess of war has her moods, that does not mean that all is lost, and I entreat you my dear sisters to remain as calm as I am. Of our good Bartholdy we have indirect *true* news. He is God be thanked in good health and not exposed to any danger – this much for the reassurance of his good mother and yourselves. In Italy Archduke Johann has had brilliant victories. He has defeated the enemy anew at Castelfranco and is over the Adige. – The French army in Italy is almost completely annihilated. With Archduke Ferdinand too all is well. – Forgive me my beloved sisters if my letter today resembles a formal bulletin. But since I surmise that you wish just as much to hear from us who always speak the truth what is happening to us as from the newspapers whose ill-informed writers do not always give you the plain truth, I have ventured to send you a newspaper rather than a letter.

After a warm spring shower we at last have a very fine day again. I shall make use of it and drive to Hitzing with my children. May you too my good sisters enjoy the fine weather and all good things in fullest measure.

Then Cäcilie sends greetings to relatives and friends, and closes:

I am sending you some letters in transcript which cast the most beautiful light on the revolution in the Tyrol. As you have in any case much to read I end here with the assurance that I am sincerely and eternally your faithful E.

Why, in this letter, the frequent references to the Tyrol, about whose uprising Cäcilie seems particularly well informed? Here one of the most astonishing episodes of Fanny's life comes to light that is the benevolent sympathy shown by herself and her family towards the Tyrolean struggle for freedom. With the energy which she applied to every enterprise directed against Napoleon, she had from the beginning supported the rebellion against the Bavarian yoke. In the first months of 1809 deputies from the Tyrolean mountains had come to Vienna, led by the innkeeper Andreas Hofer, who with his companions stayed in hiding with a man named Duschel in Mariahilf. After having procured weapons and funds in the capital they hurried back to set up their peasant regiments in great secrecy. The last of them left the city on 2 March.

Speckbacher, one of the rebels, had already travelled home in mid-February. Earlier he had frequently turned up at Fanny Arnstein's, where he not only replenished his war fund and conspired for all he was worth, but also proved very entertaining company.

'He left behind,' according to Hormayr, who for his own part had joined the Tyrolean citizens' militia, in his later biography of Speckbacher, 'a good supply of entertaining stories in one of the first houses of Vienna, that of the unforgettable Baroness Fany [*sic*] Arnstein, who was so tirelessly beneficent to the Tyroleans, where also Bartholdy was right well buttered up'. In what the buttering-up of her nephew consisted is not quite clear, unless the meaning is that the Prussian Jew Bartholdy made the 'War of the Tyrolean Peasants in the Year of 1809' his own affair, as did Hormayr, who was from Innsbruck, wrote a whole book about it and had it published under that title in 1814 by his cousin Julius Eduard Hitzig.

Fanny's husband, and probably also her brother-in-law Eskeles, had placed 'large sums' at the disposal of the freedom fighters. They were not the only men of their faith whom the Tyrol had to thank for financial help. The Jewish community of Hohenems, for example, where the most violent battles raged at the end of May, had offered the Vorarlbergers a 'loan' of 12,000 gulden, with no thought of repayment. The rich manufacturer Nathan Elias – later Brentano – alone had 'advanced' them 10,000 gulden for their fighting fund. Supplied with these and other monies the Tyroleans were ready for battle on 9 April, when the imperial armies began to march. The uprising began in the Pustertal. Five days later Innsbruck was taken and released from the power of the Bavarian soldiery. The Tyroleans were triumphant. The Bavarian lion was torn down from the post-office building of the provincial capital and the imperial two-headed eagle affixed in its place. Two burning candles stood in front of it and everyone who passed doffed his hat. At the same time looting began – and in the very places where this was habitual. When a priest named Benitzi reproved a peasant who was on the point of robbing a Jew, he received the reply: 'We've surely earned the right to do a little looting; who should we be robbing then, the Jews or the Christians?' Whom indeed? But after all, this happened in Innsbruck and not eight kilometres away in Hall, where Speckbacher, who knew better than this, was stationed.

On 18 April the Emperor, 'Franzl', as he was known to his Tyroleans, wrote them a loving and encouraging letter. He thanked them emotionally for their faithfulness and heroic deeds and assured them that of all the sacrifices he had had to make in 1805, 'that of separating myself from you' had been 'the most painful to my heart'. 'With divine assistance,' he hoped, 'Austria and the Tyrol shall always remain as united as they were for a long succession of years.' But on the day after the issuing of this document, the defeat of his army at Landshut and at Regensburg had begun. Napoleon was on his way to the capital. The only hope of restraining him lay in the reunification of the principal army with the isolated left flank, under Hiller. This was to have taken place at Linz or Krems, but the French pressed forward so vehemently that Hiller was no longer able to cross the Danube, but was forced to retreat at Ebensberg behind the river Traun.

Here, on 3 May, it came to a murderous battle, in which the Viennese militia came under fire for the first time, the writer Leo von Seckendorff fell, Maurice O'Donnell covered himself with glory and Jakob Bartholdy suffered a wound, but during a courageous skirmish in retreat succeeded so well in rescuing his troops from the battle that he received a commendation. 'About Jakob,' his sister Lea Mendelssohn wrote next day to Henriette Pereira, 'I hear only by way of Berlin . . . I tremble for him, rejoice and, at the thought of being a man and perhaps being able to achieve something, feel so elevated and enthusiastic that I can only love and praise him and say the most fervent prayers for him. "O had I only a little jacket and breeches and hat", I too, I believe, would not stay sitting here, and well for us if many think as I do.'

But their prayers, Old Testament and Christian alike, were of no avail, for the rationalist French had superior generals and better-trained soldiers. On the same day, 4 May, the Empress left Vienna with the imperial family, and on the ninth the enemy was at the gates. This time the city was defended with might and main. Volunteers and local militia were called up, the walls studded with cannons, the drawbridges of the city gates drawn up, and the suburbs, as Caroline Pichler wrote, abandoned to 'the enemy or the mob'. Napoleon's advance posts were already at Hütteldorf when the bearer of a flag of truce sent by his marshal Lannes was repulsed by the Viennese. Soon the city was surrounded. Napoleon established himself in his headquarters at Schönbrunn, and Andreossy, appointed governor of Vienna, had taken up residence at the Kaunitz *palais* at Mariahilf, not far from Fanny's country house.

On the Glacis stood the 'cannoneers with slow-matches burning, watching from the bastions, along with the strolling members of the general public, as the enemy prepared his means of attack'. The situation was, as so often in Austria, desperate but not serious: 'All businesses were on holiday; the *beau monde* put on its Sunday best.' From time to time the artillery fired a few shots, provoking a response from the French. These 'iron answers . . . however, proved to have been addressed to the houses behind, perhaps because the gallant foe noticed the many veils and feathers on the ladies' hats behind the wool-bags on the ramparts and did not wish to spoil the pleasure of the "interesting Viennese ladies"'. Pleasure in what? In their own mortal danger! Even up to the last moment these delightfully carefree people contrived to make a picturesque spectacle out of an enemy siege.

On the night of the twelfth, Napoleon resolved to break the resistance of the Viennese. He ordered an attack on the city by twenty howitzers, whereupon fourteen houses were set on fire and seventeen persons killed. Cannons had also been fired from the ramparts 'and numerous inhabitants of the suburbs killed by the city's gunners'. When, towards three in the morning, over 1,500 howitzer shells and fiery shot had descended upon the inner city, the white flag was displayed and the enemy advance posts received the report that Vienna wished to surrender.

'The more excellently,' writes the chronicler Hormayr, 'the spirit of the Viennese, to whom the bombardment as well as the deceptive wiles of the enemy had generally aroused no more than resentment and embitterment, had preserved itself in the face of all this stress, the greater must the astonishment be over such a rapid conclusion.' But, after all, the outcome of the battle had been certain, and the citizens would have been stupid to allow their beautiful city to be shot to smithereens for the sake of a few hours' delay. A carefree, but fundamentally sensible population had refrained from heroic deeds performed to no purpose.

The French were now within the gates for the second time. The local historian had much to record of 'the vicious and plebeian attacks, tyrannical expressions of power and violations, terrifying alarms' and 'Oriental ostentation'. The truth is that the occupying forces behaved as is usual in such cases; they did a little looting, shot the occasional brave protester, drank all the wine to be found in the barrels and requisitioned the greater part of the city's provisions. The people began to starve. When the municipal council opened its store-rooms, one could buy mouldy bread at colossal prices; meat was scarcely to be had. At the same time paper currency was daily falling in value. Industry in general was in a state of confusion, as the supply of goods dried up, trades and businesses came to a halt, the payment of pensions and allowances were interrupted, debts left unpaid, house-owners received no rent and millions were lost to commerce through the absence of the high nobility and the wealthy.

This time, too, Fanny had stayed in Vienna. She had given refuge in her house to all those friends who did not know which way to turn. Thus, since Friedrich Schlegel's departure for the army, his wife Dorothea Mendelssohn, now *Kriegsräthin* Schlegel (wife of the councillor for war), lived at Fanny's and 'could otherwise have existed only with great difficulty as a result of the increased cost and scarcity of foodstuffs'. How greatly these costs had increased, as Dorothea's brother-in-law August Wilhelm reported to his friend Germaine de Staël, could be seen from the fact 'that even in the rich house in which she now lives, the first concern of the morning is always to procure foodstuffs for the following day'. Together, on 21 May, a fine spring day, Fanny and the *Kriegsräthin* heard the thunder of cannon crashing across the Danube from the battle of Aspern. Together they admired the brave regiments and the legion under the command of Archduke Karl, which had imposed the first defeat of his career upon Bonaparte. The *Empereur*, to be sure, saw the battle over his abortive landing on the left bank of the Danube only as a 'somewhat lively cannonade', with 'substantial losses on both sides'. But to the ladies in the Arnstein *palais*, and to all Vienna with them, indeed to all nations hostile to the French, it appeared the signal of a liberation which now at least seemed imaginable. Meanwhile, Napoleon was right in thinking little of 'losing a battle once in a while, when one has won forty'. The forty-second, at Wagram, was another victory for him.

The renewed triumphs of the stalwart Tyroleans on the mountain of Isel, at Innsbruck and at Hohenems, the individual German rebellions in Dresden, Bamberg, Nuremberg and Stockach, and finally the courageous conquest of Znaim by Austrian troops – all these were now in vain. The war had been lost at Wagram. At any rate Archduke Karl maintained that this was the case, and he sent an officer bearing a flag of truce to entreat an armistice. At the same Znaim which had just been taken by him, the cessation of all hostilities was declared. Count Stadion, the prime minister, promptly resigned. The Archduke laid down his command. On 23 July the Viennese were once again bustling about in their Prater, and 'the new restaurant called *zum Thurm von Gothenburg* had run out of supplies within a couple of hours'.

In the days after Aspern and Wagram, Fanny had dedicated all her energy to the care and nursing of the injured. The terrors bound up with the gigantic open battles of those days were being recorded at that time by Goya in the Spanish arena of war. In the Danube valley, along the road home to Vienna, countless numbers of the severely wounded, suffocating in the intense heat, were crowding round the peasants' wagons and hackney-carriages which were the only means of transport apart from the hard, bumpy army vehicles. Whoever was beyond hope – and two-thirds of the wounded men perished – was left to his fate or even negligently thrown into the river or into hastily shovelled-up graves along with the dead and dying. The citizens of Vienna, insofar as they had the time and the devotion for the task, drove out in coaches to the battlefield to carry out Samaritan services indiscriminately and unhindered. In the city, the ladies prepared lint, helped in the hospitals or took under their wing the families of soldiers which had lost their breadwinners.

'After the war of 1809,' Varnhagen wrote about Fanny, 'whose outcome weighed upon her heart like a personal sorrow, she again devoted her most active assistance to the poor, whose number had greatly increased as a result of the war and its after-effects.' He was in a position to know this. For between the end of hostilities in July and the peace signed at Schönbrunn in October, Rahel's friend came to Vienna in an Austrian officer's uniform.

Varnhagen, twenty-four years old at the time, had for several years been involved in an intimate relationship with the very much older Rahel. A man of commonplace but ambitious disposition, he clung just as eagerly to this woman, who sparkled with wit and originality, and was esteemed by all the great men of Germany, as she herself did to the brisk young man who was totally devoted to her. Neither of them exactly loved the other, but they needed each other; it was one of those successful symbioses which are frequently found precisely among such disparate couples. When Varnhagen decided to go to Vienna at the end of 1808, like so many of his compatriots, Rahel promised him letters to her former lover, Count Finckenstein, now Prussian minister at the imperial court, to Prince de Ligne, to everyone in Vienna to whom she had any kind of access. And finally Gentz – 'my friend in Prague' – was to recommend him to the whole of the literary and the noble worlds.

Writing to him at Tübingen, the first stop on his journey, she reported proudly how many Berliners were rushing to take up arms for Austria: 'Conscription has not taken place here at all, so many persons are voluntarily enlisting: the best-educated Jews, and all; ah! everyone would like to dig up former glory out of the ground.' When, finally, shortly after the battle of Wagram, he was in Zistersdorf, still hoping that the war was not lost, she sent him words of encouragement. 'Be brave and good . . . you know I am anxious: but I would choose an unknown death, were it my own choice; and would not yield. – You know how I feel about war, about this war. War is not for any cultured person . . . Yet you could not live without proof of your courage, practical proof – so go ahead with a stout heart!' And since he suffered from the fact that he was not of noble birth, she reassured him that he 'was conferring nobility upon himself with his own blood'.

That this, however, was not enough, both knew very well. For this reason Varnhagen – like Rahel's 'friend in Prague', some of whose characteristics, though not his talent, he shared – was in later years to procure himself a patent of nobility which was totally in order, even though based on an insubstantial claim. Now however, even though Napoleon had preceded him in entering Vienna, he resolved not to let slip the opportunity of seeing the capital. Just like Gentz, he at first had some difficulty in gaining access to the high nobility. All the more friendly was his reception in a house where he had made his appearance without any recommendation. As he recalled in his *Denkwürdigkeiten*:

I had myself announced at Frau von Arnstein's, and simply told her whence and why I had come to Vienna, and that I had long wished to make her acquaintance. This experienced woman of the world was scarcely surprised, but immediately passionately delighted to see so much as an Austrian uniform again; for, weighed down by the power of the French, and swarmed around and besieged by Frenchmen, she nourished and expressed the most glowing hatred against their nation and in particular against Napoleon. I asked after Frau von Schlegel, Friedrich's wife, whom I knew to be hospitably received in the Arnstein house, while her husband had gone to Hungary to follow the events of war. She was summoned and appeared, she recognised me at first glance, but bowed her head sadly, saying in bitter reproach: I remember very well how you praised the French troops in Dresden, to my pain and annoyance, but I did not think to meet you yourself here among them. Through a singular error she took me for a French officer. 'But what are you saying,' cried Frau von Arnstein, 'do you not see he is one of ours?' Frau von Schlegel looked up, and as if freed from a burden she gave way to the loudest expressions of delight.

Now a series of questions and answers began in which all those present were soon taking part, but particularly Frau von Arnstein, whose interests were always forceful, intense and for the moment exclusive of all else. This excellent woman and her social power and effectiveness have already been described elsewhere; here I will add only the observation that the presence of the enemy did not disturb the social brilliance of the house, but in many respects actually enhanced it. One had to associate with the French, one could not repulse them, it was important, and incidentally pleasant, to be on good terms with them, their generals and high officials, as well as their elegant young people, some of them from distinguished old families, knew how to assert themselves in society so that the reason for their presence was forgotten. My hostess's hatred for the Emperor [Napoleon] was laughingly accepted as the endearing foolishness of a woman, indeed, not seldom did distinguished Frenchmen assent to the abusive remarks with which she was not sparing. It was a strange relationship which must occur to a lesser or greater extent everywhere, where the cultured persons of two inimical nations gather together peaceably, but which the French are particularly adapted to establish. The Viennese for their part, instead of withdrawing, flocked to her even more eagerly than before; it was the most evident gain to find oneself with the unavoidable and on the other hand so attractive enemy in a salon which seemed to take upon itself on behalf of many others the reception and entertainment of these guests.

If the 'cultured persons of two inimical nations' were clearly wise and superior enough not to carry over the embittered dispute of their nations into their private lives, the people in general had even fewer scruples as far as the enemy were concerned. Hardly had the French troops entered the city and bivouacked in the main squares when the first of the sausage-sellers, cobblers' lads, market women, maidservants, dandies and idle onlookers came running along. The first careful attempts at familiarity soon cooled off, as the war was still going on outside the city gates and the foreign soldiers wanted to do a bit of looting and revelling before being sent off once again to the battlefield. But as soon as the armistice was declared and Napoleon had returned to Schönbrunn, as soon as his garrison had completed their domestic arrangements, the fraternisation between French and Viennese was no longer to be restrained.

Those who had just been shooting off each other's arms and legs were now embracing each other with unfeigned amiability. 'Now life was improving daily, becoming cheaper, more amusing, indeed extraordinarily merry', writes a witness. 'The time of suffering seemed to be over, and one must therefore catch up on the pleasures one had lacked; the effervescent Gallic character mingled with Viennese liveliness in exactly the right proportions. On both sides they vied in adopting the originality of the others; the French found the Viennese, and the latter found their enemies, worthy of imitation and most delightful.'

Three Parisian restaurants 'opened their fragrant dining-halls'. Parisian lemonade-sellers offered refreshments in the private garden of the Empress who had fled her city. In the evening the *beau monde* drove to the palace theatre to enjoy German plays, Italian ballets and operas in both languages, in the presence of Napoleon and side by side with his officers. Caroline Pichler too reports such a visit, which she undertook with Frau von Fliess in the carriage of a French general, an acquaintance of Eleonore's. To be sure, the good woman was distracted less by the entertainment on the stage than by the 'well-nourished prelate's face' of the *Empereur* which she studied instead, violently repelled. 'The stalls full of staff-officers of the various weapons,' as our eye-witness describes the scene, 'a balcony full of generals, ministers and high dignitaries and all *en grande tenue* in their uniforms fitted out with the most sophisticated splendour; and in addition Vienna's female nobility in their most brilliant evening dress.'

The ladies of society were for the most part, like Fanny, anti-Napoleonic in their sympathies. Bonaparte knew this well, and after the battle of Wagram, when his General Durosnel, who had been captured, was to be exchanged for an Austrian prisoner of war, he had threatened the negotiators: 'Si la moindre chose arrive à Durosnel, je ferai massacrer tous les prisonniers autrichiens; – non! car ils sont innocents; mais je ferai violer les dames de Vienne par mes tambours.' Nevertheless they were the last persons to have refrained from attending a court entertainment in their finest evening dress, even if this was got up not by their hereditary Emperor, but by a Corsican usurper. After all, the conquerors might be impressed, if not by superior military strategy, at least by dazzling *savoir vivre*. The Apollosaal was proudly opened for them and they were heard to remark in praise that no other city, not even Paris, had such enjoyments to offer. Napoleon's birthday, too, for which, with the help of the Pope, he had commandeered the feast of the Assumption of the Virgin Mary on 15 August, was celebrated with the participation of the whole population to the sound of bells and the thunder of cannon, with splendid parades, banquets and general illuminations throughout the city. A wave of pleasure was sweeping along the victors and the defeated alike.

At the same time it was by no means a settled affair that the armistice of Znaim would really lead to peace. Negotiations were in progress, but, as Varnhagen reports, both sides were arming for renewed hostilities. No one, it is true, honestly believed any longer in the continuation of the war. 'It was not the courage of the warriors or the readiness of the people that were in doubt, but certainly the power and skill of those in the highest positions of command.' Archduke Karl was not of a mind to resume the supreme command of the troops, nor was there any intention of entrusting him with it. The knowledge of all these facts 'had already reached the lower orders, whose mood was expressed in violent diatribes against those whom they had formerly been wont to revere'.

Varnhagen himself, who had become a sort of prisoner of war through his presence in Vienna, was exchanged for a Frenchman in September and no longer prevented from travelling. Countess Engel, a friend of Henriette Pereira's, told his fortune by cards and predicted that his return to Vienna would only be a matter of weeks. Disbelieving, he left the city on 23 August. Three weeks later a peace was signed at Schönbrunn which Metternich later found to have been obtained surreptitiously, with 'undignified cunning', and of which even Napoleon said that Austria's negotiators could have achieved better. Almost one-third of the state territories, with more than 3,500,000 inhabitants, were relinquished. Salzburg and the district of the Inn went to Bavaria, the Croatian coast with Fiume, Istria, Trieste, parts of Carinthia and Carniola to the French Empire, Lublin and Cracow to Poland, and Tarnopol to Russia. Austria not only lost her naval base in the Adriatic, but was also 'encircled by a girdle of nations which lay under the sceptre or under the direct influence of Napoleon'.

By the same stroke of the pen which Prince Johann Liechtenstein placed at the foot of this shameful contract, the Tyroleans too were cast off. 'The Emperor would have done everything,' Archduke Johann wrote to them from Hungary, 'to fulfil the wishes of the state of Tyrol. However, as deeply affected as the Emperor is by the fate of the worthy inhabitants of this state, yet the necessity has arisen to make peace.' And he informed them that the wish of his Majesty was 'that the Tyroleans should behave themselves calmly and not sacrifice themselves to no purpose'. The epilogue was spoken by the proclamation of Eugène Beauharnais from Villach, recommending them to accept the peace of Vienna: 'You are the only ones who do not yet enjoy its benefits!' But these obstinate people continued to fight and gave up their weapons only when these were wrested from them by force.

At the end of November, a day after his troops, Francis I returned to Vienna. 'It was on a dull autumn day,' Caroline Pichler recalled, 'as they are wont to be at this time of year, when our beloved Emperor, presumably in order not to attract attention in any way, was driven into the city by the Stubenthor, wearing the hussar's uniform of his regiment, in which he was not commonly to be seen here, accompanied only by Count Wrbna, in an unpretentious carriage which, as was related, was even laden with his belongings, at about four in the afternoon.'

The Viennese scolded, but they cheered. 'Ils crient toujours', Napoleon had said, when their cries reached his window at Schönbrunn. This time the first and loudest applause came from disguised police officers; but they would hardly have been needed. Who would have missed the chance of festive evening illuminations – there had been no such spectacle since Napoleon's birthday! So all the citizens put their lights on, and all the street-lamps were lit, and Francis, accompanied only by a squad of the city cavalry, drove in by the light of countless torches on his usual route of honour – through the Herrengasse over the Hohe Brücke, past the town hall, by way of the Tuchlauben to the Hoher Markt, then to St Stephen's square and, making a further detour, to the Kärntnertor and back into the Hofburg.

This time Fanny was not standing on her balcony when the Emperor's *calèche* rattled over the greenish cobblestones of the Hoher Markt below. To see the face of conquered Austria had no attraction for her now.

–9–

Calm before the Storm

Years of shame, years of despondency, years of discontent! They began in Vienna as soon as the lights and torches whose gleam had brightened the dismal autumn night had been extinguished. Next morning the joyful excitement over the return of their own *Kaiser* to the Hofburg, while the *Empereur* was no longer installed in Schönbrunn, had already subsided. There was fog and drizzle. The soldiers took off their uniforms and returned to everyday life. One almost longed for the French and their fireworks. While celebrating with their conquerors the Viennese had sought to forget their own defeat. Now it stared them in the face. As if they had lost a game of cards from which their opponents had emerged with all the trumps, they accused each other of errors and omissions which could no longer be made good.

Varnhagen, who had fulfilled Countess Engel's prediction by arriving back in Vienna, borne by the current of the returning army, not only seemed, for his own part, gripped by the general disgruntled and quarrelsome mood, but also managed to intensify it in others. 'A furious hatred,' he reported to Rahel on 30 November, 'is vented upon Archduke Carl, and yet to a great extent unjustly so; one fails to appreciate that he created the army, and if he has lost, then that, for all his lost battles, so much still remains. I was at Madame Arnstein's, whom I find not at all charming, and this time found quite insufferable.' He had evidently surprised her in one of her worst fits of rage and enraged her even further by his disagreement:

> If another war should break out, she said, she knew what she would do, she would in the first instance always stay close to the Archduke, where she would be safest. This was such a thoroughly stupid thing to say that I merely retorted: if one was sitting on a silken sofa (I was seated beside her) and in handsome houses, it was easy to talk in this manner, but it would still be of no consequence. And, indeed, the Archduke is intrepid and brave like no other. I saw him on the high ground in the worst of the artillery fire, and he was wounded at Wagram, he is splendid in battle!

Certainly it was 'thoroughly stupid' of Fanny to cast doubts on the courage of a man who was above all fearless and who is rightly immortalised in bronze on the Heldenplatz in Vienna, astride a foaming charger, raising aloft the banner of Zach's regiment for the attack! But this image had not yet become engraved upon the consciousness of his contemporaries. They saw in him the vanquished general, whose incredible good fortune in having once beaten Napoleon had slipped out of his hands. And they were the more resentful of him because at first they had praised him to the skies. No, the feeling in Vienna was against poor Archduke Karl, and even wiser women than Fanny had lost their respect for him. Germaine de Staël too would have nothing more to do with him; it was only when, three years later, he refused to command the military force of 30,000 men that had been placed at the disposal of Napoleon's *Grande Armée* that she warmed to him again: 'Quand je le vis se promener seul, en habit gris, dans les allées du Prater, je retrouvai pour lui tout mon ancien respect.'

Fanny had immediately withdrawn her severest reproach, though she was not of a mind to revoke her other observations. 'But hear more!' Varnhagen wrote to Rahel.

> Madame Arnstein did acknowledge her stupidity to some extent and withdrew the accusation of cowardice, but burst forth into a flood of complaints about his manner of commanding the army, and became vulgar in her words and her tone. I had already risen from my seat; Madam, I said in a polite but firm voice, you are no doubt familiar with Goethe's verse on 'How one rises above the defeated over tobacco and beer'. I have just learnt that these two attributes are not always strictly necessary. With this excellent insult I took my leave and left her sitting there. You see, my dear, that my extempore wit had not forsaken me. I have seen Mesdames Pereira, Eskeles, Schlegel; Friedrich Schlegel too is about to arrive here. Bartholdy is a conceited ox . . .

And so on, in an irritable, unamiable tone. It is not a pleasant scene that is presented to us here, and one would be grateful not to be obliged to report it. But the times themselves were not pleasant; they were bad times and brought out the worst in people. In a further letter to Rahel, Varnhagen once more censured the woman to whom, decades later, he created such a glorious monument. At the beginning of January he writes of his social ascent in the capital:

> Here in Vienna I have this time been very preoccupied, I have of late scarcely visited the more formal gatherings . . . my colonel took me to see a Countess Fuchs, she is an amiable, humorous woman . . . and sees the best society. One could serve princes and counts, princesses and countesses there for tea instead of bread and butter . . . They *are* so

grand, these people, that it does not occur to them that anything could be injurious to their rank, while at the Arnsteins', the Eskeles' and the Pereiras' the grandeur is sustained only with difficulty, through the painfully repeated exertion each evening, and everyone trembles when a countess sits upon the sofa and a princess on the chair. Countess Fuchs is visited by young people, amiable and lively, the ladies in question almost exclusively by caricatures, old worn-out figures of society, it is pitiful to behold. What unfortunate aspirations!

Poor Fanny! Certainly it was possible to see her salon in this light too. While, thanks in part to her example, a freer sociability had developed in other, more aristocratic houses, her own was falling behind. No wonder, moreover, that her circle seemed elderly to the youthful Varnhagen. Her loyal friends, the Sonnenfels, Collenbachs, Spielmanns, Sebottendorfs were growing old with her, and the amiable gentlemen from noble houses were looking for younger ladies to pay court to. One such was the beautiful Countess Laura Fuchs, known as Lory to her many admirers, a future close friend of the man who had already, before Varnhagen, described the decline of the Arnstein salon. And these two kindred spirits were about to meet: 'I often see Gentz,' reported Varnhagen to his friend, 'and hold lively arguments with him; he considers me young and intelligent, and yesterday, at Countess Fuchs's, where there was a great party, he observed my behaviour. I love him exceptionally well.'

Gentz, the 'agent of Europe', whose hopes had now been shattered for the third, crushing time, had again settled in Vienna. What he had honestly desired and, even though in the pay of the English and on their behalf, had advocated out of his own conviction – the European revolt against Napoleon – seemed to have retreated into the sphere of the unattainable. Now the time had come for a cynical game of patience. But he had an equal talent for cynicism. Metternich, the former imperial ambassador in Paris and the successor to Stadion, was his old patron. Gentz now intended to hitch his wagon to this star. And if Metternich's first act was to give the *Empereur* an Austrian archduchess as his wife, this was equally agreeable to the former Napoleon-hater.

Two months after the peace of Vienna, the Emperor of the French had simply got rid of his Josephine – with her agreement and that of her children. When, in the following February of 1810, Gentz arrived in Vienna he was just in time to witness the betrothal of Napoleon to Marie-Louise of Austria. None other than Archduke Karl had been picked out to represent the bridegroom at the wedding on 11 March; the latter meanwhile was ensconced in Compiègne, saving himself the trouble of attending the public balls, festive banquets and gala opera performances held by Vienna in his honour.

That February, while a Habsburg and a Bonaparte were pledging themselves to each other, the Tyrolean struggle for freedom, too, came to an end. The last resistance was broken when Andreas Hofer was captured and Speckbacher fled. Hofer was brought to Mantua, where the unusual relationship between Tyroleans and Jews stood the test for the last time. He was defended by the talented Jewish attorney Baseva, who was perhaps a descendant of Jakob Bassevi, court supplier to Ferdinand II. But even Baseva's shrewd understanding could not save Hofer, and on 20 February the man who was considered the personification of Tyrolean loyalty to the *Kaiser* was shot. 'Der gute Kaiser Franz / hat uns vergessen ganz [The good Emperor Francis / has quite forgotten us]', they sang now in the valleys of the Inn and the Eisack. Not blotted from the memory of Francis I, only driven into a dark corner of his bad conscience, the Tyroleans now lived only for the day when Europe should shake off Napoleon's yoke. Fanny, however, may have quietly continued in her good deeds towards them. For her help and that of her husband were not forgotten in Tyrol, and after the liberation a mountain peak, two thousand metres high, near the Scharnitzerjoch on the Bavarian border, was named Arnstein-Spitze in their honour.

If they had been totally in agreement in their attitude towards the Tyroleans, indeed towards the whole of the last campaign, the old antithesis between Fanny and Nathan now emerged once more. In these years of discontent the line of separation between the couple, otherwise for the most part invisible, was at times dangerously highlighted. Fanny, who was by no means cynical and anything but patient, was unable, with her Prussian frankness, to come to terms with the altered situation. An emperor who had left his staunch Tyroleans in the lurch, an archduke who let himself be degraded to becoming the puppet of his former deadly enemy, aroused in her nothing but disgust. But her husband's unconditional loyalty to the house of Austria remained untouched by this. If Francis had a mind to bury the hatchet with Napoleon, the 'premier baron du vieux testament' had no objection. After all, Nathan owed everything to the Emperor: his nobility, his continuing wealth, the granting of every favour requested. Just at this moment he was receiving further confirmation of this.

When, after the peace of Vienna, the sum of 55,000,000 francs had to be raised for contributions to France, this task fell once more to the banking house of Arnstein & Eskeles, along with those of Fries, Geymüller and Steiner. A figure of authority in the bestowing of the commission was the former president of the court chamber, Count O'Donnell, father of Madame de Staël's young friend. With the help of the old Count, Nathan obtained, in March of that year, the Emperor's permission to adopt his son-in-law and for the latter's simultaneous elevation to the nobility.

Nathan's petition, forwarded with a particular recommendation by O'Donnell, contained the reasons: 'Your Majesty,' Nathan had written,

> the undersigned repeats at your exalted feet the most submissive request to be pleased to raise his son-in-law Pereira, by means of acceptance of the same in place of a child, to the rights of the status of *Freiherr*, with which your Majesty has honoured the undersigned.
>
> The feelings of a father's heart are not foreign to the best of fathers. The petitioner may therefore plead with the most respectful confidence that your Majesty may, by the gracious granting of this favour, at the same time allow him the consolation of his old age, not to be robbed of his only daughter and his grandchildren.

Count O'Donnell, in his accompanying letter, added a few points in support of a favourable outcome:

> The son-in-law pleads, in the further most obedient enclosures, that his children are already being brought up in the Christian religion, and Arnstein assures me that Pereira will have himself baptised, thereby removing a significant impediment. Arnstein has rendered substantial services through a long period of years of financial administration, and is, according to his generally recognised character, a man devoted with all his heart to your Majesty, to the imperial house and to his country. It was only in the uncertainty as to how the same should be rewarded for his services rendered during the last hostile invasion and over the negotiation of the contribution, as no decoration can be bestowed upon him as an Israelite, that I humbly petitioned for the conferment upon him of a valuable gold box bearing your Majesty's monogram. Now, however, since he has declared his wish, I respectfully ask your Majesty to be pleased to grant most graciously the requested elevation of his son-in-law to the rank of *Freiherr*, in place of the desired gift.

Whereupon, on 13 May 1810 – shortly after O'Donnell's sudden death – the Emperor's agreement was conveyed. The *Extractus Protocolli* of the court chamber three days later included an entry stating that his Majesty had been pleased to bestow the title of

Freiherr upon 'the Jew Heinrich Pereira'. And when, together with Henriette, he was baptised on 23 July, the last temptation to summon up the disagreeable memory of his origins was disposed of.

'Since the same have acknowledged their error and have been sufficiently instructed in the true Christian Catholic faith which alone leads to salvation', Henriette and 'Heinrich Pereira, an Israelite, born at Luxemburg in Holland, the legitimate son of the *Hochwohlgeboren* [right honourable] Herr Eliseus Freiherr von Pereira, of the Portuguese religion and the *Hochwohlgeboren* Frau Anna, née Machado, spouse of the same, both already dead, of the Jewish religion', received the sacrament. Henriette's godmother was her friend Countess Engel, while Heinrich's godfather was Hofrat Sonnenfels. And no less than the Prince-Archbishop of Vienna, Count Hohenwart, had taken it upon himself to perform the ceremony.

Nathan's dearest wish was now fulfilled, and the consolation of his old age had been granted. Through the idea of taking his son-in-law for his adopted son, he had provided for his succession and for the continuation of his name – as Freiherren von Pereira-Arnstein three sons of Henriette's were to form connections with the Austrian nobility. Certainly Fanny too was happy to see her daughter elevated in this way. Certainly she was content to see Henriette in the arms of the Church, although the words 'the Christian Catholic faith which alone leads to salvation' on the baptismal certificate may not have been quite convincing to her. At the same time, she now turned her gaze with greater sympathy towards Berlin, where her brother-in-law Friedländer was in the process of achieving civic equality for all those who had remained faithful to the old religion.

On 6 June Karl August von Hardenberg, who had been temporarily expelled from the Prussian government through Napoleon's displeasure, had taken over the reins from the incompetent Dohna–Altenstein administration. With the help of this outstanding man the reforms begun by Stein could be continued. Immediately after his appointment Friedländer had approached him to lay before him once more the petition of the Berlin Jews for an edict of liberation. As early as July, Hardenberg requested sight of the relevant documents, among them a draft bill from the hand of the former minister of state Freiherr von Schrötter and a commentary on this by Wilhelm von Humboldt. Schrötter had intended to deal with this matter in terms of a 'pedagogic emancipation', when he attempted to introduce a limited form of equality. Humboldt had gone significantly further in his observations set down in July 1809. He relied on the basic principle that the state is not a promulgator of education but of rights. And what he demanded was no less than the total freedom of Jews in this state.

In a calm and scientific manner Humboldt, the former student of Dohm and Markus Herz, had studied their situation anew. What the last government statement of 1798 had seen as an established impediment to their acceptance in society – the 'peculiar character of this nation' – became for him merely a historical, and thus changeable factor. Three characteristics, he explained, had distinguished the Jews since ancient times: an originally nomadic life, an ecclesiastical–political framework and a system of separation from those among whom they lived. In each case a remedy could be provided: nomadism could be countered by settlement, the ecclesiastical–political framework by the destruction of the ecclesiastical form, and separation by assimilation with the people in whose midst they were living.

As to how the second point, the most sensitive of the three, was to be handled, Humboldt had also had a proposal to make. According to him, one should encourage, not orthodoxy, but schisms among the Jews; their hierarchy would then collapse of its own accord. Conversion to the Christian faith appeared to him desirable only after equality had been achieved. In their spontaneous movement towards an enlightened Protestantism he saw the way towards a higher humanity. For it was this, the development of the individual entity, which Humboldt valued above any community, that contained for him the meaning of every reform. It was, he wrote, an 'inhumane and prejudicial way of thinking' if one 'judges a man not according to his peculiar qualities, but according to his origin and religion, and looks upon him, against all true conceptions of human dignity, not as an individual, but as if belonging to a race, and, as it were, necessarily sharing certain qualities with it'.

Humboldt's statement was a document which could not have been composed on this subject at either any earlier or any later date. It was the purest expression of that humanism which was the source of the Enlightenment, the noblest version of the final goal of emancipation. Joseph II would have rejected it out of hand – although it would have appeared to his Hofrat Greiner as the crowning of his own ideas. Fichte and Hegel in their turn would have disclaimed it. It was the good fortune of this moment that Humboldt, the 'Periclean statesman', found a kindred spirit in

Hardenberg, who, moreover, was in a position to translate their corresponding thoughts to a great extent into action. In the new Chancellor a certain deference towards the 'mighty and subtle' which had led him to conclude the peace of Basle and later, at the Congress of Vienna, to represent the ambitions of Prussia with insufficient force, was combined with a sense of the ideal, together with moral and humane convictions. Now that he gave signs of being able to solve the Jewish problem at least from the legal point of view, Friedländer's fellow-believers could hope for the realisation of their long-cherished hopes and dreams.

Not all Fanny's relatives, who for the most part had already been granted civic rights, had waited for this development. Many of her nephews and nieces had in the meantime become Protestants, some of them even with a fiery fervour which gave rise to satire. One was her nephew Julius Eduard Hitzig, son of the second eldest of her brothers, Elias. Hitzig had studied law in Halle, Erlangen and Wittenberg and had developed his leanings towards poetry through his acquaintance with Clemens Brentano and Ludwig Wieland. In Warsaw, where he afterwards practised as a young barrister, he had joined the circle of E. T. A. Hoffmann. Once more in Berlin, he founded a publishing firm which handled, among other works, Kleist's *Abendblätter*. In 1814 he again went into government service, became a criminal lawyer and finally the biographer of his friends Hoffmann, Adelbert von Chamisso and Zacharias Werner. His pietism later aroused the mockery of Heinrich Heine, which was to find expression in a poem about the origin of 'Peter Schlemihl', the story by Chamisso in which a young man surrenders his shadow to the Devil in exchange for Fortunatus's purse. But not only the devout pietist, who by means of baptism had bought that 'entrance ticket to European culture' referred to by Heine, but also Jews who persisted in the old faith, such as Julius's own cousins Moritz and Albert Itzig, joined the secret Prussian freedom movement which in these years was spreading its influence in ever-increasing circles. It consisted of the most extraordinary groups. Metternich speaks in his memoirs of the Prussian army of 1813, which was 'composed of totally national elements, prepared and worked upon over a long period by the *Tugendbund* (League of Virtue), among them numerous battalions of fanatical volunteers, such as, at that time, were the students and their professors, the men of letters and poets of every stamp'. This in fact was no longer the same League of Virtue which Henriette Herz had founded with the Humboldt brothers. At any rate Wilhelm von Humboldt, who had gone to Vienna as Prussian envoy in this summer of 1810 and maintained an attitude of reserve towards the patriotic aspirations of his country, took no active part in it. The new group, brought into being perhaps not without knowledge of the earlier one founded in Königsberg in April 1808, was used by Stein and the Prussian generals Gneisenau and Scharnhorst as a means of influencing public opinion against Napoleon. It never had more than 600 members. At the urging of Napoleon, King Frederick William dissolved the League of Virtue in December 1809. But the society continued to exist in secret and, after Francis I had come to a peaceful agreement with Bonaparte, also gave cause for concern to the Austrian police.

In August 1810 the Viennese chief of police, Franz Freiherr von Siber, reported to the Emperor on the German intrigues and the influences derived from Freemasonry which were threatening to spread to Austria. A second document of December of that year went into greater detail about the preparations being made for 'a united Germany as one nation' by the 'Society of Virtue, or German Society'. At the time 'many Prussians [were] going on journeys, which otherwise cannot be reconciled with their economic principles!' One such was the lawyer, former cabinet councillor and most recently dismissed Grosskanzler (High Chancellor) Karl Friedrich von Beyme, who had arrived in Vienna a few weeks earlier. As far as Beyme was concerned, 'he is being closely watched, and the various inquiries will in any case be presented in separate reports as we are in duty bound'. The Emperor commented in the margin: 'Yes, but when?'

But Siber's report continues:

> It is very probable that the wives of the bankers von Arnstein and Eskeles, as true Berliners, may be fully animated by the tendencies of their compatriots, only it might prove difficult to get anything out of them on this matter. They are clever, already advanced in years, and commonly surrounded by so many people that they bestow their particular confidence upon no one; the direct method would be not at all advisable with persons of this kind and would scarcely lead us to our aim. – There is also a sister of Madame v. Eskeles [sic!] here, the well-known Madame Flies, a woman of pretended learning, who also gathers a circle around herself which has Prussian leanings, but who is more open and by whom it will be easier to be received. Preparations have already been made for her to be spied upon.

The Emperor's marginal comment was: 'At last! Frau von Schilling.'

Apart from Beyme, 'Schlegel, who has travelled around Germany with Frau v. Staël' and Prince von Anhalt-Pless are named as being close to the Society of Virtue. Siber suggests that 'either the Society should be penetrated further by trusted men with whom contact has already been made in the north of Germany, or that our own persons of repute, good judgement and shrewdness should be sent to Prussia, who would allow themselves to be initiated into the Society, establish a correspondence with them, and in this way acquire an exact knowledge of their statutes and connections'. And finally, the following January, Hager, the police president himself, intervenes in the investigation and gives as his opinion that 'v. Gentz, who appears to stand in a close relationship with Beyme and his whole entourage . . . could be persuaded into confidential communications and important disclosures'. What must, however, have been unknown to Siber was the low estimation in which Gentz held Beyme. At the turn of the century he had already written of the latter that he was nothing but a 'conceited lawyer, arrogant, illiberal, endowed at most with the talent which belongs to the composition of a judicial opinion'. It was not to be assumed that he now stood in 'a close relationship' with him. But even the secret police could not know everything!

To the Emperor, these disclosures were unpleasant in the extreme. When he gave his young daughter's hand in marriage to the French usurper, he believed he had thereby bought 'some years of political freedom' for his monarchy, 'which I will be able to use for the healing of its wounds'. To see this time abridged by a precipitate war, into which he would be drawn in one way or another, was contrary to this wishes. He was, therefore, not only mistrustful but positively hostile to the League of Virtue. Besides there was, so it seemed to him and his advisers, a second danger in this movement. 'The purpose is,' wrote Hager,

to form the whole German nation, however many branches it has, and under however many governments it is divided, according to one principle, and to conduct it according to one form: in other words to bring the hitherto existing states of which Germany is composed into a new, autonomous general union. This tendency of the League's is of course in direct opposition to the aspiration towards universal monarchy emanating from France; the League together with its members is therefore an instrument of the persecution of the French government.

Moreover, as Hager warns, it also threatened 'the existing forms of government in Germany'. This was the most important reason for keeping a strict eye on the former Chancellor Beyme during his stay in Vienna.

The police reports on Beyme begin on December 17 with the indication that he – like every other German traveller of rank – had taken up residence in the hotel *Römischer Kaiser* in the Freyung, and in the morning had been introduced to Prince Metternich by Humboldt. He had also called upon the minister from Baden, the French ambassador, the Russian, the Württembergian and finally, once more, upon the Prussian envoy Humboldt. But as zealous as was Beyme's activity in high diplomatic circles, he seems to have spent his leisure time with his family in Fanny's house, where he was sure of the sympathies at least of his hostess. The communications of the informant – a certain Strasser – are surprisingly similar to that diary kept by Goethe in Franzensbad, except that the Arnstein table is preferred to the Eskeles one:

> 18th Dec.: In the evening to Baron A. on the Hoher Markt, where they supped and played. 20th Dec.: At midday to Baron A. Sunday 23 Dec.: Divine service, then midday Baron A. [. . .] Monday the 31st Dec.: Midday with his wife to the Hoher Markt to Baron Aer [Arnsteiner], where they dined. Friday 4th Jan.: Midday to A. where they dined, because it is the Baroness's birthday [*sic*!]. In the evening they drove away from there and went home.

To add some spice to the laconic reports – which, it is true, contain further mention of Beyme's movements in government, diplomatic and aristocratic circles – Siber's informant provides his own, more homely version of Beyme's intentions: 'Undersigned learned . . . that the High Chancellor Beyme is a sworn enemy of the French Emperor and has long studied means in secret of suppressing the French realm and bringing about the overthrow of the Emperor.' Beyme was now travelling 'around the world in a state of rage in order to ascertain opinions – in Italy, Switzerland, Tyrol, where he went around the villages into the poorest peasants' houses, gave people presents and tried to sound out their opinions'. He had come to Vienna chiefly 'to spend the winter and the carnival season here, but he had already inquired whether there were no meeting-places in Vienna where men of experience came together and where various current events were discussed, but where, in order to go unrecognised, one could enter masked'.

Like so many other reports by Francis's secret police, this too has a strong tinge of *Hintertreppenromantik* – backstairs, or cloak-and-dagger, romance. It was in fact by way of the back stairs that the agent Strasser obtained his information. He had bribed Beyme's hired servant to become his informant and managed to have the High Chancellor's letters, which were directed by way of Nathan Arnstein's office, intercepted and put before him. An embarrassing incident took place on 5 January, when Beyme, after his meal, instructed his servant to ask after his mail at Arnstein's. There were in fact three letters there. Strasser took charge of these and hastily placed them in the hands of the authorities. Meanwhile the High Chancellor was becoming impatient. The servant had told him that the post had not yet arrived, and after half an hour he sent him back. But the police were taking their time. It was two hours later before they deigned to return the letters to Strasser, while the servant had already been sent out a third time. Strasser reported grumpily: 'The servant told the undersigned that he would not like to submit to such danger again for a thousand fl. . . . all the more since, a few days ago, Count Humboldt's ambassadorial secretary said in the presence of the High Chancellor and all his staff that in Vienna the hired servants were in league with the police.'

Beyme stayed in Vienna until the beginning of March and continued to visit the Arnsteins, the Eskeles, the Hofburgtheater and the society balls. For no other reason than in order to attend a reception of the French ambassador's he ordered a Prussian uniform to be made for himself. On the afternoon of 29 January he stayed at home, because 'he was already making elaborate preparations for the ball at the French ambassador's'. Two days later he again supped at Fanny's where, ominously, 'apart from himself no one else was present'.

The great gentlemen meanwhile seemed to be losing their liking for him, for on 6 February he was refused admittance at Prince Lobkowitz's – nevertheless he drove in the evening 'to the ball at Baron Arnsteiner's' – and on 9 February the French ambassador had no time for him. Only Humboldt continued to give him a friendly reception, although this cosmopolitan man did not share his violent hatred for Napoleon. Beyme's mail, too, became more scanty. From 25 February up to the time of his departure 'he receives few letters either from the ambassador or from B. A. [Baron Arnstein] and himself writes rarely', and gradually begins to strike camp. On 1 March the apprehensive servant is dismissed, and soon afterwards Beyme leaves the city 'by the post-chaise'.

So much for his visit to Vienna! There was a little epilogue to the story in the summer, at the spa of Baden near Vienna, where the High Chancellor made a brief appearance, but found little approval among the distinguished visitors. A confidential agent named Schmid reported on 20 June that here too Beyme was expressing the view that the Germans should again be formed into one nation: 'I, said he, would make Spartans of the Prussians. That, answered one of the company, they already are, for they have nothing but black broth. It is superfluous to point out,' adds the informant, 'how easily a witticism of this kind is uttered here, and how foolish a Prussian, of all people, is then made to appear.'

A second verbal exchange, in which Beyme likewise drew the short straw, took place during an excursion which he took with some acquaintances to Heiligenstadt. There he announced, in connection with the current industrial and financial arrangements, that 'because there was no harmony in anything, it seemed to him as though in Austria an ass were wearing a lion's head'. In the police documents it can be seen that the Emperor, on reading this, angrily underlined Beyme's remark with his pencil. 'One who disagreed with him,' Schmid reports, 'said to him, you must be speaking of Prussia, but the comparison is not apt, that of the frog which puffed itself up until it burst fits Prussia better, and walked away. Beyme ran after him and assured him that he had misunderstood him.'

A patriot, but not a man of great sensitivity! Perhaps Gentz's judgement on him had not been exaggerated. The opinion of a third, clearly quicker-witted informer proves him right. In May a report had been received at the police headquarters from Graz, where the Chancellor was temporarily staying, presumably in order to 'sound out opinions' in Styrian farmhouses and among townspeople. The observation was made therein that Beyme 'might have quite a good brain and be a capable businessman, but that despite a goodly portion of tedious pedantry he was totally lacking in delicate tact and knowledge of human nature'. Which may serve to conclude the characterisation of the member of the League of Virtue in Austria.

In Beyme, Fanny might have found a slightly ridiculous ally. Nevertheless the comic aspects of his personality did not prevent her from working with tireless zeal during those years for the cause of Prussian resistance. Without doubt she was kept fully informed of everything that happened in Germany or that came from there through Humboldt, who was well known to her from Henriette Herz's salon. Without doubt other, more skilful emissaries of the League of Virtue than the High Chancellor sought and received help and advice from her. While Fanny conspired with her former compatriots, Nathan enjoyed himself with his noble friends around the card-table. This too did not go unremarked by the Austrian secret police.

On 5 January 1811, the vice-president of police reported:

Your Majesty! With the return of Count Genicco from the country I resolved, since the mischief of games of hazard was again becoming an everyday occurrence, to pursue him in earnest, and make a surprise attack on the revellers at their gaming.

He had rented a large apartment in Prince Palm's house, No. 54 Schenkenstrasse, and fitted it up expressly for gaming, but his partners had no liking for this place; the gaming therefore takes place at his old apartment in the Baldauf house on the Stephansplatz, and at Baron Nathan Adam Arnsteiner's on the Hoher Markt.

The confidant employed for this purpose is already making all the preparations for our visit.

A note from the Emperor which has been added to the police file gives the order 'to put an end in good earnest to the gaming, as prescribed by law'. Luckily, at the same time an informer's report had arrived, according to which a 'forbidden game of hazard' was to take place that very evening at Count Genicco's. The operation could therefore be carried out without delay, and on the following day Hofrat Siber, who was already sufficiently engaged in reading the letters of High Chancellor Beyme, reported the success of this enterprise to his much-preoccupied monarch. Since, as he recalled, the games of faro and *rouge et noir* taking place at Genicco's had been under observation for some time, he directed 'four police officers . . . thither on the preceding night'. Their report is attached to his letter:

Following the imperial commission received, those undersigned proceeded at a quarter to one o'clock in the preceding night to the apartment of Count Aloys Genicco at No. 929, Stephansplatz.

The doors to the ante-room, where the servants were, were all unlocked according to a previously made arrangement. Here the servants attempted to prevent our entry, but were immediately instructed to conduct themselves quietly; we now moved through two further rooms into that one where the players who had not already noticed the presence of the undersigned were gathered.

At one table was Count von Genicco himself with Prince von Lichnowski, Prince Wenzel von Liechtenstein and Count Przerembski, playing whist.

At a second table: Count von Triangi, Niklas von Forgats, Dominik von Kaunitz, von Athems, Baron Nathan von Arnsteiner, von Leykam Johann, Chevallier von Malliard, and Leopold Edler von Herz; these were playing faro, with Count von Triangi acting as banker.

When the undersigned were observed by the players to be entering, these were thrown into great dismay and some immediately reached for the money lying in front of them, but were reminded that everything must be left standing or lying exactly as it was found at the time, whereupon they indeed withdrew their hands immediately, but could not be prevented from mingling with each other, on which occasion Count von Athems and Freiherr Johann von Leykam slipped away through a concealed door and hid themselves in the apartment, so that although the adjoining rooms were searched, the aforesaid were no longer to be found.

As a postscript it was stated that according to another informant named Seywald, faro was being played at one table, but ombre at another. Prince Lichnowsky had been watching the latter game and had then had himself carried away in a sedan-chair. As for Count Athems and Freiherr von Leykam, 'the two gentlemen had hidden themselves in Count Genicco's bedroom, under the bed', while he, Seywald, had seen everything 'from an unremarked spot in the dark'. The whole affair must have been betrayed by Count Wrbna or Prince Kaunitz, because his son had fallen into debt, or Count Kaunitz himself, in order not to have to pay his debts, or even Leykam, who was well known as a 'bad character and a dirty fellow'. In any case it must have been one of their own circle.

This then was the company in which Nathan, the cheerful, jovial, pleasure-loving man, moved every evening. But it was not only in that circle, but also in exclusively aristocratic ones that games of hazard were played with great intensity. Even the *Oberkämmerer* (Lord High Chamberlain) Count Wrbna was said to indulge in games of chance from time to time. Nathan was therefore in the best of company – so that the whole affair gives the lie to the evil tongues of Gentz and Varnhagen, who had criticised the bad company kept by the Arnsteins.

In May Siber reported that the card parties at the homes of Prince Windisch-Grätz, of the brothers Johann and Moritz Liechtenstein, of Count Palffy and of Nathan Baron Arnstein were continuing to take place. According, however, to the informant Seywald, such precautions were now being taken that any police intervention, 'if it were not now quite impossible, would certainly miscarry'. By secret means, however, certain details had come to light, such as the circumstance that 'at Baron Nathan Arnstein's no illegal play was taking place either in his wife's reception rooms, or in the adjoining rooms particularly occupied by himself. Baron Nathan Arnstein, the merchant Neuberg etc., likewise play – like Prince

Johann Liechtenstein – only the French game of ombre, although not exactly for small stakes.'

At the end of June a sentence was finally pronounced by the Viennese magistracy, according to which 'Counts von Kaunitz and von Attems, then Baron Nathan von Arnstein' were found guilty of illegal gaming, and the 'named persons of rank' were ordered 'to forfeit a fine of 900 fl. in redeemable bills, to be paid to the poverty relief fund of this country'. All the monies found at the faro table were assigned to the exchequer as unclaimed goods.

For a man of Nathan's prosperity a fine of 900 gulden could easily be endured and hardly fulfilled the intended purpose as a deterrent. Fanny, however, may have frowned on this method of filling the purse of the poverty relief fund. She had the greater occasion to do so since she had been elected at the beginning of February 1811 to the committee of a new charitable society, the 'Society of Ladies of the Nobility for the Promotion of the Good and the Useful'.

A report in the *Vaterländische Blätter für den Österreichischen Kaiserstaat* (Patriotic Papers for the Austrian Empire), ran as follows:

The ladies who have united in this society have chosen from their midst the twelve committee members each of whom will be responsible for the business of the Society in a district of the city and of the suburbs. The votes were sent to his Excellency the Provincial Marshal Count von Dietrichstein, the Count having taken upon himself the task of ascertaining their result. The majority of votes was given to the following ladies:

Baroness von Arnstein, *née* von Itzig
Princess von Auersperg, *née* Princess von Lobkowitz
Countess von Chotek, *née* Countess von Rottenham
Princess von Dietrichstein, Regent of the Ladies' Foundation of Savoy
Princess von Esterhazy, *née* Princess von Liechtenstein
Countess von Lanckoronska, *née* Countess von Rzewuska
Princess von Lichnowsky, *née* Countess von Thun
Princess von Liechtenstein, *née* Countess von Manderscheid
Princess von Lobkowitz, *née* Princess von Schwarzenberg
Countess von Rzewusky, *née* Princess von Lubomirska
Countess von Thun, *née* Countess von Sinzendorf
Princess von Trautmannsdorf, *née* Countess von Colloredo.

These ladies will occupy the posts of honour entrusted to them by the Society for three years. As, according to their statutes, they are obliged annually to elect the chairwoman of the Society from among themselves, they gathered on Sunday 3 February at the house of Princess von Trautmannsdorf. The vote was cast unanimously for Princess Caroline von Lobkowitz, to whom the Society owes its existence.

If it was true that 'everyone trembled' in the Arnstein house as soon as 'a countess sat on the sofa and a princess on a chair', there must have been veritable earthquakes in the Hoher Markt on certain of the Society's committee days! There was not in the Austrian Empire a nobler selection of ancient names than those which were now joined with that of the lady, *née* Itzig. A consideration in choosing Fanny may have been her wealth; yet it could not stand comparison with that of the houses of Esterhazy or Lobkowitz, nor was it larger than the fortune of a Baroness Geymüller or a Countess Fries. It was not upon one of these two bankers' wives, whose husbands had the same business income as Nathan and whose blood, moreover, was 'irreproachable' or even blue – Countess Fries was by birth a Princess Hohenlohe – that the choice had fallen, but upon a Jewess from Berlin. It must have been her famous charitableness and her amiability, not her money alone, which had helped her to this position of honour.

After the foundation of the society, as is noted in its statement of accounts for 1836, 'his Majesty Francis I graciously deigned to remark that these women, who were joining an association of such benefit to the community, could count with confidence on his Majesty's goodwill and gratitude'. The sentiments he was offering to Fanny were of a kind that she was unable to reciprocate. But even if she had at that time no love for the Emperor, to whom a Bonaparte grandchild was born that March, she still sympathised with his people. A week before the birth of the King of Rome the *Wiener Zeitung* carried an anonymous, but all the more remarkable notice:

> To do good by stealth; to offer one's hand in loving kindness to suffering humanity; to help even when every prospect of help seems impossible to the fearful unfortunate is – great. – There is no expression worthy to describe the noble actions of the most noble philanthropist, Baroness von Arnstein, née Itzig. – May this noble woman forgive those families who, forced by tragic circumstances to leave their devastated homes, found their saviour in her, and, penetrated by the most heartfelt feelings of gratitude, are no longer able to remain silent.

In these months there was occasion enough for offering 'one's hand in loving kindness to suffering humanity'. Not only were the inhabitants of the war-ravaged villages of the Marchfeld still in need of accommodation and the necessities of life, not only were there deaf-mutes, blind people, convents and hospitals to be maintained, but there were the new poor – victims of the new financial charter which had recently been issued. Count Wallis, O'Donnell's successor as president of the exchequer, had attempted to control the hopeless situation of the financial economy by simply declaring the state bankrupt on 20 February. Almost all kinds of banknotes, credit notes and bonds were affected and sank to a fifth of their face value; only some older funds had remained intact.

Underhand practices were not unknown – Counts Chotek and Zinzendorf, old Thugut, even Prince Johann Liechtenstein and the Empress's mother had in good time acquired papers of stable value. The majority of the population, however, were down to their last reserves. Thousands of officials, officers and pensioners were facing ruin. The state left its citizens cold-bloodedly in the lurch. In view of such 'financial arrangements' the ungracious Beyme had not been quite wrong when he made the presumptuous remark that 'in Austria an ass was wearing a lion's head'. The Emperor, who was so angered by this impudence, was nevertheless made some-what uneasy by it.

Of all these comfortless years, 1811 seemed the worst. It was only in Spain that the conqueror of the world still met with resistance. In Prague, powerless, Freiherr vom Stein was biding his time in the circle of Prussian patriots. Gentz, who had swallowed his hatred of Napoleon as a spy once detected swallows the incriminating piece of paper, sat disgruntled and uninterested in external affairs in his 'wretched little apartment' in the Seilergasse in Vienna. Finally, Metternich, 'blasé and, as a result of his brilliant and precocious career, no longer eager for many more forms of higher ambition', wished indeed 'privately to preserve his reputation for the right ideas regarding the freedom of Europe', but went no further in this 'than can conveniently be done . . . This spoilt child of fortune has become a minister of neutrality'.

Adam Müller, the reactionary and Teutomaniac philosopher, who had recently joined the little coterie of German mystics in Vienna, gave the Prussian Chancellor Hardenberg the above de-scription of the Austrian statesman. He had even worse things to say of the ruling house: 'The behaviour of the Emperor and the Princes of the imperial house during the last war and since then, the obvious indifference to the suffering of the people and the Em-peror's personal avarice, as well as the outrageous antithesis be-tween the proclamation of 1809 and the family connection formed in 1810, have blunted the sense of national pride.' Müller, no moralist himself, reported this without emphasis. His compatriot Fanny, more impetuous and uncompromising than himself, was continually in a fury over that 'outrageous antithesis' in the imperial attitude.

The German educationist and archaeologist Karl August Böttiger often found her in a bad humour that summer, as Varnhagen had done before him. She was, as he recorded in his notebook, becoming 'more violent and caustic with the years', was 'very bitter about the great nation and its autocrat', and had also restricted her own hospitality. He had several times seen her husband in his shirtsleeves at the card-table – Böttiger's visits took place in the Arnsteins' summer residence. Nathan would soon retire from his business, but 'still [had] two millions and only Madame Pereira as his heiress'. An entry reads: 'Midday dinner at banker Arnsteiner's. Captain and Major von Hohenzollern. English Miss. – *Tous les rois que vous avez fait, pleurent.*' Did Fanny tell him this melancholic *bon mot*? He reports further only that Fanny herself showed her guests around her cowshed and pigeon-loft.

Fanny, meanwhile, had sensed during these summer months that her house and she herself were hardly able any longer to escape the reproach that they were aging or even aged. To resign herself to this was not in accordance with her temperament. Young people were needed; and as Henriette had formed her own circle, which coincided less and less with her mother's, a creature of similar beauty and gentleness was to replace her. One such was found in Marianne Saaling, Bella Salomon's niece, whose sister Regine had been living in Austria for a while. Many were to praise the charms of the pretty child; at the time of the Congress her presence enhanced the attraction of the Arnstein salon.

So the year drew to an end. In November, despite autumnal fog and cold, the noble ladies of the association assembled on an open tract of land in Baden to attend the ceremonial opening of a newly built hospital. Archduke Rudolph laid the first foundation stone in his own name, the second in that of his brother Anton, and Princess Lobkowitz, as president of the association, the third, in which a roll of parchment signed by all the ladies of the committee had been buried. Fanny had already contributed 6,660 gulden, 'which she had received as a contribution from the Israelites by means of collections', to the building fund of the future Marienspital, which had been founded by the association. Now, stirred by the moving ceremony, she undertook on the spot to provide six complete beds on her own account. Cäcilie Eskeles, too, having become an 'active member of the society', had organised support among her family and in the circle of her acquaintance for the *Elisabethinerinnen* in the Landstrasse – nurses who were later to work at the hospital. On the name-day of its patron saint she handed over to the convent more than 4,000 gulden, a bundle of wood and a supply of food.

The *Elisabethinerinnen* now became special protégées of the two sisters. Henriette Pereira emulated her mother in this as in so much else, and in later years became superintendent of the hospital at Baden. As yet she was still leaving the greater part of these good works to Fanny, looking after her beautiful town house in Grün-angergasse, bringing up her children, 'flirting', as Böttiger noted, 'with the new philosophy' – by which doubtless was meant the Catholic mysticism of Schlegel, Müller and the romantic writer Zacharias Werner – and trying ever more vainly to preserve her marital happiness. 'Pereira, her husband,' as Böttiger had also reported, 'is too lazy to do business properly, too mean to run a household, an insufferable money-counter, does not appreciate or understand his wife.' Henriette found more understanding among her friends – romantically inclined, sentimental young people, with whom she sat in a quiet circle on winter evenings, making music and telling each other ghost stories.

The 21-year-old Theodor Körner, the son of a *Konsistorialrat* (consistorial councillor) from Saxony and a writer whose dramas were performed at the Hofburgtheater, also became her frequent guest. In the carnival season, when she held larger *thés dansants*, he met influential people there such as his theatre director, Prince Lobkowitz, and Count Fries. But he preferred the more intimate gatherings where one only chatted, made music or gave readings, 'the ladies provide the inspiration for songs and Bartholdy and I saddle Pegasus'. He described Henriette and her cousin Marianne Saaling to his father in a letter as 'two great exceptions of efficient inner culture, adorned with all the good qualities of the glossy external world'. Through her, his imagination was stimulated in every way. 'I have,' he wrote to Dresden in September, 'occupied myself much with ghost stories this week. Madame Pereira has held several spiritual soirées, where I won the garland with two stories I had thought up. I put into verses a very fine story told by Marianne Saaling.'

The more tragic verses, the first impulses for which had been given to him by Henriette, had not yet been written by himself or by history.

Now, however, came 1812, and the first sign that the repose of Europe was coming to an end. Tsar Alexander had begun to relish the role of saviour and liberator. After announcing to Napoleon his withdrawal from participation in the Continental system (the closure of the Continent to British trade), and breaking off his own war against the Ottoman Empire, he eagerly prepared for the inevitable clash. Metternich, who would not have been displeased by a few more 'years of political freedom to heal Austria's wounds', observed this without enthusiasm. Later he was to say that he had 'not been able to prolong the duration of this inactivity beyond 1811'. Had he succeeded, he would have liked nothing better.

Instead, he found himself forced to adopt a politics of 'armed neutrality', which in the first instance consisted of an arms alliance with France. When Napoleon demanded 30,000 soldiers from the Emperor, and that force was supplied, it was not to be interpreted as a breach of neutrality by either of the hostile powers – an 'eccentric political stance', as Metternich himself later admitted, which had 'no parallel in history'. To his own astonishment he succeeded in securing Napoleon's assent. Thus safeguarded on all sides, the Viennese awaited the war between Russia and France.

Prussia was in a more pitiable state. At the beginning of March Napoleon had forced the King into an alliance against Alexander and had claimed his country for the deployment of his troops. Led by Stein, the 'Prussian separatists and Teutomaniacs' – in Metternich's words – betook themselves to Russia, to transform their resistance, until now passive, into an active one. In the midst of these disturbances, Hardenberg, who had just, with a heavy heart, concluded the alliance with France, with a lighter conscience brought out the awaited edict with regard to the Jews. It had been ratified on 11 March and appeared to those concerned as a great, if not wholly unclouded joy. Not everything proposed by Humboldt and approved by Hardenberg had been confirmed by the King. Certain provisos, a remnant of that principle of Schrötter's of 'pedagogic emancipation', still remained. These included the stipulations over oaths, the continued restriction on admission to certain public offices, and the increased impediments to immigration. Nevertheless much, indeed nearly everything, had been achieved.

Jews resident in the Prussian state were raised to the position of natives and citizens. They were to take surnames and use the German language. They were permitted to settle anywhere, to buy land, to hold teaching and municipal posts, to carry on business without restrictions. They were excused from special payments, but in exchange had to subject themselves to civic taxes and duties, particularly military service. Their special judicial status was abolished; the jurisdiction of the rabbis and elders was to dwindle.

Calm before the Storm

However, their religious situation remained unchanged, although prospects of reform were held out for the future, as was the case with education. All in all, the new law was a progressive step such as had never yet been taken spontaneously in Germany. When Hardenberg gave the news to the elders of the community on the evening of the very day on which he had received the royal signature, it seemed to them that they had won a finer victory than any of Napoleon's.

So it was true after all, what a Prussian minister had told the ambassador of the French Republic in the second year of this King's reign: the King was a democrat; the advantageous revolution, which over there had been carried out from bottom to top, was here being introduced by him from top to bottom, and he was on the point of 'pursuing the path of Joseph II of Austria, although more cautiously'. This was meant with reference to the privileges of the nobility, but it applied equally to the Jews. Frederick William, exactly thirty years after Joseph's edict of tolerance, had realised a thoroughgoing 'reception' going far beyond the latter. It was a daring leap from the *loi cannibale* of 1750 to this act of liberation!

Now it was the turn of the Emperor of Austria to express scepticism. He himself had not the slightest intention of extending the rights of his Jews – still no more than some 120 tolerated families. It had not been until the spring that, at his request, the law of 1764 preventing their purchase of houses had been newly confirmed. But as far as new ideas of all kinds were concerned, he had voiced his opinion at the time of the first Prussian reforms in front of a row of university professors in Ljubljana: 'There are new ideas in the air, which I shall not approve. Abstain from these and hold to the positive; for I need no scholars, but only good honest citizens. It is your duty to form our youth into such persons. He who serves me must teach what I command; he who cannot do this, or who comes along with new ideas, may go, or I will remove him!'

It was not easy to feel affection for such a ruler if one had grown up in the Berlin of Frederick the Great and been at home in the Vienna of Joseph II. The best thing to do was to refrain, as far as this was reconcilable with a highly excitable temperament, from any comparison of Francis with more enlightened and progressive princes, and to dedicate oneself instead to the more gratifying aspects of the state of Austria. One such was the love of its citizens for music. Fanny, who, although she no longer practised this art, was still passionately devoted to it, now saw an opportunity to combine its cultivation with her interest in good works. Joseph

Ferdinand Sonnleithner, secretary to the Hofburg theater and librettist of Beethoven's *Fidelio*, had taken over the administration of the 'noble women'. In April 1812, under the aegis of the association, he and Fanny discussed and organised a private concert for the benefit of the blind and those suffering from eye disease, to be given in the newly built Streicher hall.

The project was a success and aroused the general wish to bring the music-lovers of Vienna together in a closer bond. A small committee which included, apart from Fanny and Sonnleithner, Prince Lobkowitz, Count Moritz Fries and Countess Marianne Dietrichstein, now planned a second concert in a more glittering setting and style. 'A suggestion made by Frau Fanny von Arnstein and strongly supported by Sonnleithner,' writes the chronicler, 'was victoriously upheld; it was decided to prepare the performance of a comprehensive oratorio and to engage a sufficient number of instrumentalists and chorus members as well as proficient soloists for this purpose. Emperor Francis allowed the use of the Winter Riding School and its temporary adaptation as a concert-hall, and in addition gave permission for the last ensemble rehearsals to be held in the Rittersaal of the Hofburg. For the earlier choir rehearsals Prince Lobkowitz put his *palais* at the disposal of the organisers.'

The work to be performed was Handel's *Prometheus, or the Power of Music*, whose instrumental section had been strengthened and adapted by Mozart. The preparations for this concert, out of whose audience the Viennese *Gesellschaft der Musikfreunde* (Society of Music-lovers) was to develop, took up the whole of the summer and half the autumn. It was a good thing that Fanny was so fully occupied with it; that year the events of world history would otherwise have given the finishing stroke to her irritable nerves.

In May Napoleon had reached a new zenith. At an assembly of princes, which he held with great splendour and the greatest possible display of power in Dresden, he sunned himself in the anticipation of new triumphs. The Russian campaign, of whose success he had no doubt, would bring Stockholm and Constantinople into his empire; Finland, St Petersburg and the Baltic states would become a kingdom founded under the rule of one of his generals. The *Grande Armée*, given wings by the strongest fighting spirit, was stationed at the Vistula, ready for the attack. With much less enthusiasm for war, 20,000 Prussians were making their preparations under the command of Lieutenant-General von Yorck. The Austrian auxiliary corps, led by Prince Schwarzenberg, had departed for the Galician border. When Metternich, who had accompanied the imperial couple to Dresden, sat opposite their son-in-law, full of confidence in his victory, he could not doubt the wisdom of his own tactics of immobility.

Whatever might happen, this crafty man, not ill-advised by Gentz, even better by his own instinct and practical experience, had nothing to lose. If Napoleon should succeed, Austria would be on the right side. If the Russian exploit should miscarry, a pact secretly concluded in St Petersburg was enough to allow him to change sides effortlessly. And as far as the judgement of posterity was concerned, Metternich, now as later, had his justification ready: 'Was the path taken by us better than that which Freiherr vom Stein and his political friends never wearied of suggesting to King Frederick William?' Actual events were to prove it! They 'would probably have been quite other ones if Austria had not opposed her deliberate attitude to the last adventurous exploits of the conqueror. Had we given a hearing to the pressure of the impatient Prussian party, we would, without possessing the means of defence, have seen Napoleon on the battlefields of our own exhausted domains, rather than on the icy steppes of Russia. At least the attitude of Austria has not traversed the paths of destiny.'

While Napoleon joined his army and the imperial Austrian couple lingered with Marie-Louise in Prague, Madame de Staël paid her second visit to Vienna. But the atmosphere had changed. Her former lover Maurice O'Donnell had married Titine de Ligne, Napoleon-haters were out of fashion – that certain 'outrageous antithesis' to the formerly adopted attitude was noticeable even in the 'first' ranks of society – and Germaine herself, likewise, no longer had the charm of novelty. However, for the time being she saw no reason to complain about her reception. In certain circles her opinion was still shared. She therefore hastened to the side of Fanny, in whom she hoped to find a kindred spirit. 'J'étais ravie de me trouver ainsi au milieu d'une société qui me plaisait, et dont la manière de penser répondit à la mienne,' she later wrote about this time in Vienna.

Soon, however, it became clear to her that she, who on her earlier visit had been received in a friendly manner by the Emperor and by the whole court, was this time regarded as a *persona non grata*, and to her annoyance she found herself spied upon in all her comings and goings. 'Cette manière de faire la police me paraissait réunir tout à la fois le machiavélisme français et la lourdeur alle-mande.' And so, after three weeks, she left the perfidious city, to travel to Sweden, whose Crown Prince, Bernadotte, had been her idol since his courageous alliance with Russia.

Madame de Staël, it is true, did not know that Napoleon's former marshal, who had been forced upon the Swedes as heir to the throne, was at that very moment aspiring to a re-insurance with France. Shrewder than Fanny, Germaine was no more equal than she to the age of secret diplomacy; she shared with her that impulsive emotion that wraps itself like a fog around every insight of the intellect. For the rest, the deposed Swedish King Gustavus Adolphus had that summer travelled through Vienna, where he also established contact with the Arnsteins. Years ago he had bestowed upon Nathan, who was looking after the affairs of his country in Vienna, the title of a Swedish consul general. Now, clearly in financial straits, he sought out his old adviser. The following provision is to be found in a will drawn up by Fanny the following February: 'A medal which I bought from the King of Sweden on his travelling through Vienna in the year 1812, belongs to my dear niece Mariane Eskeles, who, with her intelligence, will know how to appreciate the misfortune of the man who was constrained to sell it, and will draw from it the useful observation: how transitory is the greatness of the good things of this world.'

Napoleon had crossed the Memel, and all was going well for him. In the rest of Europe his advance was being followed with keen interest, but daily life remained unaltered. Herr Geheimrat von Goethe, too, had gone to Carlsbad again this summer to take the waters, although some of Prince Schwarzenberg's troops were stationed not very far away.

It was here that Bernhard von Eskeles had called upon him at the end of August. 'Your brother,' wrote Goethe to Frau von Fliess, 'has done me the favour of seeking me out, but stayed for such a short time that I missed his instructive and valued company only too soon.' He added greetings to Cäcilie and a few polite, but easily interpreted words about Caroline Pichler's novel *Agathokles*, which he had received some time earlier, hoping for his favourable verdict:

> How much the innate talent of the author and its development prejudiced me can be seen from the fact that, in reading this charming work of nature and art, I quite forgot how little that century, and the ways of thinking that triumphantly appear in it, are actually to my taste. Indeed, our friend will value very highly the fact that I did not become in the least ill-tempered if she treated my great-uncle Hadrian and his little soul, and the rest of my heathen kindred and their spirits, rather indifferently.

But his letter was never read by Eleonore. Before this last sign of Olympian favour could reach her hands, she had died. In the midst of preparations for an outing to Hietzing, whither she had been invited by Cäcilie together with Caroline Pichler and young Körner, she had suffered a stroke. Her sister-in-law, however, felt too 'saddened and distracted' to inform the poet of the unhappy event. The task fell to Jakob Bartholdy. On 7 September, the day on which the battle of Borodino was raging, he announced Eleonore's death to Goethe in his aunt's name. Frau von Eskeles, he reported, had opened his Excellency's letter to the departed, had told Frau von Pichler immediately, to her great delight, 'everything pleasant and flattering' that it contained about *Agathokles*. For the rest, his aunt thanked him from her heart for all his friendly reminiscences and 'counted on the pleasure of repeating to you soon, in her own writing and her own words, how unforgettable the hours passed in your Excellency's company will always be to her'.

Soon afterwards Caroline also took up her pen and wrote to Goethe that Cäcilie Eskeles had given her the letter in question 'as it were, as a kind of legacy from our dear departed'. It was, she stressed, to Eleonore that she owed her correspondence with him and his verdict on *Agathokles*, which had 'deeply flattered' her. Clearly she could not or would not see in it the concealed censure of a work which, in its religious sentimentality, belittled Goethe's beloved heathen antiquity. Finally, she regretted not having been able to welcome him to Vienna that summer. 'Your arrival was already being spoken of, and everyone waited with longing for the moment of making your acquaintance in person.' Perhaps the following year would bring her what had been denied to her this year.

The ladies of Vienna tried everything to lure the poet to their city. In November Cäcilie renewed her plea that he should finally delight with his presence the imperial city to which he had already been so near on many occasions. But Goethe simply did not want to go to Vienna. He knew of its charm, its brilliance, its magic. But he had heard too much of the lack of serious literary interest which ruled there to be able to expect intellectual stimulation from such a visit. The Austrian states, he had once observed, seemed much further away to him in his imagination than other countries and cities at the same distance, they were for him 'a modern Nineveh, a dense forest through which no path was to be found through the wilderness'. And it may well be that the amiable ladies, in fact Caroline von Pichler above all, with her foolish (as it appeared to him), unctuous religiosity may even have diminished further his wish to go there. Besides, at about the same time as Eleonore and equally unexpectedly, Marianne von Eybenberg had died in Vienna. If she had not until then been able to persuade him to take that journey, no others would ever succeed.

Goethe wrote to Cäcilie once more from Weimar, to offer his condolences on the death of her sister-in-law. To his words of sympathy he added a postscript, which represented a concealed but final refusal of Vienna:

> And why should I not make use of this empty sheet to express my warmest thanks for your friendly invitation to Vienna. On such an occasion, truly, it pains me to bring to mind the loss I have suffered all my life, through never having seen the imperial city. Continually, and particularly in recent times, I feel urged to comply at last with my duty, to pay my respects to my noble well-wishers and worthy friends and make this visit. But unfortunately the prospects are no better than before, as my ailments keep me in the Bohemian watering-places in summer and at home in winter. Even there, alas, I can very rarely accomplish those things that society may demand of us; larger and broader relationships therefore always make me anxious.

One can imagine the sadness of the hospitable ladies over the elusiveness of such an illustrious visitor. Perhaps, however, his refusal had spared them, if not disappointment, at least the danger of an embarrassing difference of opinion. On that 26 November which was the date of Goethe's letter from Weimar, the fate of the Russian campaign had already been decided. While the *Grande Armée*, on the ice-bound roads and snow-covered steppes, were setting out upon the most fearsome retreat ever undertaken by any army in history, Napoleon made ready to return to Paris, defeated. His opponents scented the morning air. What had been a treacherous dream at Aspern now lay visibly, if not yet tangibly, within the realms of probability.

From Germany's greatest poet, however, a circle which was thoroughly anti-Napoleonic, and wished the French usurper in hell, could expect little sympathy. Goethe, who forbade his son August to join the army of liberation, who said the following April to Christian Gottfried Körner: 'Rattle your chains as you may, the man is too great for you, you will not break them' – Goethe was not the spirit of fire which could have kindled the patriots of the day. Arndt, Rückert, Fichte, Kleist, Fouqué and Uhland were calling the German nation to revolt. Vienna, however, had her own little poet of freedom: Körner's handsome and enthusiastic son, who sought to emulate his father's best friend, Friedrich Schiller, in youthful rebelliousness. In Fanny's house and that of her gentle, easily influenced daughter his ardour was nourished and encouraged. Here, he found more sympathy for his violently awakening desire to join the fighters for freedom, than from Toni Adamberger, the charming Hoftheater actress, to whom he had recently become engaged.

As Fanny, about midday on 29 November 1812, in the richly decorated hall of the Winter Riding School, surrounded by an audience of 5,000 and in the presence of the entire court, listened to the triumphal strains of Handel's oratorio, she experienced not only 'the Power of Music' but also the grandeur of the moment. A woman no longer young, hardly to be called beautiful any more, whose dignified appearance inadequately concealed her fiery temperament, she would probably have longed, like Goethe's Klärchen and her own niece Lea, for 'a little jacket and breeches and hat' to be able to take part herself in the coming uprising. That such an event was imminent was clear to all the world, clearest of all to Napoleon. From Dresden, which he had reached on 14 December, he was already demanding from Emperor Francis double the number of Austrian auxiliary forces and renewed proofs of friendship. About the same time his ambassador wrote to him from Vienna that 'it was unprecedented how generally one here indulged in the idea of abandoning an ally after the first misfortune suffered and of joining the ranks of the enemy'. This mood was even more evident in Prussia. While the peace-loving and anxious King might send his General von Krusemark to Paris, to assure the *Empereur* through him of his 'enduring attachment to the alliance', the people were more than ready for a defection from that bond.

Young Körner spent those weeks in a mood of cheerful, martial excitement. He gave a reading of his tragedy *Zriny* at Henriette's and wrote to his father that he had found there the most appreciative, and yet the sincerest, most sensitive audience for his work. He celebrated Christmas, too, at her house: 'I spent Christmas Eve very merrily at Madame Pereira's, where we all received presents. Mine was a large doll dressed up as Helene von Zriny, with all the instruments of murder and destruction, and with a very pretty poem written by a fair hand.' When his letter arrived in Dresden the turning-point had already been reached. Not far from the Lithuanian town of Tauroggen, the commander of the Prussian auxiliary corps, Lieutenant-General von Yorck, had entered into negotiations with the three Russian delegates, Diebitsch, Clausewitz and Dohna – all countrymen of his. On 30 December, without the King's authorisation, he concluded an armistice. The first signal for the defection and revolt of Prussia had been given.

$-10-$

Battlefield and Conference Table

Wars are made by kings, revolutions by the people. The man in the street has good reason to tear his own masters down from the throne when their rule has become unbearable to him. But it is rarely that he sees the need to take up arms in order to bring death to the citizens of another country. Yet in the Prussia of 1813 it was not high politics, but the long-dammed-up anger of the people that declared war on the French. Against the wishes of Frederick William, who apprehensively opposed himself to this uprising, his subjects – 'fanatic volunteers, students and professors, literati and poets', but also simple people, officials, manualworkers, athletes and eccentrics, rushed to don uniforms and to form an army.

Here at last was a war for cultured people! Even Rahel Levin, who had denied such a thing at the time of Wagram, had become converted to this view. For a cosmopolitan woman such as she, who had wanted to find a home in Napoleon's Europe, Prussia had become a real concept. Arndt's cry 'To all those who deserve the name of Germans' seemed directed at her too. 'The hour of Fichte' (in whose *Addresses to the German Nation* he called upon his country to resist Napoleon) became for her 'my only consolation, my hope, my riches'. Heinrich von Kleist's murderous cry 'Strike him dead! And in the world's eye / None will ask the reason why!' rang convincingly in her ear.

It was not otherwise with Humboldt, whose humanist serenity had until now enabled him to stand aside. He, too, who believed in only two beneficent powers in the world – God and the people – underwent a change of heart now that both of these tribunals seemed to desire the struggle for freedom. Moreover, as soon as Yorck's defection became known, the Prussian envoy to Vienna found his apartment besieged by his countrymen. Officers who had entered the Austrian service after Jena, civilians, voluntary helpers, flocked to him. The call to arms that was finally given by the King, who had fled Berlin and was surrounded by patriotic advisers, had not yet become public when all the able-bodied were already gravitating back to Germany.

'A great moment of my life is nigh. Be assured that you will find me not unworthy of you, whatever the proof may cost.' So wrote Theodor Körner to his father on 29 January 1813. His tender little fiancée, a girl of old Viennese stock, the daughter of the tenor Adamberger who had been a friend of Mozart and of the cabinet secretary Günther, had little time for such high flights of a German temperament. With the uninhibited *joie de vivre* which her heredity and environment had awoken in her, she resisted anything that might imperil her happiness. She had for a long time been a little jealous of Henriette Pereira, the beautiful lady in the Neuburger-hof, because of Körner's sentimental admiration for her. Now, on top of this, she bewailed the fact that he enjoyed Henriette's support for his belligerent intentions.

But how could Henriette not have encouraged an urge that corresponded to her own feelings? She might have grown up in Vienna, the daughter of the indolent, far from warlike Nathan – but it was at all times her mother who exercised the strongest influence over her. Fanny had brought her into the world in Berlin, had commended her in all her wills to the care of her 'beloved sisters', had educated her in the culture of the German world of the intellect. Frequent journeys to her native city had kept alive in Henriette her relationship with her 'Berlin *famille*'. Now that the sons of Isaac Daniel had joined the voluntary fusiliers, and another cousin, Jacob, her uncle Benjamin's son, had already fallen in Spain against Napoleon, she found it natural, even a matter of course, to see a young German hastening into active service. And if she perhaps hesitated to release from her side the handsome youth whose admiration was a comfort to her in those years of declining marital happiness, such scruples were dispelled by her mother. Weakened by an illness which had taken hold of her during those winter months, Fanny rallied under the influence of the stirring news. The enthusiasm with which she greeted the Prussian uprising was communicated by her to the whole of her acquaintance.

At the end of February, Hardenberg had met the Prussian general Kutuzov in the Silesian town of Kalisch, and concluded a treaty of alliance with him. On 17 March Prussia declared war against France and the King issued a proclamation 'To my People'. Ten days earlier, young Körner had informed his father that his purpose had ripened to maturity: 'Germany has risen up; the Prussian eagle, with the valiant beating of its wings, awakes in all loyal hearts the great hope of a German, or at least north German freedom. My art sighs for her fatherland – let me be her worthy disciple! – Yes, dearest father, I want to become a soldier, I want to cast joyfully

aside the happy, carefree life I have attained here, to gain a fatherland in battle, if need be with my blood!' He hoped to depart within
the next few days, perhaps as Humboldt's courier. At the Breslau
assembly point he would meet with the free sons of Prussia. 'Toni
has proved the greatness and nobility of her soul to me on this
occasion too. She weeps, it is true, but the end of the campaign will
soon dry her tears.'

Soon afterwards Körner left Vienna. As early as that very 17
March, he sent news to Henriette Pereira of a short stay in Troppau:

Dearest friend! Fortunately there are no horses to be had; we are staying
here for a few moments, and I have time to write to you. When I was in
Vienna, I often looked forward to this in secret; now I feel what a
clumsy pleasure it is, when one thinks instead of the beautiful moments
of free conversation.

I had a very pleasant surprise; the last familiar face to appear before me
in Vienna was that of your little coachman, who was probably driving
to Hietzing. I charged him to convey my greetings to you. – The first
hours of my journey were very sad and dull. I was at great pains to place
very clearly before my mind the necessity of leaving Vienna and all my
happiness, in order not to fall into a kind of regret, which remains the
most adverse thing to me, despite all my manly resolves.

And he closed:

Oh God, to be able to sit again this evening at the dear round table and
move your lampshade! Think of me always in the kindest way, you
lovely, amiable woman; I kiss your dear hands in my thoughts.

Five days later, already in Breslau, he wrote again:

Good morning, fairest lady! The sun has today surprised me in a bed for
the last time. From now on it will probably look more like straw
everywhere . . . In a few days, perhaps as early as tomorrow, we
march, and in ten days we face the enemy . . . My heart leaps violently
when I but see the glint of a rifle. God! what a great, glorious time this
is. Everyone goes with such a free, proud courage to face the great battle
for the fatherland. Everyone presses forward to be the first to bleed for
the good cause. There is but one will, one desire among the whole
nation, and the stale saying 'Victory or death' acquires a sacred meaning.

Henriette's relationship with the young poet is veiled by the mists
of the past. How he reconciled his inclination towards the much
maturer woman with his passion for Toni, from which of the two

he found it harder to part when he left Vienna, remains a secret. It is certain only that he wrote from the field no fewer letters to Henriette than to Toni Adamberger, and that in these he repeatedly bemoaned the loss of heartfelt joys at her side. What he wrote to his fiancée has not survived. Henriette, on the other hand, preserved every line that came from his hand. But many dedications and poems, indeed many a confidential missive to her, were never printed and rest in a casket which is still withheld from posterity by one of her heirs. Only one sonnet dedicated to her, which bears the title 'Poesie und Liebe' (Poetry and Love), has become known.

Henriette was hardly younger than her mother had been at the time of Carl Liechtenstein's love for her. But if in that *amitié amoureuse* the stress was laid on the adjective, this presumably exhausted itself in sentimental feeling. The facility with which one entered into love-affairs and liaisons in the declining Rococo era, the premeditated defiance with which one committed adultery in the early Romantic age, were both things of the past. A new morality, a return to the medieval reverence for womanhood had come into fashion. Now one poured forth sentiment, but shrank from the realisation of the yearningly expressed desire. One might hotly embrace a dainty, but down-to-earth Toni Adamberger; a Frau von Pereira was to be approached hesitantly, as if one's own imagination were to be preferred to reality.

Was she approached at all? There is nothing in the letters known to the public which allows one to make this assumption. Körner often thinks 'of dear, beloved Vienna, of many a silvery glance which shines upon me, and now passes before me in the misty form of memory'. He speaks of a 'living, clear return of feeling, of greeting; the beautiful hours rise up again, and all the peace and joy of my heart'. He implores Henriette: 'Think of me always in friendship, without resentment, and do not forget, beyond all the wildness and waywardness of a glowing heart, many a good and quiet flower which I most surely preserve in the sanctuary of my breast.' When a friend promises to bind his wounds, he says: 'At this I thought again of you. Ah, when do I not think of you? Once you promised to nurse me with mildness and gentleness; – perhaps I shall soon need it.' And finally he laments: 'Every evening I feel powerfully drawn towards the south. Now that I can no longer be in Grünangergasse [Green Meadow Street] I may perhaps soon be at peace in the green meadow.'

All the rapture, all the love of life and bliss of death experienced by the young fighters for freedom found their echo in Körner's letters to Henriette. They were and remain the most moving testimony of that time, a first noble, touching and pure manifestation of Germanness at the time of its innocent infancy. For the people from whom Fanny's daughter was descended there is a painful irony in the fact that during the Second World War these letters were circulated among students and soldiers as a National Socialist broadsheet. It is further occasion for a melancholy smile that we have Henriette Pereira to thank for Körner's militaristic poems, *Leier und Schwert* (*Lyre and Sword*), which have since become the iron rations of patriotic German songbooks. When her young friend went into battle, she gave him a little notebook whose green silk binding was adorned by a lyre embroidered by her own hand. In this she asked him to enter his notes and rhymes. This was the origin of verses which, when released from Henriette's booklet, were to pierce like a dagger the hearts of her future kinsmen. It was her face he saw before him when, during those weeks, he created his poetic transfigurations of battle, blood and victory. 'The book which is so dear to me,' he wrote to Henriette from Jauer on 30 March, 'has already been used quite frequently, for in the lonely hours of quiet remembrance which, as often as possible, I procure for myself, my heart always leads me to song and verse.' It was a prayer of thanks that he had composed that day – a song of praise to the Lord:

> Denn was uns mahnt zu Sieg und Schlacht,
> Hat Gott ja selber angefacht:
> Dem Herrn allein die Ehre!
> Er weckt uns jetzt mit Siegeslust
> Für die gerechte Sache:
> Er rief es selbst in unsre Brust:
> Auf, deutsches Volk, erwache!

[For what exhorts us now toward victory and battle / Was fanned to flame by God Himself; / The Lord's alone is the honour! / He wakes us now with lust for victory / For the cause that is just; / His own call sounds in our breast: / Up, German people, awake!]

While the Prussians – these 'Gascons of Germany', as Napoleon called them – rushed into war, resolute in the face of death, making up in courage for what their army lacked in skilful leadership, in Austria one was content to sit on the fence as before. One wanted to topple Napoleon, but was not prepared to make Tsar Alexander the mightiest prince of Europe in his stead. One wanted to help Prussia, but not at the price of a new union of German states developing under her presidency, as was Stein's ambition. If at this moment one intervened against Napoleon, one would in the end destroy that France which, for the sake of the balance of power in Europe, should not entirely disappear. If one waited too long, Alexander might possibly execute one of his customary volte-faces and conclude a peace with Napoleon, which would prove to be as favourable for St Petersburg as it was catastrophic for Vienna.

In this dilemma, Metternich created a new political concept. If in the preceding year he had invented 'armed neutrality', with whose help one could persuade first one side, then the other, that Austria's military strength was to its advantage, he now coined the phrase 'armed mediation'. To participate in this new war as a go-between seemed the most rewarding office, the more rewarding since, after an unsuccessful attempt at peacemaking and with the situation more settled, one could still take sides. The first step had been Schwarzenberg's armistice with the Russians. He was now sent to Paris to obtain Napoleon's agreement to Austria's role as a mediator. But whatever he proposed, Napoleon refused, making counter-claims, trying to bait the Emperor with an offer to return Silesia. Meanwhile Russia had publicly declared herself in agreement with Metternich's suggestion. Napoleon was, therefore, abruptly informed that Austria would henceforth act as an armed mediator, with the polite postscript that this did not imply the least antagonism against him. How much that promise was worth, he himself was best able to judge.

All this took place, almost imperceptibly, on the chessboard of diplomacy. The general public noticed little of it. Thus an equanimity and an outward calm reigned in Vienna, which stood in almost frivolous contrast to the tumultuous events beyond the borders. For adherents to the Austrian party of war, who included the Empress, and for certain other hot-headed Napoleon-haters among the population, this trial of their patience was playing havoc with their nerves. In the *palais* on the Hoher Markt the tension had become unbearable. Many intimates of the house, almost all the Prussian *émigrés*, had left the city. Bartholdy too had departed to offer his services to Hardenberg. From Berlin one heard how everyone was making ready for war, how military hospitals were being set up, money, beds and bed-linen were being donated. Rahel, the new patriot, was in her element, running about, taking collections, writing to Varnhagen of the general spirit of self-sacrifice: 'The Jews are giving all they own; it was to them that I first addressed my cries. Madame Herz is endlessly active; I spur her on even further. Oh, what a joy the city is to me!' And here sat

Fanny, in a city which was no joy to her at all, feverish with good will, condemned to do nothing!

Things became even worse. On 15 April Napoleon had broken camp at St Cloud and three weeks later inflicted a severe defeat upon the Russians and Prussians. Since the death of Kutuzov, the Russian Wittgenstein led the allied troops; but there was confusion among the general staff, the Tsar was continually intervening, and at the decisive moment the orders came from everyone or no one. Thus whole companies were senselessly sacrificed at Lützen, including the third battalion in the second regiment of the Guards, to which the Itzig brothers belonged. Moritz, wounded on 2 May, died eleven days later. Their commanding officer, Captain von Rexin, expressed his sympathy to Moritz's brother, who had likewise been wounded. He wrote that he had 'respected the deceased as a soldier, admired him as a philosopher, deeply loved him as a human being. He never caused me a troubled moment. May Heaven comfort his survivors.'

They were as little to be comforted as anyone who is robbed by war of his closest relatives. But in Berlin the event made an impression on many persons not directly concerned, and allowed them to see a justification for Hardenberg's edict in the heroic death for Prussia of Moritz Itzig. Three years earlier he had had a serious clash, though an honourable one, with the noted poet of this Romantic era, Achim von Arnim, who had uttered anti-Semitic remarks in the house of Moritz's aunt Levy. Now Arnim, who had joined the Berlin militia at the beginning of the war of independence, retreated at the first opportunity to his estate, Wiepersdorf. The *Staatsrat* (state councillor) Stägemann gave expression to public opinion when he summed up that still unforgotten affair in the words: 'Itzig and Arnim have both remained behind – the former at Lützen, the latter behind the oven.'

After their first defeat in battle the Prussians sent their severely wounded general Scharnhorst to Vienna, to persuade Austria to immediate joint action. But Metternich would not receive him, remained inflexible, refused any kind of participation, and Emperor Francis, in making renewed peace proposals to Napoleon, at the same time congratulated him on his victory at Lützen. Was it any wonder that Fanny, devastated by her nephew's fate, in despair over Austria's continued neutrality, at this moment completely lost her nerve and unrestrainedly railed at both Emperor and government? A secret report of 30 May recorded:

Madame Fanny Arnstein et sa société se permettent du propre scandaleux contre l'Autriche et surtout contre l'auguste Monarque, parce qu'on n'opère pas d'abord en faveur des Russes et Prussiens. Selon eux, ce pays sera bientôt la victime de la vengeance la plus éclatante.

It was meritorious to unite with the highest society in the land to help the poor and suffering; but this gave one no licence for free speech. Nevertheless the authorities were as considerate as possible in restraining Fanny's tirades to a more seemly measure. On the following day a document from an exalted source instructed the much-plagued police president Siber to persuade Nathan to exert his influence on his wife:

> *Frau Baronin* Fanny Arnstein, from whom we are accustomed to hear violent or biting criticisms of the French *gouvernement*, with reference to the present situation of Prussia and Russia, is now said to give herself up to outbursts against the politics of the Austrian public administration and even against H. M.
>
> It is disagreeable for me to hear that such a respectable and decent woman should not always, in the warmth of conversation, observe the bounds of political modesty.
>
> I request you therefore to make my wish known in confidence to the husband, that he should remind his wife of what she owes to the state, to herself and to her acquaintance. I have the honour . . .

The signature is illegible.

These were the last weeks of harassing uncertainty. For, very calmly, with that cold-blooded *désinvolture* which gave him such ascendancy over Russians, Prussians and French with their temperaments constantly seething to boiling point, Metternich was preparing for the attack – if necessary, even a military one. His decision was not based on sympathy with the Germans. 'With regard to Austria . . .,' he later explained, 'the expression *deutscher Sinn* [German spirit], in particular as manifested in the higher strata of the local population since the catastrophe of Prussia and of the northern regions of Germany, had merely the value of a myth.' Rather, 'Napoleon's victories in battle at Lützen and Bautzen were the sign that the hour had struck'. Alexander appeared so discouraged by his lack of success that he gave signs of wanting to make his peace with Napoleon at Austria's expense. For Metternich this was the last warning signal.

First he persuaded the allies to seek an armistice with his help. On 29 May Generals Shuvalov and Kleist had already arrived at the French camp as negotiators. At the same time Metternich sent

Count Bubna to headquarters at Dresden with his proposals for mediation. Napoleon now feared that the Austrians might turn against him if he continued to ignore them. He therefore approved a suspension of hostilities, which gave both sides time for renewed negotiations and for increased mobilisation. The armistice was declared on 4 June and was to end on 20 June. The battlefields were cleared. Once again seats were taken at the conference table.

The most dramatic encounter of those years took place between Metternich and Napoleon. A conversation between the minister and the Tsar had preceded it. He had been able for the last time to dispel Alexander's mistrust of his double-dealing – among other things, by asking him to send a trusted person into the Austrian camp. Alexander designated Count Nesselrode for this role. But now there was pressure from all sides for a decision. During these days all the princes and their advisers, on whom the fate of Europe depended, had advanced physically closer to each other. Francis I and Alexander had installed themselves on a little triangle of land on the Bohemian–Silesian border, a day's journey from Napoleon and Dresden. Between the Austrians in Jičin and the Russians in Opočno lay the country mansion of Ratibórz, the property of the Duchess of Sagan. Here sat Metternich, like a spider in a web. To this, his mistress's house, he had invited all those statesmen whose presence was now useful to him: Humboldt and Hardenberg; the latter's brother, the Hanoverian envoy; Gentz; Stadion and Nesselrode. Between them the situation was discussed yet again, not without vehemence. In the second half of June he departed from their midst to make a last attempt at peacemaking in Dresden.

This time Napoleon had not the courage to reside in the city. His quarters had been established in the Marcolini Garden beside the meadows of the Elbe. It was in two rooms of the little Rococo *palais*, the Chinese Hall and the Pompeian Room, that he received Metternich. His parley here with the Austrian minister of state is well-known – but only thanks to Metternich himself, who recorded it for posterity in a terse, epigrammatic form. For eight hours the general, usurper, visionary and enemy of all ideologies threatened, accused and entreated the smooth-tongued diplomat, though no match for the latter's cold self-assurance.

To Metternich's credit one must say that in his account he did concede a few brilliant points to his opponent. At the end of the histrionic dialogue he even allows Napoleon an effective exit speech: 'In marrying an archduchess, I wanted to blend the new with the old, Gothic prejudices with the institutions of my century; I deceived myself, and today I am conscious of the magnitude of my error. It may cost me the throne, but I will bury the world beneath its ruins.' A trump-card only surpassed by Metternich's parting words: 'You are lost, Sire. I had a premonition of this when I came; now, in going, I have the certainty.' And finally, to Marshal Berthier, Prince of Neuchâtel, who had conducted him out: 'He has disclosed all to me; the man is done for.'

The result of this rhetorical *tour de force*, three days later, was Napoleon's consent to a peace congress at Prague. Thither now departed all those statesmen, with their camp-followers, who had assembled in northern Bohemia. Meanwhile the news had spread of Wellington's victory of Vitoria, which put an end to the French campaign in Spain. No one now expected peace. 'Your conclusions of peace were never anything but armistices,' Metternich had said to Napoleon in Dresden. Now he, too, was no longer prepared to play out the comedy. And so, in case there should be no agreement in Prague, even at this stage, though in private, he concluded the long-awaited covenant with Russia and Prussia.

The agreement did not take place. The period of armistice had expired. Metternich extended it for just that span of twenty days which Prince Schwarzenberg had demanded in order to strengthen the Austrian army by a reinforcement of 75,000 men. When this had been done, he haughtily and decisively refused a last attempt of Napoleon's to negotiate further. The task of drafting a manifesto of war fell once more to Gentz; he undertook it with enthusiasm and brilliance. About midnight on the night of 10–11 August the proclamation was released to the world. Then all the fiery signals between Prague and the Silesian frontier were let off as a token that the allies were taking up the fight.

This is not the place to describe the battles and strategic manoeuvres with whose help this last coalition drove Napoleon out of Germany, chased him home to France and forced him into abdication in Paris. Only to the extent that they directly affected the small circle which is the subject of this book have the disturbances of those years so far seemed worth reporting. But from the moment at which her two fatherlands were united in that last alliance, the daily anxiety of Fanny and her family was at an end. Now it was only a question of time before the common aim should be attained and the pressure be taken off Europe. The frightful dissension which for twenty years had rent the heart of the Prussian woman in Austria, the torment of divided loyalties and constantly alternating shame, were over.

We must ask ourselves whether such an equation of one's own fate with that of the nation was not exaggerated, indeed ridiculous; whether it was not less seemly for a Jewess than for the young hotheads who, intoxicated by Fichte's speeches and Rückert's poems, thronged to make the ultimate sacrifice for the concept of their nation. But that pronounced patriotic feeling which had developed in Fanny and in many of her fellow-believers was the proud expression of their new nationality, the sign of their entry into a larger community. They had cast off what bound them to the life of their forefathers, stifling, narrow-minded and bolted inside and outside. They gave up their own national character, as was demanded of them, and, in so doing, went too far in the inordinate fervour of their nature, so alike in some ways to the German temperament.

'The wars of liberation in the years 1813 and 1814,' Varnhagen wrote in retrospect about Fanny, 'filled her heart with delight; she could take pleasure in one single emotion about her two fatherlands, the native one and the adoptive one, Prussia and Austria. She gave endless sums of money and other means of help for the wounded and other necessities of war.' More she was not able to do; she could no longer even concern herself over her nearest friends and relatives. For her nephew Bartholdy, now a veteran, was no longer at the front, but employed in Hardenberg's war office, and her daughter's young protégé had fallen in the first weeks after the outbreak of hostilities.

Even earlier, in June, in the middle of the armistice, Theodor Körner had almost succumbed to death. One of Lützow's 400 riders, he had galloped from Stendal on the lower Elbe right through the enemy ranks as far as the border at Bayreuth. His poem about 'Lützow's wild reckless chase' had immortalised this ride. Now his commandant wanted to join the infantry of the corps. Lützow's troops advanced against Leipzig. At Kitzen they suddenly found themselves surrounded by the French; Körner, who had been sent out to demand an explanation, received three severe blows about the head and fell to the ground. At this moment the attack began, and the squadrons were wounded, captured and dispersed.

Peasants had found the gravely wounded Körner and secretly taken care of him. Soon afterward he wrote to Henriette from Carlsbad, reminding her once more of her undertaking: 'You promised once to nurse me if I were wounded. – A pity I am not in

Vienna; you would have the best opportunity to do so, and I would certainly reach my goal of recovery the sooner.' Instead, his good and wise friend Elisabeth von der Recke attended to him 'with truly maternal care and gentle words', and he began to recover. At the end of July, almost fully recovered, he was in Reichenbach, where the Prussians had their headquarters and the secret alliance with Austria had been concluded. Here he met Stein, Arndt, Schenkendorff, Gneisenau and Blücher, as well as General von Pfuel, who sent 'a thousand most cordial greetings' through him to Henriette and Marianne Saaling. 'As far as the green book is concerned, it lies wonderfully preserved before me on the table; it has not left me for a moment since the 14th of March; now only a few pages of it are still empty . . .'

Only a few pages – only a few weeks of his life! The young man who had marched off so hesitantly, so 'sadly and dully' from Vienna, almost repenting the resolve which had torn him from those dearest to him, was now pressed and impelled irresistibly onward, to the end, to victory, to death! Since entering the first verse in his book he had been in that state of heroism which is similar to a continuous intoxication, an incessant ecstasy. In such a heightened mood he wrote his poems. And once he had put them down on paper they moved him no less than his comrades, spurred him on further and transfigured for him the hardships and ugly sights of every day: the sore throat in the bivouac, the rain in Jičin, the pain of the sabre wounds, the shaven head, the rough horse-blankets, but most of all his own decline. His existence had become poetry to him. There was no way back to reality.

> Soll ich in der Prosa sterben? –
> Poesie, du, Flammenquell,
> Brich nur los mit leuchtendem Verderben,
> Aber schnell!

> [Shall I die in prose? / Poetry, thou fiery source, / Burst thou forth in shining ruin, / Quickly though!]

In his worst verses he had betrayed the truth. Fulfilment was death. And it was not long in coming. 'The people rise, the storm bursts forth,' thus he greeted the outbreak of the new war. 'And should our bell toll in the red of battle / Then welcome to a soldier's blessed death!' He informed Henriette: 'We are about to march; in two days we await our marriage with death.'

What God could have denied him this hotly desired union? The God of love did not. At seven on that morning of 26 August,

Körner fell, not yet twenty-two, struck by a French bullet, in the woodland between Gadebusch and Schwerin. Three comrades, among them a Count Hardenberg, had lost their lives with him.

His family, free, despite their patriotic high flights, from the ecstasy of heroism, were plunged into profound grief by his only too real death. It broke his sister Emma's heart; she died two years later. Before her brother was laid in the grave which she was likewise to occupy, she wrote to Henriette: 'Pray for us, that I may still preserve the strength at our loved one's grave to support my dear parents.' Her father, too, expected to encounter the deepest sympathy from Henriette: 'How close you were to his heart, for you recognised his worth, he told me, and you feel his loss with me. Death cannot rob us of what was spiritual in his being, and it is preserved for us for a better world.' Körner's mother, finally, sent her back the little green book, after his verses had made their way in the world.

For Fanny's daughter it was as though her mother's story had been repeated. For weeks she avoided all society and 'the bitter pain she felt', says a chronicler, 'allows one to conclude that she had lost more than a friend in him'. Mutual sorrow now united her with Antonie Adamberger, who had more legitimate grounds to mourn Körner. They saw each other often and shared their grief. At the time of the Congress of Vienna Stägemann met them again and again in the same little circle. Toni had gone back to acting. In 1817 she married the historian von Arneth, and effaced the distressing memory of her first betrothed by burning all his letters and the other documents from his hand.

Henriette, who continued to preserve and hold sacred every word of Körner's, after a while also returned to daily life. Indeed, she even took refuge in the arms of her husband, whom she scarcely loved any more. In August 1814 she gave birth to her last child, a girl whom she called Flora, and whom from then on she idolised – her comfort in these and in future days of mourning.

The battles whose outcome could no longer influence the end of the war, which could only postpone it, took their course. On the day when Körner fell, the allied army had suffered a defeat at Dresden. In October the battle of Leipzig ended Napoleon's sovereignty in Germany. Nothing was left for him but a retreat across the Rhône and an attempt to concentrate his army at the border. At the beginning of November Emperor Francis and the authorised plenipotentiaries of the alliance went to Frankfurt to ensure that Schwarzenberg's army should now carry the war into the heart of France.

The Prussian Jews were anxious, hopeful, charitable and victorious along with their compatriots. Rahel was in Prague, where she maintained a veritable 'Prussian office'. 'Shirts, stockings, food, money are here distributed and dispatched.' Bartholdy, his sister Lea, her husband Abraham Mendelssohn, Rahel's brothers, sent or brought their financial contributions and other comforts for distribution to the troops. In her letters to Varnhagen, who was marching on Bremen in Tettenborn's regiment, she told him something of the feverishly excited, exhilarating atmosphere in which she moved, a small but important cog in the mechanism of the war of liberation: 'I am in touch with our commissariat and our staff surgeon; have a great amount of lint, bandages, rags, stockings, shirts; arrange for meals in several districts of the city; attend personally to thirty or forty fusiliers and soldiers every day; discuss and inspect everything.'

Fanny was in Vienna, further from the firing-line, but no less active at last. Her husband's banking house had earmarked 155,000 gulden for patriotic purposes. She for her part outdid herself in donating those 'means of help' of which Varnhagen speaks, and the evidence of which has been here and there preserved. On 14 October, for instance, she sent 100 ducats to Field-Marshal Bellegarde, which 'an unnamed benefactor of the needy' had given to her for 'a worthy cause', to be divided 'in equal parts among a hundred warriors of our army, from the sergeant downwards, who have been wounded in the fighting on 30 August'. She added to this sum another 500 gulden, 'which have been allotted in the same way for another hundred wounded Austrian soldiers by the gentlemen I. and A. M. [Mendelssohn] of Berlin, inspired by the spirit of unity which must fill all citizens of the allied states.'

An announcement in the *Wiener Zeitung* the following spring stated that Fanny had offered 'for the improvement of his lot, to provide a monthly allowance of 15 gulden from the day of his arrival in Vienna, to Gunner Franz Gattinger, who signally distinguished himself on 15 November 1813, in the defence of the bridge of Villa Nuova, but has become an invalid through the loss of both feet'. If the man should after all die of his wounds she wished to 'dedicate this monthly sum to the charitable fund of the Vienna *Invalidenhaus*'. It was probably not the only case in which she gave support to a war hero. And when Paris was won, Napoleon had been deposed, King Louis had arrived and all the allies assembled in the French capital to conclude the first peace for twenty-two years which was to be no mere armistice, she resolved upon a new benefaction which was characteristic of her: As the *Wiener Zeitung* of 25 May reports:

> Freyinn von Arnstein, who lets pass no opportunity to do good to every class of sufferer, has learnt that the private institute for sick and destitute army chaplains was still weighed down by a debt of 3,000 gulden; this sum had originally been intended by Frau Freyin von Arnstein for the lighting at the celebration of the conquest of Paris, but later, with her well-known patriotic sympathies, was used by her to repay the aforesaid debt of the institute for the sick clergy, in order, through the removal of this burden, to enable it to provide better care for its clergymen.
>
> This institute, as well as the whole of the clergy connected with it, wishes herewith to express publicly its well-deserved thanks to its noble benefactress.

Yes, now he had really abdicated, the man before whom Europe had trembled for so long! Now there really was peace – it was still difficult to believe. Many who had cursed Napoleon when he betrayed first the Revolution, then the great notion of the universal state, began to offer him their sympathy now that he was no longer dangerous. Many hearts were wrung by the spectacle of the fallen Titan. Others feared the vacuum left by his departure, into which the phantoms of the old regime, together with the menacing spectre of a new, nationalistic German future, were now plunging helter-skelter. Among those harbouring apprehensions was Gentz. He had urged upon Metternich in vain that the recall of the Bourbons must be prevented. If these phantoms were readmitted, the spectre of the German united state could not be held back. But Gentz's words fell on deaf ears; Francis I's minister of state desired the restoration of the monarchy, and obtained it through the other allies.

Everyone was in Paris that May. Germaine de Staël was again holding brilliant court in the Rue du Bac, where she was honoured by the presence of Tsar Alexander. Varnhagen turned up there and happened to meet Jakob Bartholdy, who was ill at ease in the company, for one always stood there 'shamefaced and humiliated, if one were not a prince or a duke and had not three or four stars'. Pauline Wiesel, too, had come to the peace negotiations with her husband, and had tried to seduce the young Varnhagen, which made him indignant, but wrested a smile of admiration from Rahel, who learnt of it from him. Pauline, she explained to him, wanted only 'a taste of Rahel's man; like iced punch'. It was no more than a proof that Pauline took a lively interest in her friend's destiny! Rahel herself was still in Prague, writing to 'Bentheim, August, Robert, Varnhagen, Gentz, Madame von Humboldt, Tettenborn, the whole *world*', for everyone wanted to know what she thought now: 'Thus it is for thinkers! But I know not what to think of many things.' Then she departed from the emptied city to take the waters at Teplitz, and finally, by way of Dresden, home to Berlin. Varnhagen, too, returned to Berlin from Paris, and began to arrange for Rahel's baptism and his marriage to her.

Rahel, too, was now manifestly seceding from her former community! She had long pondered the matter. After enduring the war, she had made her decision. External circumstances spoke in favour of a change of faith now, rather than at a later date. In the autumn Varnhagen was to go to Vienna, where a congress to determine the new frontiers of Europe was to assemble. Rahel wanted to accompany him as his wife, his spouse wedded to him by the Christian rite. They turned to the clergyman Stägemann, a relative of the Prussian statesman.

'He received me,' wrote Rahel, 'as though it were Spinoza coming to be baptised: as though crushed by the honour.' The act, a symbolic one for her, took place. Then, touchingly old-maidish despite all her wisdom and experience of the world, she bought herself 'a kind of trousseau: I am not extravagant; but in Vienna, what one must have is beyond my means.' On 27 September she stood at the altar. Shortly afterwards her husband travelled to Austria, and two weeks later she was to follow him.

Varnhagen was by no means the first Prussian to arrive in the capital that autumn. Weeks before him Hardenberg had already arrived with his staff, and on 25 September King Frederick William, side by side with his great protector, the Tsar, entered the city through the Jägerzeile. Within a few days the city began to fill alarmingly. Five sovereigns, eleven princes (either reigning or now subject to the imperial crown), ninety plenipotentiary envoys and fifty-three uninvited representatives of European powers appeared for the Congress; yet the number of their secretaries, clerks, followers, servants, and the throng of all those soldiers of fortune, pickpockets, courtesans, portrait-painters, caricaturists, commission-agents, scandalmongers, doctors, confessors, prophets and charlatans who had also streamed in, came to 100,000 persons – more than a third of the total population.

What a spectacle! It seemed as though Vienna had lived for centuries in anticipation of this moment, as if the love of pomp and enjoyment of celebrations, the refined art of enjoying oneself, to which people had been devoted here since time immemorial, had been only a rehearsal for the unique, unrepeatable performance which was being presented here with all the props of baroque theatricality. The whole city became a stage set, and all the people played their parts. Everyone knew his role – it had been handed down in the family, rehearsed for generations. Coachmen, waiters, washerwomen became their own embodiments. Every chamber-maid tripped, warbled and coquetted as though she were the prototype of Liotard's *Belle Chocolatière*. Every landlord stroked his green apron, every lemonade-seller adopted a jovial smirk as though dispensing true Viennese *Gemütlichkeit*, the 'nymphs' of the Graben winked more boldly, secret agents crept more quietly, popular singers sobbed more fervently than had been their custom till now. Rehearsals were over. The curtain had gone up. Europe sat in the auditorium.

The principals, too, played their parts with verve and conviction. The six monarchs stressed their individuality. A print which went the rounds at the end of October depicted them with the respective legends: 'He loves for all': Tsar Alexander. 'He thinks for all': King Frederick William. 'He speaks for all': King Frederick of Denmark. 'He drinks for all': King Max Joseph of Bavaria. 'He eats for all': King Frederick of Württemberg. 'He pays for all': Francis of Austria. The Emperor, not otherwise known for munificence, had this time decided to play the perfect host. Court balls, banquets, tournaments, boar-hunts and sleigh-rides were conducted in a grand style never seen before. The consumptive little Empress Maria Ludovica was constantly inventing new diversions. 'The Congress will cost me ten years of my life,' she had said. It cost the royal privy purse no small amount besides. After the potentates – private guests in the Hofburg – had departed, Count Wurmbrand, the chief master of ceremonies, reckoned the 'arrangements for the foreign sovereigns, all the fêtes, liveries, rents, board, stabling' at 8,500,000 gulden. Double that amount had been swallowed up by the whole Congress when it was all over.

And yet – yet it seemed to the Viennese as if the occasion had not been a success! Were they dissatisfied, as actors always are with themselves, no matter how loudly they are applauded? Had they expected more – a mightier assembly in the Prater than the military banquet for 20,000 soldiers which took place on the anniversary of the battle of Leipzig, a more densely attended ball than that in the court riding-school on 2 October, a finer funeral than that of Prince de Ligne in December, a more fiercely crackling fire than that in the mansion of Count Rasumovsky two weeks later, larger tips than those given by the King of Württemberg, more dazzling medals than those which gleamed on the chest of Congress Secretary Gentz, more glittering gems than those, worth 6,000,000 gulden, worn on one evening at the neck and on the arms of Princess Esterhazy? None of these things. The eternal sorrow of the Austrian soul had befallen them, the awareness that fulfilment can never be equal to expectations, let alone surpass them. In other words, that inevitable first-night failure took place, known only to initiates, when a piece has been rehearsed too often and too perfectly. One knew how it should be, which was more than it was.

The Viennese might shake their heads, begin to sigh and finally groan – their guests noticed none of this. They had no complaints about the spectacle being offered to them. Never had an audience been in more enthusiastic mood! The pressure of decades had been lifted from the world; now one abandoned oneself to all one's dammed-up appetites. Once again, in this year of 1814, the lusts and excesses of the Rococo triumphed. The princelings as well as the reigning princes, even the kings, who had met together here to divide Europe among themselves like a cake, wallowed in the beds of the *demi-monde*. Alexander, squeezing his incipient *embonpoint* into the most finely cut uniforms, patronised duchesses as well as courtesans. Frederick of Denmark, talkative, melancholy and white-blond, pursued the beauties of the street and fell in love with a creature who was thenceforth known as the 'Queen of the Flea-market'. The Grand Duke of Baden, the hereditary Prince of Hesse-Darmstadt, Prince Karl of Bavaria, Napoleon's stepson Eugène de Beauharnais, who was admitted to the Congress under the Tsar's protection, went astray 'day and night with the most vulgar females'.

Even Metternich and Gentz, who in truth were in a position to enjoy themselves at other times with Viennese wenches, had their heads as full of love-affairs as of state business. Only the industrious, deadly serious Prussians kept apart from these matters. Their King, who indeed sentimentally adored the beautiful Countess Julie Zichy because she resembled his late consort Luise, but dared to approach her only in the most respectful manner, set them a good example. Their Chancellor Hardenberg, too, who was otherwise no despiser of women, found the moment too solemn for giving way to frivolities. Those who, like them, looked into the future found little pleasure in the reawakened depravity of the *ancien régime*.

Not only at court, but also in the great private houses there were true 'festivals of the people', motley assemblies where every European nation was represented. This opportunity for salon diplomacy was all the more appropriate since the Congress met only infrequently and even then only in small committees, but otherwise consisted entirely of correspondence, separate conferences and private discussions, in fact had really never properly begun at all and was only to acquire the force of law through its final act. Although all the sovereigns and most important diplomats met each other on ceremonial occasions, at supper or in the ballroom, certain circles began to form as early as the first weeks. In most cases they collected around beautiful or influential ladies.

Until now the high nobility had resisted that more relaxed social life which had become customary since the turn of the century. Now, with the invasion of so many illustrious foreigners, most of the barriers of exclusivity were falling. There were no more 'Castle Boredoms' in Vienna. At Princess Fürstenberg's, rigid formality might still be preserved, but the Esterhazys, Colloredos and Liechtensteins, the Wrbnas and widely ramified Zichys behaved amiably to less blue-blooded visitors too. Even women of the first society thought nothing of being considered quite generally 'the six beauties of the Congress'. They were, according to the Tsar's choice and in his words, Princess Gabriele Auersperg, 'la beauté qui inspire du vrai sentiment'; Countess Julie Zichy, 'la beauté céleste'; her sister-in-law Sophie Zichy, 'la beauté triviale'; Princess Therese Esterhazy, 'la beauté étonnante'; Countess Caroline Széchenyi (Scottish by birth), 'la beauté coquette'; and Countess Gabriele Saurau, 'la beauté du diable'. They and the Duchesses of Weimar and Oldenburg – sisters of the Tsar – were visited by the princely personages whose political activity was limited and for the most part carried out by their representatives.

In the Palais Palm in Schenkenstrasse, where three years earlier Count Genicco had wanted to establish a gambling-den, resided two ladies of brilliant name and more than dubious reputation. Princess Katharina Bagration, a great-niece of Catherine II and Prince Potemkin, had lived in great style there for years. During the Congress she received chiefly her compatriots – Nesselrode, Stackelberg and Capo d'Istria in her salon, the Tsar in her bed. This bewitching woman, who was known, because of her low necklines, as 'the beautiful naked angel', had given her favours to Prince Metternich, and even borne him a daughter, long before Alexander came upon the scene. The same progression from minister to monarch was now accomplished by her rival, the Duchess of

Sagan, at whose country mansion of Ratibórz the prelude to the last war had taken place. Living next door to Princess Bagration, she captured the latter's lover, the Tsar, thereupon discarding Metternich.

The apartments of these adventuresses, whose favours were so easily obtained by high-born gentlemen, were attended almost every evening during the Congress by Friedrich Gentz. At Princess Bagration's he met all the Russians with whom he wished to converse, and at the Duchess of Sagan's the most important Frenchmen, above all Talleyrand. Two sisters of the Duchess, by birth, like her, Princesses of Courland, were staying in Vienna. One, Johanna, was married to the Prince of Acerenza-Pignatelli, that Russian agent whom Reichardt had already seen seven years earlier in Fanny's house. The other was Talleyrand's niece by marriage and his mistress, Countess Dorothée de Périgord. For her sake the old fox sometimes left his lair, the Palais Kaunitz in Johannesgasse, and held court in the intimate circle of Wilhelmine of Sagan.

A coterie which overlapped with this one had formed around the charming Laura Fuchs. Amiable and extravagant, 'Lory' still had her salon, where, as Varnhagen had written, one could serve princes and counts for tea instead of bread and butter. It was here that the indolent society so little appreciated by Madame de Staël betook itself. But besides all these ladies – Empress Maria Ludovica, the six noble beauties, the Russian grand duchesses, the princely *cocottes* and the wife of the banker–count Ignaz Fuchs – another set of hostesses were vying to do the honours at the Congress. Gone and forgotten were the days when the Arnstein house had been 'the greatest, and to some extent the only resource of the stranger arriving here'!

How was it that, nevertheless, Fanny now stood 'on the highest peak of pleasure and of fame', in 'the richest heyday of her social reputation and activity'? Varnhagen, who said this of her, was able to substantiate his remarks. It was not just that a hospitality practised to perfection over decades was now fully coming into its own. What carried greater weight was that Fanny's compatriots felt at home with her, and that therefore everyone who had anything to do with Prussian salon diplomacy visited the *palais* on the Hoher Markt every Tuesday evening, and frequently at other times too. As Varnhagen recalls:

Persons of the highest rank and the greatest distinction, ladies and gentlemen, foreigners and natives, gathered in her rooms. On the same evening one could single out from the crowded throng the Duke of Wellington, Cardinal Consalvi, Prince von Hardenberg, Counts Kapodistrias [Capo d'Istria] and Pozzo di Borgo, Baron von Humboldt, the Princes of Hesse-Homburg, Counts von Bernstorff, von Münster and von Neipperg, and many others of similar standing. The Prussians especially, as a group, had here the pleasantest abode, where they could enjoy the charms of a foreign land together with all the comfort of home. They were the more easily introduced here as the later Prussian consul-general and private counsellor to the legation, Bartholdy, Frau von Arnstein's nephew, had come to Vienna among the number of the state officials accompanying the state chancellor Prince von Hardenberg.

As early as July an informer to the police department had reported: 'Arnstein and Eskeles – both houses say so themselves – are daily keeping open house, midday and evening, throughout the time of the Congress, for all Berliners and Prussians, as their compatriots.' Conjointly with the arrival of their King, who, to be sure, was not to honour them with his presence, the two sisters also returned to the city. From the next day onwards the *Staatsrat* Stägemann, Hardenberg's trusted colleague, had become a regular guest at the house of one or the other. 'I have a standing invitation', he wrote to his wife on 26 September, 'midday and evening, to the houses of Frau von Eskeles and Frau von Arnstein. Both were residing in the country, but since yesterday both are in town.' He had also visited Gentz. 'He was very friendly, but I cannot put my trust in him. Frau von Eskeles told me that he no longer visited her or her sister, because neither of them associated with anti-Prussians.' Stägemann could not doubt her word; Gentz had for a long time been an enemy of Prussian politics. Stägemann did not indeed know, nor was there any need for him to be told, that eleven years ago the Austrian *Hofrat* from Breslau had already 'fallen out forever' with them.

The *Staatsrat* was still to report much and more frequently about Fanny and Cäcilie. Since the restaurants were 'simply not to be endured', when not with the Prince-Chancellor he ate regularly with them. At Cäcilie's he met Caroline Pichler, whom he found 'young, not pretty, but unassuming'. He preferred the ladies of the Hoher Markt: 'Frau von Arnstein is in her fifties; an intelligent woman who interests me, uncommonly vivacious, but serious and fashioned for the world by much experience, and knows how to restrain herself everywhere.' A sign that her ill-temperedness had for the time disappeared! 'She knows how to say something obliging to everyone and seems to apprehend very quickly the merit and temperament of people.' Henriette, 'who is said to have been uncommonly charming', seemed now only pretty to him, weakened by ill-health, but still 'surrounded by admirers'. Zerboni – a Prussian *Geheimrat* – 'courts her violently'. Countess Engel, 'a friend of the house, *née* Countess von Hohenfeld and related to all the great families – Princess Schwarzenberg is her cousin', seemed to him, if not beautiful, 'cultured and sensible'. He also met there Rebecca Ephraim and her daughter, a 'clever, jolly girl'. Most of all, however, he valued 'Fräulein Saaling, whom I hold one of the first beauties, because she looks like you'. He was to be one of Marianne's most enthusiastic admirers throughout the Congress.

In October Varnhagen hastened to make use of the generosity of these houses. He had arrived on the eleventh. Next day he wrote to Rahel:

> I have seen Madame Eskeles, Madame Ephraim, Mariane and Jette Ephraim, also Madame Schlegel and her husband: all well and friendly, but what is the use? I feel dreadful in front of these so-called people without truth and depth and gifts! . . . The Arnsteins seem more than usually *en vogue*, I see it from the fact that Bentheim spends every evening there; I hope to see him there this evening. All these people will be extremely friendly and well-disposed towards us. They will be pleasant exoteric company for us.

And a little later:

> I have been often at the Arnsteins' and the Eskeles', where I was well received, not in excessively friendly fashion, but sufficiently so.

Another Prussian who was received by her was General Ludwig Wolzogen. As far as possible he kept away from the great court occasions at Metternich's and Rasumovsky's, to which he was invited:

> in part because I was not at all fond of such diversions, in part because I soon had a great deal of work to do. It was only in the house of the Jewish banker Arnstein, whose wife . . . was very amiable and, supported by her clever daughter and a beautiful niece, Fräulein Saaling, was excellently fitted to conduct a salon, that I appeared frequently, and there I had the best opportunity to improve my acquaintance with all the diplomats and distinguished friends who went in and out there.

In this circle he met Count Neipperg, who was in the service of Napoleon's consort Marie Louise as her chief steward since her return to Schönbrunn. 'He often complained to me that she would have nothing to do with him and treated him badly, because she wished to see none but Frenchmen about her, and her heart still – apparently – belonged to Napoleon, so that she looked upon him as a spy.' Later, however, she married him. 'His excellent piano-playing is said to have tamed her. Moreover, Neipperg was highly intelligent.'

Wolzogen had come to Vienna, not with Hardenberg, but in the entourage of the Duke of Weimar. Goethe's Duke had also brought his own 'literary *chargé d'affaires*', the bookseller Carl Bertuch, who, two years later, published his famous *Diary of the Congress of Vienna*. On 7 October Bartholdy introduced Bertuch to Fanny. Soon afterwards he wrote to his father:

> I have just come with Cotta from dinner at the Arnsteiners', where I am beginning to enjoy myself. Baroness Arnsteiner is indeed a woman of the best society manners, full of wit and attention towards her guests. It was a party of twenty-two persons, among them Duke Acerenza-Pignatelli, some Swedish barons, the Italian poet Carpani, Stegmann, Jordan, etc. I shall visit the house more often, it is, perhaps, in view of the fine, unconstrained company one of the first in Vienna.

Bertuch, as a man of taste and an emissary from Goethe's circle, could gain admittance to Fanny's salon at any time. He took particular pleasure in her beautiful private concerts. At the first one to which he refers, chamber quartets and vocal duets were performed. Frau von Geymüller, a Fräulein von Wertheimstein and a Fräulein Olivier took part. It was the same evening of which Stägemann wrote that the queen of the party was 'the *Ministerin* Countess Bernstorff', wife of the Danish representative at the Congress. There were many other beauties, but none of these had equalled Fräulein Saaling.

The second concert presented Rebecca Ephraim's nephew, the young Berlin musician Meyerbeer. He 'showed, as a pianist playing a theme with variations, an excellent talent and great dexterity with both hands'. In addition, there were heard choruses from the oratorio *Timotheus, or the Power of Music*, which Bertuch found 'better fitted for a large company' than Handel's *Samson*, performed not long ago in the Winter Riding School by the recently formed *Gesellschaft der Musikfreunde*. Later 'the young world' danced till nearly midnight. 'On these occasions tea, then lemonade, almond milk, ice-cream and light pastries are presented. – Among distinguished foreigners I today observed Count Pozzo di Borgo . . . also Capo d'Istria, Russian envoy to Switzerland. Moreover, many generals, princes and counts.'

Aristocracy and diplomacy were common in this house! But also among those who now attended upon Fanny during the Congress were the highest members of the Catholic clergy. She had always received worldly clerics of modest rank, among them her old Abbé Collenbach, the unnamed *sous-abbé* of the papal legation, and later little Abbate Carpani – now secretly in the service of the police chief, Siber. Dignitaries such as the personal representative of his Holiness, or even the Viennese nuncio Severoli himself, were now crossing her threshold for the first time. On 31 October Stägemann wrote to Berlin:

> At eight in the evening I drove to the Arnsteins', where, to the astonishment of all of us, Cardinal Consalvi and the nuncio arrived. They conversed very civilly with the ladies for several hours. Their appearance gave occasion, particularly for Madame Ephraim, to many a *bon mot*, and Countess Engel suffered greatly. I presume, however, that they took the house for a baptised one.

It was a small supper, augmented by the presence of the Spanish envoy and that of Hedemann, later Humboldt's son-in-law. In crude contrast to the Prussian envoy, Hedemann undisguisedly declared his anti-Semitic prejudice, of which one would soon no longer need to be ashamed:

> He went home with me afterwards and expressed his astonishment when I said to him that in the Arnstein house no one, not even Marianne, was baptised. That was why he had already that evening detected the over-educated Jewess in her. So obdurate are people's temperaments becoming!

Cardinal Consalvi, whether he believed the house to be baptised or not, came again often – whether to supper or to a concert with lemonade, ice-cream and almond milk. Fanny's receptions were for the most part not ostentatious. Once, however, Nathan held a festive evening such as he believed he, as a man of wealth, owed the Congress. After all it was to him, Vienna's most prominent financier, that foreign potentates and diplomats entrusted their credit, through whom they received many of their letters and, on their departure, had *douceurs* sent to their Viennese mistresses. For this occasion even the spacious rooms of the *palais* on the Hoher Markt were inadequate: the public ballroom *Zur Mehlgrube* had to be hired. Another memoirist, Count Auguste de la Garde, reports:

> Baron Arnstein had, so to speak, surpassed himself. The rarest flowers

from all climates decked the staircases, salons and ballrooms with the richest of glowing colours and with glorious scent. Thousands of candles and mirrors, gold and silk were displayed everywhere. Excellent music, such as could then be heard only in Vienna, enchanted the ear. The most distinguished society of Vienna crowded into the salon, all the influential people of the Congress, all foreigners of rank, all heads of the princely houses were present. In fact only the sovereigns were missing. The delighted eye recognised all the charming women in whose possession Vienna took pride, and who were the soul and the most beautiful adornment of this excellent feast. In the midst of these aristocratic beauties, without fear of rivals, shone Baroness Fanny Arnstein, tirelessly greeting each stranger, and Madame Geymüller of the ethereal form which causes her to be known as the 'daughter of the air'.

The soirée began with a concert. Of this one needs only to say that it was performed by the leading musicians of Vienna. The concert was followed by a ball and the ball by a supper, at which the Baron seemed to have diverted himself by representing all the seasons of the year and all distances as non-existent. He had united the produce of all lands and all latitudes. The rooms were decked with trees hanging heavy with rich fruits. It produced an extraordinary effect to see, in the midst of winter, cherries, peaches and apricots being picked, as if in a garden in Provence.

At last we retired, less astounded at the inexhaustible variation of wonders than at the insatiable desire for diversions.

It was a grand evening, but one which was far from putting in the shade certain assemblies of the high nobility or diplomacy. Even so, it created a stir even in a city which was drowning in festivities. Siber's informers, who during these weeks included members of the highest circles, had their hands full noting down significant or even subversive remarks made at the supper-table or on the dance-floor. But Fanny and her acquaintance incessantly provided material for the police agents. This was not a salon like that of Lory Fuchs, where one simply wanted to enjoy oneself harmlessly. Here, in accordance with the hostess's inclinations, politics were conducted with burning enthusiasm.

There were two questions which caused Fanny agitation. One of these dominated the entire Congress, several times nearly caused it to founder and excited people's temperaments more than any other conflict that came to light in the course of this general 'haggling over countries'. It was the planned seizure of Saxony by Prussia, with which Russia combined its claim to the duchy of Warsaw. Tsar Alexander and King Frederick William had made the claim jointly from the beginning and immediately provoked the resistance of Austria, who wished to see neither a Prussian predominance in the German union nor a Polish domain in Russian hands.

France and England too resisted, because they saw the plan as a threat to the 'just balance of power in Europe'. The bitter debate lasted from October to January, and in its course Metternich tried to play off Russia against Prussia and Prussia against Russia, Alexander attempted to win Talleyrand to his side through bribery, Prussian and anti-Prussian pamphlets went the rounds, Hardenberg passed on a confidential note from the Austrians to the Tsar, plots were hammered out and sides changed, Metternich and Alexander twice clashed angrily, with threats of resignation, departure or even war, and finally, under pressure, a compromise solution was agreed upon. In all this, as the confidential reports attest, Fanny took a passionate interest.

The other question was such an incidental one that hardly anyone found it important or even took it seriously. Indeed, when, the first discussions about it having been broken off in the autumn, it once more came before the committee of German nations at the end of May, the Bavarian Count Rechberg began to laugh, 'and the laughter became infectious and was taken up generally, except for a few'. The objects of derision were, as of old, the Jews. Hardenberg and Humboldt had made it their business to extend their civic equality, which had been introduced in Prussia, to the rest of Germany. At the same time, representatives of several Jewish communities which, after Napoleon's fall, had sunk back into their former unemancipated state, had appeared at the Congress and for their part had requested a new settlement. Undoubtedly this matter too deeply interested Fanny and her sisters. But so little importance was accorded to it by the authorities and it was so little discussed on the Hoher Markt that Siber's informers regarded not a single observation on this subject as worth reporting. Nothing in their statements allows one to make assumptions about the way in which the Arnstein circle exercised its influence on the participants. It was only with regard to Prussia that 'la bonne enthousiaste et bavarde Mme de Arnstein' was examined under the police magnifying glass. Beyme's visit had not been forgotten, and the announcement that one would daily meet Prussians in this house during the Congress did not go unnoticed. Thus it attracted attention that on 8 October Prince Hardenberg, having consulted for four hours with Nesselrode, Castlereagh and Humboldt, invited to the subsequent dinner not only Prince Radziwill, several other gentlemen from his embassy and the Sardinian Marchese St Marsan, but also Baron Nathan Arnstein.

Two days later it was reported that 'Frau von Arnstein prides herself greatly on the fact that the hereditary prince of Mecklenburg-Strelitz has visited her'. Soon afterwards 'it is said at Arnstein's that the King of Württemberg had paid a visit to Empress Marie Louise at Schönbrunn on Friday'. Zerboni's visit, as well as those of the 'Prussian cabinet members Stägemann, Heim, Grosse and Krug', is noted. At the beginning of November 'Count Keller, Baron Bildt, Los Rios and the Prussians recently repeated at Arnstein's that the Congress will not continue'. Around the middle of the month the deterioration in the rate of exchange is associated with the frequent court celebrations. Fanny's Tuesday has this time been attended, besides 'a large and numerous gathering', by Count Bernstorff, the Prince of Mecklenburg, the British ambassador and brother of Viscount Castlereagh Lord (actually Sir Charles) Stewart, General Sinclair, Counts Medici, Degenfeld and Solms-Laubach, Prince and Princess Dietrichstein and old Prince Metternich, the minister's father. On 24 November we finally learn the situation with regard to the mood of the Prussians and Fanny's judgement of the situation.

> Prince Hardenberg, last Tuesday, at Arnstein's, expressed the feeling that his stay in Vienna was extremely disagreeable to him and was being made daily more unpleasant. Prince Pignatelli related this remark yesterday in the presence of the hostess and several distinguished persons, among whom was the Duca Serra di Capriola, who added: 'Humboldt complained of the same thing to me.' Fanny Arnstein on the other hand said: 'I am very sorry that Hardenberg and Humboldt no longer like being here; they enjoyed it at the beginning. But it is shameful how every means is being employed to rekindle the old grudge between Prussia and Austria. Unfortunately the wretched pamphlet *Saxony and Prussia* has no other purpose. There is much truth in it, but nothing new. Why bring back to people's memory that Prussia once forgot to be German? They have after all made amends for it, done penance and redeemed their errors by wonderful deeds and unmistakable devotion to the whole, to the salvation of Germany. It is not to be denied that Prussia's mania for expansion is suspicious and makes us mistrustful, yet, if one observes their situation fairly and with cool rationality, the need to give more consistency to this dispersed state, stretched lengthwise without any breadth, becomes evident. But let us hope that this may be adequately achieved through the possession of the two Lusatias and of Wittenberg, and that a venerable line of rulers should not therefore be struck from the list of crowned heads.'

This was no unreflecting opinion – fundamentally it corresponded to the eventual decision of the Congress. Moreover, in this confidential report, probably from the hand of her old friend Carpani, Fanny's gaze seems directed from Austria towards Prussia, rather than the other way around. Stägemann judged matters differently. On 17 November he wrote to Berlin that, because of the tension between the two powers:

> which must now be taken as definite, our situation here [is becoming] very embarrassing from a social point of view. For even if the ladies of the Arnstein house remain well-disposed towards the Prussians, especially since most of them come only for short visits, the men on the other hand are rabid Austrians.

And eleven days later:

> We are being driven insane here over Saxony. The Austrians are furious. Metternich intrigues for all he is worth. Gentz, although publicly discarded, still secretly continues his machinations . . . This friction tells greatly on our ladies. It is often said that the Jews have no fatherland. But Frau von Eskeles has a fit if anything is said against Prussia, and Frau von Arnstein showers abuse on people and is beside herself. She compromises one through her vehement patriotism, says Humboldt.

And on 18 December another informer reports:

> Excellency! The ladies Arnstein and Eskeles are behaving scandalously, making scandalous remarks, in order to influence opinion in favour of Prussia. They find fault quite impudently with the censorship that accepts the English articles on Saxony and Poland in the *Wiener Zeitung* and the *Österreichischer Beobachter*, and allows the pamphlet *Saxony and Prussia* to be sold openly. 'En un mot [to quote the original report] ces dames sont scandaleusement prussiennes.'

Not that the social life in the Hoher Markt suffered from such stormy exchanges. Fanny's musical Tuesday soirées enjoyed growing popularity and drew into her circle ever-more members of the highest society, who would have avoided her a few years earlier – such as Princess Marie-Caroline Palm, Prince Trautmannsdorff, Count Emmanuel Khevenhüller, Countess Colloredo-Crenneville, the representative of the Teutonic Order Baron Ulrich, and Count Schlitz-Görtz, brother-in-law to the Bavarian Rechberg who found the Jewish question so irresistibly comic. Their King, indeed, did not call on Fanny; instead, obliged to do so by the Tsar, he visited the licentious Princess Bagration. There is no mention, either, of her old acquaintance Nesselrode, which, to be sure, does not mean that he kept entirely away. At any rate the nuncio Severoli showed his face again, even though he did not stay long, 'because the throng of ladies frightened him'. Consalvi, however, had become a regular guest and conversed 'to the best of his ability with Marianne Saaling', for whom, as Stägemann proudly related on one occasion, 'he has a natural liking. After the company had left and we wanted to sup,' continues the *Staatsrat*, 'there was another concert. Flemming whistled, Radziwill sang his song of the spinner, Minckchen [Baroness Münk] hers of the *Tadedel* [a clumsy dolt], so that we did not go in to supper until 12.'

These were sparkling, enjoyable occasions. Nevertheless the thin red line of separation between the spouses sometimes flared up threateningly. A few days before Christmas Stägemann found the atmosphere unpleasantly tense:

I did not stay long, as the political dichotomy between the two parties is becoming more and more noticeable. At midday the day before yesterday there were, by chance, only Prussians dining at Arnstein's, so that he [Arnstein] refused to come to the table; Frau Ephraim persuaded him to do so only by her tears. Frau von Arnstein had known nothing about this. When she learnt of this scene, she said quite calmly: 'You are spoiling him for me; if I had known, I would have said to him: just go and eat nicely downstairs, I will send everything down to you.' To me both men are very well-behaved and obliging. Eskeles is very intelligent. Arnstein not particularly, but otherwise a good person, whom we must forgive for being an Austrian.

Poor Nathan, one must say this time! That he sometimes fled from a dinner-table where the host had to be forgiven 'for being an Austrian' seems unsurprising. But with his easy-going nature he did not make the slightest objection when Fanny proposed celebrating Christmas Eve according to the Berlin custom. Stägemann recalls:

In fact, he had counted only on the Prussians and the Sicilians [Murat's opponents], and these were indeed the only invited guests; but of course, as usual, there were many other foreigners there.

Everyone received a present:

An Italian who had made comments about Saxony a few days earlier received a book in which the Prussian battles were illustrated, with the inscription on a slip of paper: *Vengeance d'une Prussienne*. This jest must have cost a few thousand thalers. Afterwards everyone was very lively. All sorts of merriment were indulged in, and music was played.

The secret police gave a more derisive account:

At Arnstein's the day before yesterday, according to the custom of

Berlin, there was a very numerous Christmas-tree celebration. There were present Chancellor Hardenberg, Staatsräthe Jordan and Hoffmann, Prince Radziwill, Herr Bartholdy, and all the baptised and circumcised relatives of the house. All the invited guests received presents or souvenirs from the Christmas tree. According to Berlin custom, comic songs were sung; Frau von Münch sang songs about *Kasperle*. There was a *cotillon* through all the rooms with the distributed objects taken from the Christmas tree. Prince Hardenberg enjoyed himself immensely; Herr von Humboldt was not there.

It was the first Christmas tree that Vienna had seen! 'Here this celebration is not usual,' wrote Prince Anton Radziwill to his wife, 'and the Arnstein house is the only one where the women keep up the Berlin custom.' After it had been introduced to Austria by Fanny, first the nobility, then the middle class took up the north-German custom. The Princess of Nassau, Henriette, to whom Archduke Karl became engaged the following spring, having been denied the Tsar's favourite sister, Katharina von Oldenburg, transplanted the Christmas tree into the imperial household after their marriage. At the Arnsteins', meanwhile, the celebrations continued, punch was drunk on New Year's Eve and *tableaux vivants* presented on 10 January. The Swiss envoy Jean Gabriel Eynard, who was also keeping a diary about the Congress, was present with his beautiful wife – 'la belle Anna' – and found everything 'fort bien exécuté, les costumes sont superbes'. Bertuch described in detail everyone who had taken part in this 'waxwork cabinet', including Marianne Saaling as Daphne and Frau von Geymüller as the Queen of the Night. Greek and Persian gods, Indian bayadères, even Wotan and Freya were represented. Among the 200 guests was, once again, Cardinal Consalvi with his little red cap and red stockings – 'a sharp, friendly clerical face, which never forgets his church'.

As ever, an informer had the last word:

There was the greatest pomp in the preparation, decoration and illumination. It was a success; there was almost a larger audience than the room could hold . . . It was said that Frau von Arnstein's aim was to surpass the *tableaux mouvants* of the court; she achieved her aim.

But in the midst of all this – the Christmas tree from Berlin, the tableaux of Teutonic gods, the Cardinal who paid court to the beautiful Marianne Saaling – one subject remained unmentioned which must have concerned the women of the house far more greatly. Only in one small observation which, two days after

Fanny's waxwork show, Stägemann dropped into a letter to his wife, is the theme lightly touched upon:

> I spent the evening at the Arnstein's, where I also supped. Apart from Stoffregen and Ezechiel there were no foreigners present, and there was immoderate laughter. Frau Ephraim let her bolts of lightning flash and strike. Frau von Arnstein was particularly kind to me because I have worked out a very favourable resolution for the Jewish communities in Hamburg, Lübeck and Bremen.

The Jewish question had been raised at the Congress in two different ways. The first initiative came from Frankfurt, where the old form of community had been a re-established after the departure of the French in the preceding autumn. It was now a matter of concern to the citizenry to restrict once again the rights of the Jews. Some of these, who had found employment in municipal posts – such as the young police actuary Ludwig Börne – were hastily dismissed. A general regulation had not yet been issued, but all the legal proposals of the period that followed gave evidence that the hostile spirit had returned.

On 5 September 1814, the Jewish community in Frankfurt turned for help to the leader of the central administration council, none other than Freiherr vom Stein. The man who had introduced the first reforms to Prussia and prepared the ground for Hardenberg was of a different mind on this point from his successor and the latter's envoy in Vienna. He loved neither Jews nor Frenchmen, but was well-disposed towards the citizens of Frankfurt, and immediately replied brusquely 'that in consideration of the circumstances of the Israelite believers in the city, I can make no alteration or further regulation concerning the provision made for them in the constitution, but they must expect further measures in this matter from the justice and the public spirit of the constitutional city authorities'. To trust to this justice and to this public spirit did not seem a very hopeful prospect to the Jews. They therefore chose two representatives from their midst, J. J. Gumprecht and Jacob Baruch – the father of the writer Börne – and sent them to Vienna to plead for the protection of the Congress.

The Hanseatic communities were in a similar situation. In May 1814, when the French occupation forces had finally departed from Hamburg, the old regulations regarding the Jews came back into force together with the earlier municipal regulations. Even Jewish soldiers returning home were to enjoy no particular consideration. At the request of their community leader the senate was now working out a draft emancipation document according to which a favoured class of wholesale merchants, scholars and rabbis should be granted civic rights, but all other, poorer Jews should remain without rights. Even this compromise was rejected by the city council, and so the Hamburgers had no choice but to turn likewise to Vienna. The same happened in Bremen and Lübeck. In this last city, however, a Protestant was found who was prepared to appear before the Congress as representative of the Jews of the three Hanseatic towns.

Dr Carl August Buchholz was a gifted young man, a late scion of the Enlightenment and admirer of Mendelssohn, to whom it appeared an honourable task to espouse this cause. Indeed, he intended to give it a more wide-ranging significance than was attached to the request of the Frankfurters. While Gumprecht and Baruch, despite difficulties with the authorities, who at first tried to forbid their stay in Vienna, had already placed their petition before the authorities on 10 October, Buchholz did not present his application until 10 December. In contrast to them, however, he stressed the claim of all the 'Israelite communities' of Germany to equal rights. The German Jews had found their advocate.

A few days after the Frankfurters' request had been handed in, the question came up for discussion in another connection. This singular Congress of Vienna, which never held a full meeting and preferred to conspire in the wings, had nevertheless instituted two smaller committees. One consisted of representatives of the eight great powers which had concluded the peace of Paris in May – Austria, Russia, Prussia, England, France, Spain, Portugal and Sweden – and was concerned with the reorganisation of Europe. The other dealt with the constitution of the proposed confederation of German states and was restricted to Austria, Prussia, Bavaria, Hanover and Württemberg. This 'Committee of Five' held its first session on 14 October. It had before it a *mémoire préparatoire* which Humboldt had composed in the spring as the first draft of a universal 'proclamation to the German people'. It contained the provision that 'every subject of the confederation' should be 'assured of the rights of a German citizen'. The second of the twelve articles read: 'The purpose of this confederation is the preservation of outward peace and independence and the inward security of the constitutional rights of every class of the nation.' One of these classes must include the Jews.

The 'Committee of Five' had hardly begun to consult when a bitter internal conflict became evident. The representatives of Bavaria and Württemberg, previously states of the Confederation of the Rhine, came out in total opposition to the draft constitution as submitted by Prussia with the agreement of the two other anti-Napoleonic powers. Thus they objected to the second article 'with regard to the Jews', because the latter 'did not enjoy the same rights in one state as in another'. The Jewish question was by no means the only stumbling-block, and certainly the least weighty, between the two groups. But it appeared inevitably bound up with the other differences of opinion. Here, as on all other points, Metternich for Austria, Hardenberg and Humboldt for Prussia, together with Count Münster and Count Ernst Hardenberg for Hanover, supported the draft of the 'Act of Confederation', while Prince Wrede for Bavaria and Count Winzingerode for Württemberg resisted it. The disunity in this committee had not yet been resolved when a greater conflict began to overshadow it. When, in mid-November, the situation had become one of the most distressing gravity, the 'Committee of Five' broke up and adjourned its sessions indefinitely.

The Frankfurt emissaries and Buchholz had meanwhile taken care that the question of the Jews' rights as subjects should be put, even if separately, before the Congress. Thus, while the German committee was temporarily dormant, individual personalities took an interest in the matter. On 4 January Chancellor Hardenberg wrote to his envoy in Hamburg, Count Grote, that he should intercede on his behalf for the Jewish inhabitants of Hamburg, Bremen and Lübeck and call upon the magistrates and citizens of these towns 'to associate themselves with the arrangement which the Prussian state, through the edict of 11 March 1812, has deemed appropriate as much to the demands of humanity and the needs of the time as to a rational system of government'. Stägemann had composed this resolution for him and thus earned Fanny von Arnstein's particular favour. Without doubt, however, Humboldt had been the motivating force. The pupil of Markus Herz and friend of Henriette was determined to transmit the Prussian work of emancipation to the whole German Confederation, and was not even afraid of the mockery of his wife Caroline, who found his concern exaggerated and felt that the Jews should rather be brought 'step by step' and without '*salti mortali*' to the employment of civic rights.

That Hardenberg and Humboldt were fighting for this cause surprised no one. What was more astonishing was that, besides Prussia, Austria too was now raising her voice on its behalf. Indeed, Metternich himself, who at home would not lift a finger for the Jews, now intervened in their favour with the Hanseatic towns. On 26 January the minister of state instructed the imperial chargé d'affaires in Hamburg, C. L. von Höfer, 'at the moment when adherents to the Jewish faith are justified in expecting from the Congress assembled here a definition, arrived at according to liberal principles, of their conditions and rights', to secure from the Hamburg magistrate the repeal of the harsh measures taken against them. Now it appeared easy to demand of others a toleration which was not yet established to a similar extent in one's own laws. Austria had never gone beyond Joseph's edict of tolerance and had never had the remotest notion of allowing Jews civic rights. Nevertheless, Metternich's action was a sign that his own attitude differed in beneficence from that of the Emperor.

That this was so, was due not least to the influence of his banker Leopold von Herz. Nathan's nephew, to whom Fanny in all her testaments entrusted the arrangements for her funeral – in place of Pereira, who was becoming less dear to her and, in addition, was no longer a member of the Jewish community – had some time earlier got into favour with the minister of state. Gentz, of all people, had introduced him to Metternich at the time of the wars of liberation. Soon afterwards Herz, together with the usual four banking houses, had been entrusted with the winding up of the English subsidies after the battle of Leipzig. A man as clever in business as he was easy-going in private life, who like his uncle was welcome at all the gaming-tables of the nobility, and had once in Baden lost 60,000 gulden to Wenzel Liechtenstein and Count Schulenburg, he now took up a position of trust with the two statesmen. Gentz allowed himself to be bribed by Herz. And Metternich, who did not visit Fanny's salon, although his father frequently did so, went so far as to dine at Leopold von Herz's with Wellington immediately after the latter's arrival in Vienna to relieve Castlereagh. A few days earlier he had given his instructions to Höfer in Hamburg. These two astonishing events were not unconnected.

The Hanseatic towns were not in a hurry to give their answers, which in the case of Hamburg and Lübeck were evasive but friendly, in that of Bremen negative. Meanwhile Buchholz had placed before the Congress a second memorandum, in which he adduced arguments based on the dogma of the Enlightenment, on historical and political grounds, for a general emancipation of the German Jews. It ended: 'German rulers and statesmen of this great and remarkable time! The eyes of the present world accompany your steps, and posterity will judge you!' Submitted in the course of February, it could very well have served as a stimulus to a newly convened 'Committee of Five' to look at the Jewish question in a more benevolent light. But the committee remained adjourned, though not because of the conflict over Poland and Saxony. This question had already been resolved on 8 February, Austria having formed a secret alliance with the British and French and the Tsar having withdrawn from the Prussians. Russia received the lion's share of the duchy of Warsaw. Prussia received only two-fifths of the kingdom of Saxony, which she had demanded, together with certain tracts of land in Poland and Westphalia and on the northern Rhine. Humboldt and Hardenberg felt that they had been cheated; their opponents felt they had swallowed up too much as it was. At any rate the newly kindled grudge between Prussia and Austria had been buried again for the next few decades.

What was now delaying the conferences on the Act of Confederation as well as on all the other business of the Congress was an event whose sudden and violent eruption resembled a natural catastrophe. On 1 March Napoleon had landed in Fréjus, and six days later the news reached Vienna.

The Austrian court and its high-ranking guests had, however, the strength to attend a private theatrical performance in the Redoutensaal on the evening of 7 March. Gentz was among those invited. 'Assisté à un assez ennuyeux spectacle: vu sortir tous les souverains, et bien accueilli par tous', he noted in his diary. Talleyrand seemed less composed. 'He found the matter insignificant, but fear seemed to shine out of him,' observed Archduke Johann. Soon the other ministers and monarchs stopped yawning and shrugging their shoulders. Napoleon's rapid advance, his entry – thirteen days later – into Paris, caused mounting confusion, indeed at times even panic, at the Congress.

Gentz was of the opinion that he had always said the Bourbons were no bulwark against this man. Emperor Francis, with Austrian resignation, commented to Prince August of Prussia: 'If the French want Napoleon, I suppose they must be allowed to have him.' Even the Tsar vacillated and for a moment seemed prepared to recognise the *Empereur*, if the French nation really insisted upon him: 'One cannot oppose a whole nation.' This to Marie-Louise in Schönbrunn, who had just with difficulty torn her simple heart away from her husband and turned it towards Neipperg! Metternich and Wellington, not to speak of the Prussians, were all the more firmly determined to drive out the 'troublemaker', 'despot' and 'villain' as quickly as possible – they did not, to be sure, yet know how.

If the Viennese, weary of the Congress's pleasures, were less terrified than pleasantly stimulated by the new development, deep gloom reigned at least in one household. Another 'waxwork show' had just been held, at which Wellington and Sydney Smith, Eugène de Beauharnais, his secretary Méjean and the elder Metternich, apart from the usual festive complement of 200 people, had been entertained; Pozzo di Borgo, to general gratification, had told stories of himself and the friend of his youth, Bonaparte, in their early Corsican days – and that ghost, already a historical figure, had begun to haunt them again in broad daylight! Fanny, for whom Napoleon had taken shape as a personal enemy, so to speak as her own Beelzebub made flesh, hovered in a state of derangement. 'Frau von Arnstein is no longer herself,' reported Stägemann, 'so greatly have the last eight days brought her down: anger and rage.' And Rahel Varnhagen, who had spent the winter in Vienna in a most peevish and rheumatic state, excluded from the great, crowded soirées at the Arnsteins', and embittered by the neglectful behaviour of her old friend Gentz, now continually ran to the side of Fanny, who 'is more than beside herself about this event' and 'is in great need of my company'.

When, at the end of March, Bonaparte's arrival in Paris became known, the mood on the Hoher Markt sank to its lowest level. A few days earlier the four great powers had concluded a new military treaty. Nevertheless, as was rumoured, Beauharnais had expressed himself at Princess Bagration's to the effect that 'he did not see why the allied powers should not make their peace with Napoleon; if he would now content himself with France as it was, one would easily come to an understanding'. Beauharnais' secretary Méjean, according to an informer – presumably Carpani – in a report to the police minister Hager dated 31 March, 'says much worse things yet. At Frau von Arnstein's the day before yesterday a scene took place in front of a crowd of people, at which among others General Degenfeld, Count Scherr and the ladies de Bruce and Fossati were present. The matter was related to me as follows by Frau von Eskeles and Abbé von Rauen (!) [Rohan], as they had just heard it from the lips of Frau von Arnstein:'

Frau von Arnstein speaks unsparingly of Bonaparte and is furious about what has just happened. After first showering M. and Mme Méjean with amiable remarks, she says to Méjean, who hardly had time to sit down: 'Now, Monsieur, are you not ashamed to be a Frenchman, after everything that has just happened? And those traitors Ney and Suchet!'

Méjean replies that he has always considered himself fortunate to be a Frenchman, but that he now esteems France, which has declared herself for her Emperor, even more highly, just as he does the brave Marshals who have always stayed loyal to their Emperor.

Frau von Arnstein says to him: 'So you do not blush to honour those traitors?' And she adds whatever violent phrases her anger suggests to her.

Mme Méjean then says to Frau von Arnstein in German that her husband did not mean what he said, but on the contrary, honours those who keep their word, etc. In this way she attempts to smooth things over, while at the same time giving her husband a signal to drop the subject.

Frau von Arnstein replies in French: 'No, Madame, you are mistaken. I understood very well what he said . . . Do you want proof? Now, Monsieur, repeat your words, if you have the courage to do so!'

Without hesitation Méjean repeats his assertion, and everyone is outraged by the impudence manifested by this Frenchman who arrived here, became very popular and even married in Vienna, after the declaration of the Congress which was by no means unknown to him.

Frau von Arnstein was so irritated and disconcerted by all this that she had a *crise de nerfs*, could not sleep at night and is still ill. She did, it is true, take her revenge on the spot. When this scene had ended, General Degenfeld and other military persons were discussing the movements of the Austrian troops. The two Méjeans were still present. Frau von Arnstein, who heard this from a distance, raised her voice and said: 'Gentlemen of the military, you are ill-advised to speak of these things here. One must look around and see if one is among trustworthy people.' Méjean swallowed the pill without a word.

This scene at Fanny's seemed to Hager particularly suitable to open the Tsar's eyes about his favourite, Beauharnais. He, therefore, communicated the secret report to the Emperor and added that, in his opinion, it should also be brought to the attention of Alexander of Russia, 'to enlighten him about the attitude of mind and the sympathies of Prince Eugène's entourage'. Whether this was done is not known, but a few days later Beauharnais left the country together with his father-in-law, the King of Bavaria. Fanny, however, was still to hear, in her own house, a Prussian state councillor, Jordan, expressing himself in favour of making the little King of Rome regent of France. Quarrels, strife, discontent on all sides! No wonder that Rahel wrote to her brother at the beginning of April: 'Yesterday I ate very well at Fanny von Arnstein's. But nothing spoken but insults against the army, Murat, the French, etc. An abomination to me!'

Not without sadness we realise that Fanny's image, to which her early contemporaries lent so many features of charm, wit and amiability, has become increasingly severe in outline, has hardened, even darkened. Was she really such a sharp-tongued Xanthippe, an uncontrolled bundle of nerves, an implacable enemy as she now appears to us? One neither wishes nor needs to believe it. Had she become all these things, her salon would soon have emptied. Hardenberg would not have insisted, even in the times when he was most occupied with work, 'de venir passer un instant chez la Fanny', as he did, for example, to Capo d'Istria at the height of the Saxony crisis. Varnhagen would never have said of her that even at the time of the Congress 'she played the tireless hostess, bubbling with vitality, embracing all circumstances and improving them appropriately'.

The reconstruction of a human existence from circumstantial evidence is a dangerous thing. And if in those stirring 'Hundred Days' of Napoleon's restoration the hot-headedness to which Fanny was inclined came to the surface in all sorts of unpleasing ways, this does not mean that during that time she showed nothing but displeasure and ill-humour. In the midst of the first excitement over Napoleon's return Rahel Varnhagen was able to write to her brother on 12 March: 'I amused myself yesterday evening very much at an ordinary soirée at the Arnsteins'; with Frau von Arnstein, with a good French lady, with Frau von Ephr., with much looking and listening, and we laughed at table!'

Fanny's temperament, always in ferment, never at rest, was certainly so stirred up by the latest happenings that, when the Jewish question at last came up again at the Congress, she could no longer show very much interest in it. At the beginning of January 'Baroness A.' had, as the representative of Bremen in Vienna, Senator Smidt, wrote home, 'like Esther to Ahasuerus of yore, gone in person to high-ranking personages, in order to plead for the highest intercession particularly in favour of the Hanseatic Jewry'. However, her personal intervention might have been less necessary on this occasion than at the time when she appeared before Emperor Joseph for the same reason. The matter, she must have supposed, was in good hands. Buchholz, who frequented her house and that of Cäcilie, had made a good impression. Hardenberg and Humboldt, like Metternich, were of a mind to achieve a satisfactory solution through the Act of Confederation. Bernhard Eskeles and even her own husband, who was otherwise so unwilling to become involved in public matters, were preparing a separate petition over the situation of the Austrian Jews. Two influential members of the Jewish community in Prague had come to support this petition. In short, there was no obstacle to moving out of the city to the Braunhirschengrund. Garden, cow-shed, pigeon-loft and the country air in springtime would provide the speediest escape from the perfumed, spectral breath of salon diplomacy!

The Congress, meanwhile, whose business had been brought to a standstill by the landing and victorious advance of Napoleon, now hastened towards the conclusion of its activity. The allied army was in the field – more could not be done against the troublesome *revenant*. For all that, statesmen and ruling princes were eager to cut short their stay in Vienna and be at home during these decisive weeks. The aim was, therefore, to remove all outstanding conflicts, including that of the German Act of Confederation. As early as 24 April the 'Committee of Five' signed a provisional agreement, about which, however, there was still further violent discussion. Two weeks earlier a petition from the 'Austrian Jewish communities to Emperor Francis' had been received, which was delivered 'in the name of the members of the Jewish faith in Vienna' by Nathan Freiherr von Arnstein, Bernhard Ritter von Eskeles and Leopold Edler von Herz, while Simon Edler von Lämel signed on behalf of the Jews of Bohemia and Herr Lazar Auspitz for those of Moravia.

In 1797 – the year in which he had ennobled Arnstein, Eskeles and Herz – Emperor Francis had proclaimed his intention in a Bohemian edict of abolishing the legal distinction between Christians and Jews. Since then nothing had happened. But reference could still be made to it. If the Emperor lacked proofs of the Jews' entitlement to better treatment, the five petitioners believed they could now provide an adequate supply of these:

Most gracious Emperor and Lord!
The members of the Israelite faith have complied with your Majesty's expectations. Their capability in all the useful trades is proved by facts, the numerous places of work attesting to their industry in several provinces of the monarchy, their extensive factories, the scope of their external business connections, allow no room for doubt about the use that they would make of their powers and capital under liberal and egalitarian laws; in services which they have rendered to the state in all professions where their participation has been demanded or even only permitted, in sacrifices of all kinds which they have made for the general good, in love of their country and loyal devotion to their beloved monarch, they have, in proportion to their numbers as well as to their means, at least equalled their Christian fellow-citizens. The unfounded prejudice that they were not suitable for military service has been disproved by action; loyal everywhere to the call of their monarch, they have readily given their persons and their lives in the last severe wars and, like other good citizens, for the safety and honour of their mutual

fatherland, have shed their blood in the pious expectation that it would no longer treat them as stepchildren . . . We have stood every test; and if a humiliating partition still divides us from other citizens of the state, this exists only in antiquated opinions, or blind and groundless fear of competition which appears dangerous to petty private interests, but is evidently beneficial for the whole; in your Majesty's great soul this partition has long since been torn down.

The petitioners did not, however, dare to demand total and complete naturalisation. They did not expect so much favour from his Majesty's great soul. They pleaded only for a new decision, some sign from on high that equality before the law should be fundamentally recognised:

We would count ourselves fortunate enough, if only the august promise of the year 1797 should at last be fulfilled, if only the general principle which made the Israelites equal to all other believers in consideration of rights of purchase, of trade and of possession should be proclaimed by your Majesty as law.

This and no more! Even from Metternich, who, after all, dined with Leopold von Herz and who consequently had already torn down that partition, the five men had no demands to make beyond his 'decisive voice and influential intercession' with regard to a new Austrian law. They believed it necessary, however, to influence this intercession in another way, and that was with the help of Metternich's venal colleague, Hofrat von Gentz. This friend of Rahel's and admirer of the 'truly witty' and 'endlessly amusing' Grattenauer had already been approached on 19 March by the banker Simon von Lämel, who had entrusted him with the work 'dans l'affaire des juifs'.

'This summer,' Goethe had written in 1812 to Cäcilie Eskeles, 'I have become greatly indebted to the excellent house of Lämel in Prague. May I ask you at some time to remember me to them most kindly and to answer for my unswerving gratitude to the same.' At the end of the Congress Gentz was to have equal reason to be grateful to the Edler von Lämel. During the following weeks he repeatedly notes visits from him, 'arrivé de Prague pour pousser la fameuse affaire des juifs', and on 13 April he is already able to write in his journal: 'Lämel de Prague qui m'a fait un beau présent pour la mémoire en faveur des juifs.' He saw Buchholz with equal frequency, indeed at times almost daily, even if this worthy man was not aware of the reason for his particular interest in the cause of the Jews. In addition, he himself once dined ostentatiously at Leopold von Herz's with three Princes de Rohan, any number of counts and Jakob Bartholdy – 'one of the most dreadful of this depraved brood', as he had once called him. And when, on 18 June, 'après beaucoup de négociations, Lämel se chargea du payement des autres 2,000 Ducats, que m'a valu l'affaire des juifs', Gentz had pocketed, for use in that respect, almost four times as much as those 1,100 ducats which both the Russians and the Prussians had given him as a farewell *cadeau*. He had certainly talked a great deal, but achieved nothing. The petition of the five Austrian Jews was left unanswered; after an unfavourably composed provisional settlement, the Congress referred the decision on the Jewish question to the Bundestag (Federal Diet) at Frankfurt.

Even this result had come about only after violent conflict. First of all the representatives of the Hanseatic towns and of Frankfurt, which had meanwhile become a 'Free City', had managed to prevent a separate consideration of their Jewish communities. Senator Smidt, the representative of Bremen in Vienna – a friend of Freiherr vom Stein – had succeeded at the end of March, by means of a memorandum couched in apparently liberal terms, in convincing both Metternich and the Prussians that the measures they had taken in January in support of the Jews had been premature and unnecessary. When the discussions about the Act of Confederation then continued on 23 May, at which time the original 'Committee of Five' had been increased by ten delegates from other German states, a new group had congregated around the antagonists of the Jews, Wrede and Winzingerode. Senator Smidt had also appeared. It was he who was later to report that, when the draft was read out and 'the point about the Jews came up', first Count Rechberg and then nearly everyone else had laughed uncontrollably.

Humboldt, however, was determined not to give in, however unfavourable the mood had become. On 4 June he wrote to his wife about the Jewish claim to civic rights in Germany:

> I have always been inclined in favour of this cause. I know that you think otherwise, sweetheart, but I have thought about it a great deal at various times and remain faithful to my old opinion. It is, moreover, an idea of my youth, for Alexander and I, when we were still children, were considered defenders of Jewry.

Also, 'an old man from Prague, whose character pleased me quite well, since he is not one of the new-fangled Jews', had come to him a couple of times to commend the affair.

> I now composed a clause according to my convictions . . . Metternich,

Wessenberg, Hardenberg and I conducted the matter as best we could. Rechberg, Darmstadt-Hesse, the Hanseatic towns above all were against it. It came up in two sessions, Metternich, as is his custom, almost gave the matter up, but I kept it going, gave it new twists and made it innocuous, so that I only referred it to the future assembly of the Confederation, but preserved the Jews' rights which had already been won. There was a great deal of talk about the matter; everyone knows that it was only I who composed the clause and carried it through.

Humboldt, well-intentioned towards the Jews, had drafted a paragraph which he clearly considered unassailable. It read:

> The assembly of the Confederation will take into consideration how the civic improvement of those of the Jewish faith in Germany may be achieved in as harmonious a way as possible, and especially how the enjoyment of civic rights, in return for the adoption of all civic duties, may be secured for them in the states of the Confederation; nevertheless the members of this faith shall until then receive the rights already conceded to them in the individual states of the Confederation.

On 1 June, after a long debate, this clause was adopted. Four days later Metternich entered the German Confederation in the name of his court. On 8 June the Act of Confederation was at last to be given its definitive form. And now, at the last moment, on the eve of the Congress's closure, the Jews were suddenly outwitted – and this in a way which is only comparable with the ingenious hair-splitting of sophisticated casuistry. At Senator Smidt's suggestion a single word of the clause drafted by Humboldt was altered. It now read: 'nevertheless the members of this faith shall until then receive the rights already conceded to them *by* the individual states of the Confederation.' By this means, that status quo which was to prevail pending the decision of the Bundestag was defined as the situation in the nations *before* the Napoleonic invasion. The achievements of emancipation were disregarded and the old constraints were confirmed, indeed newly enforced.

This realisation may have dawned only slowly on the Jews. Lämel, who offered Humboldt a *cadeau* of the same value as Gentz's, after the former had championed their cause, was certainly not clear in his mind about it. Humboldt himself, too, who politely declined the three emerald rings valued at 4,000 ducats, probably did not immediately comprehend it. 'For myself,' he wrote to Caroline, 'I know nothing so ignoble as not to be as pure and undefiled as gold.' Such an honourable disposition was not capable of seeing through the tricks of crafty opponents.

Moreover there was no time to think through the effects of that alteration. The whole Act of Confederation was unsatisfactory to the Prussians, but for good or ill they had to acquiesce with the situation. The Congress was in the process of dispersing. On 30 May the sovereigns had departed. Now there was nothing to keep their representatives any longer. On 9 June the hastily completed documents were signed in the chancery office, two days later eleven further clauses were accepted, and on the twenty-sixth of the same month, after all the great statesmen had already left, the last signatures were appended by the Congress offices that still remained open.

At this time the battle of Waterloo had already been fought. One breathed a sigh of relief, wherever one happened to be – Gentz in the suburb of Weinhaus, the Prussians back in Berlin, Fanny and her family in Baden. The spectre had departed. Now all Europe was ready for a long sleep; for the torment of the last years had been great.

-11-

The Father's House

On the morning after the Congress ended, the Biedermeier era began in Austria.

The world of the Rococo, which had once more risen up like a spectre, the short-lived style of the *Empire* had sunk without trace overnight. A new age had begun – playful, dreamy, introspective, in which one turned one's gaze no further than one's most intimate circle. The great events were over; now little things once more gained prominence. Daily life loosened up, became simpler, more relaxed. Whatever had seemed austere and challenging now took on more peaceable features. The rigid furniture of the Napoleonic era with its fluted columns, its laurel wreaths and fasces, acquired soft and pliant outlines. In place of crossed swords, a lyre adorned the cherrywood chair. Fashion, too, was transformed at a stroke. The tight, plain, flowing garments still worn at the beginning of the Congress became puffed and flounced and *bouillonnés*, fragrant and floating, hung about with sashes and draperies. The clever courtesan became a picture of charming innocence. Her hair, until recently coiled about her head in Greek knots and garlands, now fell to her shoulders in languid ringlets.

A last euphoric glory had lingered upon the sleigh-rides and carousels, the illuminations and equine minuets that Emperor Francis had arranged for his exalted guests. Now the splendid spectacle gave way to the idyll. Following the call of the Romantics, one turned to nature; but it was neither the artificial park landscape of the Rococo nor the heroic mountain-ranges of the *Stürmer und Dränger* for which people longed. Their nature was prettified and innocuous, a series of delightful vistas, with hills not too high, valleys not too deep, rivers and waterfalls not too torrential, whose wilderness gradually subsided in quiet streams and green pools. And nowhere was it found so abundantly as on the slopes of the Vienna woods, nowhere so pleasingly dotted with villas, country houses and spas as in the purlieus of the curative springs of Baden near Vienna. On Monday, 19 June 1815, Rahel Varnhagen wrote:

After dinner to the divine, far too little renowned Helenen-Thal. Through cultivated, very agreeable pleasure-grounds, country estates, *osterie* and village houses, not a deserted spot all the way; all near at hand, along the little river Schwechat. Rocks on the left; towards evening. I drove with Mesd. de Prie, Arnstein and Mariane; another carriage followed. Frau von Arnstein brought a bagpiper, who preceded her on the stony footpath in the valley. The fine, easy paths, upwards and on the level, were bestrewn with polite and colourful walkers, whose carriages had halted at a bend of the river and the rocks. Flocks of cattle were passing under the bridge through the stony river, goats clambered above on the heights, the sun flamed, light and dark, over the foliage of trees and bushes, grass, rocks, mountains. Young girls sang comic songs to the accompaniment of harps. Frau von Ephraim was agog to show me all this. Herr von Veyder most merry. I walked a little. We drove home; walked a little more in the park in the beautiful moonlight; and so to bed.

The day before, near the inn of the Belle Alliance at Waterloo, Napoleon had been defeated for the last time. Here, two hours' drive from Vienna, he and his destiny seemed as far removed in time as in space. Here the nineteenth century had arrived, strolling on wooded paths in the wake of a bagpiper, sitting at the edge of a stream and gazing at the mild, melancholy moon. Its festivals were celebrated in village inns, over a glass of wine, in the cool breath of evening which rose up from the river and wafted through the treetops. Its misfortunes took place when a new iron bridge over the Schwechat collapsed at its ceremonial opening, after Archduke Johann, and before the Empress, had crossed it. These were everyday joys and sorrows, and they had a homely and human dimension, no longer larger than life.

Little Baden was the right place to find a transition into the comfort of the Biedermeier. Fanny had transferred her household here from the Braunhirschengrund, and Rahel had come as a guest after her husband's departure, with 'Jettchen Pereira, of whom I am very fond'. She stayed almost two months in the rambling, one-storeyed country-house which adjoined the present-day *Schlosspark*, and felt more than ever at ease among the beautiful scenery and in the atmosphere of unconstrained, friendly companionship. 'I shall live very well here,' she immediately wrote to Varnhagen, 'I am lodged at ground level, comfortably.' Henriette and Marianne Saaling, Madame Ephraim and her daughter also had accommodation in the house. Their constant companions, at table or on pleasure outings, were a Marquise de Prie, Baroness Münk (who

sang that song of the *Tadedel* with such comic effect), the merry
Lieutenant-Colonel von Veyder, Count Keller and Countess Dietrichstein. At times they were joined by camp-followers from the
time of the Congress, gentlemen such as the Prussian General
Wolzogen, the Neapolitan Duke of Serra-Capriola or the Spanish
Marquis Marialva, Marianne's admirer and later fiancé. Apart from
these they saw only friends of long standing and travelling companions, the narrowest circle in which a familiar *Gemütlichkeit* was
still possible.

They visited Count Fries at his country house at Vöslau and old
Baron Braun at his famous castle of Schönau. As Rahel reported to
her sister-in-law in Berlin:

> A garden of the gods, visited by kings and emperors. Our hosts showed
> it to us. The whole district round about is like this, and the owners are
> all friends and guests of the Arnsteins'. There is a temple of night in a
> rocky maze, with moon and stars inside; altars, a Queen of the Night
> and a harmonica-organ on which Salieri composed some very fine
> pieces. A great book lies upon an altar, in which Braun's guests make
> inscriptions. The Emperor, the princes, scholars, everyone. I wrote: 'A
> saying of Goethe's! Ah, who would not gladly invoke what cannot come
> again!' The date and underneath: 'Even more so!' Because of our battle.

For in the meantime the news of Waterloo had reached Baden, and
was received on returning to the house after a drive in a high wind
to the village of St Helena. 'We met all Vienna in Helena' – the
prophetically named spot lay in that valley which Rahel too had
found so divine. 'Thank God,' she wrote about the outcome of the
battle, 'that it is not the opposite! But how dreadfully, in un-
wonted, ambiguous circumstances which shocked my every fibre,
did I feel the whole of the preceding war.'

It was the last time that one would be shocked in every fibre by
the memory of the past. In October the ghost finally departed on
the island which bore the name of the village in Lower Austria. But
as early as July in Baden he was no longer given a thought. The
weather was alternately fine and cloudy; it provided a calmer theme
for conversation. Rahel's journal continues:

> Rain-showers, wind, long discussions about going out, finally with the
> Arnstein, Münk and Ephraim ladies to Leesdorf. Frau von Arnstein
> greatly in fear: rainbows, beautiful play of sunlight, corn, clover,
> vineyards . . .

They visited the castle of Rauheneck:

A wide, wide prospect: many horizons one after the other. The most wonderful play of light: on the ruins, trees, valleys, corn, grass edges. Sheep, bells, silence; friendliness and comfort, ingenuousness and jests. At home General Wolzogen, who told me how he had delivered the captive Vandamme to Emperor Alexander. Frau von Jäger, who sang and played the guitar, Frau von Münk also.

Idyll upon idyll! Rahel – who had found Vienna as unbeautiful as had Nicolai or at first Gentz, accustomed, like all Berliners, to wide prospects and the fresh air of Brandenburg, and for whom the whole brilliant social life of the past winter had been spoilt by her coughing and rheumatism – could not find sufficient words of praise for country life at Baden. She was uncommonly happy 'to enjoy all this here in such a genial comfortable way'. Time and again in her letters to Varnhagen she raved about the 'path of the Gods' of the Helenental:

> where there were many people, goats climbing, horned cattle stepping through the stony streams, bagpipes playing, singers yodelling to the harp, Levantines wandering about. Close to the stream which separates the mountains from the valley, we drank coffee at an inn. I saw only the objects. The company was good and unaffected, their only pride that of the valley. The ladies desperate to show me all the beauties! Frau von Arnstein a thousand times better than in town; and not the remotest thought of pretension in her household guests, who enjoy complete freedom and only the good things which the comfortable house offers with its numerous servants and horses. They wished for nothing but to entertain themselves and the guests without anxiety.

Nathan too, who was often mildly ridiculed or even reviled, came off well with her. It seems that Varnhagen had borrowed 500 gulden from him, which General Tettenborn was to repay on his behalf through the banker Bethmann, but this had been overlooked. 'It is of course very embarrassing for me,' wrote Rahel, 'and certainly for you as well. The more so since Arnstein behaves in the most gallant way to me, particularly where money, exchange and like are concerned, and in all things!' She had learnt only indirectly of the oversight and soon managed to arrange the settlement of the debt by means of a draft on Bethmann's bank. But otherwise 'I cannot tell you how much cause I have to be satisfied with our ladies; no unpleasantness of any kind takes place. Nothing but good things.' The only trouble she had was that of changing her clothes once a day: 'Our hostess has invited the whole of Baden to tea; this requires a special *toilette*.' The little spa was in fact full of the elegant *monde*. Somewhere nearby Mesdames Sagan and

Bagration were in residence, though indeed they were seen only when taking the waters. Napoleon's consort, Marie-Louise, lived five houses away; daily Fanny and her guests saw innumerable couriers hastening to her and suspected what was still a closely guarded secret – that she nourished 'the most raging passion for General Neipperg, who was her chamberlain or something of the sort. He too is quite electrified, and knightly, the way she condescends to him. She is completely happy, quite romantic.'

Romantic – she too, who had lost an empire! But the Biedermeier lifestyle had taken hold of her also, so that Marie-Louise preferred a country house at Baden, and later her little residence in Parma at the side of the clever Count Neipperg, to the splendour of the Tuileries and the presence of the genius Napoleon – *Gemütlichkeit* rather than grandeur! Thus there were plenty of empresses, duchesses and noble personages in this little wateringplace. Moreover, there was a charming theatre, not far from the Arnstein residence – 'the best theatre in the spas that I know: the hall too is fine, the audience distinguished'. The great actress Sophie Antonie Schröder came as a guest artist and declaimed Schiller: 'The whole salon wept bitterly. She is a god.' There was a casino too, where balls took place on Sundays, at which one might meet the Duchess of Sagan and her sister, or even Princess Hohenzollern. And if despite all this one had attacks of boredom, one drove to the Braunhirschengrund in Vienna, visited the Schlegels, Pauline Wiesel and Adam Müller, returning late at night. 'We then spent the evening at Frau von Arnstein's bedside. I always merry.' For Rahel was merry here as she had never been before:

I am much healthier here than in Vienna. Very merry; and [I am] the entertainment of the whole house and all its guests; in whose company I am capable of verbal preludes! My whole existence, my every activity and utterance is their continuous amusement . . . And this only because I am sincere and have my own ideas. It even extends to my demeanour. I am the only one there to have an opinion. The day before yesterday I was even able to defend the French nation, in a guest-room which was far from empty, and with the greatest success: the counts were quite satisfied: and smiled at the novelty which they did not have to think out for themselves; our fiery hostess, when I fell silent, said approvingly: 'Do continue! We should all rather listen in silence!' Another proof for me of the success with which men holding official positions can speak and behave if they are upright enough and in particular have an opinion: which for the most part is missing.

Here, in a smaller circle, Rahel was at last able to impress, and could play the part from which she had been restrained during the winter in the densely filled salon of the Hoher Markt. Fanny, known hitherto only as a blind Francophobe, had since Napoleon's final fall regained her old amiability and gladly withdrew in favour of the eloquent and imaginative Rahel. The latter now launched forth into a long defence of the French peasants, who could not be patriotic because this class 'has only the oppression, the burden, of working for the few, the cream of mankind, who wallow and revel in ambition and enjoyment' – inflammatory speeches which were heard with respect by the Austrian counts.

> Earlier they were all of another opinion; as soon as I dared to express it, [they became] their own opponents, with laughter and applause; and silence! – But to dare something like that, one must judge the moment well, see in one's mind's eye the edge on which the bored spirits are standing; and not be able to be accused of personal interest, even of being opinionated. Oh! why am I not a person in office! Why not a princess! (You are right about me – in this.) So help me God! I impressed them; I see it. – So I am well liked throughout the house.

So well liked was Rahel, and so impressive in her refound self-esteem, that the Arnstein ladies vied to go travelling with her in the late summer. Since mid-July Varnhagen had been in Paris, where the monarchs and statesmen of Europe were to meet once more, this time to make a lasting peace with France. The ladies were tempted to be there too. 'The whole house here wants to go to Paris,' wrote Rahel to her husband. Meanwhile 'Frau von Arnstein positively begs for something striking, cut out [*Ausgeschnittenes*], from Paris' – by which she meant, not some dramatically *décolleté* gown, but some significant passage or other from French journals. At the same time plans were being made. Henriette Pereira wanted to accompany her in her carriage:

> at least as far as Frankfurt. But Marianne Saaling wants to go with me too: and so does Frau Ephraim. All the ladies, because they think I will be a good travelling companion and because I have no detrimental pretensions. But there is great strife between them. I don't know which of them will come with me. Baroness Arnstein wants to follow, so as to go to Paris. She would like Jettchen Pereira to go with me. I will be governed by your letter and your health.

Varnhagen encouraged her in his letters – 'tell everyone we want to lead the merriest life in the world here'. He mentioned that Chancellor Hardenberg had asked after Rahel and 'the ladies of the Arnstein circle, whose presence here he would find very acceptable'.

And he sent, if not yet the desired striking cut-out passage – as he had not been able to find anything 'piquant from here' – for the time being 'the ship that is to bring Bonaparte to St Helena, the *Bellerophon*, which happens to be lying on my table'. At the house in Baden they had to be content with this replica carved in wood. At the beginning of August the Duchess of Sagan, that tireless camp-follower of modern wars, had already arrived in Paris, while Humboldt, Bülow, Pfuel and Bentheim had also established themselves there. 'Bring your dear women friends!' Varnhagen repeated on 8 August. 'They will enjoy themselves here, despite all the decay of the once flourishing conditions of the capital.' On the same day Rahel had already left Vienna with the younger ladies.

She herself had no inclination for Paris. 'I cannot decide myself for France,' she had written to a friend in Frankfurt, the Prussian chargé d'affaires there, Baron von Otterstedt. At least until this goal should be reached they kept together. Rahel drove in a carriage lent by Fanny with her servant Johann and her maid Dore. Henriette Pereira followed in her own 'with Jettchen Ephraim and her domestics. Frau von Pereira goes to Spaa, and after taking the waters either to southern France or to Italy; her mother, and the Ephraim mother, follow'. It was not without an effort that the ladies had torn themselves away from Vienna and Baden. Only a week earlier Rahel had reported to her husband that 'suddenly Frau von Arnstein with all her ladies and the whole house, because of a *tracasserie* that she had had with her son-in-law Pereira concerning the journey' had left 'immediately after dining for the garden' (near Vienna), and 'everyone here is in a ferment of packing'. For good or ill, Pereira had after all allowed his wife to go. Rahel's comment casts new light on the bad terms between him and Henriette, undoubtedly stirred up by her mother.

It is to Rahel, too, that we owe the last glimpses of Fanny's life, before the contemporary reports on her final years fall silent. First of all, with Henriette Pereira and the latter's cousin, she had arrived safe and sound in Frankfurt, 'Goethe's city', put up at the *Englischer Hof* and immediately become enchanted by the 'manifold magic within magic' of the district. On the evening of 20 August 'the Jetten' (the two Henriettes) drove on. Rahel meanwhile had on the same day set off for Niederrad, a village which was transfigured for her by memories of Goethe's youth. Strolling in his footsteps, she noticed a low-built carriage, in which a gentleman sat on the coach-box with the coachman, and behind him three ladies in mourning: 'I look into the carriage, and see Goethe. The shock and the joy transform me into a savage: I cry with the greatest force and haste "There is Goethe!". Goethe laughs, the ladies laugh: but I grasp hold of the Vallentin woman and we run ahead of the carriage.'

This slightly undignified encounter with the man she had once met briefly as a young girl, but admired for a lifetime, was to be followed by a second one, under hardly more favourable conditions. Informed that she was staying in Frankfurt, on 8 September Goethe called upon Rahel, who was not yet dressed. Once more in a state of panic, she rushed to him – her hair loose, still in her *négligé*, her appearance, small and unpretty, as little advantageous as she could have feared. Dumbstruck by the overpowering encounter, she had scarcely gathered her wits together before the poet was already taking his leave. 'I could say nothing to him of Frau von Pereira, nothing of Frau von Grotthuss, nothing at all! Only, just at the beginning, I said to him: "It was I who called out to you in Niederrad; I was there with strangers, just because you had spoken of the place; I was too surprised."'

A lamentable, touching scene! What would she have given to have been for ten uninterrupted days in Goethe's company, like the worthy, good-natured Cäcilie Eskeles! But so badly does Fate sometimes direct such dramatic climaxes, or so pitilessly does she reduce them to their human minimum, that a moment hoped for, longed for, dreamt about for decades is blown away in an instant, ignominiously, to one's eternal sorrow. What had fallen into Cäcilie's lap remained denied to Rahel. Thus once again she succumbed to despondency, and nourished a renewed unspoken resistance against those Arnstein ladies whose wit fell so far below her own, yet whose demeanour and reputation, indeed whose happiness, so greatly surpassed her own influence and meagre portion of *joie de vivre*. When, shortly afterwards, Fanny came to Frankfurt with her sister, Rahel's reports to Varnhagen about her amiable hostess of Baden had once again taken on that mockingly captious tone which she and her husband adopted towards everyone who was outwardly more successful.

Meanwhile she proudly recorded how much she meant to Fanny: 'Frau von Arnstein writes to me constantly, most affectionately . . . Here you have the letters from mother and daughter, see how I stand with them . . . Frau von Arnstein, for instance, who writes to no one, announces that she is writing to me . . . Just now I have received again the most loving letters from Frau von Arnstein and Frau Ephraim.' And on 25 September the Viennese ladies had finally arrived in Frankfurt. Even through the light veil of ill-will in which Rahel now clothes Fanny's activities, one senses her appearance, already growing hazy, vanishing in a last breath of living presence:

> Frau von Arnstein came today; more unsettled, indeed I might say unhappier than ever; she wants to leave as early as the day after tomorrow. To Mainz, to Heidelberg, to anywhere, except only Paris; anything but to stay here, to see people! 'Dear child! I want peace and quiet, that is why I travel; who cares for landscapes?' In short, for someone who can observe her agitation without sympathy, it would be comical. The point is this: she can no longer remember why she undertook the troublesome journey; and she quite forgets Jette's pleasure. 'Why do you put up with all that in Paris?' and she asks this quite seriously. In a word, [she is] as you know her, except while travelling; and now I must be with her for two days; for her comfort; with her and Madame Ephraim.

To this description Varnhagen later added a few sidelights, as he had taken them from Rahel's oral rendering:

> Frau von Arnstein had hardly arrived in Frankfurt when she was already in complete despair as to how and where she should spend her day. She overwhelmed Rahel with her caresses and complaints, and when she saw Dore, she threw her arms around her neck, weeping, and crying repeatedly: 'Dore, dear Dore! can you not tell me why I went travelling! Oh do tell me, why am I travelling? Children, don't you know? I don't know the reason any more!' All of which was endlessly comical and yet incidentally truly sad to hear.

It was not a well-meaning report. But better than all the declarations of her admiring friends he conveys Fanny's particular charm, her changeable, sparkling moods, her childlike, yet not quite unconscious, indeed slightly affected state of distraction, the sudden alternation between laughter and weeping, the aura of this much preoccupied, absent-minded, and at the same time extravagantly affectionate woman – an expression of personality that she shared with many great ladies and women of talent or even genius. One can imagine her: slim and agile, the somewhat protuberant blue eyes still beautiful in the ageing face, her travelling gown fluttering about her, caressing Rahel, embracing Rahel's maid, demanding sympathy from all and sundry, confused, unsettled by an excess of social life, by her own restless temperament, then again enraptured by Rahel's dry wit, crying with laughter over the latter's *bons mots*, thirsting for peace, solitude, rest and yet irresistibly driven to make the round of the houses of Frankfurt, to run to the Otterstedts' and the Hügels', to Joseph Mendelssohn's wife, whose attire was insufferably Teutonic, to the Herz family, the

Jewish patricians transplanted here from Hamburg.

On one occasion, Rahel was unwelcome at the Hügels', which gave rise to even greater malice: 'Today I want to annoy other people, and not myself . . . The Hügels were so uncivil as not to invite me as well, when they invited the Arnsteins.' The next day, 30 September, was one of 'balmy weather', which helped Rahel to bear everything more easily, and in the morning at 8.30 she went once more 'to Frau von Arnstein, who was to leave at about 9, that is, nearly 10; great turmoil, almost merriment . . .'

A few days later:

> I have already had to reply to Frau von Arnstein, from whom I had just received a letter from Heidelberg; and how tenderly and severely she was already complaining that I did not write. There she saw Frau von Stägemann, who had made Goethe's acquaintance. Frau von Arnstein is waiting for her daughter, *au désespoir*, and somewhat ill . . .

Au désespoir, and somewhat ill! Thus we must leave Fanny. Now and then, only fleetingly and amorphously, she will appear again from the obscurity into which she has already slipped away. Her physical image fades. Even in public life she no longer takes up any space, no longer is room set aside for her, and world history is already rushing past her. What she thought of the strange, religious–moral Holy Alliance which Prussia had concluded in Paris with Austria and Russia, we do not know. How she felt about the new German Confederation and its constitution cobbled together in Vienna, in which the Biblical nation was cheated out of its so recently acquired freedom, we can only surmise. And yet, now that Prussia had regained her glory and was taking up her hegemony in Germany, while Austria, once the heart of the Holy Roman Empire, had turned into a separate multi-ethnic state, doomed sooner or later to disintegrate, she began to ponder once more over her double, indeed triple loyalty – as far as her restlessness allowed her time to do so!

Austria, Prussia, the Jews: the destiny of all these was now being determined anew. Humboldt's wife Caroline wrote that year: 'Austria is so diversely and heterogeneously mixed in its forces, in the nationalities of which it consists, that I would wager everything on its ceasing in this very century to be a German power. National *Deutschheit* is clearly still growing, and Austria is not keeping step.' On the one hand, a nation was confidently rising out of the European chaos of the past century. On the other, a conglomerate of peoples, straining asunder, were being held together by police power and lulled by the foolish illusion that the superficial enjoyment of life was a sufficient substitute for intellectual and political freedom. It was a frivolous system which might last for a while. 'It will just see out me and Metternich,' said Gentz, or in other words: *après nous le déluge.* In the midst of their wine-bibbing and guzzling of roast chicken, the Austrians did not notice with what cynicism their future was being neglected and left to the blindness of providence.

The Viennese were the last to notice. Their particular atmosphere, that 'element in which the days drift away here; the genial sensuality directed towards robust enjoyment, the strongly appealing love of jests and laughter, the cheerful good nature nourished by a life of ease, the half-Italian indolence and the half-Italian capriciousness which goes with it', which Varnhagen had observed during the Congress, had even intensified since the Congress's end. The Emperor – 'Papa François', as Napoleon and Alexander of Russia had called him – kept his Viennese in chains of roses, under which the iron fetters were concealed. But they went carefree about their business, averted their gaze if a disturbance should break out anywhere and the grenadiers take some rebellious Slav, Italian or liberal student into custody, and knelt down in unbounded servility if an archduke rode past. The Jews meanwhile flocked to 'grow into' them, to become like these who spent their days on earth in so cheerful a manner.

Why indeed should they hold out further against a people, a government, which accepted them with open arms as soon as they had thrown off their old worn-out religion, indeed, which no longer even bore them ill-will if they persisted in their religion, as long as their general way of life was not at variance with the prevailing one? During those unfree but light-hearted years of the Biedermeier, in this Viennese *Vormärz* or pre-revolutionary epoch, in which every new idea, every modern opinion was tabooed and exposed to persecution, a more friendly attitude towards the Jews had become general. Not that this was based in any way on law! The request of the five petitioners had been greeted with neither agreement nor refusal. A commission set up by the Emperor under the title *Zentralorganisierungs-Hofkommission* (Court Commission for Central Organisation) had been instructed to work out the principles of an egalitarian and liberal treatment of the Jews in the federal state. This task had been shelved and the Commission managed to nourish and spin out the conflict of opinions in such a way that its disunity offered the Emperor sufficient occasion to apply to this case his well-loved policy of procrastination.

So the old state of outlawry continued – no naturalisation, no permission to own land, no community life, and no residence without tolerance money! But since in Austria everything forbidden by the authorities was at the same time allowed, since the severity of every government ordinance was always softened by *Schlamperei* (sloppiness), the Jews of Vienna during the *Vormärz* lived in a more salutary atmosphere than ever before, or frequently since. Between toleration and naturalisation there was a fundamental, yet not continuously perceptible gap. As far as house-purchase was concerned, the authorities often turned a blind eye to it – as, for example, in the case of the unbaptised silk-merchant Isaac Löw Hofmann, who owned a freehold farm at Perchtolds-dorf, or that of the Arnsteins who not only owned a country house, but also soon acquired, even if they did not occupy, certain buildings in the outskirts of the city. Finally the Jews had been permitted to form the nucleus of a community in the Seitenstettengasse where, in the former Dempfingerhof, an infirmary, a Hebrew seminary, a prayer-room and a women's bath-house were being established. The influx of new immigrants was, however, not perhaps entirely welcome to the Jews of Vienna themselves.

And so, as it were underhandedly, a situation had been created which was hardly unfavourable any more compared with the Prussian one. The 160 tolerated families of the capital could hope with time to merge ever more closely, and probably one day with legal authority, with their compatriots. By now the more prosper-ous among them were no longer exposed to mockery or insult, and even the poor and the orthodox, who still kept themselves separate in their clothing and customs, thereby giving occasion for ridicule, knew that their incorporation into Christian society depended upon themselves and was possible, if desired. Much the same went for the provincial Jews and those of other Austrian territories, even for the most wretched of them in Bukovina, in Hungary and Galicia. The best surety for an unhindered completion of their emancipa-tion seemed to lie in the fact that the stern, indeed ever more cruel Metternich, for whatever reasons, was well-disposed towards them. Even this would not have helped if the people had continued to be hostile to them. But the people, in their well-fed, sleepy Biedermeier fashion, were inclined to live and let live. The Viennese of all classes of society had watched the children of the Old Testament coming to resemble them more and more, and they did not oppose what was so near to their own likeness.

Fanny had contributed decisively to this transformation of atti-tudes. According to the already well-known words of Varnhagen 'the free, respected position, removed from the constraint of prejudice, which the adherents of the Mosaic faith have enjoyed and now enjoy in Vienna was quite undeniably won only with and through the influence and activity of Frau von Arnstein'. It was the finest obituary, it was the justification of her whole existence that was here pronounced.

In Germany, even in her beloved Prussia, things were otherwise. Here, now that the state of Frederick the Great once more sat victorious in the saddle, a new wave of anti-Semitism was breaking out. A professor who occupied the chair of history in Humboldt's newly founded university, Friedrich Rühs, had in February 1815 published a pamphlet, *Jewish Claims to German Civic Rights*, in which he advised the reversal of all the newest reforms and the reintroduction of protection money and special distinguishing marks. With the same methodology which had been applied for more than four decades to the improvement of the Jews' civic circumstances, this educator of youth now dedicated himself to the justification of its opposite. His pamphlet met with approval. Arnim's 'Christian-German Dining Society' had long been out of bounds to 'women, Frenchmen, Philistines and Jews'. For the Romantic Teutomaniacs who had been kindled by Fichte's concept of the state, the renewed rejection of their alien fellow-citizens became a commandment.

Not only at Humboldt's university, but even in his immediate circle the new ideas were gaining ground. A few days after the end of the Congress, Varnhagen wrote from Paris to Rahel:

I find Frau von Humboldt very much altered in her character; she must have been following the example of bad lovers, at least she shares the un-German Germanness and the un-Christian Christianity which are now in vogue, together with her daughters. She hates the French with the fury of a Schleiermacher, the Jews, etc., and always likes only individuals. I have observed with sadness how dreadful and abominable are the prejudices which one can denote as aristocratism, since even the best are corrupted, infected and ruined by them.

Dreadful and abominable prejudices were now rife not only among the nobility, which had once been the first connecting link between the Jews and society. The Prussian people too, stirred up by new voices of mockery and contempt, turned against those who for so long had been allowed to live peaceably among them. How many years earlier was it that 'the sage Mendelssohn's fellow-believers' had begun to be 'prized at higher rate by wise Berlin'?

Now, in the same National Theatre in which the actor Fleck had once spoken his Enlightenment-inspired prologue to *The Merchant of Venice*, a common farce, written in ridicule of the Jews by a deceased Breslauer, entitled *Unser Verkehr (Our Social Circles)*, was after some resistance allowed to be staged. Varnhagen, who reported this first to Rahel and later in his memoirs, was shocked to the core of his being.

He found the event:

> very unseemly at that time and in the capital city where the Jews vied gloriously with the other inhabitants in sacrifices offered and in their personal eagerness to take up arms, a number of Jews became officers or won the Iron Cross, and were now again opposing the foe in battle. But a pride which put on superior airs, which pretended to be Christian, was stirring, and on many sides there was unconcealed pleasure in seeing a troublesome class of fellow-citizens deeply wounded in their feelings and humiliated. The Chancellor, to whom appeal was made at the right moment, had the performance prohibited . . . There was now a great uproar about this in the city, people cried that Hardenberg was assuming a power which was not his by right, he was restricting freedom, and even such people who did not support the views of the wretched play, indeed who should have hissed it off the stage, violently condemned the prohibition. Here was matter for melancholy observations; Ölsner said it showed at what a low stage of the development of freedom the people of Berlin still were: no one was interested in the freedom of the press, no one in public proceedings, one put up with the unconditional exercise of power by the police, but when the freedom of despicable mockery on the stage was justifiably forbidden, the common and the high-born mob all cried out as though one were wantonly attacking their special privileges!

Stägemann too, who had once already, when Achim von Arnim expressed himself offensively in the presence of Moritz Itzig, publicly taken the part of the Jews, reminded the Berliners of the recent past.

> He said that if the bloody shades of Moritz Itzig and of Hauschildt, who fell in battle at Lützen, should become visible in the audience, the latter would soon lose their taste for this crude entertainment. Many of our most respected men spoke with the same indignation. For the moment, indeed, good sense prevailed. But some time after the Chancellor's departure the opposing faction nevertheless managed to have the farce performed, and a not unskilled, but deeply vulgar comedian by the name of Wurm celebrated his worthy triumph in it!

In the rest of Germany there was no reputation for particular tolerance to be lost. Of all the regions formerly sympathising with Napoleon or occupied by him, which were now relying on the sophistry of the Confederation's constitution in order to revoke the rights of the Jews, the Hanseatic communities dealt most severely with them. In Hamburg the Jewish community fell back into its old condition within a self-governed city, without retaining its former privileges. Bremen, the city of Senator Smidt, drove out its few Jews without further ado. And Lübeck, which had provided them with an advocate, also turned them out of its gates and left only one protected Jew with his family remaining from the pre-French time.

In Frankfurt the first action to be taken, as early as July 1815, was to deprive the dismissed police actuary, Ludwig Baruch (Börne), of a pension. At the same time it was decided to obtain a judicial opinion from three universities as to whether the civic rights granted to the local Jewry by the former Grand Duke should be recognised by the present government or not. Before these judgements had been received, the Jews were excluded in October from participation in townspeople's meetings, a number of trades and businesses were forbidden to them, their applications to be married were refused with medieval heartlessness, they were driven out of certain parts of the city and generally treated as though they were still minions. Hardenberg and Metternich, who had probably not realised until weeks after the end of the Congress how skilfully Senator Smidt and his Bavarian and Saxon helpers had rendered vain their own efforts on behalf of the Jews, tried to exercise their influence on the Frankfurt senate. When this proved ineffective, the community of that city prepared a memorandum for the assembly of the German Confederation, which had met on 3 November. Its author was young Börne. But the Bundestag's decision was delayed for as long as that of Francis's *Zentralorganisierungs-Hofkommission*, and it took years before a more favourable solution was found at least for Frankfurt.

Meanwhile further poison was being brewed in every quarter of Germany. In the summer of 1816, a physician and professor of natural science in Heidelberg, Friedrich Fries, published a treatise, *Threat to the Welfare and Character of the Germans by the Jews*, in which he recommended exterminating this people, root and branch. Not just an occasional teacher but even the student body, usually so full of grand speeches about freedom and human rights, turned in their 'Teutomania' – Gentz's word! – against the tribe which had lived in their midst since Roman times. The academics in their *Wichs*, the student garb copied from the uniform of the

Lützow volunteer corps, who declared battle against government tyranny on the Wartburg at the end of 1817, called themselves, and probably were, Heralds of the Revolution in Germany. But at the same time they were marching, with faces forward, back into the Middle Ages, and no power on earth seemed able to stop them. Börne, who as a youth in the house of Henriette Herz had inhaled the last breath of the German Enlightenment, who for a few years had been stirred in Frankfurt by the intoxication of total equality of rights, turned his sorrow into wild lamentations. The hero in one of his novels, a Jewish officer, voiced his own bitter disappointment:

> You have stolen the games of my childhood, you evil scoundrels! You have thrown salt into the sweet cup of youth. You ask me why I flee my fatherland? I have none, yet I have never seen a foreign land. Where there are dungeons I recognise my native land; where I find persecution, I breathe the air of my childhood. The moon is as near to me as Germany.

Reaction was moving ever faster. In Prussia the ageing Hardenberg could not prevent his benign law from becoming a dead letter; through all the loopholes it contained a new coercion emerged, and everything for which express permission had been accidentally forgotten was now forbidden with the greatest severity. Even the designation 'Jew' was re-introduced in public documents; no new settlers were allowed in towns where there had previously been none; moving from one province to another was forbidden; and in Poznań the purchase of houses, residence in the country and free practice of trades were forbidden. In the Rhineland, which had been won by the decree of the Congress of Vienna, they had even newly confirmed a restrictive edict from the last, no longer pro-Jewish years of Napoleon, although in all the other regions on the left bank of the Rhine – just as in the France of the restored Bourbons – the Jews had been allowed to retain the total freedom they had won in the Revolution. Long before the spirit of tolerance vanished from Prussia together with Hardenberg, the new intolerance had begun in this state. It was again, in Klopstock's phrase, 'rattling its chain around the wretches', as it had before the times of Joseph II.

In the spring of 1819, a mentally disturbed young man who was a member of the group of activists called the *Unbedingten* (the 'Unconditionals') broke into the bedroom of the dramatist Kotzebue and stabbed him to death because he was receiving money from Russia for minor confidential political reports – a long-standing favoured source of income for German writers. The execution of the murderer Karl Ludwig Sand became a storm-signal. By making him the martyr of their national movement, the *Deutschtümler* or Teutomaniacs were announcing that their 'Christian hate will call down the Day of Judgement upon the Jews, the accomplices of profiteering'. In Würzburg, at the University, the first cries of 'Juda verrecke' (Judaism must perish) were heard. Shops were broken into, Jewish fellow-citizens mistreated and 400 of these finally driven out of the town. The persecution continued in Bamberg and was taken up throughout Franconia, in Bayreuth and Meiningen, Darmstadt and Karlsruhe, Düsseldorf and finally Hamburg. All summer the anti-Jewish riots raged, stirred up by students and petty bourgeois, quelled at last by the town council with an order for the expulsion of the Jews. As in ancient times one saw figures drifting like the Wandering Jew through the German dominions and resting in open fields with what possessions they had with difficulty rescued. In Frankfurt, too, Jewish houses were destroyed. While James Rothschild received the great world at a ball in Paris, his residence at home was invaded and plundered. In Heidelberg it would likewise have come to acts of violence, had not the students, led by the two upright professors Daub and Thibaut, themselves protected the defenceless.

Now a flood of pamphlets poured out, such as had once before welled up at the beginning of the century, but not then spread more widely. In November 1819 a *Judenspiegel* ('Mirror of the Jews') appeared, from the hand of a man calling himself 'Grattenauer II'. No such malicious attacks had been mounted since the inflammatory writings of Pfefferkorn, Margaritha and Carben in the days of Charles V. But, of course, there had not been such a general and bloody persecution of the Jews on German soil since the Middle Ages! And the worst of it was that it could no longer be averted by baptism. When Dr Koreff, a co-founder of the Romantic movement, a physician, man of the world, member of the Serapion brotherhood and friend of beautiful ladies, was made professor of medicine in 1816 at the instigation of Hardenberg, neither his Christianity nor the Iron Cross which he had received for his valour in the war of independence was able to prevent the hate-filled resistance against his appointment.

This too happened at the University of Berlin, the institution which had been intended as an immortalisation in stone of enlightened science. But even its founder, the great Humboldt, who had with his brother Alexander been a protector of the Jews since his childhood, now seemed tempted to lay down his arms. He wrote to his wife at this time:

> I can imagine your hatred of the Jews. It has everything which new Christians actually believe in. And I resign myself to being the loser where the old faith is concerned, one cannot prevail against it. In fact I only like the Jews *en masse*; *en détail* I avoid them.

And finally he confessed to Brinckmann his change of heart, for which he gave a strange justification:

> I have very much withdrawn from the Jews. Not that I share the present fury against them, rather that is one of the things that the newer sect holds against me. But I maintain that no more real Jews are being born. They all come into the world with a bit of Christianity about them, and the old ones are disappearing one by one.

So it all ended – the proud humanism, the bright beacon of the Enlightenment, the appeal of Lessing, Mendelssohn and Kant to reason and human dignity – in a relapse into dark primeval instinct, an escape into misled and misleading emotions. The Jews themselves, in their compassionate Romantic enthusiasm and genuine love for a fatherland which they believed to be theirs, had helped to prepare the ground in which this seed was nurtured. Rahel, horrified at the fury against the Jews, wrote to her brother:

> I am infinitely sad, as I have never been before. Because of the Jews. They want to keep them; but in order to torture them, to despise them, to kick them and throw them downstairs . . . the hypocritical new love for the Christian religion (God forgive me my sin), for the Middle Ages with its art, its writing and its horrors, spurs the people on to the only horror to which, reminded of past experiences, they can still be spurred on.

Rahel was still there to experience that bloody summer and to see the edifice of her patriotism fall into ruins. Fanny, who had fought for the Prussian cause long before her and with greater vigour, was spared the worst. The cries of hate which rang out for the first time at the University of Würzburg in August 1819, and soon afterwards found an echo throughout Germany, no longer reached her ears.

Did she realise in her last years what a chimera she had been pursuing? Or did she believe the new delusive madness of the

Germans to be a temporary one, and persist in an allegiance which had been self-evident to her all her life? The temptation suggested itself, now that the tumult in her own soul was subsiding and she felt a great weakness coming upon her, to turn to all those things which she had always esteemed rather lightly while she was achieving them. The frivolous, compromise-loving charm of the Viennese, that soft and indulgent character which had so often irritated Fanny in her husband and had in general given her occasion for impatience, the slackness and shapelessness of conversations, the deliberate meaninglessness of polite phrases, the graceful shrug with which one excused onself from ever expressing a decided opinion, the smiling lie with which one got rid of uncomfortable facts, the shying away from any irrevocable deed – now she might have begun to appreciate their value. Here there were no 'Unconditionals', in either a good or a bad sense. Anyone who saw in Prussia the noblest intentions, which had been seriously and systematically defended, transformed into their opposites, must be much more, and more sincerely, attached to an Austria which did not set up rules of conduct in the first place, in order not to have to break them.

But was she so attached? One would like to think so. For what Fanny had until now neglected in a life full of turmoil, full of people, travel, art, music and politics, had now been given to her. At last she had time to come to herself and to her senses – to get to the root of certain matters which she had hardly ever thought through. She had returned from her last journey to the Rhine and to Italy in poor health. The Viennese disease, which here took hold of everyone, high or low, young or old, flared up in her. The damp houses, the eternal wind blowing from the woods, the constant dust of the capital affected her lungs. Fanny had always been *poitrinaire*, suffering from a weak chest, like Emperor Joseph and his first consort, like Empress Maria Ludovica, and like the little Duke of Reichstadt, Napoleon's son. The restlessness by which she was so frequently pursued, her hectic activity were probably also due to this. Even in the poem Alxinger dedicated to her in earlier days, her ill-health was mentioned. In her wills she constantly foresaw an early death. But so little attention had she ever paid to her malady, so little had she spared herself on its account, that it was only now, when she could no longer deny it, that it gained the mystery over her thoughts and actions.

Lying on a *chaise-longue*, in the garden at the Braunhirschengrund or in her park at Baden, above her the mild sunlight of these wide spaces, around her a landscape deep in a Biedermeier sleep, she reflected once more on the relationships of her life. Not her tragic love affair with young Liechtenstein – there was nothing to be added to or taken away from that; it was an unalterable part of her past. But her persistence in the old faith, her passion for Prussia, her furious hatred of France and her always a little condescending, always a little superior relationship with Austria needed to be examined. Did they still stand up to the light of the present day, or even to the prospect of eternity? Presumably Fanny now felt she had much for which to apologise to her second home; she had, after all, to thank it for an existence in which the feeling of well-being far outweighed the times of discomfort. Towards the French people, who had freed the Jews as much as a quarter of a century earlier, even towards Napoleon, who had brought emancipation with him in his triumphant progress through Germany, she was probably, upon quieter reflection, more charitably inclined. But to tear from her heart her love of Prussia, let alone her religion, certainly did not now enter her head. Her undiminished inclination was towards a Berlin which had been wise and magnanimous and might become so again, in which the heritage of the Enlightenment had perhaps been cast away, but not destroyed for ever. To preserve this faith it was necessary for her also to hold true to the faith of her fathers. If Lessing's *Nathan* was to be honoured again by posterity, then a mother must be allowed to remain Jewish, her daughter to become Christian, without there being any difference in piety between the two.

Strangely, the only letter from Fanny to survive to our own time was written, on 26 December 1816, to the 'Honorary Representatives of the tolerated Israelites in Vienna'. Neither before nor since had she found it necessary to assure her community that she was still one of their number. Indeed, she had spent more time in churches and cathedrals, in convents and hospitals staffed by nuns than in a prayer-house of the Mosaic confession. Now she dictated to her maid or her foster-daughter Marianne a few lines which signified neither more nor less than a proof of loyalty:

Gentlemen! I should have thanked you earlier for your obliging letter of the 17th instant and for the kind remarks contained therein, had not an indisposition requiring rest kept me to my bed. I can now no longer delay communicating my feelings to you through the pen of another: how happy I feel when I am in a position to be able to do something for the suffering humanity to whom you so efficaciously dedicate your active concern; how ready I shall be in the future to do everything in my power, if you will lay claim to my good will; and how sincere are the expressions of esteem with which I have the honour to remain, gentlemen, your devoted servant, Fanny Freyin v. Arnstein Itzig.

In the following year, she was probably not constantly bedridden, for the Danish national poet Adam Öhlenschläger, when visiting Vienna during the summer, found the ladies of Barons Arnstein and Eskeles 'at her pretty country-house in Hietzing . . . very cultured and full of love of poetry'. Fanny had gathered up her strength once more in order to entertain a distinguished foreigner. Nevertheless, Öhlenschläger noted neither her name nor any further remarks about her appearance in his memorandum book. The last recorded utterance of our heroine, by that time already deceased, is reported by Countess Thürheim, a talkative lady of the high nobility, to whom we owe particularly informative memoirs from the times of Joseph II and Francis I. At the end of 1817, after a little disquisition about the blessings of Christianity she wrote:

> And yet there are people who do not even superficially touch upon such serious considerations. The other day, for instance, someone said to Frau Arnstein, a Jewess, that she should have herself baptised, as the rest of her family had already done. 'No,' she replied naïvely, 'I am too old.' At all events she saw in this change of faith nothing else but what her *soi-disant* converted parents [*sic!*] had seen, namely a way of increasing her fortune.

So different does the world appear to us sometimes! But how should the good Lulu Thürheim know what considerations, by no means naïve, lay behind Fanny's attitude? At least her love for Prussia was no longer held against her, even if, in the evening of her life, she was now considered only *scandaleusement juive*. She wished to be so even in death, and had some time ago taken care of this. Her nephew Leopold von Herz, Metternich's friend, was to arrange her funeral according to the custom of the Old Testament. And this he did, afterwards himself converting to Christianity. A year before the German persecution of the Jews, which presumably influenced Herz's decision, Fanny lay upon her deathbed. In the early summer of 1818, with her sixtieth birthday only a few months away, at the Braunhirschengrund, she had become ill with a 'suppuration of the lungs' by which she, as her brothers and sisters wrote in an obituary in the *Königlich-private Berlinische Zeitung*, 'was instantly fatally attacked'. She died on 8 June. Her sarcophagus was set up in the new Jewish cemetery at Währing which Nathan had helped to found in 1784. Her funeral rites, conducted by Herz Homberg, the friend of Mendelssohn and Wessely and religious representative of the Berlin Enlightenment in Vienna, took place ten days later at the prayer-house in the Seitenstettengasse.

With funeral hymns and music, with psalms and prayers, she was commemorated according to ancient ritual. Herz Homberg spoke the fourth verse of Psalm 84: 'Yea, the sparrow hath found an house, and the swallow a nest for herself, where she may lay her young, even thine altars, O Lord of hosts, my King, and my God.' And he said in his address:

She was a refuge in the times of affliction; in the times of the all-destroying war. How did not her sense of citizenship manifest itself then, her love of her country, and her active zeal to do all she could to heal the wounds of sufferers and to support energetically the defence of the imperial state! She was a refuge in the times of affliction; in the years of the bad harvest. The magnanimity with which she rescued thousands from the evils of starvation was that of a queen.

Her tomb bore the words:

Wie im Leben allgemein verehrt
So im Tode allgemein beweint
Den Armen Mutter –
Gleich groß an Kopf und Herz
Ihr Name ist ihre schönste Grabschrift.

[Mourned by all in death / As she was respected by all in life, / A mother to the poor – / Equally great in head and heart / Her name is her finest epitaph.]

So she had departed from the temporal world, as had the era to which she had belonged. Her life had lasted exactly as long as emancipation in Germany. And German emancipation had disappeared with her from the face of the earth. Many others who had experienced the transformation from the enlightenment of the spirit to the new darkening of feeling also made their exit: Sonnenfels and Madame de Staël shortly before her, Hardenberg a few years later. She was the only one among the women of Berlin for whom the Old Testament dirge was still sung. Sophie Grotthuss, Dorothea Mendelssohn and Rahel had all been baptised long ago. Now Henriette Herz's conversion took place – not long after Fanny's death! But the next generation had become totally Christian: all her brothers' and sisters' children, soon her Viennese nephew Leopold too, Marianne Saaling, even Ludwig Börne, who 'did not wish his well-aimed arrows to be checked by the prejudice that it was a Jewish marksman who shot them'.

Only fellow-believers had accompanied Fanny on her last journey;

her daughter, her grandchildren were denied access to the prayer-house and the cemetery. Indeed, Henriette's own resting-place was to be far from hers – in the Pereira family vault on the estate of Schwarzenau, in the reddish glow of the ever-burning light that reminds the devout of the blood of the Redeemer. At the price of such an outward separation Fanny had set an example. The meaning of her sacrifice became clearly evident when Nathan, donating a precious curtain for the Ark of the Covenant to his community in Fanny's memory, wrote in his accompanying letter:

> To contribute to good works for the outer splendour of our house of God and for the glorification of the Creator is the duty of every feeling person. And if my late wife lived according to these principles, if I follow her example and my inward voice in this, I may assure you at the same time that my daughter, inspired by the same principles, will never differentiate on the grounds of religion, will according to her powers give comfort and alms to those in need of help, whatever faith they may profess, and so always remain worthy of her unforgettable mother.

The mantle was now to descend upon Henriette. But however gentle and kind-hearted she was, still quite under Fanny's spell, she nevertheless already belonged to a world which no longer had any interest in the equality of all religions before God. Her mother, in her final will, had bequeathed the same sum of 5,000 gulden to the 'Israelite hospital and to the worthy *Elisabethinerinnen*'. When she herself, four decades later, made her last will and testament in the name of the triune God, to whose mercy she commended her soul, she left substantial sums to the *Elisabethinerinnen*, to the Sisters of Mercy or *Soeurs grises*, the Sisters of the Holy Redeemer, the *Maria Elisabeth Verein*, the Society of Jesus as well as to the poor on her estates, to all her staff, which no longer included any Jews, and to two Christian god-daughters – but not a penny to any Jewish charity, unless to those which she still administered on behalf of her parents.

In other ways, too, she was hardly suited to carry on Fanny's influence and activities. Indeed, intimidated by her mother's over-powering personality, she herself hardly had the confidence to be able to take up Fanny's position in life. At first she did have some thoughts of doing so, and initiated her cousin Lea Mendelssohn-Bartholdy into her plans. Lea had adored Fanny, called her daughter after her, brought her four-year-old son Felix to his aunt Arnstein, who grew fond of him; and she was so shocked by the news of Fanny's death that ten days later she suffered a miscarriage.

Now she again conjured up Fanny's image:

> She was inexpressibly dear and admirable to me; her reflected splendour seemed to shine upon me too, I was proud to be related to her and to be able to boast of her love. It is for me as though Vienna's bright sun has set, the shimmering glory departed! What a mother have you lost, you poor creature! Never, probably, has the passing of a woman caused a greater sensation. She was the most interesting woman in Europe, a miraculous phenomenon in our stupid, egoistic times.

Yet it was just for this reason that Lea doubted that Henriette would be able to replace her: 'God preserve in you your noble, strong feelings and your fine intentions,' she wrote. 'In this way your actions will most worthily honour and praise the departed. But have you, my dear child, after the first transport of emotion, which seems to give us strength for a new existence, really considered carefully what it would mean to take up a totally altered way of life?' Would she above all summon up the courage, the patience and the endurance, Lea asked, to lead that tiring existence which the custom and the connections of her father demanded, to 'do the honours of the noisy paternal house', since she 'had always shown an aversion to it', and her 'plan of education' for her daughter could not be reconciled with such a role?

She was right. Henriette knew it well and resolved not to take more upon herself than her mother's benevolent care for the poor and sick. She took her place in the committee of twelve ladies of the nobility, superintended the Marienspital (Hospital of the Virgin Mary) at Baden, and, as Caroline Pichler reported, with her father annually donated substantial sums to people in need. To practise the same degree of hospitality, to be the centre of a large and glittering circle, was not her role in life. As a mature woman she was probably still a little helpless, a little gauche, with a sweet childlike quality. At the time of the Congress, while dancing with Prince Dietrichstein at a ball in the Geymüller house, she had become entangled in the folds of her gown and fallen at full length to the ground with her partner. It was a mishap which could never have befallen the ladylike Fanny, but was more likely in her shy daughter, who would rather sit communing with herself at the piano or listen attentively with a few friends to a young writer reading his plays.

The social life in the Grünangergasse, at Baden and in the Braunhirschengrund became more muted, dedicated much more than before to art, music and unpretentious entertainment. At the Neuburgerhof the nearly deaf Beethoven, who had been scared off by noisier assemblies, played to Clementi's pupil on her pianoforte and showed his gratitude for the help her father had conferred upon him years earlier. Grillparzer came, introduced by his uncle Sonnleithner or by Caroline Pichler, cracked almonds with Henriette and, in June 1820, dedicated to her two poems, 'Das Vielliebchen in der Doppelmandel' ('The Philippina in the Double Almond') and 'Das elegante Frühstück im Kuhstall' ('The Elegant Breakfast in the Cowshed'). Twenty years later the novelist Adalbert Stifter was to meet him at her *Geist-Salon* ('Salon of Kindred Spirits') and admire in him a modesty, calmness and goodness which is possessed only by true genius. At Baden Henriette's young cousin Felix Mendelssohn appeared, to whom Caroline Pichler ascribed an exceptional talent for composition, praiseworthy execution and a corresponding simplicity. Foreigners, too, were seen at her house, such as the English eccentric James Holman, who travelled the whole of Europe 'in total blindness' and made the acquaintance in Baroness Pereira of 'an accomplished woman, well acquainted with English language and literature'. Field-Marshal Radetzky sought her out. And finally, when Goethe's daughter-in-law Ottilie spent some years in Vienna, Henriette became the best friend of this original woman.

Frau von Goethe left behind some notes which bring to life the Pereira house around the year 1840. The noble connections of her son- and daughter-in-law, her old friend Countess Engel and the connoisseur of art Prince Fritz Schwarzenberg frequented Henriette's house just as freely as her cousin 'Frl. Epraihm' [*sic*]. Every Friday was an 'artists' soirée'. Grillparzer, though he came less and less often, or Freiherr von Feuchtersleben took Ottilie in to dinner. The ladies Julie Rettich and Auguste Brede, or Heinrich Anschütz, of the Hofburgtheater, were guests no less honoured than the painters Schwind, Schnorr and Amerling or the portraitists Daffinger and Kriehuber. Occasionally a son of Mozart's was present – it may have been Wolfgang, the musician – and once Liszt appeared for a few minutes. The mood was often merry, as when Frau von Münk, who had occasioned jollity many years ago at Baden, read the jokes in the Post Office annual. But often Baroness Pereira was indisposed, would not admit Ottilie when the latter wished to visit her, and next day as a consolation sent her an invitation to her box at the opera, the 'Burg' or the Theater am Kärntnertor. She would rather have invited the Kammerrätin Goethe to see her alone, but unexpected visitors always interrupted the tête-à-tête. Once they succeeded in telling each other 'in great confidence much night gossip from our lives', and she even lent Körner's little green book to Ottilie, who examined it 'at home with most devout attention'. For the most part, however, more company appeared at her Fridays than might have been pleasant to Henriette, and so she seemed, as Ottilie noted, from time to time 'very preoccupied'.

Even so the tradition was preserved for a while, if in more modest fashion. And if one were to bemoan the passing of all the splendid banquets, the receptions day after day, the balls, suppers and soirées for which all Vienna had gathered in Fanny's apartments, one might as well mourn the way of the world in general. For the 'golden age of the salon' now began to give way to the 'silver age of the literary coffee-houses and societies'. Poets were no longer intent on shining in society, they began to shun the light, trusted no one and fled from censorship to sheltered spots – to satire, like Nestroy, to the magical farce like Raimund, to nature like Stifter, or into their own four walls like Grillparzer, who buried his works in the drawer of his desk. Even Caroline Pichler, whose gatherings were always a little prosaic, finally complained about the dearth of salons, blaming the great quantity of coffee-houses, restaurants, assembly-rooms and public gardens. Meanwhile she stayed faithful to Henriette, formed a 'little Baden coterie' with her, drank with her on 23 September to the memory of 'our dear Körner', on which occasion they both agreed 'that probably apart from her and me, no one else would have given a thought to Körner's birthday', nurtured other old memories with her and began to avoid her house only when Henriette's children grew up and married, and a new young world was romping around her which was foreign and even distasteful to Caroline. She wrote to her friend Dorothea Schlegel:

> What formerly appealed to me there has gradually disappeared, through death, distance, changed circumstances . . . In this circle one has now completely adopted the way of life of the *haute volée*. One dines at half-past five, gathers for tea at about half-past eight, then sits in the salon, without any general conversation giving us the impression that anyone is concerned about our entertainment; rather, the lady of the house is there like any other stranger and leaves it to her guests to amuse themselves here and there as best they can, for which purpose journals, portfolios containing etchings, keepsakes and so on lie upon the table. But this is simply not my style, and the division of time is not agreeable either to Pichler or myself at our advanced age.

When she uttered this lament, the 'good Emperor Francis' had just gone to his grave, leaving the throne to his more kindly, but somewhat simple son Ferdinand. Eighteen years after Fanny's death things looked no different in Austria from the way they were in her lifetime; the same pressure from the authorities still reigned here, as did the 'clever leading by the nose' and 'lulling to sleep of the noblest powers' which had enraged Ernst Moritz Arndt at the beginning of Francis's reign. If Caroline Pichler thought that for this reason nothing in private life ought to have changed either, this was a false conclusion such as one often draws in old age.

For the Arnsteins, however, too much had changed for Fanny's tradition not to become threadbare and finally break off altogether. Her daughter's marriage deteriorated more and more: 'Henriette a pris son mari en dédain,' said a family letter of the early 1820s. Pereira became unbearable, stingy, eccentric, neglected his business, collected property, acquired, like his father Eliseus, one estate after another (at the end of his life he was lord of Schwarzenau and Allentsteig, of Erlakloster, Dobra, Wetzlas, Tiefenbach, Krumau, Neudegg and Waldreichs on a high hill); in eating, drinking, riding and talking he knew neither moderation nor boundary, could order his carriage at two in the morning and drive to Erla 'pour y planter dans douze jours un jardin', plagued his wife and children with his moods and headstrong ideas, and in a word was 'incorrigible', as Henriette herself wrote in the end to her sons. They, however, and even more her pretty little Flora, were to a certain extent a comfort to her, if not an unqualified one. Her eldest, Louis, took a Freiin von Diller as his wife. August married a Countess Amadé de Varkony, and Flora was to marry a younger son of the recently ruined Count Fries, of whom Caroline 'heard nothing but good', but whom Henriette found unhandsome, with a disagreeable voice and no more than plain common sense.

Not an unqualified comfort! For Freiin von Diller became sickly and finally died childless, whereupon a Countess Larisch became Louis' second wife. Adolph, the second son, was also in poor health and slipped early out of this world without giving her a grandchild. And, finally, August too prematurely followed his brother, after Seraphine Amadé had given him five children. None of her sons was to survive Henriette! All this sorrow, present and anticipated, constantly overshadowed her days, so that one could hardly reproach her for being often 'very preoccupied' or forgetting to enliven her guests. When August became engaged, she wrote to him: 'Your father is more moved than I have ever seen him, he weeps at every moment, *il paroit que nous avons changé de rôle.*' And she implored him: 'Be faithful to each other in trust and love. Avoid the great world, it is commonly the grave of happiness and of harmony and gives us nothing in return for the joys of which it robs us.'

Nathan, too, robbed of his beloved, though intimidating companion, went into a decline after her death. 'Your father has not known misfortune until today, and now this heavy blow!' Lea had cried out sympathetically at the time. 'I know how much he was enslaved in heart and mind and all his senses to this enchantress, and can judge how infinite must be his sorrow.' Well, outwardly one would not have noticed it. He continued to live, to gamble, gave up his town house and lived at his daughter's or in the country, went to the theatre almost every evening, retired completely from all business activity and, after Charles XIV had bestowed on him in 1824 the knightly cross of the order of Vasa, relinquished the Swedish consulship to Pereira. He also gradually reduced his expenditure – since he had ceased to be a merchant, Henriette complained, it was difficult to get money out of him. Cards remained his favorite pastime. At Baden Varnhagen saw him, now at an advanced age, sitting at a game with Countess Fekete, 'a couple of such a strangely fairy-tale appearance that one could easily believe they had been sitting there in this way for a hundred years, and could sit for another hundred'. And he loved above all to visit old friends and relatives, where he was left in peace at the ombre table, while the rest of the company surged through the other rooms.

He also at times attended dinner-parties. In early 1829, on such an occasion, he was encountered by old Hofrat Gentz, who had not entered his house for a quarter of a century. 'At Frau von Neuwall's (daughter of my friend Herz),' reads an entry for 9 January in the latter's journal, 'ate with a great party of bankers, among whom were Rothschild, Arnstein, Eskeles, Sina, the Liebenbergs, Löwenthals, etc.' And the following December: 'At eight to Frau von Neuwall, where I expected an intimate little soirée, instead of which I found a rout of more than a hundred persons, which gave me but little pleasure. I had meanwhile to consent to an ombre party with Baron Arnstein, Herr von Neuwall and Käser, which luckily was over by eleven.'

Not only the lives of Nathan and his daughter had changed against the constant background of the *Vormärz*. The destiny of the banking house of Arnstein & Eskeles too now took a different, disturbing turn. Even Cäcilie's wise husband had not been able to prevent the firm from irresistibly losing its pre-eminence. 'Do not forsake Arnstein,' Fanny had cried out to him in her will, 'be his inseparable friend, make Frau von Eskeles as happy as she deserves

to be, and I will lay myself down calmly to sleep my long sleep.'
Had she known what was now to happen, her sleep would have
been badly disturbed! For a new financier had appeared, made of
slyer, more ruthless stuff than the upright Bernhard and good-
natured Nathan. His name has already been dropped in Gentz's
journal. Salomon Rothschild came to Vienna from Frankfurt in
1821, ousted Herz from Metternich's favour, was able to make
more generous presents to Gentz than he, managed to become
settled in Vienna without the usual document of tolerance and
authority to conduct a wholesale business, had already procured
himself a title by the following year – becoming the third Jewish
Freiherr in Austria, Eskeles having meanwhile been granted the
same title – and lived there alone, without social pretensions,
obsessed and stubborn, first in lodgings at the *Römischer Kaiser*,
then in a *palais* which he had created by rebuilding the house next
door to the old inn. In every respect he was now competing with
the native houses of Arnstein, Sina, Steiner and Geymüller, managed to drum up sums of money that they would not have been
able to find anywhere, entered into neither business nor family
relationships with them, but nevertheless extorted from them the
place of honour in their circle, so that in 1830 J. F. Castelli was able
to report: 'I was invited to a ball at the merchant A.'s. The whole of
the aristocracy of money was gathered there. The king of Jews and
Jew of kings, Baron Rothschild, was present too.'

Not only he, but other immigrants were now also streaming into
that Vienna where one lived so much better than in German cities
or in the Austrian provinces. In a document of the court chancery
of 1833 it is stated: 'The local Israelites are in constant communication with all classes of residents of the capital, and not only in the
life of business, but also in that of society; their earlier isolation has
for some time almost completely ceased. The aversion of Christians from Jewish believers, which kept the latter at a distance from
them, has for the greater part disappeared.' The 'local Israelites'
very soon no longer included the Arnsteins, Pereiras and Eskeles,
for not only Nathan and his son-in-law but also Bernhard and
Cäcilie died during the 1830s, and their children and grandchildren
all became absorbed into the nobility – apart from the young
Pereiras there was also Daniel, now Denis, von Eskeles, who had
married a Freiin Brentano-Cimaroly-Visconti, and his sister Marianne, who became the wife of a Count Wimpffen. They, who bore
the names of their Itzig grandparents, were soon at the greatest
distance from their tradition! Side by side with the Ritter von
Liebenberg and Freiherr von Wetzlar, the Pereira brothers took

part in the sessions of the Vienna Landtag (Provincial Diet), and it was Louis who, in 1845, unsuccessfully proposed the motion that men of particular knowledge, experience and patriotism from the 'fourth estate' should be admitted to the Landtag. Not they, therefore, but the recently arrived Königswarters from Frankfurt, the Todescos from Pressburg, the Springers, Gompertzes, Auspitzes, Liebens, Figdors and Trebitsches from Bohemia and Moravia, together with the few still unbaptised families who had been settled here for over 150 years, formed the present Jewry of Vienna.

More and more descendants of the original tolerated families defected. The son of the orthodox Isaac Löw Hofmann, Edler von Hofmannsthal, for instance, who had been persuaded to the strictest observance of his faith by his friend Marcus Benedict, the chief provincial rabbi of Moravia, had undergone conversion immediately after his father's death. But the descendants of Samson Wertheimer, among them the Wertheimsteins, mingled and connected by marriage with the new arrivals, clung to their old religion and together leapt over the last hurdles of Jewish equality of rights in the imperial state. In 1846 they secured the abolition of the old Jewish oath. In March 1848 they surrounded the biers of the Jews whose blood had flowed for the Revolution, and were proud of the fact that two leaders of the insurrection were called Fischhof and Goldmark, that their own poet, L. A. Frankl, had written the fiery rebel hymn of the university students. The following year they thanked the young Emperor Franz Josef for the fact that his new constitution had at last given them the longed-for civic and political rights, and were deeply disappointed, with all the rest of his subjects, when everything was revoked. They, too, were affected by the pendulum-swing of reaction, which was to repeal twice more the conditions which had already been granted. And it was not till 1867, when Franz Josef, after defeat by Prussia and the separation from Germany, offered a Federal Council to his people, joint status with Austria to Hungary and unrestricted, complete and fundamental equality of rights to the Jews, that they regarded emancipation in Austria as complete.

A liberal era began, kindled by the ideas of Joseph's time. Now there was once more room for Jewish salons of wit and intellect, where it was no longer the nobility, but the intelligent bourgeoisie who mingled with poets and artists. Fanny's place was taken by Josephine von Wertheimstein, like Nathan's mother a scion of the Gompertz family. At her villa in Döbling and her sister Sophie von Todesco's mansion in the Kärntnerstrasse, a young man calling himself Loris, the great-grandson of the pious silk-merchant Hofmann, read his first poems. So it was that from this circle there arose Hugo von Hofmannsthal, in whom the multifarious heritage of the old Austria was united.

By the time that all this happened, every trace of Fanny's sojourn on earth had long since vanished. Since 1859 Henriette had lain beside her sons in the vault at Schwarzenau, while Pereira, self-willed even in death, awaited the resurrection near the altar in the church of Allentsteig – he, too, in the light of an eternal lamp, and comforted according to his last wish by a weekly mass. In the Jewish cemetery at Währing rested Fanny and Nathan, Cäcilie and Bernhard in splendid stone tombs which seemed as indestructible as once had their own financial power. But the power of the house whose foundations had been laid by the court agent Isaac Arnsteiner had already passed away. Louis von Pereira and Denis von Eskeles, two sensitive, refined, fastidious characters, had not known how to guard their inheritance. To hold their own against the Rothschilds, to whom their change of faith and noble connections were a particular thorn in the flesh, to invest daringly in railways, as was now becoming the fashion, or to speculate on slumps or booms when rumours of war or peace were abroad – these were things of which they had no understanding. When, at the beginning of 1859, Napoleon III revealed his decision to join with Sardinia in attacking Austria, Arnstein & Eskeles had provided themselves too abundantly with funds in expectation of quiet times. All paper money became worthless. The house was ruined. What remained after the forced settlement was lost in the stock-exchange crash of 1873.

Those earthly possessions, the lengthy and difficult acquisition of which had smoothed the entry of Fanny's family into the highest circles, fell away as soon as they had become superfluous. The later heirs of its founder, hardly distinguishable now from the Wimpffens and Larisches, the Széchenys and Strachwitzes, the Wittgensteins, Schloissniggs and Czernins into whose families they had married, now turned to other professions and occupations. They managed their own and other people's estates, became soldiers, racehorse-owners, state officials and diplomats. They forgot their origins, or did not care to remember them. Once there was a sufficient streak of blue flowing in their objectionable blood, they had escaped the destiny which had been such a heavy burden to their ancestors. With their former companions, the Wertheimers and the Gomperzes, the Herzes and Ephraims, they needed to have no more dealings, and the 'Berlin *famille*', to which Fanny had clung so devotedly, were strangers to them.

This too had changed to the point of being unrecognisable! To those families of the Catholic country nobility, what were those Hitzigs and Ebertys and Schmidts who were the descendants of the two mint-masters of Frederick the Great? Among them were police officials, town councillors, architects and physicians, who belonged to the Berlin bourgeoisie and brought up their children in the Lutheran faith – an alien world, with which their Viennese second and third cousins had nothing in common. They would not have known what to make of the ancient Sara Levy, who sat in solitude at the Packhof, 'her noble countenance clouded with sorrow', lamenting that she felt 'like a leafless tree, now that all my family have converted to Christianity'. Bartholdy, who had once fought in Austrian uniform and dedicated a book to the Tyroleans, was the one they might have got on with best. But he was long dead, and his nephew Felix Mendelssohn, of whom, even as a member of the Austrian nobility, one could have been proud, had also prematurely passed away. The beautiful Marianne Saaling, on the other hand, lived until 1869 – unmarried, after her first fiancé, Marquis Marialva, had died and her engagement to Varnhagen, soon after Rahel's death, had been broken off. Fanny's great-grandchildren could have learnt from Marianne's own lips how all Europe had gathered in the house of their ancestor. But who, in those days, made the journey from Vienna to Berlin? The gulf between the two cities had opened once again.

Since the Jewish persecution of 1819 the poison mixed by Professors Rühs and Fries had circulated in the German bloodstream. In Austria, too, its traces were found and persons called Quirin Endlich or August Rohling wrote threatening pamphlets in which the beginnings of racialism and anti-Semitism were to be found. But here Jewish emancipation, like the Enlightenment in Berlin, was bound up with the progressive forces in the land, while in Berlin it was the so-called reformers who bore ill-will against the Jews. Whoever strove for the greatness of Prussia, whoever descended into Germany's past, spurred the people on, in Rahel's words, 'to the only horror to which, reminded of past experience, they can still be spurred on'. The descendants of Veitel Ephraim might now be called Eberty, the heirs of Daniel Itzig take the name of Hitzig – in Gustav Freytag's *Soll und Haben*, the first great novel since the vagaries of the Romantics and at the same time the first glorification of the German bourgeoisie, their ancestors were together besmirched in the detestable figure of Veitel Itzig! And the more that state in the north of Germany grew, the more its national consciousness increased, the more warlike and belligerent it became, the less it could endure the Jews in its midst, although their love of fatherland if possible even surpassed that of their fellow-citizens! When France was defeated, the Empire formed and Berlin made the German Emperor's capital, the court preacher Stöcker could fulminate against them from the pulpit, as once the Great Elector's merciless contemporary, Bishop Kollonitsch, had done.

And finally – with the turn of the century in sight – anti-Semitism awoke again in Austria. The liberal era had freed the victims of persecution. Now their long-stored-up urge towards action, their talent, which had long lain fallow, burst out in new ways. Whereas they had once been either pariahs or servants of princes and friends of aristocrats, they now pervaded all classes. More and more, hungry for education and eager for work, came to Vienna, to settle again in their old quarter, the Leopoldstadt, and turn to the trades newly open to them. The intellectual *grande bourgeoisie* watched this calmly. But the little people felt threatened by the influx and were scandalised by the frequently uncouth figures of the new arrivals. The *petit bourgeois* movement grew. It found its leaders in Schönerer and Lueger, its mouthpiece in the Christian Social Party. The *Burschenschaften* or students' associations, which had once marched to Frankl's university song during the Revolution, became Pan-Germanic and excluded Jewish students. But with the increasing prosperity of the *Gründerzeit* – the 'epoch of the founders' – both factions, those of the immigrants and of their opponents, increased in numbers ever more mightily.

It was a race against time which was not to succeed. A process of speeded-up assimilation took place, but it was still not fast enough to be over by the time the Middle Ages re-awoke with a cruelty increased a hundredfold in the 'Third Reich'. The distance was still too great between the way of life which had already been attained and that which was still being striven after, between the refined sons of the old-established tolerated families and the rough hordes of the Polish, Ruthenian, Russian and Rumanian borderlands who now also wanted their place in the sun. When Hugo von Hofmannsthal spent a few days of his military exercise in the little Polish village of Tlumacs, he shrank away in disgust from the 'stinking Jews' with whom he had been quartered, and found his host Schwefelgeist as contemptible and ridiculous as though the same 'weariness of quite forgotten peoples' did not lie upon their eyelids, as if this man was not as closely related to his own 'ancestors in their shrouds as their own hair'.

The 'imperial-royal' lieutenant of dragoons, who got drunk on Polish schnapps with young Haugwitz, O'Donnell and Starhemberg, and then, helplessly befuddled, 'as all the doors are open, stumbled into a number of Jewish interiors, with their ritual candles alight', was as far removed from the steadfast fellow-believers of Isaac Löw Hofmann as they would have been from themselves after a hundred years – whether they had trodden the path of assimilation or returned to the land of their fathers. But those hundred years that they needed to make their choice were not granted to them. Not even half that number! When the most cold-blooded mass murder in human history began, they were the first to fill the gas-chambers.

In a Vienna torn apart by many opposing forces, in which a Lueger and a Herzl, a Bielohlawek and a Freud represented polarities of world outlook, in which the newly destitute battled against the *nouveau riche*, the worker against the exploiter, and there were Jews in both camps, a Vienna in which the old Emperor died and the young one was forced to abdicate, whereupon, after the collapse of the monarchy, ever more Jews streamed to the impoverished capital from the new succession states, because, more than their soil, the German language, the German spirit was their home – in this Vienna Fanny's children's children had disappeared in the throng. They were not seen again. Those men in brown shirts, who sought in faces rigid with fear or in dusty registers of births for the clues to possible victims, discovered nothing to distinguish the Pereira-Arnsteins from their fellow-citizens. Many of these, daughters or sons of daughters, were, moreover, obscurely disguised, bore the titles of counts and barons, were called Galen and Beroldingen, Eiselsberg and Pirquet, Coronini and Czernin, Hiller and Arx, Blaskovics and Skrbensky. But it was one of Fanny's heirs who still bore her name to whom a Habsburg finally paid a visit.

In the years before the warning signal-fire which preceded the darkness, Freiherr Ferdinand von Pereira-Arnstein was living in Berlin, the native city of his ancestress. There, between 3 and 27 January 1933, the eldest son of the Emperor of Austria, upon whose shoulders the purple robe had not been destined to descend, came to stay as his guest. The lady of the house which for three weeks harboured Otto von Habsburg was by birth a Countess Mensdorff-Pouilly, and had before her marriage been a lady-in-waiting to Empress Zita. But Baron Pereira-Arnstein had no need of her ancient aristocratic descent in order to merit this belated honour. His own could even compete with that of his exalted guest

– through his great-grandmother, Seraphine Amadé, he was able to derive them from King Attila, Charlemagne and St Elizabeth of Thuringia. The 'blemish' of his origins was blotted out in this generation. Now that there were no longer any imperial receptions, Fanny's descendant had become presentable at court!

If the vestiges of a life are blown away, no one can ever succeed in faithfully retracing them. Every life becomes a legend. However many pictures, letters and accounts one may possess from which to conjure it up again, however many witnesses one questions, the living and breathing present, the daily fluctuations of mood, the intellectual horizon, the sphere of feeling of the being whom one is trying to reawaken can never be comprehended nor exhausted. Why, then, make the attempt? Because in most cases, when a form of existence is to be newly outlined, it is not its true nature but its symbolic content which is worth unravelling. Not what Fanny was like, but what effect she had on others, concerns us here.

One must almost be grateful that so few of her own utterances are preserved. If those handwritten documents addressed to Rahel and to Sophie Grotthuss, which Varnhagen guarded for decades, as Fafner did his hoard, together with many other collections of the correspondence and journals of his contemporaries, had not been lost in the confusion of the last war – would we really know more? Would that strong-box full of old documents which a Count von Galen still preserves and keeps to himself really yield up allusions to this or that event, this or that characteristic – would anything definite really be found to be add to Fanny's portrait? Perhaps, on the contrary, it would become so confused by a multiplicity of incidental disclosures that we would lose sight of her general impression. We must see Fanny as her own age saw her: as a 'fair Hebrew', even if we are not prepared to grant her the adjective, as 'queen of every feast', as a 'pretty woman with an excellent address', a 'wondrous vision of curving lines', as the 'bonne et bavarde Madame Arnstein' as well as the 'scandalous Prussian', the 'fiery hostess' and the 'enchantress'. While her great contemporaries rose up to pedestals in bronze and stone – the victor of Aspern high on his horse in the Heldenplatz in Vienna, Joseph von Sonnenfels, his foot placed upon crushed instruments of torture, in front of the Rathaus – a monument was raised to her in the memories of her friends.

There, however, the story of her life is freed from those faults and shortcomings which should not cling to a statue or to a symbol. Varnhagen rightly refrained, when long after her death he sketched her portrait, from mentioning that scene upon the silken sofa. That was beside the point; it belonged to the transitory part of her personality. What was relevant was that 'since Frau von Arnstein, no lady of this kind had again penetrated the circle of the high nobility' and that in this she 'succeeded almost unintentionally, through self-assertion over many years in brilliance and dignity, through outstanding beneficence and social influence, with which, at the right time, were united sharp intellectual courage and significant worldly wisdom'. For Fanny was irritable and moody on her own behalf, but brilliant and dignified, intellectual and worldly-wise in the name of her fellow-believers. Her hatred of Napoleon bore the stamp of an often childish and self-willed temperament, but she was a German Jewess in her great and unreciprocated love for Prussia.

Rightly, too, did the gentlemen who prepared a 'historical–genealogical almanac of the entire nobility of Judaic origin', for publication by the house of Kyffhäuser, place Fanny's portrait at the front of their *Semi-Gotha* of 1914. With as much justification a similar production, *Sigilla Veri*, fifteen years later poured out its mockery upon her 'tapir-like face with pendulous-tipped nose, large mouth, generous cheeks and below them long spidery arms'. For this woman was a concentration of all her kin – she had to be jeered at and humiliated when that class of mankind was once more to be crushed into the dust. Had not Jewish historians such as Grätz, Grunwald and Bermann proudly claimed her as their own? Even worse: did she not live on in venerable compilations such as the *Austrian National Encyclopaedia* as an embodiment of all virtues, as a woman who was distinguished by 'beauty and charm, intelligence and kind-heartedness, imagination and culture, vivacity and talent, refinement and wit, tact and skill, nobility and aestheticism to a high, rare degree'? Was not her house described in the same volume as 'the dwelling-place of good breeding', as a 'Palladium of the noblest and finest delights, the most respectable freedom, the most piquant social entertainment', even as 'the most beautiful pattern of higher conversation'?

Those who praised her and those who abused her were agreed in one thing, that her destiny was to be seen as a parable. In her, for a short span of time, the whole Biblical people had taken on a serene, contented, confident form. She had led the great ones of this world to whom she opened her doors to wonder whether or not there was room in the community of mankind for the children of the Old Testament. For this was what it amounted to – a piece of earth, a few untroubled breaths of air, a roof over one's head like everyone else in this transitory state that we call life. What did Christ say? 'In my Father's house are many mansions.' Should only this one be uninhabitable for all eternity?

Bibliography

Fanny von Arnstein and her Family

Alxinger, Joh. Bapt. von, *Gedichte* (vol. VIII of Complete Works) (Vienna, 1812)

Anon., *Bemerkungen und Briefe über Wien etc. eines jungen Bayern* (Leipzig, 1800)

Anon., *Handzeichnungen aus den Kreisen des höheren politischen und gesellschaftlichen Lebens* (Vienna, 1816)

Anon., *Vaterländische Blätter vom österreichischen Kaiserstaat* (Vienna, 1811)

Anon., *Journal kept during a Visit to Germany in 1799, 1800* (1861)˙

Auerbach, Baruch, *Zwölfter Jahresbericht über das jüdische Waisenerziehungs-Institut für Knaben zu Berlin* (Berlin, 1945)

Bermann, Moriz, *Österreichisches biographisches Lexikon* (Vienna, 1851–2)

——, *Ein Concert bei Baronin Fanny Arnstein*, supplement to *Blätter für Musik*, nos. 89, 91, 93, 95 (Vienna, 1855)

Bertuch, Carl, *Tagebuch vom Wiener Kongreß*, ed. Egloffstein (Berlin, 1916)

Böttiger, Carl August, 'Memorandenbuch', 13th annual of the Grillparzergesellschaft (Vienna, 1903)

Dörr, A. von, *Genealogisches Quellenmaterial* (Vienna, 1927)

Eggers, C. V. D. Freiherr von, *Reise durch Franken, Bayern, Österreich etc.* (Leipzig, 1810)

Erman, Paul, 'Erinnerungen', *Schriften des Vereins für die Geschichte Berlins*, no. 53 [n.d.]

Erman, Wilhelm, *Paul Erman. Ein Berliner Gelehrtenleben 1764–1851* (Berlin, 1927)

Eynard, Jean-Gabriel, *Journal* (Paris, 1914)

Fournier, August, *Die Geheimpolizei auf dem Wiener Kongreß* (Vienna/Leipzig, 1913)

Franzl, Franz, *Die Gesellschaft adliger Frauen zur Beförderung des Guten und Nützlichen in Wien 1811–1835* (Vienna, 1836)

Friesz, Edmund, 'Die Darlehen der Wiener Großhändler und Niederleger, Juden und Griechen zum Wiener allgemeinen Aufgebote im Jahre 1797', *Adler* (monthly publication) (Vienna, 1923)

Fuchs, Joh. Bapt., *Erinnerungen aus dem Leben eines Kölner Juristen* (Cologne, 1912)

Gentz, Friedrich von, *Briefe von und an . . .*, ed. Wittichen (Munich, 1909–10)

Gerning, J. J., *Reise durch Österreich und Italien* (Frankfurt, 1802)

Goethe, Ottilie von, *Tagebuch* (Vienna, 1961)

Gonord, François, *Silhouetten aus dem Jahr 1781* (Vienna/Berlin 1922)

Gräffer, Franz, *Kleine Wiener Memoiren zur Geschichte und Charakteristik Wiens und der Wiener* (Vienna, 1845)

Grunwald, Dr Max, 'Arnstein. Nachtrag zur Familiengeschichte einiger Gründer der Wiener Chewra Kadischa', *Mitteilungen zur jüdischen Volkskunde*, nos. 32, 33, 35 (Vienna, 1910)

——, 'Samuel Oppenheim und sein Kreis', *Quellen und Forschungen zur Geschichte der Juden in Deutsch-Österreich*, vol. V (Vienna/Leipzig 1913)

——, *Die Feldzüge Napoleons nach Aufzeichnungen jüdischer Teilnehmer und Augenzeugen* (Vienna, 1913)

Gundlach, Wilhelm, *Geschichte der Stadt Charlottenburg*, vol. II (Berlin, 1905)

Hiller, Gottlieb, *Reise durch einen Theil von Sachsen, Böhmen, Österreich und Ungarn* (Köthen, 1807)

Holman, James, *Travels through Russia, Siberia, Poland, Austria, etc.* (London, 1825)

Homberg, Herz, *Rede zur Totenfeier der Freiin Fanny von Arnstein* (Vienna, 1818)

Hüffer, Hermann, *Rheinisch-Westfälische Zustände zur Zeit der französischen Revolution* (Bonn, 1873)

Illustrirte Monatshefte f. d. gesamten Interessen des Judentums, vol. I (Vienna, 1865)

Iris, Graz ladies' periodical, vol. II (Graz, 1854)

Jagemann, Karoline, *Memoiren* (Dresden, 1926)

Jahrbuch der Tonkunst von Wien und Prag (Vienna, 1796)

Kaufmann, Prof. David, *Aus Heinrich Heine's Ahnensaal* (Breslau, 1907)

——, and Freudenthal, Max, *Die Familie Gomperz* (Frankfurt, 1907)

Kerst, Friedrich, *Die Erinnerungen an Beethoven* (Stuttgart, 1913)

Küttner, C. G., *Reise durch Deutschland, Dänemark, Schweden etc. in den Jahren 1797, 1798* (Leipzig, 1799–1801)

Mendelssohn, Moses, *Gesammelte Schriften*, vol. V (Leipzig, 1843–45)

Nesselrode, Comte Charles Robert de, *Lettres et papiers du Chancellier Comte de Nesselrode, 1760–1850. Extraits de ses archives, publiés et annotés avec une introduction par le Comte A. D. de Nesselrode* (Paris, 1904)

Olfers, Hedwig von, *Lebensgeschichte v. Fr. H. v. Stägemann*, vol. I (Berlin, 1908)

Öhlenschläger, Adam, *Meine Lebenserinnerungen*, vols. 1–4 (Leipzig, 1850)

Österreichische Nationalenzyklopädie, ed. Gräffer-Czikann (Vienna, 1835)

Perger, Richard von, *Geschichte der k. k. Gesellschaft der Musikfreunde in Wien von 1812–1870* (Vienna, 1912)

Pichler, Caroline, *Denkwürdigkeiten aus meinem Leben* (Vienna, 1844)

Bibliography

Rachel, Hugo, and Wallich, Paul, *Berliner Großkaufleute und Kapitalisten* (Berlin, 1938, privately printed)

Reichardt, Joh. Friedr., *Vertraute Briefe, geschrieben auf einer Reise nach Wien etc. am Ende des Jahres 1808 und zu Anfang 1809* ed. Gustav Gugitz (Munich, 1915)

Röder, Philipp Ludwig, *Reisen durch das südliche Teutschland*, vol. I, *Leipzig* (Klagenfurt, 1789–95)

Rühl, Franz (ed.), *Briefe und Aktenstücke zur Geschichte Preußens unter Friedrich Wilhelm III, vor allem aus dem Nachlaß Stägemanns* (Leipzig, 1899, 1902)

Schopenhauer, Arthur, *Reisetagebücher aus den Jahren 1803–1804* (Leipzig, 1923)

Staël, Madame de, *Dix Années d'Exil* (Paris, 1904)

Stern, Ludwig, *Die Varnhagen von Ensesche Sammlung in der Königlichen Bibliothek zu Berlin* (Berlin, 1911)

Thürheim, Countess Lulu, *Mein Leben, 1788–1819* (Munich, 1913)

Varnhagen von Ense, K. A., *Denkwürdigkeiten des eigenen Lebens*, vols. I–V, VII–VIII (Leipzig, 1843)

——, *Briefwechsel zwischen Varnhagen und Rahel* (Leipzig, 1874, 1875)

——, 'Fanny von Arnstein', in *Ausgewählte Schriften XVII* (Leipzig, 1875)

Weckbecker, Wilhelm, *Von Maria Theresia zu Franz Joseph. Zwei Lebensbilder aus dem alten Österreich* (Berlin, 1929)

Weil, Commandant Maurice-Henri, *Les Dessous du Congrès de Vienne* (Paris, 1917)

Wolzogen, Ludwig Freiherr von, *Memoiren des Königlich-preußischen Generals der Infanterie . . .* (Leipzig, 1851)

Zinzendorf, Carl Graf von, *Journal* (unpublished)

Contemporaries and Other Personalities

Alxinger, Johann Baptist von
Alxinger, Joh. Bapt. von, *Briefe* (Vienna, 1899)
Wilhelm, Dr Gustav, *Briefe von Joh. Baptist Alxinger. Aus dem josephinischen Wien* (Berlin, 1888)

Bartholdy, Jakob
Jacob, H. E., *Felix Mendelssohn und seine Zeit* (Frankfurt, 1959)

Gentz, Friedrich von
Gentz, Friedrich von, *Tagebücher, Aus dem Nachlaß Varnhagen von Enses* (Leipzig, 1873)
Mann, Golo, *Friedrich von Gentz* (Zurich/Vienna, 1947)

Goethe, Johann Wolfgang von
Bab, Julius, *Goethe und die Juden* (Berlin, 1906)

Sauer, August, 'Goethe und Österreich', *Schriften der Goethe-Gesellschaft*, vol. 18, II (Weimar, 1904)

Grillparzer, Franz
Glossy-Sauer, *Grillparzers Briefe und Tagebücher* (Stuttgart/Berlin, 1903)
Grillparzer, Franz, *Sämtliche Werke*, vol. I (Munich, 1961), p. 126

Herz, Henriette
Fürst, J., *Henriette Herz, Ihr Leben und ihre Erinnerungen* (Berlin, 1850)

Hitzig, Julius Eduard
Erman, Wilhelm, *Paul Erman* (Berlin 1927)
Heine, Heinrich, *Gedichte* (Juda ben Halevy IV [n.d.])

Hofmannsthal, Hugo von
Hofmannsthal, Hugo von, *Briefe 1890–1901* (Berlin, 1935)
——, *Gedichte. Ges. Werke* (Berlin, 1934)

Humboldt, Wilhelm von
Grau, W., *Wilhelm von Humboldt und das Problem der Juden* (Hamburg, 1935)

Körner, Theodor
Körner, Theodor, *Sämtliche Werke*, ed. Dr Karl Macke (Berlin, *c.* 1908)
——, *Briefe und Lieder aus dem Feld* (Munich, 1813)
Peschel, Dr W. E., and Wildenow, Dr Eugen, *Theodor Körner und die Seinen* (Leipzig, 1898)
Wedler-Steinberg, Augusta, *Theodor Körners Briefwechsel mit den Seinen* (Leipzig, 1910)

Liechtenstein, Carl Fürst von
Wolf, Adam, *Fürstin Eleonore Liechtenstein 1745–1812* (Vienna, 1875)

Mendelssohn, Moses
Hensel, S., *Die Familie Mendelssohn* (Berlin 1908)
Kayserling, Dr Meyer, *Moses Mendelssohn: Sein Leben und seine Werke* (Leipzig 1862)

Mozart, Wolfgang Amadeus
Mozart, Wolfgang Amadeus, *The Letters of Mozart and His Family*, ed. Emily Anderson, 3 vols. (London, 1938)
——, *Briefe*, ed. E. H. Müller v. Asow, vols. I, II (Berlin, 1942)
Gugitz, Dr Gustav, 'Zu einer Briefstelle Mozarts', *Mitteilungen des Salzburger Mozarteums*, year III, February, May (Salzburg, 1921)

Bibliography

Schlegel, Dorothea von
Geiger, Ludwig, 'Dorothea Veit Schlegel', *Deutsche Rundschau Berlin*, year 40, issue 10 (Berlin, 1914)
Körner, Josef (ed.), *Briefe von und an Friedrich und Dorothea Schlegel* (Berlin, 1926)
Raich, J. M. (ed.), *Dorothea v. Schlegel geb. Mendelssohn und deren Söhne Joh. und Phil. Veit* (Mainz, 1881)
——, *Dorothea v. Schlegel, Briefwechsel* (Mainz, 1884)

Sonnenfels, Joseph von
Kann, Robert A., *A Study in Austrian Intellectual History* (London, 1960)
Lessing, Gotthold Ephraim, *Gesammelte Werke*, vol. 12 (Berlin, 1840)

Staël, Madame de
Herold, J. Christopher, *Mistress to an Age. The Life of Madame de Staël* (London, 1939)
Mistler, Jean, *Madame de Staël et Maurice O'Donnell, 1805–1817* (Paris, 1926)
Pange, Pauline de, *August Wilhelm Schlegel und Frau v. Staël* (Hamburg, 1940)

Stägemann, Fr. H. von
Assing, Ludmilla, *Briefe von Stägemann an Varnhagen* (Leipzig, 1865)

Varnhagen von Ense, K. A.
Leitzmann, Albert, *Briefwechsel zwischen Karoline v. Humboldt, Rahel und Varnhagen* (Weimar, 1896)
Varnhagen von Ense, K. A., *Denkwürdigkeiten des eigenen Lebens*, vol. VIII (Karl Gust. Fr. v. Brinckmann)
—— (ed.), *Galerie von Bildnissen aus Rahels Umgang und Briefwechsel* (Leipzig, 1836)

Varnhagen von Ense, Rahel
Arendt, Hannah, *Rahel Varnhagen, Lebensgeschichte einer deutschen Jüdin aus der Romantik* (Munich, 1959)
Badt, Bertha, *Rahel und ihre Zeit*, ed. O. Walzel, Pandora series, vol. VIII, (Munich, 1912)
Schmidt-Weissenfels, Eduard, *Rahel und ihre Zeit* (Leipzig, 1857)
Varnhagen von Ense, K. A. (ed.), *Rahel Levin und David Veit, Briefwechsel* (Leipzig, 1861)

Bibliography

Judaica

Arendt, Hannah, *Privileged Jews* (New York, 1946)

Arenhof (Arnstein), (Ein jüdischer Jüngling [A Jewish youth]), *Einige jüdische Familiensszenen bey Erblickung des Toleranzpatents* (Vienna, 1782)

Baron, Prof. Salo, *Die Judenfrage auf dem Wiener Kongreß* (Vienna/Berlin, 1920)

——, *Unveröffentlichte Aktenstücke zur Judenfrage auf dem Wiener Kongreß (1814–1815)* [n.p., n.d.]

Bato, Ludwig, *Die Juden im alten Wien* (Vienna, 1928)

Corti, Cäsar Conte, *Der Aufstieg des Hauses Rothschild* (Vienna, 1953)

Dohm, Christian Wilh., *Über die bürgerliche Verbesserung der Juden* (Berlin/Stettin, 1781–83)

Dubnow, Simon M., *Die neueste Geschichte des jüdischen Volkes 1789–1914* (Berlin, 1920)

——, *Weltgeschichte des jüdischen Volkes*, vol. VIII (Berlin, 1925–29)

Freudenthal, Dr Max, *Aus der Heimat Mendelssohns* (Berlin, 1900)

Friedländer, David, *Ein Sendschreiben an die Frau Kammerherrin von der Recke etc. Beitrag zur Geschichte der Verfolgung der Juden im 19ten Jahrhundert* (Berlin, 1820)

Geiger, Ludwig, *Berlin 1688–1840* (Berlin, 1892)

——, *Geschichte der Juden in Berlin* (Berlin, 1871)

Gelber, N. M., *Aktenstücke zur Judenfrage am Wiener Kongreß* (Vienna, 1920)

Grätz, Prof. Heinrich, *Geschichte der Juden*, vols. X–XI (Leipzig, 1873–1900)

Grunwald, Dr Max, *Geschichte der Wiener Juden bis 1914* (Vienna, 1926)

Jacobson, Jacob, *Jüdische Trauungen in Berlin 1723–1759* (Berlin, 1938)

——, *Some Observations on the Jewish Citizen's Book of the City of Berlin*, Leo Baeck Year Book I (London, 1956)

Jäger-Sunstenau, Dr Hanns, *Die geadelten Judenfamilien im vormärzlichen Wien* (diss.) (Vienna, 1950)

Jüdischer Plutarch (Vienna, 1848)

Kaufmann, Prof. David, *Die letzte Vertreibung der Juden aus Wien und Niederösterreich* (Vienna, 1889)

Kayserling, Meyer, *Der Dichter Ephraim Kuh* (Berlin, 1864)

——, *Die jüdischen Frauen in der Geschichte, Literatur und Kunst* (Leipzig, 1879)

——, and Dr Max, *Jüdische Geschichte und Literatur* (Leipzig, n.d.)

Kobler, Dr Franz, *Jüdische Geschichte in Briefen aus Ost und West* (Vienna, 1938)

—— (ed.), *Juden und Judentum in deutschen Briefen aus drei Jahrhunderten* (Vienna, 1935)

König, Joh. Balthasar, *Annalen der Juden in den deutschen Staaten, besonders in der Mark Brandenburg* (Berlin, 1790)

Bibliography

Mayer, Sigmund, *Die Wiener Juden* (Vienna, 1917)

Pribram, A. F., *Urkunden und Akten zur Geschichte der Juden in Wien 1526–1847*, vol. 8, II (Vienna, 1918)

Samter, N., *Judentaufen im 19. Jahrhundert* (Berlin, 1906)

Schirnding, F., *Die Juden in Österreich, Preußen und Sachsen* (Leipzig, 1842)

Sendschreiben an Seine Hochwürden Herrn Oberkonsistorialrath und Probst Teller zu Berlin von einigen Hausvätern jüdischer Religion (Berlin, 1799)

Sigilla Veri (1929)

Tietze, Hans, *Die Juden Wiens* (Vienna, 1933)

Weimarer historisch-genealoges Taschenbuch des gesamten Adels jehudäischen Ursprungs (Weimar, 1912)

Wolf, Gerson, *Geschichte der Juden in Wien 1156–1876* (Vienna, 1876)

Wolff, Dr Alfred, *Der Toleranzgedanke in der deutschen Literatur zur Zeit Mendelssohns* (Berlin, 1915)

Wyking, A., *Die Juden Berlins* (Leipzig, 1891)

General History

Vienna and Austria

Anon., *Galanterien Wiens, Briefe eines Berliners an einen Freund* (Vienna, 1784)

Anon., *Reise eines Engelländers durch Mannheim, Baiern und Österreich nach Wien*, ed. L. A. F. v. B. (Amsterdam, 1790)

Anon., *Lamentabel der gnädigen Frauen der gegenwärtigen Zeit* (Vienna, 1791)

Arndt, Ernst Moritz, *Bruchstücke aus einer Reise von Baireuth bis Wien im Sommer 1798* (Leipzig, 1798)

——, *Reisen durch einen Teil Deutschlands* (Leipzig, 1804)

Bauer, Wilhelm, *Briefe aus Wien* (Leipzig, 1908)

Bibl, Viktor, *Die niederösterreichischen Stände im Vormärz* (Vienna, 1911)

Blümml, Emil Karl, and Gugitz, Gustav, *Alt-Wiener Thespiskarren* (Vienna, 1925)

Castelli, J. F., *Aus dem Leben eines Wiener Phäaken, 1781–1862* (Stuttgart, 1912)

Gräffer, Franz, *Josephinische Curiosa* (Vienna, 1848)

——, *Kleine Wiener Memoiren und Wiener Dosenstücke* (Munich, 1922)

Fischer, Jul. Wilh., *Reisen durch Österreich, Ungarn etc., 1801, 1802* (Vienna, 1803)

Friedel, Johann, *Briefe aus Wien verschiedenen Inhalts an einen Freund in Berlin* (Leipzig/Berlin, 1783)

Holzer, Rudolf, *Villa Wertheimstein* (Vienna, 1960)

Hormayr, Joseph Frh. von, *Wien, seine Geschicke und seine Denkwürdigkeiten*, vol. V (Vienna, 1823)

Krones v. Marchand, Franz Xaver, *Aus Österreichs stillen und bewegten Jahren 1810–1812 und 1813–1815*, vol. I, *Aus dem Tagebuch Erzh. Johanns v. Österreich* (Innsbruck, 1892)

Bibliography

Mayr, Josef Karl, *Wien im Zeitalter Napoleons* (Vienna, 1942)

Metternich, Clemens, Fürst von, *Denkwürdigkeiten*, ed. Otto H. Brandt (Munich, 1921)

Nicolai, Friedrich, *Beschreibung einer Reise durch Deutschland und die Schweiz in Jahre 1781* (Berlin/Stettin, 1783)

Perinet, Joachim, *Annehmlichkeiten in Wien* (Vienna, 1788)

Pezzl, Johann, *Skizze von Wien* (Vienna/Leipzig 1787)

Richter, Josef, *Briefe eines Eipeldauers an seinen Herrn Vetter in Kagran* (Munich, 1917)

Riesbeck, Johann Kaspar, *Briefe eines reisenden Franzosen über Deutschland . . .* (Zurich, 1783–84)

Schönholz, Friedrich Anton von, *Tradition zur Charakteristik Österreichs* (Leipzig, 1844)

Tietze, Hans, *Alt-Wien in Wort und Bild* (Vienna, 1924)

Werner, Richard M., *Aus dem josephinischem Wien* (Berlin, 1888)

Woinovich, General von, and Veltzé, Major (eds.), *1813–1815. Österreich in den Befreiungskriegen* (Vienna/Leipzig, 1911)

Wolf, Dr Adam, and Zwiedinek-Südenhorst, Dr Hans v., *Österreich unter Maria Theresia, Josef II und Leopold II, 1740–1792* (Berlin, 1884)

Berlin and Germany

Archenholtz, Johann Wilhelm von, *Geschichte des Siebenjährigen Krieges* (Berlin, 1793)

Hillebrand, Karl, *Unbekannte Essays. Die Berliner Gesellschaft in den Jahren 1789–1815)* (Berne, 1955)

Mann, Golo, *Geschichte des 19, und 20. Jahrhunderts* (Frankfurt, 1959)

Nicolai, Christian Friedrich, *Beschreibung d. kgl. Residenzstädte Berlin und Potsdam . . .* (Berlin, 1786)

——, *Wegweiser für Fremde durch Berlin* (Berlin, 1835)

Staël, Madame de, *De l'Allemagne*, in *Oeuvres complètes de Mme la Baronne de Staël* (Paris, 1820–1)

Frederick II

Carlyle, Thomas, *History of Friedrich II of Prussia called Frederick the Great* (London, 1858–65)

Dilthey, Wilhelm, *Friedrich der Große und die deutsche Aufklärung*, in *Gesammelte Schriften*, vol. III (Leipzig/Berlin, 1927)

Mann, Thomas, 'Friedrich und die große Koalition', in *Rede und Antwort* (Berlin, 1922)

Maria Theresa, Joseph II and Francis I

Bermann, Moriz, *Maria Theresia und Kaiser Josef II in ihrem Leben und Wirken* (Vienna, 1881)

Frank, G., *Das Toleranzpatent Kaiser Josephs II* (Vienna, 1882)

Karajan, M. G. von, *Maria Theresia und Josef II* (Vienna, 1865)

Bibliography

Schimmer, Karl August, *Kaiser Josef II* (Vienna, 1879)
Wendrinsky, Johann, *Kaiser Josef II* (Vienna, 1880)
Wolfsgruber, Dr Cölestin, *Franz I, Kaiser von Österreich* (Vienna, 1899)

Congress of Vienna
Bourgoing, Freiherr von, *Vom Wiener Kongreß* (Brno/Munich/Vienna, 1943)
Garde, Count Auguste de la, *Gemälde des Wiener Kongresses*, ed. Effenberger (Vienna, 1912)
Leisching, E., *Der Wiener Kongreß* (Vienna, 1898)

Tyrol
Bartholdy, J. L. S., *Der Krieg der Tyroler Landsleute im Jahre 1809* (Berlin, 1814)

Miscellaneous
Böttiger, Karl August, *Literarische Zustände und Zeitgenossen* (Leipzig, 1838)
Körner, Josef, *Krisenjahre der Frühromantik* (Brno, 1936)
Kralik, Heinrich, *Das Buch der Musikfreunde* (Zurich/Leipzig/Vienna, 1951)
Lang, Carl Heinrich Ritter von, *Memoiren* (Braunschweig, 1842)
Schulze, Friedrich (ed.), *Napoleon's Briefe* (Leipzig, 1812)

Periodicals, Encyclopaedias, Archives, Documents and Registers

Wiener Großhandels-Schematismus und Hof- und Staatsschematismus
Wiener Handelsalmanach
Vienna City Archive: *Fassionsbuch* (register of taxable properties)
Portheim Collection: Harrer (compiler), *Wien, seine Häuser, Menschen und Kultur* (Vienna, 1953)
Austrian State Archive: police records, records of the *Finanzhofstelle*, register of the nobility
Rolls of the *Gesellschaft der Musikfreunde der österreichischen Kaiserstaates*.
Museum der Stadt Wien: catalogue
Königlich-private Berlinische Zeitung, June 1818
Ost und West, year X
Sulamit, year V, 2
Vossische Zeitung, May 1865
Wiener Zeitung or *Wiener Diarium*
Große jüdische Nationalenzyklopädie, 1925

Index

Index

Index

Index

Index